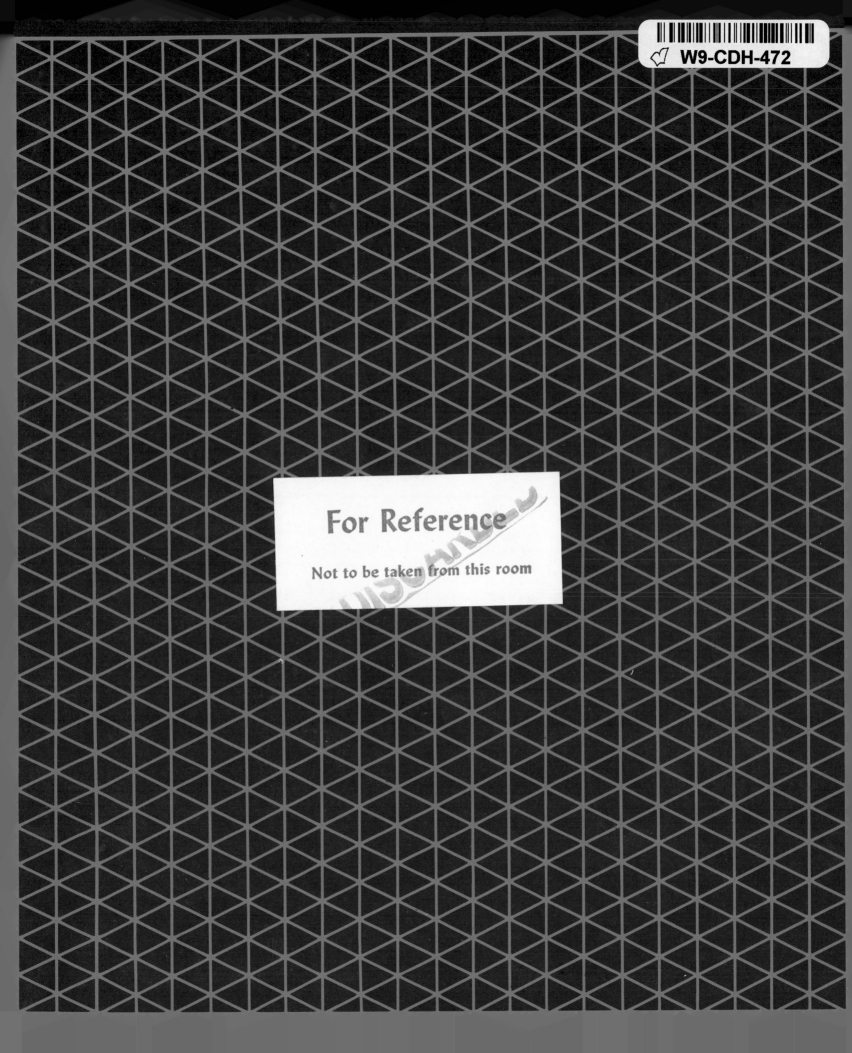

THE CONRAN DIRECTORY OF DESIGN

EDITED BY STEPHEN BAYLEY

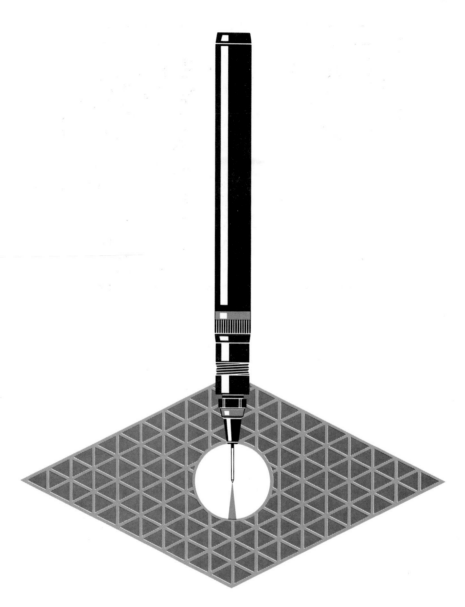

"... good design is 98 per cent commonsense and 2 per cent aesthetics."

THE CONRAN DIRECTORY OF DESIGN

EDITED BY STEPHEN BAYLEY

Villard Books
New York 1985

Library of Congress Cataloging in Publication Data
Conran, Terence.
  The Conran directory of design.
  Includes index.
  I. Design—Dictionaries. I. Bayley, Stephen.
II. Title.   III. Title: Directory of design.
NK1165.C6   1985   745.4'03'21   85-40181
ISBN 0-394-54698-9

Conceived, designed and produced by
Conran Octopus Limited
28–32 Shelton Street
London WC2 9PH

Art director Douglas Wilson
Designed by Mel Petersen Associates
Design assistant Mark Richards
Picture research by Nadine Bazar and Anne-Marie Ehrlich
Edited by Stephen Adamson and Sarah Bevan

Manufactured in England

First Edition

CONTENTS

Foreword by Sir Terence Conran   6

Introduction   8

1
Art & Industry   10
– the beginnings of design

2
Mass Consumption   18
– the beginning of the consumer age

3
The Craft Ideal   26
– survival and revival of old values

4
The Romance of the Machine   32
– the Modern Movement

5
Putting on the Style   40
– America in the thirties

6
A Modern Renaissance   50
– Italy since the fifties

7
The Language of Objects   58
– symbolism and consumer psychology

A–Z Contents   66

A–Z Entries   68

General Bibliography   248

Museums and Institutions   248
with a special interest
in the history of design

Acknowledgments   249

Index of Products and Designs   251

FOREWORD

Everything that man makes is designed, but not everything is well designed. Good design only comes about when things are made with attention both to their functional and their aesthetic qualities. Designers are necessarily concerned with the ordinary, everyday things that we use, but design is by no means a purely utilitarian discipline. Quite the opposite; good design starts from the premise that living is more than just a matter of existing, and that everyday things which are both effective and attractive can raise the quality of life.

This book is largely about the design of products — of the objects we have in our homes and workplaces and the vehicles which carry us around. It looks at the products themselves, the people who designed them, and the artistic, cultural and technical influences which formed them. It is called a 'Directory' because no book with such a huge compass could hope to be encyclopaedic, but its purpose is precise: to promulgate the idea of 'good' design. It has been written to present and discuss those designs and designers of the last hundred years or so that I, and others, consider great in the hope that it will help establish a consensus about what is and what is not good. This is because I believe that things designed with commonsense and with style are better than those made without them, and that the more things that are designed this way, the better for everyone.

Design is more than a particular style, it is an attitude to a product's intrinsic qualities. This is why we react against things which are coarse, bogus or puny, and are drawn to things which have guts, wit and ingenuity. If this sounds more a moral than an aesthetic attitude, then that is how it should be because design affects more than just our eyes.

The term design is itself a modern invention, a product of the machine age; before then the same person who created an object in his mind went on to build it. The great achievements in design of the nineteenth century were civic monuments, the bridges, structures and steamers of Telford, Paxton and Brunel; those of the twentieth century are far more personal, even domestic, in scale: think of Richard Sapper's 'Tizio' lamp, or Ferdinand Porsche's Volkswagen, or the Sony 'Walkman'. In today's mass market every consumer can be a design critic. That gives the consumer the power to affect his or her environment. The more discriminating people become, the more manufacturers will have to realize that merchandise must meet the demands made of it; as a result good design will have to become a fundamental part of any successful business.

Standards and expectations about design are constantly evolving, but one thing is certain: while styles may come and go with the changes of fashion, the essentials of good design remain the same. Things must do the job they were intended to do; they must be well made and efficient; they must also be pleasing to use and to the eye. To paraphrase Edison, good design is 98 per cent commonsense and 2 per cent aesthetics.

Despite its significance, the study of design is in its infancy. Unlike painting and architecture, there are not yet many books or articles on the subject. *The Directory of Design* is just a beginning. It is a book intended to clarify some of the diffuse complexity of a subject that embraces technology, art and anthropology. Like good design itself, this Directory should help you discriminate among the visual clutter of the modern, man-made world.

Terence Conran.

INTRODUCTION

This is a book about design and designers. Although the words are familiar, the concepts are less clear and mean different things to different people. To some, the word 'design' evokes the idea of pattern-making, an idea that can be traced back to the Middle Ages and the Italian word *disegno* (which means 'drawing'). In this sense the tapestries and stained glass windows of the great cathedrals can be said to have been drawn, or designed, in the same way that contemporary industrial designers try their ideas for mass-produced objects in preliminary sketches and working drawings. To others, the modern concept of 'design' is inseparable from the division of labour and the other economic changes brought about by the Industrial Revolution.

What is certain is that with mechanized mass-production and the new industrial and social arrangements it entailed, design and the designer achieved a new and unprecedented status. Just like the cathedral craftsmen of old, the modern designer was someone who *gave form to an idea*. In his book, *The Problems of Design* (1957), the American architect and critic George Nelson even went so far as to write: 'the designer is in essence an artist, one whose tools differ somewhat from those of his predecessors, but an artist nonetheless . . .'.

This directory of design assumes that design is inseparable from modern industry and the modern economy, and that as a fundamental part of the process which brings mass-produced artefacts to us all it is a significant component of contemporary material culture. It sets out to provide factual information and critical opinion about the people, companies, societies, movements and products which have contributed to the character of the modern world and to the climate of ideas which surrounds it. But while the directory aims to offer essential facts and opinions, no claim is made to comprehensiveness. Any directory is necessarily selective and a directory of design especially so. The subject of design covers a wide range of activities, from materials technology at the hard end to styling and marketing at the soft one, and the number of people who have made a contribution to the history of design at any of these levels is vast. This book is limited to the people who had the ideas and who invented the forms which changed our taste.

But the story of design in the twentieth century is not just one of facts and ideas. According to George Nelson, 'design . . . is a manifestation of the capacity of the human spirit to transcend its limitations'. It involves a complex network of ideas which create and define the material content of the modern world. Until now no book has been published to act as a guide to modern design. This book intends to do just that in two ways. While the alphabetical entries give specific

'Design is first and foremost an attitude.'

Roger Tallon

information, the introductory chapters both provide a general outline of the most important changes in the recent history of design, and describe in particular some of the significant moments when structural changes occurred in thinking about and making mass-produced consumer goods. These are the moments which helped create the character of modern design.

The book begins with an account of the marriage which took place in Britain between fine art and the activities of the first industrialists, a group of free-thinking entrepreneurs and inventors produced by Britain's provincial Enlightenment. With the international growth of industrialization, activity in design spread to the other European countries and to the United States. At this point the story of design changes from being one of production to one whose subject is *consumption*, for even from its earliest days the process of design was as much concerned with selling as with making. It was not simply industrial, but also social, change which determined the evolution of design. Succeeding chapters deal with two of the opposing views which influenced modern thinking about design: the craft ideal, another example of a pattern of ideas developing in Britain which became influential abroad, and the romance of the machine, an expression of taste which more than any other style has helped determine the appearance of the things we buy. Other chapters are concerned with the emergence of the professional consultant designer in the United States, the renewal of Italy's industry and culture after the Second World War (which actually made 'design' into a genuine household word), and the subtle issues of symbolism and the condition of design today.

These chapters have been written to provide a succinct and efficient framework for the entries in the alphabetical dictionary, where more details about people and ideas mentioned in them might be found. Taken as a whole, these introductory chapters and the entries which follow should provide the reader with a comprehensive account of modern design, the people, and the firms, ideas and events which created it.

'We don't expect everyone to become expert designers; that is neither possible nor desirable. We cannot all become accountants, but we can learn enough to read a balance sheet.'

Gordon Russell

I

ART
&
INDUSTRY

– the beginnings of design

Modern design is rooted in two distinct developments. One was the division of labour, the industrial process of breaking down manufacturing into its component tasks, which the eighteenth-century Scottish economist Adam Smith said could make manufacturing more profitable. The other was the refinement of techniques of high-volume production prompted by the assumed correlation between high volume and low unit costs. The consequences – long lead times and standardized products – imposed a discipline which called for careful product planning. The technological and social changes which arose around these developments are familiarly known as the Industrial Revolution. They occurred when certain technological processes were noticed and exploited by engineers and entrepreneurs in Britain. Although these same technological processes were known to men of science in all Europe, the British enjoyed a background of political stability, a centralized government, a tradition of free enterprise and of utilitarian philosophy, and also an abundance of natural resources, which together enabled these engineers and entrepreneurs to take the first commercial advantage of industry. And because Britain faced the artistic and social consequences of the Industrial Revolution before any other nation, it was in Britain that design developed first.

In the eighteenth century there was a dominant belief in the power of reason. It went hand in hand with a desire to enquire

'Arkwright's Cotton Mill by Night' by Joseph Wright, 1782–3
Joseph Wright of Derby (1734–97) was one of the first artists to sense the aesthetic opportunities offered by the Industrial Revolution. In a series of remarkable oil paintings he catalogued the scientific experimentation of the later eighteenth century. This painting is one of the first depictions in art of an industrial scene.

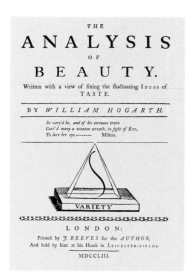

'The Analysis of Beauty' by William Hogarth, 1753
William Hogarth's Analysis of Beauty *was one of the first works to look at emerging consumer products. It is also significant in the history of design in applying rational principles to the discussion of art. Hogarth discussed in a direct and uncomplicated way the process by which certain forms appear pleasing and others displeasing. The implied suggestion was that 'art' was not necessarily constrained by traditional, classical culture. The pyramid contains Hogarth's 'line of beauty'.*

into the nature of both the natural world and the man-made one. Literature was alive with metaphors of industry, the earliest factories offering poets spectacular visions of the future world. For example, in *The Seasons* (1726–30) James Thomson wrote, 'These are thy blessings, Industry, rough power!' It was this sort of investigative, artistic awareness that led the painter William Hogarth to write his book, *The Analysis of Beauty* (1753), in which he set out to quantify the laws which govern our responses to art. Elements of appropriateness and fitness dominate the texts; he is aware that forms which are in themselves elegant can excite disgust if they are misapplied. The book exhibits a new element of informed criticism of the arts such as in its views on Rococo architecture: 'Twisted columns are undoubtedly ornamental; but as they convey an idea of weakness, they always displease, when they are improperly made use of as supports to anything that is bulky.' But he also provided a comment on the emergent phenomenon of consumer products. For his frontispiece he chose to use an illustration of John Cheere's sculpture yards at Hyde Park Corner, where reproduction lead statues of ancient Greek and Roman originals were being fabricated to cater for the demands of the growing middle-class market. Their purchasers could not afford to go on the Grand Tour to buy real antiques with the *milordi*, but nonetheless wanted to show that they were people of taste and discrimination. These *reproduction* classical statues were among the first tokens of taste in the modern world. They were symbols of an age when art met industry, and showed that when mass-production began, manufacturers and artists became *self-conscious* about the style and meaning of what they were making. The development was crucial because the introduction of culture into industry was the beginning of design and marked the start of the process that was to see the disappearance of the simple working craftsman from the economy.

While Hogarth considered these issues at an abstract level in London, in Britain's soon-to-be industrial Midlands **Josiah Wedgwood** was coming to terms with the reality of the early

'The Analysis of Beauty' Frontispiece
Hogarth's frontispiece showed John Cheere's sculpture yards at Hyde Park Corner. Cheere reproduced classical statues in lead, providing the first reproduction 'antiques' for the new middle-class markets.

Wedgwood Factory, 1769
In pursuit of his classical ideal, Josiah Wedgwood called his factory in Staffordshire Etruria. By the early nineteenth century it had become a major centre of British industry.

John Flaxman, 1755–1826
Primarily a sculptor, Flaxman also worked for Josiah Wedgwood and was one of the first industrial designers.

Industrial Revolution. The sculptor John Flaxman was to inscribe on his monument to Wedgwood in Burslem church: 'He converted a rude and inconsiderable manufactory into an elegant Art and an important part of National commerce'. Before mass-production craftsmen controlled every aspect of making, from invention to merchandising, whether individually or in groups. After the Industrial Revolution the designer assumed the role of planner, as distinct from the craftsman 'maker', in the manufacturer-to-consumer cycle, and the new manufacturing and commercial processes had the effect of separating inventing from making and making from selling. Wedgwood was the first to exploit this division of labour in the production of consumer goods. To design his wares he employed practising artists, such as the sculptor John Flaxman, the painter George Stubbs, and countless anonymous Italian modellers, all of whom worked out the appearance of the goods but were not actually involved in making them. In so doing he was the first man to introduce working artists into the industrial process, and he called into existence a new class of being: the designer.

Although where marketing was concerned Wedgwood's achievements all looked forward, there was a substantial element of revivalism in his business because the style his fine artists followed was the current fashion of neo-classicism. This is typical of the age, for although there was a widespread belief in the necessity of progress, artists in the later eighteenth century could only see 'progress' as an interpretation of the art of Greece and Rome. Wedgwood's most famous production was appropriately the reproduction 'Portland' vase of 1790, and he named his Staffordshire factory 'Etruria' in order to evoke the Etruscan art that was in part his model.

Josiah Wedgwood, 1730–95
A pioneer of mass-production techniques, Wedgwood exploited with lasting success the practical innovations of industrialization as well as the social changes it brought about.

'Portland' Vase by Josiah Wedgwood, 1790, and its Original

The taste for 'antiques' among the emerging bourgeoisie in the later eighteenth century was exploited by Josiah Wedgwood. One of the most remarkable productions of his factory was the creation of a facsimile 'Portland' vase, from an original Roman piece of the first century BC (below). Wedgwood's reproduction of 1790 was a deliberate tour de force *intended to demonstrate that the new British manufacturers were at least the equal of the ancients.*

Wedgwood made prodigious contributions to the techniques of mass-production (he kept an 'Experiment Book' where he catalogued his various technical innovations), and was made a Fellow of the Royal Society to acknowledge his work on the development of the pyrometer. It has been said that Wedgwood's research and self-education were inseparable from his commercial ambitions. In this respect, he was a pioneer of marketing, too. To realize the potential of what he had achieved in mass-production he opened a shop to sell his wares in London. These wares were separated by Wedgwood into 'useful' and 'beautiful' ones, evidence that to this eighteenth-century mind a distinction existed between the aesthetic and the practical aspects of design.

Both the moral and the mercantile components of the new phenomenon were sensed simultaneously at an 'official' level. In an ambitious programme to unite commerce with art, William Shipley founded the Society of Arts in 1754 (granted a Royal charter in 1908 and since known as the **Royal Society of Arts**). Its objectives were 'to embolden enterprise, to enlarge Science, to refine Art, to improve Manufactures and extend Commerce', thus summarizing the material and metaphysical aims of Britain's Industrial Enlightenment. It was established in imitation of the more exclusive Royal Society, an elected academy of distinguished scientists, but with more democratic, popular and practical aspirations. As such it gave Britain an institution which did justice to her international industrial lead, and the Society set about administering the Industrial Revolution and regulating its aesthetics.

However, the Society of Arts' results were sadly and ironically more cerebral than practical. Eighty years after the Society was founded, Great Britain's arts might have been doing well enough, and her manufactures and commerce were well-established, but her products were not setting standards which provided models for future generations. When France, Germany (and later the United States) industrialized they proved better able to make fine consumer products than Britain. A Parliamentary Select Committee was appointed in the 1830s to consider the problem of an increase in foreign imports and to find the answer to 'the best means of extending knowledge of the Arts and of the Principles of Design among the People (especially the manufacturing population)'. Distinguished foreigners were called in to give evidence to the committee, which had the doleful business of hearing a formidable weight of evidence suggesting that the quality of French and German education and manufacturing was so far in front of Britain's that there could be little chance of her ever catching up. France and Germany's better design owed much to their schools where models of excellence were collected together to provide examples for the new industrial classes, and where young designers were given training and manufacturers exposed to models for imitation. When the committee published its *Report on Arts and Manufactures* in 1836 its conclusions were that the only chance of saving Britain's industrial future must be 'to infuse, even remotely, into an industrious and enterprising people a love of art'. The *Westminster Review* remarked, 'Enough! and more than enough of testimony to the combined

degradation of taste and national profits! The admonition it conveys is bitter, but wholesome.'

The 1836 Report was the beginning of a Government initiative to sponsor new **Schools of Design** in Ornamental Art. (It also prompted the creation of the first museums in the belief that definite benefits would accrue from gathering together artefacts of high quality from across the ages and exposing the nation's youth to them.) In 1837 the old premises of the Royal Academy in Somerset House were made available for the first School of Design (which was one of the origins of the **Royal College of Art**). Some of the more perceptive critics saw this as a substantial symbol that in the new machine age, fine art would have to move over for industrial design; the painter William Dyce even set up a Jacquard loom in the London School of Design and his successor abolished life drawing in favour of painting on glass and ceramics. But despite these heroic initiatives, and despite the seventeen

Coffee Service, 1909
The Wiener Werkstätte, founded in 1903, demonstrated its distance from Viennese traditions in the decorative arts by specializing in simple geometrical forms. The workshops produced goods that predicted the machine aesthetic but were made by hand – like the artefacts of the Arts and Crafts movement that influenced them strongly.

'Pursuit of excellence is no guarantee of its achievement. It will require both talent and diligence . . . accumulated experience should be a foundation, not a roof.'

Eliot Noyes

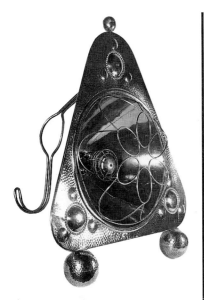

Electric Heater by Peter Behrens, 1907–8
Behrens fused classical, Renaissance and natural elements in his designs for AEG.

ELEKTRISCHE TEE- UND WASSERKESSEL
NACH ENTWÜRFEN VON PROF. PETER BEHRENS

Messing glatt, matt achteckige Form				Kupfer flockig gehämmert achteckige Form				Messing vernickelt, glatt achteckige Form			
Pl. Nr	Inhalt ca. l	Gewicht ca. kg	Preis Mk.	Pl. Nr	Inhalt ca. l	Gewicht ca. kg	Preis Mk.	Pl. Nr	Inhalt ca. l	Gewicht ca. kg	Preis Mk.
3588	0,75	1,75	20,—	3589	0,75	0,75	22,—	3587	0,75	0,75	19,—
3598	1,25	1,0	22,—	3599	1,25	1,0	24,—	3597	1,25	1,0	22,—
3608	1,75	1,1	24,—	3690	1,75	1,1	26,—	3607	1,75	1,1	23,—

ALLGEMEINE ELEKTRICITÄTS-GESELLSCHAFT
ABT. HEIZAPPARATE

Price List for AEG Electric Kettles by Peter Behrens, 1910–13
Behrens controlled AEG's graphics as well as its product design and architecture. In his search for a clear and striking typeface he went back to a fifteenth-century Venetian original.

other Schools of Design set up across the country, by 1846 another Parliamentary Committee was announcing the bold experiment a failure. The initiative had failed to such a degree that when the Prime Minister asked the painter Benjamin Robert Haydon whether the 'people will ever have any taste' his answer was, 'How should they, if no means are taken to educate them?'

Among the reasons for the failure was the fact that the teachers at the Schools of Design were mostly fine artists who had little idea of real commercial needs, and that increasingly, where 'official' opinion was concerned, industry and culture were thought to occupy different areas of social life. Thus, while designers did begin working at ground level within the new ceramic, textile and metal industries, they were not given the same status or titles as fine artists and architects. The expansion of trade during the nineteenth century should have enabled British designers to become fully integrated with the processes of mass-production and marketing, but because the authorities were more concerned with public taste and with the promotion of exports, little was done to realize the practical opportunities for artists working in industry.

The same cannot be said of Germany and the United States. These countries industrialized very rapidly during the second half of the nineteenth century and were more able, or at least more inclined, to adopt a practical approach to design. From the start they were more willing to integrate design into manufacturing, particularly in the emergent electrical industries (where Britain lagged far behind). It was in Germany that an architect, **Peter Behrens**, for the first time took entire control of the appearance of an industrial corporation. For the Allgemeine Elektrizitäts Gesellschaft (**AEG**), Behrens designed everything from posters through kettles to buildings. This ambitious venture, sometimes seen as the first ever **corporate identity** programme, marked Britain's industrial decline relative to her neighbours. From the start Germany's interest in design was stimulated by a national commitment to the idea that industry was not separate from culture.

Electric Kettle by Peter Behrens, 1910
The designer's role in industry was realized early in Germany, where Peter Behrens was given complete charge of design for AEG in the first decade of the twentieth century. Behrens' product designs were adapted to machine production but this did not mean any compromise in elegance.

'We have no choice but to make our lives more simple, more practical, more organized and wide ranging. Only through industry have we any hope of fulfilling our aims.'

Peter Behrens

18

2

MASS
CONSUMPTION

– the beginning of the consumer age

The story of taste in the nineteenth century is one of confusion and crisis. It can be seen as a two-part drama. The first act was the undermining by archaeology of the classical values which sustained Sir Joshua Reynolds and his academicians, especially when an expedition to Sicily by the Franco-German architect Jakob-Ignaz Hittorff (1792–1867), designer of Paris' Gare du Nord, discovered that the ancient temples of the Greeks were not the austere, white edifices which the neo-classicists and academicians had fancied, but were in fact garish and polychrome. The second act was the opening up of consumerism to more than one social class as manufacturing exploded.

The reasons for the growth in consumerism were multiple: they included huge increases in the mass-production of consumer goods because of technological improvements in manufacturing, a rapid rate of increase in population during the second third of the century, a generally improving standard of living, and the growth of urbanization which brought with it the implications of increased consumption of material goods, especially as status objects. By roughly 1860 more people from more social classes were regularly buying more products than ever before. The implications for design were enormous. It was no longer possible to maintain, as Reynolds had done a century earlier, that there was a single standard of taste and that any man could achieve it; quite evidently, there were many standards. Artistic and philosophic attempts to rationalize these different standards form a fundamental part of the story of design in the following century.

Under the influence of mass-consumption the refined, confident elegance of Regency style, which was essentially aristocratic, gave way to a multiplicity of styles that reflected the social and industrial upheavals of the age of Queen Victoria.

With the loss of classical standards, many nineteenth-century designers began to look to other sources for authority for their ideas. Some were led into eclecticism, deriving inspiration from this or that style of the past, while others chose to be guided by 'moral' standards rather than

'The boundless evil, caused by shoddy mass-produced goods and by the uncritical imitation of earlier styles, is like a tidal wave sweeping across the world.'

Josef Hoffmann and Koloman Moser

A Greek Temple envisaged by Jakob-Ignaz Hittorff
When the architect Jakob-Ignaz Hittorff showed that the ancient Greek temples had been polychrome, and were not originally austere and white, the discovery blew apart every assumption of neo-classicism and opened the door to all manner of Victorian excess. This illustration is from his Restitution du temple d'Empédocle à Selinonte *(1828).*

The Great Exhibition, 1851
*The organization of the Great
Exhibition of the Industry of All
Nations in London's Hyde Park
was typical of imperial
Victorian grandeur of purpose.
Intended as a demonstration of
national pride, the Exhibition
left people bewildered by the
undisciplined excess of
nineteenth-century design.*

archaeology. Among the first to react to the explosion in
housing and consumer design was the eccentric architect
Augustus Pugin, who turned to an idealized model of the
Middle Ages (which he imagined as an era of perfect social
harmony) to serve as a didactic contrast to the world of the
'depressed people' which he saw all around him. He was the
major intellectual force behind, and perhaps the greatest
creative genius of, an ethical campaign, concentrated on
architecture, which we call the Gothic Revival. Although
essentially less practical than **Henry Cole**, the Victorian
official who was most active in promoting design as a solution
to Britain's export problem, Pugin's thought was a profound
influence on Cole and his group: the **Journal of Design and
Manufactures**, founded by Cole in 1849, is full of Pugin's
thought translated into 'sound principles', but contained a
hard, commercial sense quite alien to Pugin's medievalism.
Both men were implacable critics of the Government's
Schools of Design. Pugin wrote:

'I have almost given up my hope of seeing any real good
effected by the Schools of Design . . . [they are] a hindrance

*'How many things can you
do to enhance life, and how
do you avoid those things
which do not? If there is a
moral commitment – or an
opportunity – for a designer,
that is it.'*

George Nelson

to the revival of true taste and feeling, for the minds of the students are perverted by copying the same stale models that have been used for years without producing a single artist capable of designing anything original or appropriate.'

Henry Cole shared his view.

Pugin's solution to the disorders of the day was a happy rediscovery of the architecture of the Middle Ages. He believed that 'good' societies produced 'good' people and that 'good' people necessarily produced 'good' design. But this was not merely backward-looking romanticism: Pugin had sophisticated ideas about the propriety of form. In his book, *Christian Architecture* (1841), he wrote:

'It is impossible to enumerate half the absurdities of modern metal workers; but all these proceed from the false notion of *disguising* instead of *beautifying* articles of utility. How many objects of ordinary use are rendered monstrous and ridiculous, simply because the artist, instead of seeking the *most convenient form*, and then *decorating* it, has embodied some *extravagance to conceal the real purpose for which the article was made!*'

This strain of thought passed directly to **William Morris**, who absorbed the ideas wholesale. Pugin thus has a claim to be the founder of the entire sensibility that was later to give nineteenth-century design theorists their views on propriety and from there fed directly into the **Modern Movement**, but he also has a claim to be the creator of that backward-looking sentiment which ultimately sucked life out of it. That he could do both is a testament to the fecundity of his thought and its influence.

Pugin was also a major influence in the form and the content of the **Great Exhibition** of 1851, a lesson in taste conceived for

'You cannot bore people into buying your product, you can only interest them in buying it. You cannot save souls in an empty church . . .'

David Ogilvy

Augustus Pugin, 1812–52
Architect and theorist of the Gothic Revival, Pugin argued that there was a strong connection between morality and design.

Revolver by Samuel Colt, c. 1849
The most perceptive critics of the Great Exhibition realized that, while some of the furniture was got up to look like the west front of Lincoln Cathedral, there was often a more authentic type of design among the utilitarian objects on display. Samuel Colt's 'Navy' model revolver, designed on a modular system, attracted praise for its functional elegance and simplicity.

Henry Cole, 1808–82
Cole was a civil servant who both conceived the idea of a Great Exhibition and created the Victoria and Albert Museum in order to promote good design in Britain.

the British nation by Prince Albert, Henry Cole and their circle of friends. It was to be a didactic *tableau vivant*, one of the first major trade exhibitions, but it proved to be something of a shock. Just as Pugin had said, industry appeared to be out of control: the mass-produced objects on display were scarred by vulgar and inappropriate ornament and too many of them were concerned with extravagances which concealed their real purpose. While many of the Indian products were 'rude' in workmanship, it was agreed that they very often displayed an understanding of the 'correct principles of ornament' superior to anything made in Britain. Gottfried Semper, a German architect resident in England, noticed (as **Horatio Greenough** had in America) that it was only purely utilitarian objects, like Samuel Colt's .36 'Navy' revolver from the United States, which was also being manufactured on a small scale in Pimlico, that seemed to be pleasing and appropriate.

One result of the Great Exhibition was that sensitive individuals in the circle of Prince Albert were prompted, a century after Hogarth, to analyse anew the aesthetic principles which govern our reaction to pattern and design. The most remarkable and influential publication to result from this was a book called *The Grammar of Ornament*, compiled by a Welsh architect called **Owen Jones**. Another result was a renewed impetus to create an educational institution that would cater for Britain's needs in the area of design. This was to be a museum run by Henry Cole.

A committee, which included Pugin, was set up to select exhibits from the Great Exhibition to put into Henry Cole's new museum. They were chosen in order to counter the malaise which they considered to have afflicted contemporary industry, and in order to teach the public some lessons in taste. Of £5,000 made available, almost twice as much was spent on Indian products as on British ones selected 'without reference to styles, but entirely for the excellence of their art or workmanship'. Under the auspices of the Government's

'Sunlight' Soap
The age of mass-consumption introduced the consumer to new types and families of product. William Hesketh Lever's 'Sunlight' was the first soap to carry a brand name; until the last quarter of the nineteenth century soap had been merely a generic product.

Linley Samborne's House
The other extreme of London accommodation during the mid-nineteenth century to that depicted by Doré was the house in Kensington occupied by Punch *illustrator, Linley Samborne. The High Victorian taste for clutter was amply satisfied by thriving manufacturers of furniture and fabrics.*

'Fine art deals with internally imposed problems. But if there's no external problem, there is no design.'

Milton Glaser

Department of Practical Art (which became the Department of Science and Art in 1853), this collection was assembled into the Museum of Manufactures at Marlborough House on Pall Mall the year after the exhibition closed. The germ of the collection grew by gifts and acquisitions, all the time maintaining adherence to its founding idea that 'Each specimen has been selected for its merits in exemplifying some right principle of construction or ornament . . . to which it appeared desirable that the attention of our Students and Manufacturers should be directed.' In addition, in order to emphasize some lessons in design, Henry Cole set up a 'Chamber of Horrors' in the Museum of Manufactures. Here he would demonstrate how the mass-produced metalware of Birmingham (which Pugin called an 'inexhaustible mine of bad taste') was inferior to the 'rude scarfs of Tunis'. It was an inspired reversal of the principles of the traditional academy: instead of setting up examples for imitation, Cole set up some examples for avoidance, 'bad' designs, full of false principles, put on display to be reviled and to excite higher ambitions.

With all the moral certainty of the age, Cole and his colleagues set out to look for some aesthetic certainties too. They were absolutely sure that they knew what was good and what was bad in design, and what was bad was lack of symmetry, disregard of structure, formless confusion and superficial decoration. Although Cole's efforts aroused public ridicule (and most of the manufacturers insisted on having their products withdrawn), he got the sort of response that betrayed deeply suppressed instincts and fears. Five years after the 'Chamber of Horrors', he was able to set up his grander museum in rural Brompton on land owned by the Commissioners of the 1851 exhibition. With great clarity of vision he wanted his new museum to be 'specially commercial in so commercial an age'. At first known as the South Kensington Museum and then as the 'Brompton Boilers' (on account of its apparently makeshift construction in iron), the Museum which Cole founded was renamed the **Victoria and**

Benz Car, 1883
The Benz factory was founded in Mannheim in 1883 and within two years the first automobiles powered by internal combustion engines began to appear. Initially cars were such a radical innovation for the consumer that novelty alone determined their appeal, and their appearance was drawn straight from the horse-drawn carriages they were about to supersede.

National Telephone Company Exchange, c. 1900
Along with the other late-nineteenth-century inventions of the typewriter and the automobile, the telephone changed the normal way of life. The great electrical combines, such as AEG in Germany and Westinghouse in the United States, helped shrink the world by making nationwide systems. The telephone provided an important component of the modern office: instant communication.

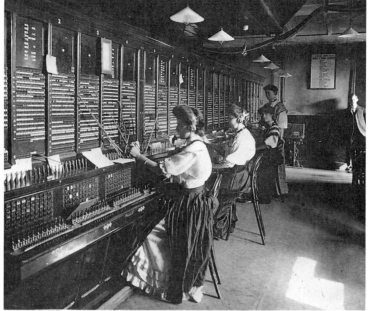

Remington Typewriter, 1870s
The age of mass-consumption saw the introduction of machines which changed the character of work. The first workable typewriters were perfected in the United States during the 1870s by arms manufacturers such as Remington.

'Two innocent articles of American life – the Sears, Roebuck catalog and the phonograph record – are the most powerful pieces of foreign propaganda in Russia . . . the catalog comes first.'

Franklin D. Roosevelt

Sears, Roebuck Catalogue, Fall 1897
Along with branded products, another innovation that provided a basis for the development of design was the creation of modern mass-distribution. This was perfected in the United States, where Sears, Roebuck used the new railway system to distribute goods sold through a mail order catalogue which provided even inhabitants of remote rural communities with the same choice as in the world's largest department store. The illustration shows the title page of their Fall 1897 catalogue.

Albert Museum in 1899. But Cole and his fellows did not realize that the emerging world economy meant that the market was likely to dominate taste and that it was no longer possible for a small elite, no matter how well-intentioned, to set universal standards.

While in Britain the problems of design reform and public taste preoccupied the authorities, in the United States a less self-conscious attitude towards mass-production and consumption developed. While Britain led in the manufacture of goods in some traditional applied art industries (of ceramics and textiles, for instance), during the second half of the nineteenth century new companies in the United States surged ahead in the making of mechanical and electrical goods. Add to this the relative wealth and homogeneous character of a population sharing the same basic economic circumstances, and the picture of a country ready for huge innovations in mass-consumption is complete.

The United States was the first nation to produce and consume new appliances such as vacuum cleaners, sewing machines, typewriters and washing machines. At the same time it developed a 'culture' of these goods for the home and the office. The early emancipation of women and the smaller numbers of servants after the Civil War encouraged the growth of these manufacturing industries and meant that new merchandise was to acquire a role in everyday life three quarters of a century before it happened in Europe.

At first the design of the new American products was determined by the manufacturing processes by which they were made. Samuel Colt's elemental 'Navy' model revolver which had shocked the British in 1851 was a remarkable example of how the aesthetic character of the product could be determined by machine-made, standardized parts. This approach pervaded the early production of all mechanical and electrical goods in the United States, but was moderated as mass-consumption increased. Soon the new products were decorated with surface patterns, applied as a marketing strategy to enhance their appeal to female consumers. American design was to develop in a more pragmatic way than in Europe, and designers and manufacturers were always aware of the demands of the market place and were quite unashamed to respond to them. In early American design theory, there was none of the need to make moral statements, as did Pugin, Morris and their followers. From this moment, design in America had a special quality. The United States was uninhibited by the cultural and political boundaries that constrained the Europeans. Influenced only by manufacturing processes and motivated by marketing needs, American industry enjoyed the opportunity of supplying a vast, homogeneous market with unique modern products. It is not surprising that when the first industrial design studios appeared, it was in America.

Hoover Factory, West London, 1940s
Patterns of manufacturing and assembly derived from nineteenth-century experience lasted until well into the twentieth. The methods and means of production influence the character of products we use.

3

THE

CRAFT

IDEAL

– survival and revival of old values

In the later nineteenth century British design became more involved with morals and ideology than even **Pugin** could have envisaged. To the leading writers of the age, the major challenge was to establish a simple and rational way of life but, in contrast, the most celebrated contemporary designer **William Morris** offered what was basically an exclusive and elitist pseudo-medieval fantasy world.

Morris and his contemporaries inherited a considerable amount of their theory from Pugin, especially his hatred of the city (whose image he liked to draw as a stack of sooty factory chimneys, a soulless non-conformist chapel and tenement housing). Pugin and, later, **John Ruskin** were High Tories who despised the crude middle classes and the modern innovation of joint-stock capitalism, and each found distant prospects (of either the Middle Ages or the countryside) to act as symbolic cures for contemporary ills. Their views took root to such an extent that in the next generation the leaders of taste in Britain became spokesmen of the back-to-the-land disposition, inspired by culturally complex and essentially fanciful rural ideals.

From Pugin via Ruskin and Morris a movement called the **Arts and Crafts** arose. The protagonists were **C.F.A. Voysey**, **C.R. Ashbee**, **A.H. Mackmurdo**, **Ernest Gimson** and the **Barnsley Brothers**. As its historian, Gillian Naylor, has said, the movement was 'based in part on a generation's preoccupation with doctrine and "style" in architecture and design, and in part on reactions . . . to the facts of life in a machine age'.

Its members promoted the crafts and repudiated industry. They considered craft activity superior to alienated divided labour and believed that design should be based on craft principles, such as 'truth to nature' and 'fitness to purpose'. In many ways their ideas were strongly in the utopian socialist mould, as they often maintained that simple design meant democratic design, no matter what the logical flaws. Similarly, work was organized into pseudo-medieval 'guilds' rather than modern hierarchies. In the event their ideas were far

'Forget the spreading of the hideous town;
Think rather of the pack-horse on the down.'

William Morris

'Fruit' Wallpaper by William Morris, 1864
Morris excelled in the design of flat patterns, derived from fruits, flowers and animals. His utopian socialism and his love of natural details made him the spiritual leader of the Crafts Revival of the twentieth century. The 'Fruit' wallpaper was still in production in the 1980s.

27

more radical than their actual designs (which remained traditional, even historicist).

Arts and Crafts principles reached the public with the work of **Ambrose Heal**, a shopkeeper and furniture-maker and founder member of the Design and Industries Association. His store in London's Tottenham Court Road was seen as an island of civilized values in an ocean of reproduction mediocrity – indeed, *The Artist* called the furniture stores neighbouring Heal's 'slurs on civilization'. Heal's honest designs with his unpolished, unstained oak were the expression in furniture of the taste for things natural and simple that had made the socialist thinker Edward Carpenter wear sandals and a Saxon tunic, and turned George Bernard Shaw into a disciple of Gustav Jaeger's sanitary woollen systems, which declared that animal fibres were more healthy to wear than

William Morris, 1834–96
Poet, pamphleteer and craftsman, Morris provided the role model for later artist-craftsmen.

Tiles by William Morris, 1870s/80s
William Morris' tiles, fabrics and furniture were much favoured by the urban middle classes of his day. It is ironic, if perhaps inevitable, that the social group which benefited most from industrialization should choose to surround itself with tokens of a quasi-medieval rural Arcadia.

Morris Workshops at Merton Abbey, 1880s
Morris was less able to create an effective medieval atmosphere in his workshops. Economic realities forced him to practise the division of labour as ruthlessly as any manufacturer from Birmingham.

The Lygon Arms, Broadway, Worcestershire
This hotel became the symbolic home of the modern crafts tradition in British furniture-making. Owned by the Russell family since 1904, the Lygon Arms was the seat of Gordon Russell who established his furniture workshops in the village. The picturesque Cotswold stone building was an emblem of the craftsman's idealistic vision of returning to an imaginary world of the past.

dead vegetable ones. Heal was himself exposed to these theories, but was particularly inspired by the theories of W.R. Lethaby, the architect-educationalist and pioneer member of the DIA. Lethaby looked around at the products of High Victorian mass-consumption and observed that the chief characteristics were 'extravagant expenditure on the worthless; the lowering of our demands to a penny picture postcard level; and overcrowding with trivialities'.

Although Heal's introduction of simplicity into the market was a radical departure for a conservative industry, the fact that his Arts and Crafts inspiration was, however distantly, derived from the past drove British taste, because of its very success, down a blind alley of nostalgia. This prevented it in subsequent decades from responding to the more modern impulses coming from continental Europe. Although ideas about fitness and propriety which had originated in Britain were taken up with enthusiasm in the German-speaking countries and in Scandinavia, where they were translated into the **Modern Movement**, there was so little response in their native country that **Nikolaus Pevsner** could declare in the mid-thirties that Britain was at least twelve years behind the rest of Europe in accepting modern design. The British heritage was a rag-bag of clubs and guilds, sentimental relics left behind after the wave of Arts and Crafts enthusiasm had receded.

Perhaps the keenest response to the demand for simplicity was found in Austria, a country whose relative industrial primitiveness offered a firmer basis for innovation. It was in Austria that **Michael Thonet** had begun his successful manufacture of bentwood furniture in the middle of the nineteenth century. It was also in Austria that the architect **Adolf Loos** adapted the Arts and Crafts view about simple materials, blended it with his own slick and idiosyncratic view of manners and style, and turned it into a 'philosophy' that was to be profoundly influential on the Modern Movement. He wrote in 1898, 'What is worth more, a kilogram of stone or a kilogram of gold? The question probably seems ridiculous. But only to the merchant. The artist will answer: all materials are equally valuable as far as I am concerned.'

This taste for simplicity reached such an extreme state with Loos that in 1908 he wrote an esssay which he entitled

John Ruskin, 1819–1900
Ruskin turned art criticism into social criticism.

'It is already becoming possible to point out that helping the Modern Movement is by no means a commercially unsound proposition. The large number of industrialists who followed the new path as a logical decision have obtained significant financial success.'

Hermann Muthesius

Painted Earthenware Tiles by William De Morgan, 1880s
De Morgan (1839–1917) was one of the most skilled craftsmen designers in the Morris workshops, which began selling his tiles in 1872. In the 1880s he set up his own pottery near William Morris' Merton Abbey workshops.

Cabinet by Walter Gropius, c. 1910
Walter Gropius' style and direction emerged from the German neo-classical tradition, and his evolution towards the Modern Movement was gradual. This handsome cabinet of about 1910 is entirely neo-classical in spirit.

'Ornament and Crime'. His thought became one of the strongest esoteric influences on **Le Corbusier** and the others who used Loos' fevered proclamations as the ideological basis for 'progressive' European architecture and design between the Wars.

The impact of British ideas was felt strongly in Germany. One of the transmitters of the influence was the diplomat **Hermann Muthesius**, whose book, *Das Englische Haus* (1905), with its explanation of the Arts and Crafts, contributed to the climate of ideas surrounding the creation of the **Deutsche Werkbund** in 1907. However, the German Werkbund was far more committed to industrial production than were any of the British design reformers, and Muthesius himself made a profound contribution to **German design** and education in his elaboration of the theory of *Typisierung* (standardization). This theory ultimately emerged in **Walter Gropius'** syllabus at the **Bauhaus** together with some Arts and Crafts principles about form and materials, which meant that in a roundabout way the backward-looking theories of the British craft enthusiasts contributed directly to the chief creative group of the Modern Movement.

Arts and Crafts principles were imported, too, into the United States at the turn of the century, influencing the ideas and work of **Frank Lloyd Wright**, whose maverick ideas and inspired leadership were to have a fundamental effect on **design theory** in the twentieth century.

The Scandinavian countries were also deeply influenced by British ideas. They all had equivalent indigenous craft movements and, as in Britain, the promotion of craft ideals became a sort of statement about national values. In Finland the craft movement centred around Eliel Saarinen, in Denmark around the silversmith **Georg Jensen**, and in Sweden (which was more industrially advanced than its neighbours) around the industries of **Gustavsberg**, **Orrefors** and **Rörstrand**.

The Scandinavian interpretation of the craft ideal was, perhaps, the most genuinely successful one. These countries succeeded in forming a genuine alliance between craft

'*Not only is ornament produced by criminals, but also a crime is committed through the fact that ornament inflicts serious injury on people's health, on the national budget and hence on cultural evolution.*'

Adolf Loos

Adolf Loos, 1870–1933
Viennese architect and polemicist, Loos was the éminence grise of the Modern Movement.

Carl Larsson's Country Home, Sweden, 1885
A powerful influence on European interior decoration in the early decades of this century was the work of Carl Larsson (1853–1919). A series of books appeared between 1899 and 1910, all illustrated with views of his house, and the new ideals that Larsson set forth reached a wide audience through German editions. The interiors of Larsson and his wife Karin embraced light and air; they exemplify the Scandinavian craft ideal, where traditional techniques blend with modern needs.

practice and industrial production, at the same time evolving a democratic, modern design which respected traditional materials and production techniques, but which responded, nonetheless, to the social and economic requirements of the twentieth century.

Scandinavian furniture designers never entirely rejected wood in favour of tubular steel, nor did they do away with natural patterns or colour. Their solution was to combine the best of the old with the best of the new and to move gently and gracefully into the twentieth century.

Crafts ideals still exist today, having been artificially stimulated by the **Crafts Revival**. In reality craft and design can never be entirely separated: the craft ideal remains a means of moderating the loss of humanism in mass-production, while providing objective standards of quality for industrial designers to emulate.

A Door Knocker in the form of a Lizard by Lavirotte, on a House in the Avenue Rapp, Paris, 1900
Although its parentage was in the Arts and Crafts movement, Art Nouveau showed no interest in simplicity: it was rather the last manifestation of the nineteenth century's love of decoration.

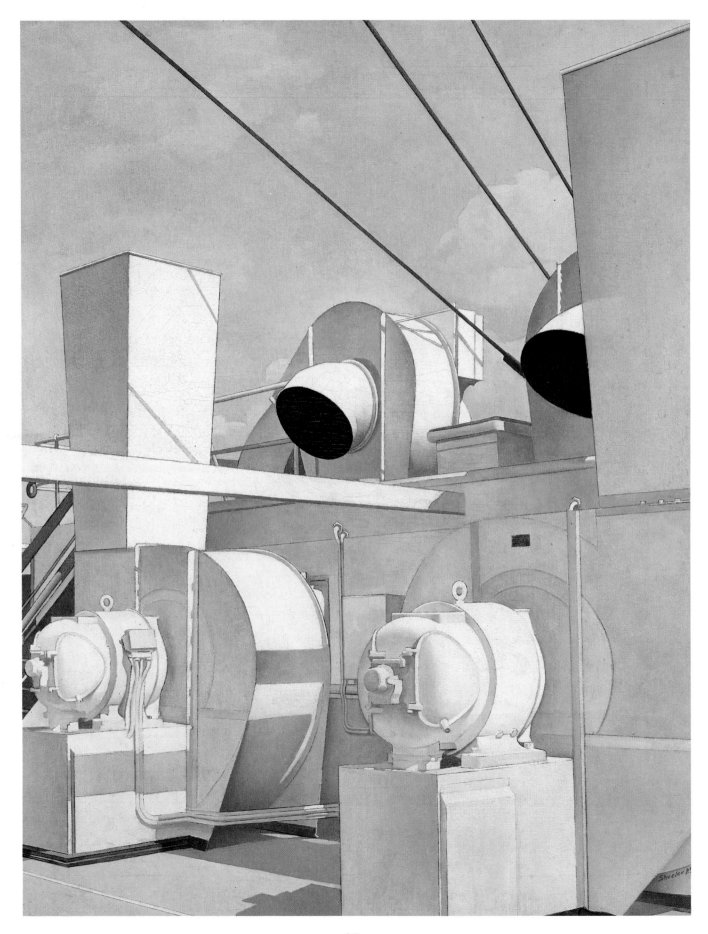

4

THE
ROMANCE
OF THE
MACHINE

– the Modern Movement

The taste for simplicity and for first principles in matters of design predisposed many architects and designers throughout Europe and the United States to an awareness of the machine, both as a means of achieving rational modern design (in mass-production) and as a metaphor of that achievement (when mechanistic details were adapted for everyday things).

Although the proponents of this machine style believed they represented the unalterably correct expression of the modern world, like **Functionalism** (with which machine romanticism is sometimes confused) the style was itself no more than an expression of a particular taste. But unlike Functionalism, which is a philosophical attitude more than two hundred years old, the romance of the machine has developed solely in the twentieth century. The Victorians believed that when machines were consumer products they should be disguised; the promoters of the **Modern Movement** believed that machines should speak for themselves (and, occasionally, for other things too). The rationale was that the visual character of any product should be determined by the internal logic of its construction and mechanism. In architecture this approach had deep-seated and strong social and aesthetic implications, in product design it was usually interpreted more in terms of symbolically effective styling.

The First World War brought about major structural changes in industrial production. The military demand for high-quality, mass-produced components created a need for standardization which after the War provided a tangible ideal for modern mass-produced consumer products. Even before the war the **Deutsche Werkbund** had promoted the idea of *Typisierung* (standardization of objects) and the architect Bruno Paul had produced *Typenmobel* (standardized furniture); but the most vigorous innovations came

'The Machine Aesthetic . . . was . . . selective and classicizing, one limb of the reaction against the excesses of Art Nouveau, and it came nowhere near an acceptance of machines on their own terms or for their own sakes.'

Peter Reyner Banham

'Upper Deck' by Charles Sheeler, 1929
Various twentieth-century painters have taken their inspiration from the machine; the American artist Charles Sheeler (1883–1965) is the most outstanding of them. (Oil on canvas, 74 × 56.3 cm. Courtesy of the Fogg Art Museum, Harvard University/Purchase – Louise E. Bettens Fund.)

about in 1927–8 when the Deutscher Normen Ausschuss (German Standards Commission) produced proposals for the A-standard paper sizes which were used by the Reichskuratorium für Wirtschaftlichkeit (State Efficiency Board) in its programmatic introduction of standardized procedures into book-keeping.

Although the Germans had the greatest practical successes with the impulse to standardize and to tidy up, it was with a Swiss architect, **Le Corbusier**, that the same impulse reached its extreme. Le Corbusier was heavily influenced by his contact with German architects, but his work was to exceed theirs to an immeasurable extent in romance and poetry. To the German industrial ethic he added style, verve and wit. He made houses look like aeroplanes and ships and he analysed eighteenth-century architecture in pseudo-scientific terms so as to demonstrate that a taste for order was omnipresent in beautiful things. In his magazine, *L'Esprit nouveau*, he liked to publish cut-away drawings of stub axles, presenting a banal component from a modern car factory as an image as worthy of contemplation and as likely to exalt as great sculpture or great painting.

'Air Pullman' by William Stout, 1920s
The first generation of aeroplanes excited the admiration of designers, although few were the sleek machines of the artists' imaginations. One man who did produce such shapes was the pioneer in the construction of all-metal monoplanes, William B. Stout. His 'Air Pullman' first flew in the early twenties, and its corrugated duralumin fuselage and geometrical arrangement were a 'real world' equivalent of contemporary Bauhaus educational theory.

'The eighteenth century Age of Reason was followed by the nineteenth century Age of Scientific Inquiry, which exploded, in the twentieth century, into the Age of Perfectability through Science and Art. It was, of course, an impossible dream . . .'

Ada Louise Huxtable

'Tank' Watch by Louis Cartier, 1917
One of the greatest cultural effects of the First World War was to force an awareness of the machine on to civilization. A trivial, although fascinating, footnote to this is the development of the wristwatch. Before the First World War wristwatches had been considered effeminate, but after they were used by German gunners, who did not have the time to fumble for pocketwatches, they gained greater acceptance. The Parisian jeweller Louis Cartier named his 'Tank' watch after the US Army Tank Corps. In name and in style it reflected the romance of the machine.

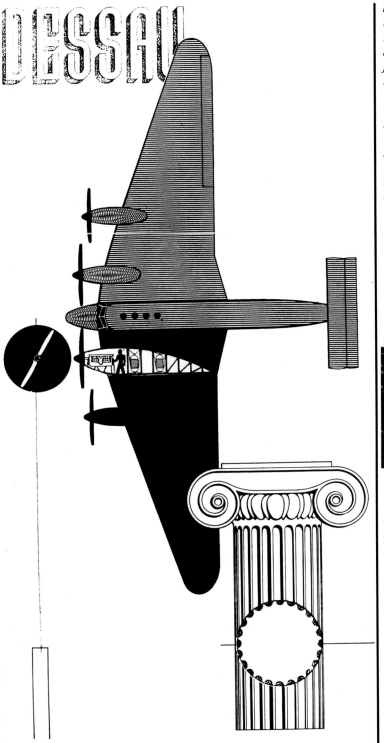

Brochure for Verkehrsbüro, Dessau, by Joost Schmidt, 1930
Elements of classical tradition and Modernism can be seen in Joost Schmidt's design of a brochure for Dessau's Transport Office. Dessau was the home of both the Bauhaus and the Junkers aircraft factory, but the city fathers were anxious to emphasize that it was also a city of traditional culture: hence the Ionic column.

Villa Savoie, Poissy, by Le Corbusier, 1929–31
A tour de force of the machine aesthetic, the house that was a machine for living in.

Le Corbusier followed the **Werkbund**'s austere *Typisierung* in looking for objects suitable as the chic French *objet-type*: he used the café wine glass and the **Thonet** chair both in his architectural interiors and in his Purist paintings. He believed that engineers were 'healthy and virile, active and useful, balanced and happy in their work', and he coined the ultimate expression of the machine-romantic sentiment when he declared that 'a house is a machine for living in'. Misquoted and taken out of context this remark brought about such abuse that **Frank Lloyd Wright** rejoined, 'Yes, but

'If the artist is really to function in the modern world, he must feel himself a part of it, and to have this sense of social integration he must command the instruments and materials of that world.'

Laszlo Moholy-Nagy

Bauhaus Exhibition Poster by Laszlo Moholy-Nagy, 1923
After beginnings influenced by the Arts and Crafts and by Expressionism, the Bauhaus graphic style was given its modern direction by Laszlo Moholy-Nagy. His own paintings were all formal experiments with colour and line, diagrams of ideas about light and space. He translated the same aesthetic into his graphics. For the Bauhaus Exhibition of 1923 he designed a series of posters whose geometricism, like that of his fine art, was a graphic symbol of the machine aesthetic.

Laszlo Moholy-Nagy, 1895–1946
A Hungarian artist and pedagogue, Moholy-Nagy put the Bauhaus ideal into practice.

'The school is the servant of the workshop.'

*Walter Gropius
(on the Bauhaus)*

'The Bauhaus was not an institution . . . it was an idea.'

Mies van der Rohe

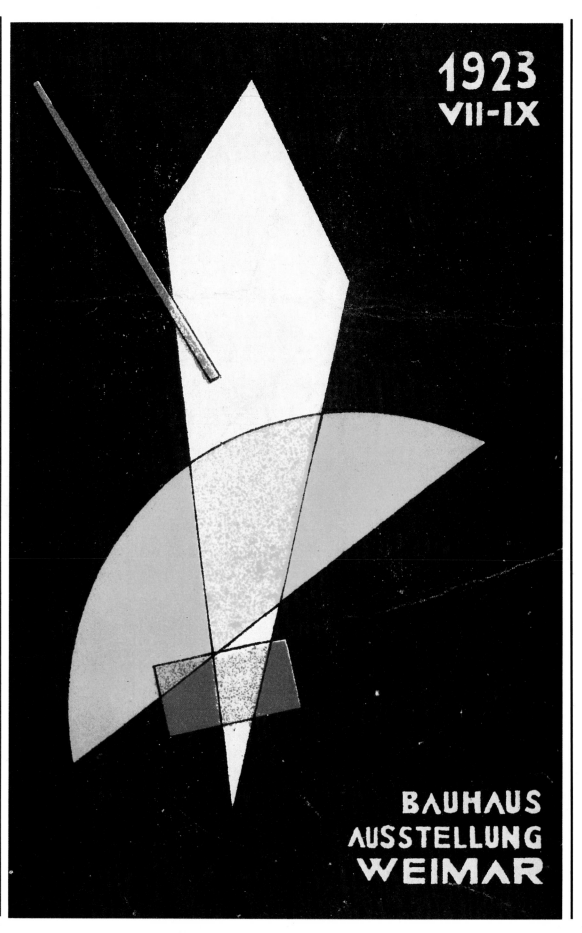

only insofar as the human heart is a suction pump', and **Marcel Breuer** added, 'and you don't want to get greasy if you lean against a wall'.

The machine aesthetic influenced fine art and art education. In Holland a group of architects and painters called **De Stijl** evolved a simple visual language based on primary colours and black and white horizontal and vertical (and, only later, diagonal) lines. **Gerrit Rietveld**'s 'Red-Blue' chair of 1918 was the supreme example of this aesthetic, a rigorous language which made furniture design into a theorem: the overlapping planes of this remarkable and unlikely chair were intended as a demonstration of chair construction and as a diagram of the route of forces. Early contacts with members of the De Stijl group influenced the development of the foundation course at the **Bauhaus**, where students were introduced to ideas about 'basic' design, to geometrical shapes which, at least in metaphorical terms, suggested the rationality of the machine. Conducted by painters such as Wassily Kandinsky and Paul Klee, and guided by the mystic pedagogue **Johannes Itten**, students at the Bauhaus were taught how to construct two- and three-dimensional compositions from basic geometrical units in simple, yet expressive, ways. It was these pseudo-mechanistic forms that the students later translated into

The Schroeder House by Gerrit Rietveld, 1923
The architects, designers and artists of the German Bauhaus were not the only exponents of a style that was inspired by the machine. In Holland a group of similarly inspired artistic radicals called De Stijl was founded in 1917. Among them was cabinet-maker, designer and architect Gerrit Rietveld, who designed and built the Schroeder House in Utrecht in 1923. At the time it was the most rigorous statement of the new aesthetic.

'How to Live in a Flat' by W. Heath-Robinson and K.R.G. Browne, 1936
Tubular steel was only a rational material for furniture in certain respects and the zealots who promoted it were an easy target for lampoon. In Heath-Robinson and Browne's satire, the authors say that if conversation at dinner lapses an interesting diversion can be trying to find the joins in the metalwork.

'Model B33' Chair by Marcel Breuer, 1930
It was from the nearby Junkers aircraft factory that Bauhaus designers learnt to use the new tubular steel. First employed in aircraft, tubular steel became one of the emblems of the Modern Movement. Marcel Breuer was perhaps the most accomplished exponent of its language. This chair was manufactured by Thonet.

objects – desklights and kettles – which they made in the craft workshops of the Bauhaus where the philosophy of their early training was put into practice.

The taste for machine living was never fully accepted in the United States, despite the success of the 1934 'Machine Art' exhibition at New York's **Museum of Modern Art**. Nor was it ever fully accepted in Britain (except by local authority architects who imitated only the superficial aspects of Le Corbusier's architecture, ignoring his refinements and lacking his sophisticated cultural references). Sir Reginald Blomfield said that most modern interiors designed on the Le Corbusier model looked as though they were fit only for 'vegetarian bacteriologists'. At about the same time Heath-Robinson and K.R.G. Browne published a satire, *How To Live in a Flat*, finding tubular steel furniture the most risible of all the machine-romantics' inventions. Indeed, the tubular steel chair, derived from the technology of aircraft production, was, both its champions and its enemies agreed, the most characteristic symbol of a taste for the machine . . . and the absurdities which sometimes arose from it.

There is a sense in which the roots of the Modern Movement can be found in neo-classicism. Not just in the way in which Le Corbusier ascribed to Blondel the same impetus that inspired him, but also in the sense that both the neo-classical architects and the designers of the Modern Movement were searching for authority. One looked for it to the past, the other looked around and saw it in the unself-conscious products of industry.

Ironically, it was some time before the machine aesthetic was actually applied to machines themselves. It first found expression in architecture (and paradoxically in some applied art industries) where the references to 'the machine' were really little more than a justification of a taste for simple, abstract forms.

After the Second World War the machine style reached its most highly developed state, especially in the products of the Frankfurt electrical company **Braun** and those of all its imitators from Britain through the United States to Japan. It fell to **Dieter Rams**, Braun's chief designer, to introduce some Bauhaus principles to the consumer. Rams believes that appliances should be discreet, 'like the good English butler', and not dominate their surroundings. Preferably, they should

'Bestlite' Lamp, 1930s
The 'Bestlite' is a classic whose uncluttered design has seen it remain in continuous production for more than fifty years.

'*Thomas Aquinas said that reason is the first principle of all human work. Now, when you have grasped that, you act accordingly. So, I would throw anything out that is not reasonable. I don't want to be interesting. I want to be good.*'

Mies van der Rohe

be black, white or grey. This refined minimalism was the starting point of the phenomenon of the 'black box' in industrial design. Successive reductions of detail created an anonymity that was, in fact, a curious reversal of the expressive principles which had originally inspired the campaigners for the machine style. Taken to its *reductio ad absurdum*, Rams' spare, angular designs showed that the machine style did not produce 'rational' consumer products, that somehow reflected the function of the machine itself, but only very stylized ones.

Boulder Dam, Colorado, 1936
Henry J. Kaiser's Boulder Dam was often illustrated in books and magazines when writers wanted to justify design experiments by referring to great feats of engineering. Kaiser's achievements, and those of aircraft pioneers, were common examples for the first generation of industrial designers.

'Nighthawks' by Edward Hopper, 1942 (detail)
Hopper's paintings capture the tawdry reality of the consumerist American Dream of the forties and fifties. (Oil on canvas, 76.2 × 152.4 cm. Friends of the American Art Collection. Copyright the Art Institute of Chicago.)

5

PUTTING
ON THE
STYLE

– America in the thirties

The concept of design in the USA has always been somewhat different to that held in Europe. Edgar Allan Poe outlined the American attitude in an essay, 'The Philosophy of Furniture': 'We have no aristocracy of blood, and having therefore as a natural, and indeed as an inevitable thing, fashioned for ourselves an aristocracy of dollars, the *display of wealth* has . . . to take the place and perform the office of heraldic display in monarchical countries.'

Around the time of the First World War, what professional design there had been in consumer products was directed at what was imagined to be, and unself-consciously declared as, 'women's tastes'. This taste was assumed to be wantonly eclectic, decorative and superficial, but represented a significant market. When the publisher **Condé Nast** took over **House & Garden** in 1915 it was with the intention of showing women that the home could be just as effective an expression of self as fashion. It was these 'tastes' and this market that the first generation of professional industrial designers began to attack.

At the end of the War America began to sense some of the symbolic requirements of the new machine age. The Metropolitan Museum in New York appointed a young curator, Richard F. Bach, with a special brief to encourage 'the application of arts to manufactures and practical life', rather as **Henry Cole**'s Museum of Practical Art had striven to do in London sixty years before. In Bach's imagination factories were to become provinces of art and imagination, the assembly lines empty canvases. By 1925 he had assembled more than one thousand examples of industrial art in the Met and arranged them to demonstrate his passionately held belief that the relevant medium of the twentieth century was not oil on canvas or sculptured marble, but mass-produced consumer goods. At a time when the department stores were filled with ugly, crude, revivalist styles – apparently reflecting 'women's tastes' and ironically looking rather like conventional museums – Bach was pleased to be able to claim that his

department at the Met was beginning to look more and more like a real, modern store. A colleague of Bach's at New Jersey's Newark Museum called John Cotton Dana also sensed the spirit of the age and in an emotional appeal to businessmen, published in *Forbes* magazine in 1928, spoke of the importance of design to a lively economy and coined the memorable phrase 'the cash value of art' to describe to *Forbes'* readers what might be gained from applying design to manufacturing.

The problem that Dana was addressing was that the success of the mail order businesses of Sears, Roebuck and others had satisfied the day-to-day material needs of the nation and the production/consumption cycle had become static. There was no growth in output so manufacturers had to compete amongst themselves to capture whatever was available of the consumer's disposable income. The situation worsened during the Depression; then the National Recovery Act stabilized prices, removing even price differential from the customer's horizon of choice. Manufacturers could now compete on appearance alone and, hence, the concept of design was introduced. 'Design' here meant determining the appearance of a product not only along aesthetic lines but with a view to stimulating sales – a characteristically American compromise between idealism and profiteering.

Soon the idea got around and American magazines frequently ran articles with headlines like 'Best Dressed Products Sell Best'. One of the pioneer designers who first established a New York studio, **Henry Dreyfuss**, said that design was 'the silent salesman' – he might have added that beauty was his business tool. The term 'industrial design' first appeared in around 1919, and **George Nelson** tartly observed what it meant in reality when he said that the first generation of American designers were business consultants who specialized in taste.

Dreyfuss was introduced to design while working with **Norman Bel Geddes** on the stage set of the play *The Miracle*, whose successful Broadway run in 1923 translated the protean Bel Geddes into a national celebrity. Although the theatre offered Bel Geddes a broad canvas for his liberal imagination, being the 'first American to feel the cultural surge of the twentieth century', as Arthur Pulos put it, he soon began to look for opportunities 'more akin to life' than the stage. He met the German architect Erich Mendelssohn, and his influence together with a well-thumbed copy of **Le Corbusier**'s *Vers une architecture* introduced this first twentieth-century American to European culture – and incidentally brought an element of social responsibility into a reckless life.

Under Bel Geddes' influence, Dreyfuss set up his own design practice in 1929, but had very little work until one day in 1930, according to a well-used anecdote, a representative of the Bell Telephone Company walked into his office and announced a $1000 prize for the design of a new telephone. Somewhat influenced by the stylistic excesses of his mentor Bel Geddes, Dreyfuss tried the opposite approach and said that he believed in human engineering and that a machine should be designed from the inside out. The Bell rep took him

to be insane and left, believing that such a mechanistic strategy of design would rob the telephone of the popular appeal it would need to be successful during the era when 'women's taste' was still influential. However, it was Dreyfuss' conviction that you could make a consumer product every bit as seductive if you paid attention to the details and to the performance. Working on this basis, Dreyfuss prepared a design for the Bell desk telephone that remained in all its essentials the standard American phone for the next forty years.

Dreyfuss had become aware that to be successful in a flamboyant world he had to offer his clients a commodity more enduring than the ephemeral glitter of a tinsel **styling** job. He offered them human engineering, or **anthropometrics**, a set of formulae based on research into human dimensions which he developed in his office and are still in use today. The importance of human factors in design was trumpeted by Dreyfuss and his press agents in routine announcements about convenience, utility and safety in design: an example of his approach was the headlight he incorporated in his design of the Hoover upright vacuum cleaner for the benefit of the woman of taste pursuing dust in gloomy corners.

Unlike his pioneering contemporaries **Raymond Loewy** and **Walter Dorwin Teague**, Dreyfuss was never completely seduced by **streamlining** and other styling motifs which had such an appeal to the mass market. His office was run with strict controls and a lot of probity: to ensure that a conflict of interests might never arise, he restricted his client list to a mere dozen or so major companies. Raymond Loewy did quite the opposite.

Loewy combined in one publicized and stage-managed personality the flair of Bel Geddes and the practicality of Dreyfuss (but added to the severe bone structure and muscle tissue of anthropometrics the seductive flesh of styling). As an immigrant, Loewy could see America afresh and he found the experience moving:

'There is something about a large up-to-date American plant in action that deserves the descriptive attention of

NCR Pavilion, World's Fair, by Walter Dorwin Teague, 1939
Together with Dreyfuss, Loewy and van Doren, Teague was one of the pioneers of consultative design in America in the thirties. His pavilion for National Cash Register at the New York World's Fair of 1939 was a witty and heroic celebration of the triumph of consumerism. Daily attendance figures were rung up on a seven-storey model of NCR's new Model '100' machine.

Stapler by Orlo Heller for Hotchkiss, 1936
One effect of the rise of the industrial designer in America was that everyday products suddenly became styled. The particular style chosen during the thirties was most often streamlining, which flattered the consumer into believing he had something new. It was usually the case, however, that sophisticated, geometrically complex shells were merely added as shrouds to existing products, as with this stapler.

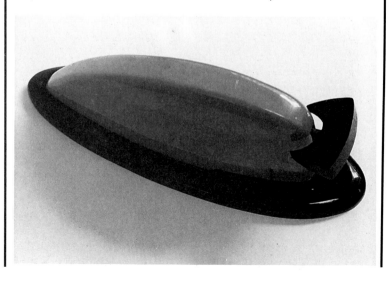

'You can design a car so that every time you get in it, it's a relief – you have a little vacation for a while.'

Harley Earl

Raymond Loewy's Design for the Electrolux Logotype, c. 1939

'This is where dishonesty came into the American world.'

R. Buckminster Fuller (on styling)

Raymond Loewy (right) with Sigmund Gestetner

Gestetner's Duplicator Transformed by Raymond Loewy, 1929
The first set-piece of consultant industrial design in America was Loewy's transformation of the old clunky Gestetner duplicator into a sleek, streamlined product (right).

some great writer. It is one of the most exciting sights in the world, and one that America alone can offer. A remarkable thing, and one that impresses me still after thirty years, is the natural elegance of the American workman. . . In their well-cut overalls, gauntlets and peaked caps, they look like the ambassadors of a great industrial nation . . . I have seen assembly line or spray booth operators that would make movie stars look like tired head waiters. They have poise and dignity. They . . . represent the working aristocracy of the world.'

With his career comes the great distinction, whether real or assumed, between styling and design. In his first major design job, in 1929 for the English reprographic machine manufacturer Sigmund Gestetner, he fused the spirit of the times with 50lbs of modelling clay and made the first piece of

'It is futile to pretend that industrial design or styling has any other function than to support marketing.'

Ford executive

office equipment to rely on streamlining. Of all the pioneer consultant designers who set up their studios in New York in the late twenties it was Loewy who realized to the fullest extent the commercial possibilities of the new trade. He also commanded fees to match. His clients all paid him retainers of between $10,000 and $60,000, plus royalties. By 1946, the year when he told the London *Times*, 'I do not ever remember designing anything purely for appearance,' Loewy had built up an enormous client list of seventy-five international corporations for whom his designs were grossing, he claimed, $900 million annually. He shared the attitude of the normally less business-like Bel Geddes who, in a letter to his lawyer, summed up the character of the pioneer American designers when, referring to some dealings with a client, he wrote:

'You misunderstand the point of my letter. Perhaps if I state it more briefly, you will not.
Get as much money out of them as you can.'

The thirties in America was a decade when licensed artists went out and sold themselves, and their vision of the future, to their clients. This commercial phenomenon was paralleled in a reflective way by the **Museum of Modern Art** in New York, which was far more interested in European than in American design.

Alfred H. Barr, the Museum's director, considered streamlining an absurdity and criticized Loewy for being highly paid and having a 'blind concern with fashion'. His response was the celebrated 'Machine Art' exhibition in 1934, organized by **Philip Johnson**. This exhibition was based on some rarefied assumptions about the inevitable beauty of pure engineering products derived from the books and manifestos of the machine-romantics of Europe. It made no reference to commercial, popular or industrial considerations in design, but was instead an elegant essay by an aesthete temporarily consumed by a taste for ships' propellors, ball races and gears.

The distinction implied in the exhibition between styling

Eliot Noyes, 1910–77
The outstanding American designer of the post-War years was Eliot Noyes. Trained at Harvard by émigré European architects like Walter Gropius and Marcel Breuer, Noyes had little time for American vulgarity and was committed from the start to reforming American design. In his studio at New Canaan he kept a child's model of a Harley Earl car fascia to demonstrate to his staff and his clients what he regarded as 'false principles' in design.

Cadillac 62 Sedan, 1956 and A4 Skyhawk, 1957
Harley Earl was fascinated with flight. His designs for General Motors' cars frequently aped the appearance of military jets, with scoops, bulges and vents for details, as here in his 1956 Cadillac 62 Sedan de Ville. It is photographed next to the Douglas A4 Skyhawk, which went into production in 1957.

Norman Bel Geddes, 1893–1958
Thespian and mountebank turned consultant industrial designer, Bel Geddes was the first American designer to recognize and respond to twentieth-century concerns.

'A Douglas transport plane presents a thrilling aspect of complete unification . . . yet in spite of this superb unity there is no monotony whatever in its aspect.'

Walter Dorwin Teague

Mobil Filling Station by Eliot Noyes, 1964, and its Predecessor
During the sixties Eliot Noyes applied Bauhaus principles to the design of Mobil filling stations throughout America and the world.

'Brno' Chairs by Mies van der Rohe, Manufactured by Knoll
The chairs Mies van der Rohe designed for a house in provincial Czechoslovakia in 1928–30 became New York status symbols in the sixties and seventies through Knoll's merchandising.

and design was becoming more clear. It became clearer still when **Walter Gropius** and **Marcel Breuer** arrived in New York from London and made the Museum their spiritual home. They carried with them the principles of European Modernism, firmly founded on morals and not on Mammon. It was into this atmosphere that **Eliot Noyes** turned up for his first job. He absorbed at first hand the **Bauhaus** ethic and after that he could never be satisfied with pioneer American industrial designers because he said they were 'not motivated by a high enough intent'. Then he went on to apply the Bauhaus to big business . . . and could never again use the word styling without wincing.

Whatever one's feeling about styling, America's contribution to twentieth-century design was the crucial one of allowing the professional designer to develop as an integral part of the process of making mass-produced consumer goods. The involvement became yet greater after the Second World War when European (and European-trained American) designers, men such as **Eero Saarinen** and **Charles Eames**, began designing furniture eventually put into production by **Herman Miller** and **Knoll**. There was an element of commercial realism to design that was always missing in Britain, and irrelevant to the more severe concerns of the Germans. In the United States design has been a fundamental part of modern business, one of the engines that powered the economy. At one extreme this degenerated into the crass commercialism of planned **obsolescence**, but at the other it has enabled the designer to become a serious professional, with an efficient business-like structure to support him, and with status conferred on his work. Knoll was the first furniture manufacturer to sell its wares under designers' names, so that there was 'the Mies chair' and 'the Breuer chair'. When the cult of 'the designer' emerged in the seventies as an important marketing tool it was the Americans who led the field.

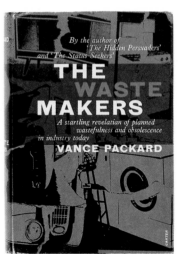

'The Waste Makers' by Vance Packard, 1960
The commercial success of American designers, credited with the manipulation of the market through planned obsolescence, brought a reaction from moralists. Vance Packard's The Waste Makers was published in 1960, a searing analysis of the presumed evils of an over-heated economy. It was one of the first popular treatments of consumerism.

CINTURATO PIRELLI

6

A
MODERN
RENAISSANCE

– Italy since the fifties

If Britain had her industrial revolution in the middle of the eighteenth century, and gave the world an example for imitation, then Italy had its industrial revolution two centuries later and gave the world something different to imitate: the first coherent design style for consumers – a culture of design so complete in its embrace of fashion, products, cars and business equipment that Lombardy and Piedmont produced what amounted to a modern renaissance.

In terms of the international market, Italian design only emerged after 1945, during the period which the Italians call the *ricostruzione*. It was a period of industrial and social renovation that was a spiritual and practical rejection of the pompous absurdities of Fascism. Typical of its spirit was **Gio Ponti**'s magazine **Domus**, edited by the architect **Ernesto Rogers**. *Domus* promoted Rationalism (the Italian version of the **Modern Movement**) in architecture as the antidote to what remained of the collapsed social order. In the first edition in 1947 Ponti wrote, 'Our ideal of the good life and a level of taste and thought expressed by our homes and manner of living are all part of the same thing.' This was not indulgent philosophizing, for the mood in post-War Italy invited speculation about how best to organize life and art together.

Although there were isolated examples of design excellence from Italy before the Second World War – **Marcello Nizzoli**'s work for **Olivetti** is one example, **Franco Albini**'s another – it is only since 1945 that it has been possible to speak of 'Italian design' and summon up an image that is universally understood. Although the post-War generation was heavily influenced by the pictures of American products, such as **Charles Eames'** chairs, and by Henry Moore's sculptures, the synthesis they created was uniquely Italian. **Alberto Rosselli** typified the aims of the new generation in a *Stile Industria* editorial: 'Industrial design in the United States represents one of the fruits of a free competition system in which peculiar economic and production conditions have led to a continuous

'I despise provincial utopias. I know that every man has his memories . . . Other people, too, have lived in particular circumstances . . . but there is absolutely no reason, for me or for them, to immure ourselves in defensive fortresses in which to play and replay ad nauseam *the scratchy record of our singularity.'*

Ettore Sottsass, Jnr

Poster for Pirelli by Bob Noorda, 1956
Noorda's poster captured the flair of Italian industrial culture as surely as did Nervi's celebrated Pirelli Building in Milan.

51

'Stile Industria', 1954
The design culture of modern Italy has been publicized and stimulated by an abundance of well-produced glossy magazines. New products and new furniture which were to set international standards often first appeared in the pages of magazines like Domus and Stile Industria.

market expansion . . . In Italy, by contrast, the true nature of design . . . results from a harmonic relationship between production and culture.'

Milan, and to a lesser extent Turin, enjoyed a particular set of socioeconomic circumstances which nurtured the creation of this sophisticated material culture. Milan not only had an enlightened business class which was prepared to use the fruits of its industry to realize some social objectives which the Italian state was likely to ignore, but the city also produced waves of architect-designers from its Polytechnic. Moreover, 'official' culture was poor and this encouraged the development of strong architecture-based subcultures. Similarly, the *carrozzerie* of Turin gave form to a nation's artistic traditions and future industrial aspirations in a succession of exquisite car designs which emerged from the shops of **Pininfarina** and the factories of **FIAT**. On a visit to Italy in 1950 the American designer **Walter Dorwin Teague** was so taken aback by the energy displayed by the Milanese that he said, 'Since the War the artists have been frolicking like boys let out of school.'

By the late forties Italy had developed a design style which was characterized by an elegant modification of American **streamlining**, found in a range of products from Nizzoli's 'Lexikon 80' typewriter to **Piaggio**'s 'Vespa' motor scooter.

Between 1951 and 1957 Italian design became firmly institutionalized: Alberto Rosselli founded the journal *Stile Industria* in 1953 (it folded in 1962); the Associazione Disegno Industriale was set up in 1956; in 1958 the large department store chain **La Rinascente** inaugurated the **Compasso d'Oro** awards, following a successful in-store exhibition of 1953 called 'The Aesthetics of the Product'; and at the ninth, tenth and eleventh **Triennales** the new Italian designs were shown to the world in a stimulating atmosphere of criticism, discussion and demand.

By the fifties the style of the forties had been consolidated and was joined by a rich and complex furniture aesthetic which owed a debt to **Surrealism** and to organic sculpture. Certain designers became associated with specific manufacturers, producing a fertile marriage of art and industry (although **Vittorio Gregotti** pointed out that, at first, as far as the companies were concerned this was more of an exercise in public relations than in enlightened sponsorship): Marcello Nizzoli continued his association with Olivetti, but also worked for **Necchi**, the sewing machine manufacturer; **Marco Zanuso** worked for furniture manufacturer Arflex; and a younger generation of designers, including **Ettore Sottsass** (who once said 'industry should not *buy* culture, industry should *be* culture'), established their own connections with manufacturers. The degree to which the Milanese designers identified with and showed affection for local industry even brought about a temporary split in the Italian radical establishment, with the more doctrinaire Roman Rationalist accusing the urbane Milanese of selling out to the agents of capitalism – the dispute was resolved in favour of the North.

As the designer and writer **Andrea Branzi** wrote, the styles of the winners of the Compasso d'Oro and of the goods shown at smart exhibitions of the Triennale filtered down through

FIAT Lingotto Factory, Turin
Designed in 1914 by Matte Trusco, for nearly sixty years Lingotto was FIAT's biggest plant. In keeping with the Futurist world-view that focuses on the dynamism of modern life, Trusco built a test track on the factory roof. It was this kind of daring that made FIAT a leading force in the post-War years.

FIAT 500, 1959
Along with the Vespa motor scooter, FIAT's 'Nuova' 500, introduced in 1957, became a symbol of the ricostruzione.

La Rinascente Carrier Bag by Max Huber, 1952
In Italy interest in design is a normal part of commercial life. La Rinascente, one of the biggest stores, is an active promoter of design through competitions and awards.

'Sistema 45' Secretary's Chair by Ettore Sottsass, 1973
Sottsass is a guru-like figure who always tries to re-interpret familiar products. This typist's chair has feet like Mickey Mouse's.

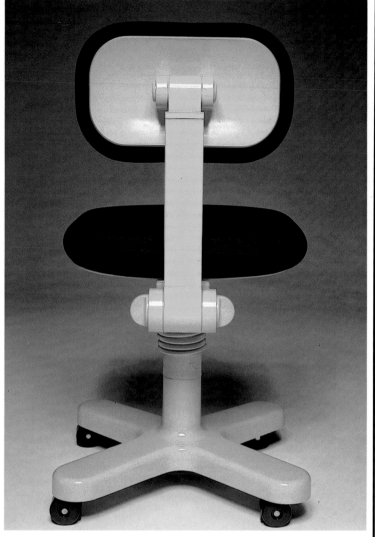

'Cab' Chair by Mario Bellini, 1977
The career of Mario Bellini typifies the versatility of contemporary Italian designers. Although much of his work has been in designing typewriters for Olivetti, he has also produced the 'Cab' chair in leather and steel for Cassina.

'Dublin' Sofa by Marco Zanini for Memphis, 1981
The avant-garde design group Memphis prefers ironic names for its furniture, such as this wood and laminate sofa.

products made for all levels of Italian society:

'Even the smallest joiner's shop soon learnt how to make bar counters that looked like Gio Ponti's own designs, the smallest electric workshop soon learnt to make lamps that looked like **Vigano**'s, and upholsterers played on armchair models that might be reminiscent of Zanuso's. This sort of indiscriminate profane looting afforded a formal renovation of the entire middle layer of Italian society. It was a style that finally replaced Fascist tinsel, and the provincial neo-classical, thus creating an opportunity to shape our first draft of a modern Italy, in a temporary but complete manner.'

During the sixties, a chasm appeared in Italian design between chic mainstream products and the more experimental pieces created in the interests of radical design. But by the seventies the same workshops which helped spread Italian 'high' design across the country also sustained the avant-garde furniture makers Studio **Alchymia** and **Memphis**, which emerged in the late seventies from a background established by the radical-**Pop** groups **Archizoom** and **Superstudio** in the

previous decade. Without the artisan-based workshop facilities which support even the big design-based manufacturers like **Artemide**, **Kartell** and **Flos**, Memphis' extravagant ideas would have remained sketches or conversation pieces, but instead they have achieved international celebrity. For Sottsass, who once said, 'I have never made monuments for the public drama, only fragile sets for private theatre, for private meditation and solitude,' the success of Memphis has been acutely ironic.

The Italian design culture has spread across international, cosmopolitan, middle-class markets, but it is essentially inseparable from the unique social and cultural structure of the city of Milan. Designers like Sottsass operate at three distinct commercial levels, each one nourishing the other. He has a studio in a large company, at Olivetti, where with **Mario Bellini** and **Hans von Klier** he is one of the three independent designers; he also runs an entirely separate studio, as Sottsass Associati; and simultaneously he gives a portion of his time to Memphis.

In fashion progress has been equally great. When an **Emilio Pucci** dress was first photographed for *Harper's Bazaar* in St Moritz in 1947 Paris was scandalized, but the centre of gravity

'Affluence offers the kind of freedom I am deeply suspicious of. It offers freedom from restraint, and virtually it is impossible to do something without restraints.'

Charles Eames

Bicycle by Piero Fornasetti, 1984
Fornasetti is one of several creative influences who work outside the mainstream of Italian design. He has produced quirky ceramics, furniture, and even a series of hand-painted bicycles. He is influenced by Surrealism.

Necchi 'Logica' Sewing Machine by Giorgio Giugiaro, 1982
When ItalDesign's Giugiaro was commissioned to design a replacement for Necchi's classic 'Mirella' model, designed by Nizzoli a quarter of a century earlier, he found an appropriately technical look to match the mood of the times.

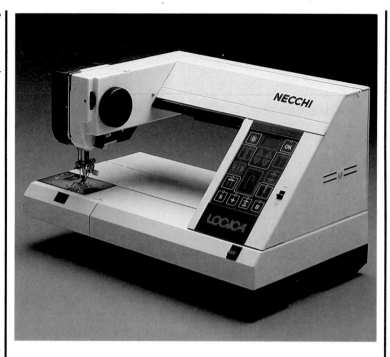

Scales and Timer by Richard Sapper and Marco Zanuso for Teraillon, early 1970s
Richard Sapper and Marco Zanuso are among the most accomplished exponents of the modern Italian High Style. Together they have designed superb quality kitchen and domestic equipment.

has switched to Milan now to such an extent that when a conference was held in the spring of 1981 to discuss the setting up of a Museum of Fashion, the unchallenged assumption was that the city had become 'the unrivalled fashion capital, not just of Italy, but of the world'. And again in this there is a unique fusion of big business and design: Montecatini Edison, one of Italy's great industrial concerns, was a major shareholder in **Elio Fiorucci**'s chain of clothes shops, but so far from hindering the progress of his colourful business, its ownership enhanced it.

Like the radical objects of Archizoom, Fiorucci's fashion design was greatly influenced by the England of the sixties: **Mary Quant**, Mr Freedom and the King's Road (or, at least, a particularly vigorous interpretation of it). Fiorucci's style was what he called '*discomoda*'; he interpreted American blue jeans for Italian youth. During the early seventies these became the most familiar symbol of the increasing domination of Italy – and in particular of Milan – over the world of fashion. Fiorucci has been joined by the Venice-based **Benetton** family, now his part owner, with their standardized shops filled with budget knitwear in strong, sophisticated colours. The success of Benetton has meant that there is a symbol of Italian design on high streets and main streets across Europe, the United States and Japan. In 1975 the Italian National Chamber of Fashion emphasized the increasing importance of ready-to-wear over *haute couture* by moving the nation's premiere dress show to Milan from Florence.

By the beginning of the eighties Italian design had emerged from what now looks like a period of febrile experimentation during the fifties and sixties, into a position where it is perhaps the major influence in international material culture, a phenomenon acknowledged by Italy's huge success in the new electronics industries where Olivetti rose from nowhere to become one of Europe's leading computer manufacturers in less than five years. The prestige of Italian design has been

Olivetti 'Divisumma 18' Calculator by Mario Bellini, 1972
Mario Bellini, like Sottsass, is a consultant to Olivetti. He is a great inventor of slick, highly finished forms.

'In America I brazenly sell my jeans for fifty dollars and they're so perfect I even get requests by mail for them. If you think about it, fifty bucks isn't a hell of a lot to pay for a lovely ass.'

Elio Fiorucci

further enhanced by the success of the new generation of car-body studios, in particular **Giorgio Giugiaro**'s ItalDesign which has been responsible for such important products as **Volkswagen**'s Golf, and which is also retained by manufacturers from Japan, Sweden and the United States.

The hard-edged success of these international businesses provided a backdrop for the experimentation of Studio Alchymia and its less pretentiously intellectual rival Memphis. Just when Italian design appeared to be reaching a plateau of respectability, the appearance of these two remarkable and highly provocative groups proved that the restless creative vigour apparent since the forties still existed. Although the precise differences between the products and the manners of each will, to future historians, be topics providing a rich subject for debate, both really represented the same thing: evidence that within Italian industrial culture there are still all the sources and resources, both practical and creative, for new ideas about design to flourish.

Nikon 'F3', 1982
Giorgio Giugiaro is Italy's outstanding car designer, but success has brought him clients from outside the automotive industry. For Japan's Nikon company Giugiaro redesigned the 'F3' camera, making it both more attractive and more ergonomically sound.

Coffee Service, 1983
Italian companies take a very positive interest in design. In 1979–80 Alessi invited eleven top architects and designers to design a Post-Modern tea or coffee service. One response was this interpretation by Michael Graves, put into production three years later.

7

THE

LANGUAGE

OF

OBJECTS

– symbolism and consumer psychology

In the two hundred or so years since 'design' emerged from the crafts of the pre-industrial world to its present position as a major force in all mature economies one central phenomenon is very apparent: Sir Joshua Reynolds' certainty about standards of taste, which was being eroded a hundred years after his death, has in recent times disappeared altogether.

When Reynolds spoke of there being one standard of taste, the processes which brought about the Industrial Revolution had only just begun. Although in his day the ceramic industries of Staffordshire were using some power machines and semi-mechanized transfer printing, most manufacturers of consumer goods were using processes no different to those employed in the Middle Ages. But with the subsequent industrialization and the depopulation of the countryside, mass-production accompanied by mass-consumption has come to mean that for the first time in history every social class could be consumers. With the growth of consumerism the taste for moral and critical certainties, beloved by classicists of Reynolds' colour and set by the educated minority, was lost.

In a sense, the **Modern Movement** can be seen as an attempt to restore that lost order. It was necessary in the struggle to clear the air for the Modernists to overstate their case, and like all overstatements their argument has been susceptible to parody, as it was in the satire of the Anglo-American designer-decorator **T.H. Robsjohn-Gibbings**. *Homes of the Brave* (1954) made fun of a number of Modernist darlings, including **Horatio Greenough**, Victorian itinerant sculptor and prophet of Modernism, of whom Robsjohn-Gibbings wrote, 'Greenough believed that form should follow function as in nature and as in the sailing ships. Though hardly news to American shipbuilders, to American architects it was a startling idea.'

'If today somebody comes to me for a new lighting fixture, we will work on it for at least 2–3 months. There was a time when I would have known at once what this fixture should look like. It was enough to know what the product was supposed to do and what were the production facilities and . . . avanti! Today I am not sure I know what to do and in what style to work . . . the relationship with the public which is going to use the product has grown so complex . . . that I simply don't know how to touch people I am not familiar with . . .'

Ettore Sottsass

Advertisement for Sony 'Walkman', 1980

The poster to launch Sony's 'Walkman' personal stereo neatly captured the way the new product straddled the cultures of East and West.

59

'TS 502' Folding Radio by Marco Zanuso and Richard Sapper, 1965
Designed for the Milanese firm BrionVega, this radio became an international cult object, not only on account of its hinged construction but also because of its clean and sophisticated appearance.

'First and Chief Grounds of Architecture' by John Shute, 1563
The European tradition has often depended on symbolism: Vitruvius compared the orders of architecture to the human form. This is a late version of Vitruvius' conceit.

In recent years, Modernism has come in for much more criticism, especially from Post-Modernists. Progress in technology has dated some of the Movement's assumptions, for 'truth to materials' makes some sense when you are dealing with elemental substances like marble or iron which have properties made familiar by tradition, but Teflon or Kevlar pose awkward questions about exactly what their natures are that designs can be 'true' to them. Although **Functionalism** attempted to re-establish standards of 'good form', now it is seen, as **Gaetano Pesce** has noted, that function 'is only one facet of the materials which men use and achieve'.

The most stimulating achievement of **Post-Modernism** is that it has forced a revival of interest in symbolism, an element of Western culture which the Modernists (although not **Le Corbusier**) overlooked in their enthusiasm to prove their point. Symbolism underwrites the majority of our attitudes to material culture: the Vitruvian tradition in architecture, for example, is based on a language of forms which identifies the Doric order with manly beauty and the Ionic with feminine charm. Even **Eliot Noyes**, the man who created the **corporate identity** for **IBM**, and who inherited the ethic of the **Bauhaus** from his teachers **Walter Gropius** and **Marcel Breuer**, actually told the company that its buildings lacked symbolic value. Without betraying any of his principles, he then went about – in Ursula McHugh's memorable expression – applying the Bauhaus to big business and turned the German Modern Movement into the *style* of corporate America.

Now it is possible to see that just as it was sentimental cultural provincialism that made spokesmen for the **Arts and Crafts** movement anti-machine, so it was a reductive fanaticism that led the Modern Movement to see machines as ends in themselves. **Henry Ford** said, 'A piece of machinery or anything that is made is like a book, if you can read it,' and now

'Less is more.'

Mies van der Rohe

'. . . less is a bore.'

Robert Venturi

'You would prefer neatness.'

*Eliot Noyes
(to the chairman of IBM)*

'We are selling diamonds.'

Akio Morita

'We do what others don't.'

Masaru Ibuka, co-founder
of Sony

*Sony 'TC 50' Tape-Recorder,
1970*
Japanese manufacturers
understand consumer
psychology perhaps as well as
any. Their products always
appeal on the basis of
'professionalism', or offer
radical innovations in service.
Sony's 'TC 50' tape-recorder
was used by NASA astronauts
on the Apollo 10 mission, a fact
exploited in the company's
advertising.

Sony 'Walkman', 1980
Sony's 'Walkman' personal
stereo is perhaps the
outstanding product
development of recent years.
Proposed in 1979 and
manufactured from 1980, it is a
high quality tape-recorder that
employs the latest techniques of
miniaturized electronics and
does not actually record. The
'Walkman' developed from
being a marginal product to a
central contributor to the
company's profits.

we can see that the most successful manufacturers of
consumer products have adapted their design policies to
allow for symbolism. The degree to which manufacturers such
as **Porsche**, **Sony**, **Braun** and **Ford** understand consumer
psychology and use design as an important aspect of their
marketing (as well as their production) processes is shown by
the elements of metaphor in the design of their products. In
producing one of the world's most desirable sports cars,
Porsche is justly proud of the company's unimpeachable
engineering credentials. But none of the elements in
Porsche's design are dictated by functional considerations
alone. **Anatole Lapine**, head of the studio, says that his
assignment is to design a car that will still be visually
interesting in twenty years' time. This is a reversal of **Mies van
der Rohe**'s celebrated remark – the emotional foundation of
Modernism – that when it came to the appearance of things he
didn't want to be interesting, he just wanted to be good.
Moreover, Lapine (who was trained at **General Motors**) has
none of the horror of **styling** that would have been expected
of a purist of the previous generation: 'What is the difference
between a stylist, a designer or a what-have-you? I don't think
it's so important what we call each other, but what we do and
what we have to show for it . . . I know just as many bad
designers as I know good stylists.'

It is not only makers of exclusive products like Porsche who
are aware of visual metaphor. The Japanese, manufacturers to
the entire world, have produced remarkable achievements in
consumer psychology: they know exactly how to make their
products *speak* to their consumers. It is perhaps Sony more
than any other manufacturer that has dangled the carrot of
appearance before the consumer. Being smaller than most
Japanese electronic companies, Sony has been forced to
compete not only by complementing the product lines of its

Sony 'Walkman', 1984
With characteristic ingenuity,
Sony has continually introduced
new models of the 'Walkman'.
Each has new features and even
more of the allure of
professionalism of its
predecessors. Not a single
segment of the market has been
left unexplored.

rivals, but by concentrating on the special language of successful consumer products. It was the first Japanese company, and the first mass-market producer anywhere, to realize how appealing the *semantics* of technology were to the customer. First of all Sony pioneered the selling of unusual new products (sometimes not containing any special technical novelty, but always employing a novel synthesis, the first clock-radio being an obvious example) and then complemented this marketing strategy with bold innovations in appearance. These innovations always evoked some technical mystique and gave a Sony product a special presence denied to other manufacturers, but which the other manufacturers soon copied. For instance, Sony provided VU-meters for the first domestic stereo tape-recorder so that a suburban drawing room might look a little bit like a studio console. At the same time the company invented the satin anodized aluminium hi-fi amplifier with its familiar array of knobs, flickswitches, tumblers, levers and dials which, while fully satisfying the customer's taste for symbolism, often paid no attention whatsoever to the mechanism within.

Sony designers understand to the full how to arouse the customer's desire by an artful display of textures and details, and other Japanese manufacturers have learnt the same trick. Their culture's traditional preference for miniature forms has given to cameras and other high-quality consumer durables an almost obsessive attention to tiny details, an attention extended from small to large objects when **Honda** interior designers were briefed to look at Nikon cameras before starting to sketch. Whether it is a car, a camera or a tape-recorder, the single element which unites all successful Japanese designs is that the customer is always flattered by being made the possessor of an optimistic, sophisticated product where minute attention to detail gives him the satisfying feeling of rubbing up against professionalism.

German product designers, more than any others, have acquired a reputation for working within the inflexible rules of function. Inheriting some of the tradition of the Bauhaus and a lot of the practice of Ulm's **Hochschule für Gestaltung**, the Germans have been able to maintain the widespread belief that the study of the end-use of a product and a consideration of the materials available will, as if by some semi-mystical process, reveal the perfect form of a timeless, unimprovable design.

However, the evolution of Braun electric razors over the past thirty years betrays this philosophy for what it really is, an exercise in style. Since about 1950 there have been no fundamental changes in the mechanism of the electric razor or, indeed, in the landscape of the human face, but the fact that the form of their razors has changed since then demonstrates that they, as much as any other interested group, are sensitive to subtle aspects of appearance. **Dieter Rams**, Braun's chief designer, has even admitted making last minute adjustments to a razor design because the almost finished product did not achieve the effect he had in mind. He did not admit to having *styled* it, but that was what he meant! This fact that German Functionalism is a style and not an austere result of engineering is further demonstrated by the Braun ET44 electronic

'Designers should not be artists. Particularly industrial designers should be the creators who understand fully all the facilities available for them within the company. They should be market creators who can make new products by combining the social trends and the inner factors of their own corporation . . . The dynamism which organizes all these factors effectively is what I call "design management".'

Yasuo Kuroki

Braun Electric Razors, 1950, 1962, 1984
The shapes of the electric razors manufactured by Braun in Frankfurt have been continuously evolving, but retain a strong brand identity. From top to bottom: 'S50' was the first post-War model, introduced at the Frankfurt Spring Fair, 1950; Hans Gugelot's 'Sixtant' of 1962 created an international stereotype, and Dieter Rams' 1984 model shows even further refinement of the form.

calculator and the Braun PI, AI, TI, CI, hi-fi system. Both are impressive and attractive machines but the 'functionalism' has been reduced to a stylistic language. The designer, no matter what he says, cannot claim to have studied at any very great length the engineering components within either the hi-fi or the calculator and to have evolved from them a corresponding form to fit the function: both machines were actually made in Japan. The designers at Braun dressed them up.

The same attention to symbolism takes place in the design studios of Ford, the third largest industrial undertaking in the world. When it came to replacing the successful Cortina with the Sierra, Ford of Europe faced special problems and new preoccupations. The Cortina had been an extremely successful product which integrated American style into an efficient package of European standards in terms of space and efficiency. But twenty years later, instead of fashion and glamour, market research had determined that the customer of the eighties was more interested in economy, safety and quality. While Ford's engineers were well able to come up with the technical solutions to the problems, it was up to the designers to make these qualities apparent to the public, both inside and outside the car. Part of the designers' brief was 'to make the driver feel important', and to meet the tastes of the eighties Ford invested more time and effort than ever before in giving their new Sierra an ergonomically sound and well-detailed cabin.

Yet this goal was not a purely scientific one, susceptible to a single scientific solution, but involved emotion and intuition. The designers decided to make the body of the Sierra a semantic vehicle for announcing Ford's new commitment to technology and design. **Aerodynamics** was known to be technically important and also to have a high profile in terms of public relations. Yet aerodynamics was itself something of a black art, as the general physics of airflow were well known, but the specific behaviour of air over a moving car was not understood. This, in fact, left the designers a great deal of creative scope. From the concept sketches through to the clay models, aerodynamic theories were teased out but only scientifically tested after the shape had been determined on subjective, aesthetic grounds. Only when management had

Braun 'Control ET44', 1978
This calculator was designed by Braun's chief designer Dieter Rams, and Dietrich Lubs.

'I want to make things that recede into the background.

Dieter Rams

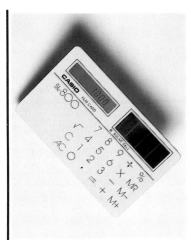

Casio 'SL-800' Calculator, 1984
New technology offers designers extraordinary opportunities. The Casio 'SL-800' has the power of a computer in a package the size of a credit card . . . but what should it look like now that function has nothing to do with form?

Technics '315' Stereo, 1984
Some Japanese manufacturers, such as the Technics division of the electrical giant Matsushita, use technological imagery as a form of Baroque decoration. The apparently professional details on the Technics '315' bear no real relationship to functional necessity but are forms of decoration.

Ford Cortina, 1964
The original Ford Cortina had American details in a package of European proportions. This happy combination made it Britain's best-selling car for nearly twenty years.

approved the full-scale models which the designers offered was the car passed through a computerized bridge called a scan mill so that accurate technical drawings could be generated.

Throughout the process of modern car body design, symbolism, allusion and metaphor are the bases of management discussion. The question of how light falls on curved surfaces, of how 'gentleness, tautness and strength', to use Ford designer **Uwe Bahnsen**'s words, might be invested in a windscreen pillar, and how the transition from a complex curve to a flat plane might best be handled to give an impression of sinew under flesh, are everyday considerations in a car design studio.

Bob Lutz, who was chairman of Ford of Europe when the Sierra programme was going through, has spoken of the mystical component in successful car design. His words apply with equal validity to all product design:

'There's a very fine line between doing a movie that gets out there and fails and doing a movie that's *Star Wars* . . . and yet the celluloid's the same, the actors are the same and so is the amount spent on special effects. One film's good,

Ford Sierra, 1982
The design of the Ford Sierra reflected a belief that the public was becoming increasingly aware of at least the symbolism of efficiency. As usual in car design, a full-scale model in clay (above) was made before any engineering drawings. In the interior the brief to designers was: 'make the driver feel important'.

the other isn't because there is that creative and psychological content in any product programme that defies a totally systematic approach.'

The design of consumer products is a partly rational, partly artistic process. Of course, machines should work efficiently, economically and safely; furniture should be comfortable and, if at all possible, inexpensive. But design is much more than merely a matter of catering for essential needs: just as important is its aesthetic function. **Frank Lloyd Wright** once said he didn't care much about the essentials of life – provided that he had an adequate supply of its luxuries.

In a sense, thoughtful design is a luxury, but it is a luxury which no civilized person can afford to be without. It is a form of communication which takes place without words.

In the first chapter there was a quotation from Hogarth's *Analysis of Beauty*, a book that was an early and successful attempt to discriminate about the material world. In the two hundred and more years since that essay, mass-production has evolved and has been perfected, and in the course of this evolution the designer has been variously an artist, an architect, a social reformer, a mystic, an engineer, a management consultant, a public relations man and, perhaps, now a computer engineer. In this way design reflects the preoccupations of its age. Certainly, design in the future will change in accordance with technology and social conditions, but in important respects it also remains the same as it was in Hogarth's day. Just as no form of communication has ever entirely replaced the one it succeeded (so that today we have books *and* television), so whatever new machines will come along to pose design problems, the designer will still also have to think about things for people to sit on, eat with, drink from, and so on. The designs of the past have contributed ideas about form which are a part of our language of objects, and which are the bases for solutions to these problems.

New developments in technology and in the means of production are going to mean an enhanced role for the designer, not a diminished one. He will still have to find forms to express new ideas for objects as yet unforeseen. The example of the calculator shows just how rapidly technology can create new mass-market products: in 1957 a calculator weighed 130 kg, cost more than $2000 and was produced at an annual rate of no more than 1200 units. By 1983 a technically superior machine weighed less than 0.02 kg, cost $26 and more than 30 million were made in the year. Moreover, advancing technology is tightening the loop between the manufacturer, the retailer and the consumer. As product life-cycles become shorter, the designer is in ever more demand to interpret the products of industry for the public. As new products emerge, markets expand. Each new product and each new market needs a 'language' and it is the designer's job to provide it.

This book is an attempt to explore the rudiments of that language, and the careers and achievements of the men and women who have developed the language over the years.

Audi Advertising Campaign, January 1985
Advertisers know that in the eighties the public is as fascinated with technology as it once was with sun, sex and speed. Audi's 'Vorsprung durch Technik' campaign (by Bartle, Bogle, Hegarty) made a self-conscious appeal to this taste.

A

Alvar **Aalto**
Eero **Aarnio**
A&E Design
AEG
Aerodynamics
Otl **Aicher**
AID
Franco **Albini**
Don **Albinson**
Studio **Alchymia**
Alfa Romeo
Aluminium
Emilio **Ambasz**
American design
Anthropometrics
Arabia
Bruce **Archer**
Archigram
Architectural Review
Archizoom
Egmont **Arens**
Giorgio **Armani**
L. & C. **Arnold**
Art Deco
Art Nouveau
Art Workers' Guild
Artek
Arteluce
Artemide
Arts and Crafts
Charles
Robert **Ashbee**
Aspen
Gunnar **Asplund**
Sergio **Asti**
Gae **Aulenti**

David **Bache**
Uwe **Bahnsen**
M.H. **Baillie Scott**
Bakelite
Cristobal **Balenciaga**
Peter Reyner **Banham**
Oscar **Barnack**
Barnsley Brothers
Alfred H. **Barr**
Barron and Larcher
Roland **Barthes**
Saul **Bass**
Bauhaus
Herbert **Bayer**
BBPR
Peter **Behrens**
Norman **Bel Geddes**
Mario **Bellini**
J.H. **Belter**
Benetton
Walter **Benjamin**
Ward **Bennett**
Berliner
  Metallgewerbe
Harry **Bertoia**
Nuccio **Bertone**
Flaminio **Bertoni**

Biedermeier
Max **Bill**
Misha **Black**
BMW
Cini **Boeri**
Rodolfo **Bonetto**
Borax
Michel **Boué**
Pierre **Boulanger**
Marianne **Brandt**
Andrea **Branzi**
Braun
Carl **Breer**
Marcel **Breuer**
BrionVega
British design

CAD-CAM
Cantilever
Pierre **Cardin**
David **Carter**
Cassandre
Cassina
Achille **Castiglioni**
CCI
Central School of Art
  and Crafts (Art and
  Design
Gabrielle **Chanel**
Colin **Chapman**
Pierre **Chareau**
Chermayeff &
  Geismar
Fede **Cheti**
Chiavari
Walter Percy **Chrysler**
CIAM
Aldo **Cibic**
Citroën
Clarice **Cliff**
Stafford **Cliff**
Wells **Coates**
Luigi **Colani**
Henry **Cole**
Colefax & Fowler
Collier Campbell
Gino **Colombini**
Joe **Colombo**
Compasso d'Oro
Constructivism
Contemporary
Cooper-Hewitt
  Museum
Hans **Coray**
Corporate identity
Council of Industrial
  Design (CoID)
Crafts revival
Cranbrook Academy
Walter **Crane**

Danese
Danish
Corradino **d'Ascanio**
Robin **Day**
Michele **de Lucchi**
De Pas, D'Urbino,
  Lomazzi
De Stijl
Elsie **de Wolfe**
Paolo **Deganello**
Design Council
Design management
Design theory
Donald **Deskey**

Deutsche Werkbund
Niels **Diffrient**
Christian **Dior**
Walt **Disney**
Nana **Ditzel**
Jay **Doblin**
Domus
Gillo **Dorfles**
Lou **Dorfsman**
Donald Wills **Douglas**
Jan **Dranger**
Christopher **Dresser**
Henry **Dreyfuss**
DRU

Charles **Eames**
Harley **Earl**
Tom **Eckersley**
Fritz **Eichler**
Kenji **Ekuan**
Electrolux
Bjorn **Envall**
Erco
Ercol
Ergonomi Design
Ergonomics
Vuokko **Eskolin-**
  Nurmesniemi
Virgil **Exner**

FIAT
Finnish design
Leonardo **Fioravanti**
Elio **Fiorucci**
Richard **Fischer**
Alan **Fletcher**
Flos
Paul **Follot**
Henry **Ford**
Ford of Europe
Fordism
Foreningen
  SvenskForm
Piero **Fornasetti**
Mariano **Fortuny**
Kaj **Franck**
Josef **Frank**
Berndt **Friberg**
Frogdesign
Adrian **Frutiger**
Maxwell **Fry**
Roger **Fry**
Shigeo **Fukuda**
Buckminster **Fuller**
Functionalism
Funkis
Futurism

Emile **Gallé**
Abram **Games**
Gatti, Paolini,
  Teodoro
Antoni **Gaudí I Cornet**
Dino **Gavina**
General Motors
German design
Ghia
Dante **Giacosa**
Sigfried **Giedion**
Eric **Gill**
Ernest **Gimson**
Alexander **Girard**
Ernesto **Gismondi**
W.H. **Gispen**
Giorgio **Giugiaro**

GK Industrial Design
  Associates
Milton **Glaser**
John **Gloag**
G-Plan
Kenneth **Grange**
Michael **Graves**
Eileen **Gray**
Milner **Gray**
Great Exhibition of
  the Industry of All
  Nations
Horatio **Greenough**
Eugene **Gregorie**
Vittorio **Gregotti**
Hermann **Gretsch**
Walter **Gropius**
Group of Ten
Gruppo Strum
Gucci
Hans **Gugelot**
Lurelle **Guild**
Hector **Guimard**
Gustavsberg

Habitat
Edward **Hald**
Katherine **Hamnett**
Ambrose **Heal**
Deryck **Healey**
Jean **Heiberg**
Piet **Hein**
Poul **Henningsen**
Henri Kay
Frederick **Henrion**
René **Herbst**
Robert **Heritage**
Erik **Herlow**
David **Hicks**
High-Tech
Oliver **Hill**
Hille
Hochschule für
  Gestaltung
Josef **Hoffmann**
Hans **Hollein**
Knud **Holscher**
Honda
House & Garden
Johan **Huldt**

IBM
ICOGRADA and
  ICSID
IDZ-Berlin
IKEA
Industrial design
Innovator AB
Institute of Design,
  Chicago
International Style
Iron
Isokon
Alec **Issigonis**
Italian design
Johannes **Itten**

Arne **Jacobsen**
Japanese design
Paul **Jaray**
Charles-
Edouard **Jeanneret**
Jeep
Jenaer Glasverein
Georg **Jensen**

Jakob **Jensen**
Betty **Joel**
Clarence L.
'Kelly' **Johnson**
Philip **Johnson**
Edward **Johnston**
Owen **Jones**
**Journal of Design
and Manufactures**
Jugendstil
Finn **Juhl**
Dora **Jung**

Wilhelm **Kåge**
Wunibald **Kamm**
Tom **Karen**
Kartell
Masura **Katsumie**
Edward
McKnight **Kauffer**
Kenzo
Frederick **Kiesler**
Perry **King**
Rodney **Kinsman**
Kitsch
Poul **Kjaerholm**
Calvin **Klein**
Kare **Klint**
Hans **Knoll**
Mogens **Koch**
Erwin **Komenda**
Henning **Koppel**
Kosta
Friso **Kramer**
Yrjo **Kukkapuro**
Shiro **Kuramata**

Karl **Lagerfeld**
René **Lalique**
Lamborghini
Lambretta
Lamination
Allen **Lane**
Anatole **Lapine**
Jack Lenor **Larsen**
Ralph **Lauren**
Bernard **Leach**
Le Corbusier
Liberty's
Stig **Lindberg**
**Lippincott &
Margulies**
Raymond **Loewy**
Adolf **Loos**
Herb **Lubalin**

Charles
Rennie **Mackintosh**
A.H. **Mackmurdo**
Marshall **McLuhan**
Vico **Magistretti**
Louis **Majorelle**
Tomas **Maldonado**
Robert **Mallet-Stevens**
Carl **Malmsten**
Angelo **Mangiarotti**
Enzo **Mari**
Marimekko
Javier **Mariscal**
MARS
Enid **Marx**
Bruno **Mathsson**
Herbert **Matter**
Syrie **Maugham**
David **Mellor**

Memphis
Alessandro **Mendini**
Roberto **Menghi**
Hannes **Meyer**
Giovanni **Michelotti**
Ludwig **Mies van der Rohe**
Herman **Miller**
Missoni
Bill **Mitchell**
Issey **Miyake**
Modern Movement
Moderne/Modernistic
Børge **Mogenson**
Laszlo **Moholy-Nagy**
Hanae **Mori**
Stanley **Morison**
William **Morris**
Motorama
Olivier **Mourgue**
Alfonso **Mucha**
Hermann **Muller-Brockmann**
Peter **Muller-Munk**
Bruno **Munari**
Keith **Murray**
**Museum of Modern
Art**
Hermann **Muthesius**

Ralph **Nader**
Condé **Nast**
Necchi
George **Nelson**
Marcello **Nizzoli**
Isamu **Noguchi**
Bob **Noorda**
John K. **Northrop**
Eliot **Noyes**
Antii **Nurmesniemi**

Obsolescence
Ogle
Olivetti
Omega
**OMK Design
Workshop**
Brian **O'Rorke**
Orrefors
Amedée **Ozenfant**

Vance **Packard**
Verner **Panton**
Victor **Papanek**
Parker-Knoll
Gregor **Paulsson**
PEL
Penguin Books
Pentagram
den **Permanente**
Charlotte **Perriand**
Gaetano **Pesce**
Michael **Peters**
Nikolaus **Pevsner**
Piaggio
Frank **Pick**
Pininfarina
Giancarlo **Piretti**
Plastics
Warren **Plattner**
Plywood
Paul **Poiret**
Gio **Ponti**
Pop
Porsche
Post-Modernism
Jack **Pritchard**

Ulla **Procopé**
Jean **Prouvé**
Emilio **Pucci**
A.W.N. **Pugin**
Jean **Puiforcat**
Push Pin Studio
Pyrex

Mary **Quant**
David **Queensberry**

Ernest **Race**
Dieter **Rams**
Paul **Rand**
Rasch Brothers
Armi **Ratia**
Herbert **Read**
Paul **Reilly**
Retro
Richard **Riemerschmid**
Gerrit **Rietveld**
La Rinascente
Terence
Harold **Robsjohn-Gibbings**
Ernesto **Rogers**
Rörstrand
Rosenthal
Alberto **Rosselli**
David **Rowland**
Royal College of Art
Royal Society of Arts
John **Ruskin**
Gordon **Russell**

SAAB
Eero **Saarinen**
Giovanni **Sacchi**
Bruno **Sacco**
Roberto **Sambonet**
Astrid **Sampe**
Richard **Sapper**
Timo **Sarpaneva**
Sixten **Sason**
Ferdinand de **Saussure**
Afra and
Tobia **Scarpa**
Carlo **Scarpa**
Xanti **Schawinsky**
Elsa **Schiaparelli**
The **Schools of Design**
Douglas **Scott**
Semiotics
Peter **Shire**
Joseph **Sinel**
SIAD
Silver Studio
Erich **Slany**
Sony
Ettore **Sottsass**
Yves **St Laurent**
Mart **Stam**
Stockholm Exhibition
Giotto **Stoppino**
Streamlining
Studio Alchymia
Styling
Superstudio
Surrealism
**Svenska
Sljödföreningen**
Svenskt Tenn
Swedish design

Roger **Tallon**
Ilmari **Tapiovaara**

Taste
Taylorism
Walter
Dorwin **Teague**
Technès
Guiseppe **Terragni**
Benjamin **Thompson**
Michael **Thonet**
Matteo **Thun**
Total Design
Touring
Triennale
Jan **Tschichold**

Unimark
Utility

Pierre **Vago**
Gino **Valle**
Henry **van de Velde**
Harold **van Doren**
Andries **van Onck**
Victor **Vasarely**
Thorstein **Veblen**
Venini
Robert **Venturi**
Vespa
**Victoria and Albert
Museum**
Jacques **Viennot**
Vittorio **Vigano**
Vignale
Massimo **Vignelli**
Vistosi
Vogue
Volkswagen
Volvo
Hans **von Klier**
C.F.A. **Voysey**
Vuokko

Wilhelm **Wagenfeld**
Otto **Wagner**
Ole **Wanscher**
Neville **Ward**
Josiah **Wedgwood**
Hans **Wegner**
Weissenhof Siedlung
Gunnar **Wennerberg**
Werkbund
Wiener Werkstätte
Yrjo **Wiherheimo**
Tapio **Wirkkala**
Tom **Wolfe**
Wolff Olins
Frank Lloyd **Wright**
Russel **Wright**

Sori **Yanagi**

Zagato
Marco **Zanini**
Zanotta
Marco **Zanuso**

Z

Alvar **Aalto**
Eero **Aarnio**
A&E Design
AEG
Aerodynamics
Otl **Aicher**
AID
Franco **Albini**
Don **Albinson**
Studio **Alchymia**
Alfa Romeo
Aluminium
Emilio **Ambasz**
American design
Anthropometrics
Arabia
Bruce **Archer**
Archigram
Architectural Review
Archizoom
Egmont **Arens**
Giorgio **Armani**
L. & C. **Arnold**
Art Deco
Art Nouveau
Art Workers' Guild
Artek
Arteluce
Artemide
Arts and Crafts
Charles
Robert **Ashbee**
Aspen
Gunnar **Asplund**
Sergio **Asti**
Gae **Aulenti**

Alvar Aalto

1898–1976

In the years after 1917, when Finland gained its independence from Russia, its designers were trying to find an expression for their national identity. Alvar Aalto was an important part of this movement. During the period up to the end of the thirties he produced his best designs, combining natural materials and romantic values.

Aalto set up an architectural office in Helsinki in 1923 and made his reputation with two public buildings, a sanatorium at Paimio (1929–33) and a library at Viipuri (1927–35). The sanatorium in particular was widely published throughout the world, and dramatic monochrome pictures in the **Architectural Review** and elsewhere helped establish Aalto's architecture as a symbol of the **International Style** in Finland. However, the real essence of his work is somewhat different from pure Modernism. Although Finland had a small and vociferous **Functionalist** lobby (known as the Funkis), Aalto did not belong to it, and was never driven to any extremes: his

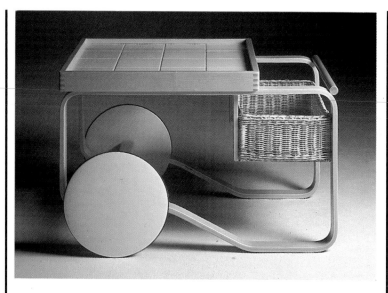

Tea Trolley, 1936
Alvar Aalto's tea trolley was designed for Artek, the Helsinki shop. Appearing first in 1936, it has remained in continuous production ever since. Its use of bent, laminated wood both as structure and as decoration is a characteristic of Aalto's style in furniture design: natural materials are used ingeniously, but unpretentiously.

Armchair, 1931–2
Cantilevered chair by Aalto in laminated wood and lacquered plywood.

architecture mediated between modern forms and traditional materials, and his furniture followed the same path.

In 1927 Aalto met Otto Korhonen, the owner of a furniture factory, and while working for him on a design for the firm's stand for the 700th birthday of the town of Turku, Korhonen introduced him to the techniques of the furniture industry. They were to work together on both Paimio and Viipuri. For the sanatorium Aalto designed a chair with a birch frame and a moulded **plywood** seat, reminiscent of the 'Luterma' seats produced by an Estonian company called Luther and used in tramcars and railway carriages throughout Europe and America. With its concept of a seat 'hanging' in a frame Aalto may have been influenced by **Marcel Breuer**'s metal 'Wassily' chair, although he was not attracted to tubular steel because 'the rational methods of creating this furniture style have been on the right track, but the result will be good only if rationalization is exercised in the selection of materials.' To Aalto this meant using wood.

For the library furniture Aalto again collaborated with Korhonen, designing a new stacking stool with legs of solid wood, bent at the top to form an attenuated 'L' shape by an

ingenious new technique of sawing and gluing. The 'L' legs were fastened directly to the stool seats (which were available in a variety of materials and finishes). This 'L' leg provided a basis for a whole range of furniture, including cocktail cabinets and side chairs, which was developed between 1933 and 1935. The furniture was typical of Aalto's design in the thirties: functional, but not utilitarian, and while the 'L' leg was a standardized component (allowing for high-volume production at low unit cost), its flexibility did not compromise either the designer's or the consumer's range of options.

In 1935 Aalto met his future wife, Maire Gullichsen, and together they established **Artek**, a store in Helsinki which still sells Aalto furniture made by Korhonen's factory.

During the thirties Aalto also designed some glassware. The most celebrated piece was first known as 'Eskimoerins skinnbuxa' ('Eskimo's skin trousers'), but is better known now as the 'Savoy' series of vases, after the exclusive Helsinki hotel interior which Aalto designed. The asymmetrical, organic, irrational design of the glassware was a refutation of geometric formalism.

Aalto's later buildings include students' quarters at Boston's MIT (1947–9) and a Pensions Building in Helsinki (1952–7). Around 1947 he tried developing his furniture ideas of the thirties, but none of his later work had the poetry and purity of his earlier designs. (See also **Finnish design**.)
Bibliography Paul David Pearson *Alvar Aalto and the International Style* Watson-Guptill, New York, 1977; Secker & Warburg, London, 1978; Karl Flieg *Alvar Aalto* Praeger, New York, 1975; Thames & Hudson, London, 1975; Quantrill *Alvar Aalto: a critical study* Secker & Warburg, London, 1982

Eero Aarnio

b. 1932

Eero Aarnio is a Finnish chair designer, who became famous for his chairs during the sixties. The 'Ball' (1965) and 'Gyro' (1968), both designed for Asko, were, according to the *New York Times*, 'the most comfortable forms to hold up the human body'. However, they now look like essays in period style, props from *Barbarella*. While in the sixties Aarnio was interested in developing a new aesthetic for plastic furniture, his recent return from Finland to Germany has found him concentrating on computer models for chair design.

'Kimara' Chair, 1983
Eero Aarnio's 'Kimara' (cocktail) chair, designed for the Asko furniture company. Aarnio is one of the few furniture designers to use computer aided design. This advanced technique allows designers both to develop the shape and to anticipate loads on the structure.

A&E Design

Tom Ahlstrom and Hans Erlich, two graduates of the Swedish Konstfackskolan (design school), founded A&E Design in Stockholm in 1968. They have specialized in the design of plastic brushes for Jordan A/S and sanitary equipment, often very novel in form, for handicapped people. With other groups, such as **Ergonomi Design**, A&E has made Sweden into a leading centre of experimentation in design for the disabled.

AEG

AEG stands for Allgemeine Elektrizitäts Gesellschaft. It grew out of DEG (the German Edison Company for Applied Electricity), formed by Emil Rathenau in 1883 after he had seen, and been impressed by, Edison's light bulb at the 'Exposition Internationale d'Electricité' in Paris in 1881. The company hired **Peter Behrens** to execute the first ever **corporate identity** programme. Behrens took the old logotype by the curlicues and turned AEG into one of the first modern companies, with a fully integrated and designed range of products, buildings and graphics. (See also p. 17.)

AEG Handbill by Peter Behrens
AEG was, like Siemens and Daimler-Benz, one of the huge industrial enterprises founded at the beginning of German unity. Its product range extended from turbines to kettles, spanned the world, and included instruments for commercial vehicles, such as the truck speedometer of c.1912 for which Peter Behrens designed this handbill.

AEG Logotypes, 1896, 1900, 1907, 1908 and 1912
The development of AEG's logotype (left) is symptomatic of the company's growth in awareness of design. The curlicue design (top) by Franz Schwechten dates from 1896. For the Paris exhibition of 1900 Otto Eckmann designed a special trademark with some of the characteristics of Art Nouveau (below Schwechten's). Peter Behrens started designing logotypes for AEG in 1907 (middle), producing some quite different designs, such as one of the ones from 1908 (below), before reaching a final form with his 1912 version, which is still in use (bottom). Behrens also designed the alphabet he used for the final version, basing it on a fifteenth-century typeface used by the Venetian printer, Aldus Manutius.

A
B
C
D
E
F
G
H
I
J
K
L
M
N
O
P
Q
R
S
T
U
V
W
X
Y
Z

A
B
C
D
E
F
G
H
I
J
K
L
M
N
O
P
Q
R
S
T
U
V
W
X
Y
Z

Aerodynamics

Aerodynamics is the scientific study of how bodies pass through air. Certain superficial elements of the science passed into the repertoire of design when **streamlining** became fashionable during the thirties. Streamlining applied some of the features of aerodynamic bodies to objects that were not aerodynamic – and often never could be.

The first aerodynamic car was patented in 1922 by **Paul Jaray**, who made revolutionary claims for the enhanced fuel economy which his efficient shape would produce. Jaray's influence was passed directly into the **Porsche** studio by **Erwin Komenda**, who had also known the work of **Wunibald Kamm**; but after the commercial failure of **Carl Breer**'s Airflow design for **Chrysler**, aerodynamics was not taken as a serious option for popular cars for many years. Although **Citroën** has continuously experimented with aerodynamically efficient shapes, it was not until **Ford** introduced the Sierra in 1982 that a mass-market vehicle was designed with aerodynamic efficiency in mind; the Sierra's designer, **Uwe Bahnsen**, then said, 'I believe we might even have underestimated . . . the willingness of the public to accept the effect of functional requirements in the aesthetic execution of a motor car.'

Otl Aicher

b. 1922

The German graphic designer Otl Aicher studied in Munich and was involved in the planning of Ulm's **Hochschule für Gestaltung**, where he became a professor in 1955 and was rector in 1962–4. He had already married Inge Scholl, the school's founder. At Ulm Aicher helped develop a highly rational approach to design, which was to characterize the work of the school.

Aicher taught at Yale from 1958 and in 1972 received the commission to design the graphics for the Munich Olympic Games. His professional objective has always been to devise clear, rationalized graphics, integrating imagery with typography, and for the Munich Olympics job he designed a system of symbols which was effective but not intrusive. From 1952 to 1954 he was a consultant to **Braun**, and has subsequently been retained by the Dresdner Bank, Frankfurt Airport, **Erco** and **BMW**, where he has used graphics to create the public character of his clients. His name has become synonymous with the restrained, severe, austere 'school' of German typography. Although considered dated by some, Aicher's graphics are a monument to clarity.

ERCO

Erco Logotype, late 1970s
Otl Aicher designed the logotype for Erco, the West German lighting company. Aicher specializes in a rational style of typography, always in sans serif faces (and very often in Frutiger's 'Univers' of 1954). However, the Erco logotype is emblematic as well as rational: the different weight of the four characters suggest a visual diminuendo, or fading, appropriate to a company whose business is lighting.

Pictograms, Munich Olympics, 1972 and Montreal Olympics, 1976
As well as typography, Otl Aicher also designed pictograms for the Munich Games of 1972 and the Montreal Games of 1976. Pictograms are an especially taxing job for a graphic designer, as the brief is to develop a set of symbols which an international audience can 'read' without words. Aicher's solution has great simplicity and purity.

Mercedes-Benz 190/190E, Final Wind Tunnel Measurement, 1983
Efficient aerodynamics are fundamental to car design. Although the general behaviour of air passing over a moving vehicle is understood, designers are less certain about its specific characteristics and can spend a great deal of development time in establishing empirical data in a wind tunnel. Aerodynamic efficiency was a fundamental part of Bruno Sacco's design brief for the Mercedes-Benz 190, seen here being tested in the company's wind tunnel; every detail, shape and contour of the car was moderated by the laws of aerodynamics.

AID

Allied International Designers was founded in London by James Pilditch in 1959. Its original name was the Package Design Association. Pilditch has been a pioneer in importing the model of American consultant design into Europe. AID is now one of the largest design consultancies specializing in packaging in the world. Pilditch has written several books on product design.
Bibliography James Pilditch *The Silent Salesman* Business Books, London, 1973

Typhoo Tea Packets from the Late Nineteenth Century to the Present
In 1980 AID became the first British design consultancy to get a Stock Exchange listing, an achievement which reflects its professional dedication to commerce. The company believes in cautious evolution rather than radical change, an approach to design which marries well with conservative, blue-chip clients such as Typhoo Tea, a leader in a static market. When Typhoo wanted a new packet for the eighties, AID rejected the idea of bringing back a historic design, but still aimed to produce something that would reflect Typhoo's heritage in a way that would be up to date.

Franco Albini

1905–77

Franco Albini was born near Como, north of Milan, and graduated in architecture from Milan Polytechnic in 1929. Until the end of the War he concentrated on interior and exhibition design, only later broadening his concerns to cover town-planning, architecture and product design. He was professor of architectural design at Milan Polytechnic from 1963 to 1975.

Albini was one of the first Italian rational architects to apply his skills to products. He designed a remarkable 'Mobile Radio' in 1941, with the components squeezed between glass, and a 'tensistructure' bookcase – in which the essence of the structure was tautened wires – which was frequently illustrated in Italian architectural magazines. It was after a meeting with Albini that **Cassina** decided to devote its corporate energies to 'innovative modern design'.

Albini's major architectural works were the **La Rinascente** department store in Rome (1957, p. 160) and the interior of the Milan underground (1962–3). In 1950 he won the 'Low Cost Furniture Competition' in New York. For him modern taste was 'against exceptional things, the search for novelty for novelty's sake, technical acrobatics, unique pieces, and, on the contrary, prefers ordinary and poor materials, simple and neat technical solutions, mass-produced objects', and his own designs always employed an economy of means, their structure being an expressive part of the design.
Bibliography G.C. Argan *Franco Albini* Milan, 1962; 'Il disegno del mobile razionale in Italia 1928/1948' *Rassegna*, number 4

Franco Albini's Apartment, Milan, 1940
Two elements of Albini's personal style – the expressive, sculptural furniture, designed by Albini himself, and the mixture of antique and modern – predicted the design of the '50s

Don Albinson

b. 1915

Don Albinson studied in Sweden, at the **Cranbrook Academy** and at Yale. He was **Charles Eames'** assistant and made the prototypes of many of his master's celebrated chairs. The contact with Eames also brought Albinson in touch with **George Nelson**. Albinson became design director of **Knoll** in 1964, where he stayed until 1971. He was especially skilled in production engineering, and his work at Knoll involved not only producing his own stacking chair but mainly getting other people's tricky designs – he cites **Warren Plattner**'s 'wire stuff' – through the engineering process and into the stores.

Stacking Chair, 1964
Don Albinson's ingeniously stacking chair for Knoll first went into production in 1964. It has a steel frame and a plastic moulded seat.

Studio Alchymia

Studio Alchymia was founded in Milan in 1979 by the architect Alessandro Guerriero, but its moving spirit has been **Alessandro Mendini**, an architect who is editor of **Domus**. It was intended to function as a gallery for designers, where avant-garde prototypes could be exhibited free from industrial constraints. The name was chosen so as to confront the assumptions of Modernism: a title that was mystical and suggested magic, although Alchymia has also promoted what it called the '*banale*', the design of the everyday.

Alchymia inherited both ideas and personnel, including **Andrea Branzi**, from the Italian radicalism of the sixties. Its first two collections were self-consciously intellectual and given the ironic names 'Bauhaus 1' and 'Bauhaus 2'; they consisted of a group of bizarre furniture pieces characterized by expressive forms and covered with plastic laminates. Since one of the original participants of the studio, **Ettore Sottsass**, left in 1981 to

form a more commercial avant-garde group called **Memphis**, Studio Alchymia has become less concerned with three-dimensional design and more with sub-political radicalizing and performance art, under the increasing influence of Mendini.
Bibliography Barbara Radice *Ologia del banale* Studio Alchymia, Milan, 1980; Andrea Branzi *The Hot House: Italian New Wave Design* MIT, Cambridge, Mass., 1984

Sideboard for Juliette's House by Alessandro Mendini, 1978
Alessandro Mendini's decorated, second-hand sideboard is an example of Studio Alchymia's irreverent approach to design. Self-consciously celebrating the everyday, designers who contributed to Studio Alchymia's exhibitions and its collections made witty references to the vernacular, but also treated history with amused and amusing contempt. Like his other exercises in 'redesign', Mendini's sideboard is a second-hand piece of furniture which he has decorated, in this case with a pattern loosely derived from a painting by Wassily Kandinsky.

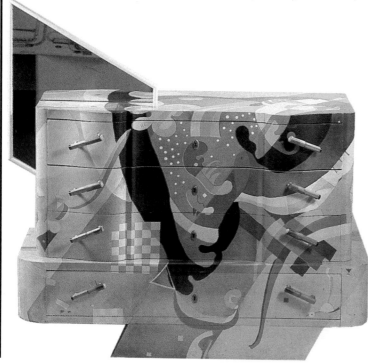

Alfa Romeo

Alfa Romeo is the second largest Italian car manufacturer and has a long tradition of employing outstanding coachbuilders and designers. Unlike **FIAT**, which is based in Turin, Alfa Romeo's home is Milan and the city's seal is used on the manufacturer's badge. 'Alfa' stands for the Anonima Lombardi Fabbrica Automobili, which took on the engineer Niccolò Romeo in 1914 (although his name was not incorporated until after the Second World War).

Alfa Romeo gained considerable mystique from its involvement in motor-racing in the years immediately before and after the Second World War. Although the nationalized concern has been in a parlous financial state for decades, its

commitment to excellence in engineering and its continued patronage only of outstanding body designers, including **Touring**, **Nuccio Bertone** and **Giorgio Giugiaro**, have won it a high critical reputation. Its sophisticated automotive image epitomizes the European 'sculptured' approach to car design.

The company's first volume car was the Giulietta Sprint, with body by Bertone, which appeared in 1954. It established standards for the small sports coupé that lasted a decade. Similarly, the Alfasud, with body by Giugiaro, defined the small advanced European car for more than a decade after its introduction in 1971.

Alfa Romeo 2500S cabriolet, 1946
The bodywork is by Pininfarina.

Aluminium

Aluminium (or aluminum, as it is known in the USA) is a metal produced from bauxite ore whose chief properties are lightness and heat-resistance. Electricity had made volume production feasible by the 1860s. At first its applications were purely industrial, but by the 1930s it began to be used for consumer goods, particularly in the United States. It can be spun, pressed or cast and it became a favourite material for kitchenware and small decorative objects. **Donald Deskey** and **Lurelle Guild** were

notable among the designers who used aluminium during the thirties. At about the same time it began to appear as a fashionable wall-cladding for interior designs.

Before the Second World War aluminium was used quite extensively by avant-garde European designers. **Gerrit Rietveld** designed a chair in aluminium, but **Hans Coray**'s 'Landi' chair is the most famous and enduring application of the metal to furniture. After the Second World War aluminium was generally displaced by cheaper plastics, and its use was again limited to industry.

Emilio Ambasz

b. 1943

Emilio Ambasz was born in Argentina and studied architecture at Princeton. He was curator of design at New York's **Museum of Modern Art** from 1970 to 1976 where he mounted the influential exhibition in 1973, 'Italy: The New Domestic Landscape'. It was the first celebration of the recent cult for Italian design and designers.

After leaving MoMA Ambasz became an independent industrial designer, rather as **Eliot Noyes** had done thirty years before. In 1977 he designed the 'Vertebra' chair with **Giancarlo Piretti**, which represented a radical re-think about the essential properties of and problems presented by the design of an office chair, and combined these with a pleasing aesthetic; it won a **Compasso d'Oro** award in 1981. His 'Osiris' low voltage spotlight, also designed with Piretti for **Erco**, won a 'Designers' Choice Award for Excellence' in 1983.

Ambasz is a quixotic and mercurial figure: he finished the undergraduate course at Princeton in just one year and, at MoMA and with his own Institute of Architecture and Urban Studies, has been a strong, though independent, creative force in the New York design world.

He has summed up his view of design: 'I believe the designer's real task begins once functional and behavioural needs have been satisfied. We create objects not only because we hope to satisfy the pragmatic needs of man, but mainly because we need to satisfy the demands of our passions and imagination. . . . The designer's milieu may have changed but the task, I believe, remains the same: to give poetic form to the pragmatic.'

'Vertebra' Chair, 1979
This was one of Ambasz' first ventures as an independent furniture designer. The idea was to produce a chair that worked like a glove, moving with the body. In this case the designer took the product all the way from conception to production: by getting toolmakers to cost his design Ambasz was able to present the manufacturer, Castelli, with a complete package (he also provided market projections). The chair went on the American market in 1977.

American design

There have been two main streams in American design during this century: the first was the industrial design movement, which peaked in the thirties and aimed to satisfy the mass-market by using **streamlining** and other **styling** clichés to stimulate demand; the second was a movement more oriented towards Europe which found expression in furniture and interior design.

The industrial design movement brought designers who had been trained perhaps as advertising draughtsmen, perhaps as stage designers, into contact with the manufacturers of hard goods such as washing machines, refrigerators, and cameras. These manufacturers had expanded after the First World War, but were caught by the Depression and needed an extra quality to add to their merchandise. They found it in this first generation of consultant industrial designers who sold them their expertise in styling. The style which emerged from this flirtation was essentially commercial and created a mass aesthetic which ▶

Lucky Strike Cigarette Pack by Raymond Loewy, early 1940s
Loewy turned the Lucky Strike pack into a bright and appealing symbol of American culture.

Cadillac, 1954
Throughout the fifties cars were America's key product. Automobile production reached its all-time peak in 1955 and it was said that anything wrong with Detroit was wrong with America. Rarely has one machine characterized a nation's preoccupations so completely.

A
B
C
D
E
F
G
H
I
J
K
L
M
N
O
P
Q
R
S
T
U
V
W
X
Y
Z

was the first democratic style of the twentieth century. Although the work of its practitioners such as **Henry Dreyfuss, Raymond Loewy** and **Walter Dorwin Teague** was widely imitated across the world, institutions which existed to reform design found it meretricious and vulgar and refused to have any association with it.

In contrast, the second American design movement was enthusiastically accepted by both the American design establishment, fascinated by all things European, and by the Europeans who were lost in admiration for the Americans' ability to implement their own ideas with such effect. The second movement is characterized by the exhibitions and the personnel of New York's **Museum of Modern Art**. The Museum gave **Charles Eames** a major exhibition and selected furniture manufactured by **Herman Miller** and **Knoll** as recipients for the prizes offered in its 'Good Design' competitions of the early fifties. The spindly legs and bent **plywood** of this furniture style soon became a familiar sight in many interiors and, combined with plants, room dividers and 'organic' coffee tables, populated many illustrated features in **House & Garden** magazine. It quickly degenerated into yet another

mass interior style.

The later fifties, America's most prosperous years, were, perhaps, best characterized by the extravagant automobile designs of **Harley Earl**. Using the imagery of space rockets, Earl proved H.L. Mencken's dictum that 'nobody ever went bust underestimating the public's taste'. However, with the rise of consumer protection and conservation movements, the bullish exuberance of American automobile styling was condemned as immoral and American design lost its primitive dynamism.

Since then American design has been predominantly a corporate matter. After **Eliot Noyes** came from the Museum of Modern Art to transform the entire image of **IBM**, the dominant American designers have tended to concentrate on **corporate identity** rather than products or furniture.
Bibliography Arthur J. Pulos *The American Design Ethic* MIT, Cambridge, Mass., 1983

Greyhound Bus by Raymond Loewy, 1946
The Greyhound bus was designed by Raymond Loewy on a General Motors chassis. Made distinctive by its fluted aluminium body panels, it became a symbol of democratic mobility.

Fanta Bottles by Raymond Loewy, mid-1960s
Loewy had already crisply redesigned the Coke bottle for Fanta's makers, but this time failed to capture the international cachet of its predecessor.

'Organic Design in Home Furnishings' Exhibition, 1940: Furniture by Charles Eames and Eero Saarinen
This exhibition was held at New York's Museum of Modern Art, the first exhibition of the design department under the curatorship of Eliot Noyes. The idea behind it was to show how the spirit of modern art could have a practical effect on the domestic environment. It displayed for the first time bent plywood chairs by Charles Eames and Eero Saarinen that were later to become classics.

Anthropometrics

Anthropometrics is the name of an interdisciplinary science which seeks to rationalize and quantify the dimensional aspects of the human form. In the USA it is more commonly known as 'human engineering'. It is the study of human physical dimensions in relationship to the objects used on a daily basis. It is purely concerned with measurements, whether, for example, a chair is high enough or a knife handle long enough to fit the palm of the hand.

Only a few designers have made a study of anthropometrics, most notably the Scandinavian furniture designers in the twenties (especially **Kaare Klint**). **Henry Dreyfuss** in the United States and **Ergonomi Design** Gruppen in Sweden have also used the science.

In his book, *Designing for People* (1955), Dreyfuss described how he used maquettes of a male and female – whom he called Joe and Josephine – to determine the functional layout of various designs, whether a control console for Bell Telephone, a tractor seat or an aeroplane seat.

Anthropometrics is related to **ergonomics**.
Bibliography Henry Dreyfuss *Designing for People* Simon & Schuster, New York, 1955

Bell 'Star' Helmet, 1966; Emery Air Freight Corporate Identity by Landor Associates, 1976; Citibank Logo by Anspach Grossman Portugal, 1970s; Cummins Diesel Engine by Eliot Noyes, 1964

American design combines high technology with slick commercialism. The Bell 'Star' helmet first appeared in 1966, about the time that Eliot Noyes redesigned a Cummins diesel engine to make it more 'rational' (see also p. 197). During the seventies American designers did more work with corporate identity than with products.

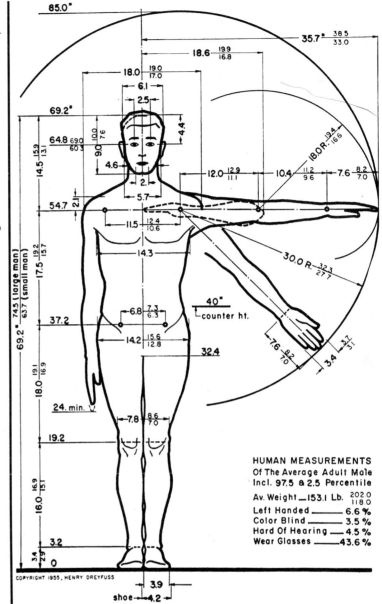

HUMAN MEASUREMENTS
Of The Average Adult Male
Incl. 97.5 & 2.5 Percentile
Av. Weight — 153.1 Lb. 202.0 / 118.0
Left Handed — 6.6 %
Color Blind — 3.5 %
Hard Of Hearing — 4.5 %
Wear Glasses — 43.6 %

COPYRIGHT 1955, HENRY DREYFUSS

Drawing of 'Joe'

Of all the American design pioneers Henry Dreyfuss was the one who was most interested in anthropometrics. In his book, Designing for People *(1955), he gave the names 'Joe' and 'Josephine' to a pair of fantasy maquettes which embodied the criteria he used in establishing the human scale of products he designed. This attention to human engineering was remarkable for its day.*

Arabia

The Arabia pottery factory was founded in Finland in 1874 by the Swedish firm **Rörstrand**, and took its name from the Helsinki suburb where it was based. By 1916 it had broken away from Rörstrand. Although it had been producing table and kitchenware in undecorated, glazed stoneware for some time it was not until the thirties that it began to gain an international reputation for promoting modern commercial ceramics. In 1946 **Kaj Franck** became chief designer, and Arabia began to produce textured stoneware in natural, earthy colours which (with its oven-to-table practicality) did much to persuade the rest of the world about the character of Scandinavian modern design. As chief designer, Franck also commissioned work from **Ulla Procopé**. Like Rörstrand and **Gustavsberg**, Arabia practises a sophisticated sort of design patronage, allowing ceramic artists studio space in its factories as well as involving them in the design and manufacture of mass-produced ware.

Bruce Archer

b. 1922

L. Bruce Archer has been a pioneer in England of systematic design. He was educated as a mechanical engineer and taught at London's **Central School of Arts and Crafts** and at Ulm's **Hochschule für Gestaltung**. In 1964 he published *Systematic Method for Designers*, an attempt to quantify and analyse every step in the process of design, but his method has not been widely adopted. He now has a chair at the **Royal College of Art**, and is involved in the educational implications of his theoretical work.

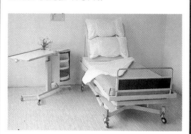

Hospital Bed with Side Table, 1960s
Bruce Archer developed a systematic approach to design which he applied in the creation of this hospital bed and side table. However, although fashionable in the fifties and early sixties, his approach found little application in the area of consumer goods. Here it has produced objects with neutral colours and flexible use, designed with ergonomic measurements.

Archigram

Formed in 1961, Archigram was a group of architects consisting of Warren Chalk (b. 1927), Peter Cook (b. 1936), Dennis Crompton (b. 1935) and David Greene (b. 1937). They married fifties **Pop** with what later became known as **High-Tech**, in an attempt to integrate architecture with mass culture. Archigram did not construct edifices, but drew imaginative, utopian essays of what might be. Their most published project was the Plug-in-City of 1965. Archigram was a major influence on Italian radical designers in the sixties.

'University Node' Architectural Sketch by Peter Cook, 1965
Peter Cook's 'University Node' was one of his technophiliac architectural fantasies from his speculative 'Plug-in-City'. Invented in 1965, this characteristic Archigram vision of the future fused the imagery of Pop with high technology.

Range of Ceramic Plates, 1876–1920
Like many other Finnish enterprises, Arabia manages to combine tradition and innovation in the design of its products. The new ceramics produced by Kaj Franck, Ulla Procopé and others were not seen as a break with the past, but as an inevitable development from it. The range of Arabia's ceramic ware illustrated here was produced in the period 1876–1920, before Finnish design had developed an independent character.

Architectural Review

The *Architectural Review* is Britain's premier journal of architectural criticism. It was founded in 1896 and at the time of its first issue was remarkable in that, unlike existing popular journals such as *The Builder*, it was concerned with the creative rather than the technical aspects of building. At first, in the hands of editor Mervyn Macartney, its bias was to the classical, but around 1930 it became directly connected with the promotion of the **Modern Movement** in Britain and it is in this respect that the *Review*'s importance lies in design: it was a very substantial influence on the history of taste through its tireless and polemical proselytizing for Modernism. The proprietor, a reclusive man called Hubert de Cronin Hastings, was responsible for bringing in a highly distinguished range of writers to the *Review*'s pages: poet John Betjeman, oenologist Philip Morton Shand and Byzantine enthusiast Robert Byron; **Nikolaus Pevsner** was on the editorial board. Even D.H. Lawrence and Evelyn Waugh contributed articles. **Moholy-Nagy** took photographs and did layouts, while the *Review*'s house photographers, Dell and Wainwright, used panchromatic film and red filters to make **International Style** buildings in Harrow and Pinner look as though they were photographed in the strong sunlight and shadows of the Mediterranean.

The *Architectural Review* continued as a campaigning journal throughout the fifties, when its star writers included Pevsner, **Reyner Banham** and Ian Nairn, but by the sixties the formula was becoming tired and the lack of conviction throughout architecture was reflected in lacklustre and directionless features.
Bibliography David Watkin *The Rise of Architectural History* The Architectural Press, London, 1980; Eastview, New York, 1980

Pages from Architectural Review *by Laszlo Moholy-Nagy, early 1930s*
In the thirties the proprietors of the Architectural Review *discovered Modernism and commissioned Laszlo Moholy-Nagy to design certain issues of the magazine. He used his own photographs and ambitious cut-out effects to make a magazine spread into something approaching a work of art.*

Archizoom

Archizoom was founded in Florence in 1966. Together with the other radical groups of architects, **Gruppo Strum**, **Superstudio** and NNN, it formed the basis for the sophisticated Italian response to **Pop**. It was greatly influenced by the English group of architectural designers, **Archigram**.

Archizoom's founders included **Andrea Branzi** and **Paolo Deganello**. It promoted what they chose to call 'anti-design', and for the 1968 Milan **Triennale**, the year of the *événements* in Paris, they established a 'Centre for Eclectic Conspiracy'. Archizoom's 'Mies' chair of 1970 was typical of their work: it was uncompromisingly irreverent, both to **Mies van der Rohe**'s memory and to the nature of sitting. Upholstered Dacron was slung across a triangular, chromium-plated frame. Their aim was design which was anti-status, anti-consumer and anti-chic. Archizoom was dissolved in 1974, but was an influence on the later Italian radical furniture designers, **Studio Alchymia** and **Memphis**.
Bibliography 'Italy: The New Domestic Landscape' exhibition catalogue, Museum of Modern Art, New York, 1973

Plastic Laminate Screens, 1970s
These vividly coloured screens, made from laminates manufactured by Abet (who later produced Memphis designs), show Archizoom's combination of British Pop imagery with Italian flair.

Egmont Arens
1888–1966

Egmont Arens typified the American commitment to the style of **streamlining** and to the marriage of design with commerce. Like the other first generation American pioneer consultant designers, he started by doing something completely different, and only became a packaging and product designer after a career in journalism. He worked for a number of short-lived firms desperate to design themselves out of the Depression. He designed several spun-aluminium saucepan sets and wrote a book, *25 Years of Progress in Package Design*.
Bibliography Arthur J. Pulos *The American Design Ethic* MIT, Cambridge, Mass., 1983

A
B
C
D
E
F
G
H
I
J
K
L
M
N
O
P
Q
R
S
T
U
V
W
X
Y
Z

Giorgio Armani

b. 1935

A fashion writer in the English newspaper the *Guardian* once claimed: 'If **Chanel** means the twenties, Dior the fifties and **Quant** the sixties, Armani could come to mean the eighties.' If this is to be proved true, it will be because of his propagation of a casually elegant, formal-informal style in fashion, typified by his unstructured jacket, which produces a sloppy refinement which only bespoke tailoring could achieve before, and by unconventional combinations such as gilets worn over coats.

He was born in Piacenza and studied medicine, but instead of practising as a doctor took a job as a window display artist at **La Rinascente**, Italy's leading chain of stores. He worked his way up to Rinascente's fashion and style department and then joined Nino Cerrutti as a designer in 1961. At Cerrutti's textile factory Armani learnt to respect materials: 'That's why today whenever I see anyone throwing away a sample of cloth, it's like cutting off my hand.' In 1970 he set up a salon of his own and started trading under his own name in 1975, now running a chain of shops under the name Armani Emporio, for which he designs both menswear and womenswear. He admits they are for the wealthy: 'My clothes are for women who have money. They are not for a teenager who expects novelty.' **Elio Fiorucci** added that they are 'over serious and not for the many who like to have fun'.

L. & C. Arnold

With **Berliner Metallgewerbe** and **Thonet**, the Arnold company was one of the pioneer manufacturers of tubular steel furniture in Germany in the twenties.

Art Deco

In the histories of design which see progress as just a succession of style labels, Art Deco has, since the later sixties, been seen as the successor to the **Arts and Crafts** movement and to **Art Nouveau**. This is to overestimate the importance of Art Deco itself and, by extension, of journalistic taxonomy.

Art Deco is not really a single style, but the name given to the fashions which dominated the decorative arts in the years between the First and Second World Wars. It is also known as Jazz Modern, and as **moderne**; in both incarnations it derives its force from the more philosophically severe experiments in art and design taking place at the time in such places as the **Bauhaus**, as well as from the contemporary influences of Cubism, Diaghilev's 'Ballet Russe' and Egyptology. But Art Deco was at the same time another phenomenon as well: much of what the sale rooms now call Art Deco is in fact not the popularization of the **Modern Movement** but the exquisite, decadent furniture of the French classes who consumed luxury – chairs by E-J. Ruhlmann, interiors by Süe et Mare and silver by **Jean Puiforcat**.

The name Art Deco derived from the 'Exposition Internationale des Arts Décoratifs et Industriels Modernes', held in Paris in 1925, where the architecture was characterized for the most part by faceted forms, complex silhouettes and decorated surfaces. Art Deco is in origin a French style; it was imported *en masse* into a number of other countries, particularly Britain and the USA, where it can be seen, for example, in the ceramics of **Clarice Cliff** and in **Donald Deskey**'s interiors for Radio City Music Hall.

Rosenthal ceramic ware, 1930s

Staircase, Strand Palace Hotel, London, 1929–30
Oliver Bernard's Strand Palace Hotel was one of the highlights of London Art Deco, a style characterized in architecture by dramatic angles, decorative curves and sensuous, glittering materials.

Art Nouveau

Art Nouveau was the first twentieth-century popular style, a mass-produced and effete successor to the rustic-biased **Arts and Crafts** movement. The name derived from a shop, opened in Paris in 1895 by the publisher of *Artistic Japan*, Samuel Bing; in Italy it is called *Stile Liberty*, after the London shop, while in Germany and Scandinavia it is known as *Jugendstil* (literally, 'youth style').

Art Nouveau reached its climax in the goods and architecture on display at the Paris Exhibition of 1900. When the official English collector brought back prize selections and presented them to the South Kensington Museum, official attitude was so outraged that they were banished to the outstation at Bethnal Green on the basis that the firescreens by **Emile Gallé** might deprave the workers and provide, contrary to **Henry Cole**'s wishes, inferior models for imitation. **Walter Crane** saw Art Nouveau as the last manifestation of the nineteenth-century interest in decoration and described it as 'a strange, decadent disease'.

The chief characteristics of

Art Nouveau appeared in a curvilinear version, recognizable by a 'whiplash line' and represented in France by **Hector Guimard** and in Spain by **Gaudí**, and in a more rectilinear version represented in Britain by **Charles Rennie Mackintosh** and in Austria by **Josef Hoffmann**. Art Nouveau responded to new materials – particularly wrought iron in architecture – and was well adapted to glass, a medium in which Gallé in France and Louis Comfort Tiffany in the USA excelled. But despite the use of new materials, Art Nouveau was also the last manifestation of the interest in decoration and its sinuous shapes look like overcooked asparagus or organisms viewed through a microscope. Tendrils abound, and there is an occasional sperm-like detail. In France these tendrils were applied to everything from vases to fire stations. At its most refined, Art Nouveau approaches the elegant simplicity of Josef Hoffmann who transformed the style into a disciplined repertoire of geometric forms.
Bibliography Robert Schmutzler *Art Nouveau* Thames & Hudson, London, 1964

House in Avenue Rapp, Paris, by Lavirotte, 1901 (above right)
The Art Nouveau in its most vegetative manifestation. Art Nouveau flourished only briefly, but was an important source – as well as a liberation – for designers. (See also p. 31.)

The Yellow Book, Cover Design by Aubrey Beardsley, 1894
Aubrey Beardsley's style, exaggerated, dramatic and effete, was the graphic expression of Art Nouveau. His techniques were soon picked up by commercial illustrators.

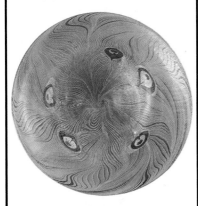

Favrile Glass Plate, 1894
The decorator Louis Tiffany founded the Tiffany Glass Company in 1885. His iridescent Favrile glass was first shown at Samuel Bing's Paris shop, Art Nouveau, in 1895. Thereafter Tiffany glass became an international symbol of Art Nouveau.

A
B
C
D
E
F
G
H
I
J
K
L
M
N
O
P
Q
R
S
T
U
V
W
X
Y
Z

A
B
C
D
E
F
G
H
I
J
K
L
M
N
O
P
Q
R
S
T
U
V
W
X
Y
Z

Art Workers' Guild

The Art Workers' Guild is a private club founded in 1884 by five assistants working in the studios of the architect Norman Shaw, including W.R. Lethaby. They were united in the conviction that architecture was an art rather than a profession, and this was the theme of an important tract they published in 1892, intended to state their implacable opposition to the Royal Institute of British Architects.

The Art Workers' Guild was formed, in Gillian Naylor's words, to promote 'the breakdown of relations between the artist, the architect and the craftsman'. It was responsible for the **Arts and Crafts** Exhibition Society, which held its first exhibition at the New Gallery in Regent Street in 1888 under the presidency of **Walter Crane**. Like Freemasonry, there is a lot of ritual and paraphernalia attached to the mystique of being a Guildsman: the Master and his acolytes all wear ceremonial robes (designed by **C.F.A. Voysey**) and there used to be a virtual vow of silence.
Bibliography Gillian Naylor *The Arts and Crafts Movement* Studio Vista, 1971; MIT, Cambridge, Mass., 1971

Artek

Artek is a Helsinki furniture store set up by the architect **Alvar Aalto** and Maire Gullichsen in 1935. (See also p. 125.)

Arteluce

Arteluce is a firm in Milan, active since the forties, which specializes in lighting. Together with some other Milanese companies it has been an influential patron of designers during Italy's modern renaissance. Its first designer was Gino Sarfatti, who made highly expressive lighting inspired by the contemporary sculpture of Alexander Calder.

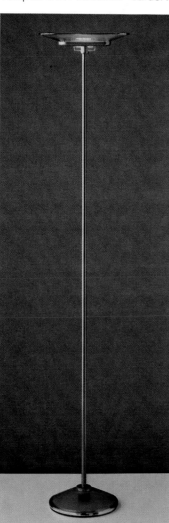

'Jill' Light for Arteluce by King, Miranda, Arnaldi, 1980
Milan has perhaps more furniture designers than any other city. Pressure for novelty can turn design into fashion in a rush for prominence at the annual furniture fair. This light, however, combines novelty with concern for the object's essential function.

Artemide

Artemide is a Milan furniture store and manufacturer, owned by **Ernesto Gismondi**, professor of rocket technology at Milan Polytechnic. It was established in 1951 and committed itself from the outset to modern design. Since then it has employed the leading product designers in Italy, including **Vico Magistretti, Ettore Sottsass** and **Richard Sapper**. Gismondi also gives financial support to **Memphis**.

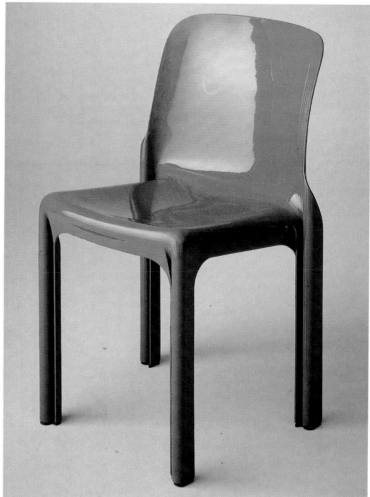

'Selene' Chair by Vico Magistretti, 1968–9
Artemide furniture is well established within Milanese modern design, and Magistretti one of its most established designers. The high finish of the 'Selene' chair, in glass-reinforced plastic, is an emblem of Milanese high style.

Light Fitting by Carlo Forcolini, 1984 (top)
Producing avant-garde lighting is an initiation rite of Milanese architects and designers. This fitting in painted and perforated metal with a glass diffuser was designed by Carlo Forcolini for Artemide in 1984.

Arts and Crafts

'Arts and Crafts' was a term coined to replace the clumsier 'Combined Arts' when an offshoot of the **Art Workers' Guild** held its first exhibition in London in 1888.

The philosophical background to the Arts and Crafts movement lay in the polemics of **John Ruskin** and **William Morris**, and its chief practitioner was **Charles Robert Ashbee**. Its fundamental premise was that industrialization had debased ornament and design and had, therefore, also debased English culture and society. For artistic inspiration it had a fuzzy vision of the Middle Ages, when, as Ruskin, Morris and to a lesser extent Ashbee supposed, man was in harmony with his labour and working life was a continuous idyll of happy, wholesome, uplifting handicraft. The model for this commonly held misconception was the Gothic Revival architect **A.W.N. Pugin**, who had first declared the architecture and design of the Middle Ages to be both cause and symptom of ideal social conditions.

In imitation of the Middle Ages, the Arts and Crafts movement created a number of guilds, populated by decent craftsmen and pretentious middle-class world-improvers. These included the Century Guild, the Art Workers' Guild and the Guild of Handicrafts. Although some of the activities were London-based, the leading lights ignored the fact that in the Middle Ages all crucial creative developments took place in cities, and sought the comfort of the countryside and, in particular, the area to the west of Oxford known as the Cotswolds. This was convenient because it combined the opportunity of maximum picturesque charm with the temptation of nearby train links to the fleshpots of the capital city, and the heroes of the Arts

and Crafts, Ashbee, **Ernest Gimson** and Lethaby, did not disdain to use the railway. Similarly, there were few active Arts and Crafts practices exposed to the meteorological rigours of the Yorkshire Dales (or the scorn and ridicule of the real workmen of Sheffield and Doncaster).

The Arts and Crafts practitioners aimed to produce designs for furniture, glass, silver and other areas of the applied arts inspired by the craft values of 'truth to materials' and fitness for purpose. Simplification and honesty of decoration, derived at all times from the natural world, were essential to all Arts and Crafts activity. However, the Arts and Crafts was not really one style, but many. At its base was a social experiment intended to reform society through art and design and to establish handcrafting as the dominant mode of manufacture. It grew out of Pugin's Gothic Revival, but absorbed the *japonisme* of Edward Godwin and the Queen Anne of Philip Webb on the way. In the 1890s it merged stylistically with **Art Nouveau**.

The polemics of the Arts and Crafts were more influential than its actual products. The romantic notions of Ruskin, Morris and Ashbee were balanced by an attention to detail and the attitude of 'truth to materials'. When translated to Germany by **Hermann Muthesius** these elements laid the basis for a more practical revolution in production and education which found its fullest expression in **Walter Gropius'** curriculum at the **Bauhaus**.

Bibliography Gillian Naylor *The Arts and Crafts Movement* Studio Vista, 1971; MIT, Cambridge, Mass., 1971

Buckler's Hard, Hampshire, 1937
Baillie Scott's architecture helped popularize the Arts and Crafts, and this house shows the Arts and Crafts at its most evocative and most nostalgic.

Wooden Dresser, 1902
Peter Behrens designed this impressive dresser in 1902, while he was working in the artists' colony assembled in Darmstadt by Grand Duke Ernst Ludwig II von Hessen. Its monumental style contains elements which betray Behrens' allegiance both to neo-classicism and to the Arts and Crafts.

Charles Robert Ashbee
1863–1942

Charles Robert Ashbee was one of the principal forces in the **Arts and Crafts** movement. In 1888, after an apprenticeship to the architect G.F. Bodley, he founded the Guild and School of Handicrafts at Toynbee Hall, moving it in 1891 to premises in the Mile End Road in London's East End. His mission, derived from reading **John Ruskin** and **William Morris**, was to teach what he called the British Working Man about the finer things in life, at least as they were understood in Chelsea. It was from there that he cycled to the Mile End Road every day, to read his British Working Men extracts from Ruskin. He would also tell them that manual labour was an exalting activity and that a revival of medieval trade practices was the best way to counter the evils of industrialization.

In 1902 he left London altogether and moved to Chipping Campden in the Cotswolds where he established a School of Arts and Crafts, and continued to design furniture and silver in an effete variation of the style of William Morris. Here his Guild of Handicrafts satisfied the market's temporary demand for the products of 'art workers', while Ashbee himself

satisfied his own demand for comradeship with sturdy British Working Men. The astonished townsfolk of Chipping Campden watched the bemused urban workers, led by a daffy intellectual, descend on their sleepy main street, taking part in a social and artistic experiment that was to become the prototype of the **Crafts Revival** in Britain and in America. It lasted seven years before it went bankrupt. By 1915 Ashbee had become disillusioned with handicrafts and went to Cairo University to be a lecturer in English.

Ashbee's designs themselves were derivative and not especially significant, but his Chipping Campden experiment and his writings on art and society had considerable influence, particularly in Austria, on **Josef Hoffmann** and the other designers of the **Wiener Werkstätte**, and in Germany, Scandinavia and the USA. In many ways Ashbee's importance is in giving form to

Two Silver Bowls, c. 1901 and 1904
The furniture of Ashbee's Guild of Handicrafts may have been humdrum, but in his silverware he achieved an individual, if somewhat derivative, style, combining traditional motifs with Art Nouveau curves.

Arts and Crafts principles, inspiring others to fight against the alienating aspects of industrialization and to base twentieth-century design values upon an ethical system inherited from an imaginary world of the crafts. From this complex net of ideas which lasted so briefly Britain has inherited the country cottage cult, the attire of the artistic radical and a reinforcement of the English taste for the picturesque.
Bibliography Alan Crawford *C.R. Ashbee* Yale University Press, New Haven & London, 1985

Aspen

Aspen was a defunct silver-mining town in Colorado when Walter Paepcke, founder of the Container Corporation of America, decided in 1946 to develop it as a centre for civilized resort. Paepcke employed **Herbert Bayer** (who had come to the United States from the **Bauhaus** in Germany) to design the Aspen Institute for Humanistic Studies. From this base Aspen became the centre for a major international design conference, organized every year by the IDCA (International Design Conference at Aspen), which, being to the United States what the **Royal Society of Arts** is to Britain, represents the entire American design profession.
Bibliography Reyner Banham *The Aspen Papers*, Pall Mall Press, 1974; James Sloan Allen *The Romance of Commerce and Culture* University of Chicago Press, Chicago, 1984

Gunnar Asplund

1885–1940

A Swedish architect, Gunnar Asplund first became known as a designer for room sets he designed for a 'Home' exhibition at Stockholm's Liljevalch's Gallery in 1917. They attracted attention because of their crisp, blue and white wallpaper and curtains, simple spruce furniture and cupboards filled with **Wilhelm Kåge**'s working man's dinner services. He was then commissioned by **Gregor Paulsson** to be the architectural designer of the highly influential **Stockholm Exhibition** of 1930 and was, therefore, responsible for helping publicize international modern architecture to an entire generation. Earlier, Asplund also designed furniture for the Nordiska Kompaniet in which he revived neo-classicism as a decorative style. **Cassina** has recently reissued some of his pieces from this period.

'Senna' Chair, 1925
Gunnar Asplund's 'Senna' chair in modern reproduction by Cassina. Although he is often identified with the Stockholm Exhibition of 1930 and therefore with the Modern Movement, Asplund was no radical. This chair, designed for a public library, shows his twenties style of simplified classicism.

Sergio Asti

b. 1926

Sergio Asti graduated in architecture from Milan Polytechnic in 1953. Of all the Milanese designers of his generation, he has been the most independent, apparently unwilling to align himself with any particular group or theory (although he *was* one of the founders of the Italian Association of Industrial Designers in 1956). His designs have been predominantly for ceramic tableware and each has a strong sculptural character. He has designed light fittings for **Arteluce**, **Artemide** and **Kartell** and his 'Marco' glass vase for Salviati won a **Compasso d'Oro** award in 1962. **Ettore Sottsass** says that Asti's designs 'explain to you what you are doing while you are doing something; they are provisions, diagrams for your life, they disclose possibilities, they let you participate'. On the other hand, **Vittorio Gregotti** wrote 'Obsession with quality has been the essence of Sergio Asti's work for thirty years . . .', and added that his work 'opposes the proletarian trend of the **Modern Movement**' and that it exemplifies 'that state of confusion which is typical of the middle class today'.
Bibliography 'The World of Sergio Asti' exhibition catalogue, International Craft Center, Kyoto, 1983

Fruit Bowl, 1984
This marble bowl was designed by Asti for Up & Up.

Gae Aulenti

b. 1927

Gae Aulenti was born near Udine and graduated in architecture from Milan Polytechnic in 1954. She first worked in the neo-Liberty style, a **Pop** version of **Art Nouveau**, then as an unpaid assistant to **Ernesto Rogers**, and then in exhibition design on her own account until 1967, when she began to undertake the same work for **Olivetti**. It is as an exhibition designer that she has made the greatest impact, and her work combines a purity of line with the use of rich textured materials. She designed the Olivetti showroom in the rue Faubourg St Honoré in Paris in her first year with the company, and then, in 1969, the travelling exhibition 'Concept and Form' which showed many people the role that Olivetti has played in modern design. In 1968, 1969, 1970, 1976 and 1978 she designed stands for FIAT at the Turin Motor Show and in 1968, 1969 and 1970 at Geneva. In 1975 she designed a range of furniture for **Knoll** (see p. 171).
Bibliography 'Gae Aulenti' exhibition catalogue, Padiglione d'Arte Contemporanea, Milan, 1979

Exhibition Design for Olivetti, 1970
Gae Aulenti's stylish exhibition designs have dramatically promoted Olivetti's corporate image in cities all over the world.

B

David **Bache**
Uwe **Bahnsen**
M.H. **Baillie Scott**
Bakelite
Cristobal **Balenciaga**
Peter Reyner **Banham**
Oscar **Barnack**
Barnsley Brothers
Alfred H. **Barr**
Barron
and Larcher
Roland **Barthes**
Saul **Bass**
Bauhaus
Herbert **Bayer**
BBPR
Peter **Behrens**
Norman **Bel Geddes**
Mario **Bellini**
J.H. **Belter**
Benetton
Walter **Benjamin**
Ward **Bennett**
Berliner
Metallgewerbe
Harry **Bertoia**
Nuccio **Bertone**
Flaminio **Bertoni**
Biedermeier
Max **Bill**
Misha **Black**
BMW
Cini **Boeri**
Rodolfo **Bonetto**
Borax
Michel **Boué**
Pierre **Boulanger**
Marianne **Brandt**
Andrea **Branzi**
Braun
Carl **Breer**
Marcel **Breuer**
BrionVega
British design

David Bache

b. 1926

David Bache is the only British car body designer ever to have achieved international celebrity.

His career as an apprentice began in Britain's industrial Midlands in the late forties, in the context of the merger in 1949 of the Austin and Nuffield manufacturing concerns. Austin already had an Italian designer, Riccardo Burzi, on the pay-roll; he had joined the Birmingham outfit from Lancia in the twenties. Burzi was responsible for the astonishingly extravagant Austin Atlantic and the delightfully minimal Austin A30, for which Bache designed the instrument panel. This was one of Britain's first serious small cars, making a credible rival to **Issigonis'** Morris Minor.

Bache joined Rover in 1954. His first cars to go into production were the cleaned-up Series II Land-Rover and the Rover P5 of 1959, known familiarly as the Three Litre. It was followed by the P6, or Rover 2000 of 1963, perhaps the most sophisticated British production car ever. Like his other designs, the P6 was invested with much symbolism, conscious and unconscious: the **Citroën** DS that he admired and the Ferrari that he drove both donated details.

Although this was a brilliant start, Bache's position as Britain's leading car designer was compromised by the catastrophic series of mergers which brought all the disparate manufacturing groups into a mismatched, muddle-headed and under-financed assemblage called British Leyland. This merger meant that 126 separate product lines from Austin, Morris, Rover, Triumph and Jaguar had to be rationalized and some brilliant designs by Bache and his engineering partner Spen King were casualties. Two lost designs included the P8, a 4.4 litre V8 saloon, and the P9, a rear-engined sports car that was judged to be superior to the **Porsche** 911. However, Bache produced two designs in the autumn of Britain's motor industry which were excellent by even the most severe competitive standards: the Range Rover of 1970 and the P10, or Rover SD1, of 1975. The P10 was one of the chief influences on **Uwe Bahnsen**'s design for the 1982 **Ford** Sierra.

In any other country Bache would be a national hero, but in Britain his name is scarcely known. Besides the much-admired products which went into production, Bache can claim impressive innovation in many details of car design, including instrument logic and **aerodynamics**. He left British Leyland in 1981, although both the Metro and Maestro show strong signs of his hand.

Uwe Bahnsen

b. 1930

Uwe Bahnsen was educated at Hamburg Academy of Fine Arts and since 1976 has been vice-president in charge of design at **Ford of Europe**. He is the first man to emerge as a personality from the anonymous mass of Ford senior management.

Bahnsen has strong rationally based views about design, dismissing **Giorgio Giugiaro**'s style-based approach with ItalDesign as the 'origami school of car design'. His most distinctive design has been the 1982 Ford Sierra, which is the most radical mass-produced car ever to emerge from a British factory. The Sierra is an expression of Bahnsen's belief that the customer can always be flattered into accepting more advanced products. (See p. 64.)
Bibliography 'The Car programme: 52 weeks to Job One or how they designed the Ford Sierra' exhibition catalogue, The Boilerhouse Project, Victoria & Albert Museum, London, 1982

Land-Rover 88-inch Hard Top
The definitive version of the original Land-Rover, the 88-inch hard top was the result of redesign by David Bache. Bache took the original agricultural vehicle and altered the proportions, changed the cut-lines, and added flash-gaps, transforming a tentative product into a timeless piece of British design.

M.H. Baillie Scott

1865–1945

Mackay Hugh Baillie Scott was an English architect of the **Arts and Crafts** movement whose work became well known in Germany and Austria after he built a palace for the Grand Duke of Hesse at Darmstadt in 1898 and furnished it with furniture made to his own designs by the Guild of Handicrafts. From the Künstlerkolonie (artists' colony) the influence of Baillie Scott's monumental yet folksy style spread across the German-speaking world at a time when English art and the English gentleman were idols revered by the continental avant-garde. One further influence of Baillie Scott's work in Europe was the publication in two volumes of the drawings for a competition organized by the magazine *Innen-Dekoration* called '*Haus eines Kunstfreundes* (A House of an Art Lover) in a series edited by **Hermann Muthesius**.

However, in spite of his strong influence abroad, his individual designs were unremarkable. His main contribution to the history of style was to legitimize the English domestic villa.
Bibliography James D. Kornwulf *M.H. Baillie Scott and the Arts and Crafts* Johns Hopkins University Press, Baltimore, 1971

'House of an Art Lover', 1902
Baillie Scott's entry for the Viennese 'Haus eines Kunstfreundes' (House of an Art Lover) competition, 1902. Illustrated in Hermann Muthesius' book, Das Englische Haus *of 1905, Baillie Scott's essay in the Arts and Crafts style was to have a strong influence on continental taste.*

Bakelite

'Carvacraft' Desk Set, John Dickinson & Co., 1948–51
Bakelite was the first cheap, popular plastic. It made hitherto luxury products widely available. In this sense it was a 'good thing', but Bakelite was also debasing because it tempted designers and manufacturers to ape traditional materials instead of inventing a 'language' appropriate to its own nature. This 'Carvacraft' desk set, however, is a rare example of integrity in early plastic design.

Bakelite was one of the first generation **plastics**, invented by a Belgian-American chemist called Leo Henricus Baekeland (1863–1944) in 1907. 'Bakelit' was the German form of his family name.

Used at first only in electrical engineering, Bakelite soon began to appear in consumer products. In the thirties its malleable properties were ideal for designers looking for new materials to give dramatic presence to the first generation of self-consciously 'designed' consumer products. With Bakelite rapid variation was possible, and it facilitated the production of many new shapes. Without its technical properties, **Jean Heiberg**'s telephone and **Wells Coates'** radio would not have been possible. Bakelite was also significant in that it made luxury items, such as bangles and cigarette cases which had hitherto been made out of ebony or ivory, available in vast numbers for the mass market.
Bibliography 'Bakeliet, techniek, vormgeving, gebruik' exhibition catalogue, Boymans-van Beuningen Museum, Rotterdam, 1981; Sylvia Katz *Plastics* Studio Vista, London, 1978

A
B
C
D
E
F
G
H
I
J
K
L
M
N
O
P
Q
R
S
T
U
V
W
X
Y
Z

Cristobal Balenciaga

1895–1972

Cristobal Balenciaga was a Basque who opened a couture house in Paris in 1936, after tailoring in San Sebastian and Madrid. He soon established a reputation there for his 'demanding' clothes of supreme cut and elegance. In his personal and his business affairs Balenciaga brought *hauteur* to new heights. He was indifferent to the press, to certain potential customers who did not reach his standards of perfection, and to the protocol of the Paris fashion season, but his clothes transcended criticism. They had a strong Spanish influence, evident in the use of lace, satins and brocades, and in shapes reminiscent of a bull-fighter's cape. Balenciaga was also entirely indifferent to fashions in fashion and created gowns that have a timeless artistry; his colour sense was strong, and he frequently used reds, rich browns, turquoises and black. In 1957 he introduced the 'sack' dress, prefiguring fashions of the sixties. He retired in 1968.

Evening Dress, c. 1955
Immaculate cut, elaborate detail, dramatic profile and bold Spanish colour are typical of Balenciaga's couture work.

Peter Reyner Banham

b. 1920

With **Sigfried Giedion** and **Nikolaus Pevsner**, Peter Reyner Banham is the most important twentieth-century writer on design.

Before the war he served an apprenticeship with the Bristol Aeroplane Company, where he gained a familiarity with technical objects that has seen him through many a tortuous metaphor. Banham became a staff writer on the **Architectural Review** during the '50s and in successive milestone articles rethought the entire history of the **Modern Movement** from first principles. These same articles were published in 1960 as *Theory and Design in the First Machine Age*, which was also the subject of his doctoral dissertation. Although Banham has no sympathy with **Post-Modernism**, his book was the first to undermine the credentials of **Functionalism**. Banham was associated with the founding of **Pop** at London's Institute of Contemporary Arts in 1956, and all his subsequent articles have explored one or other theme concerned with everyday architecture and design, in particular expendability and symbolism.

Banham can be said to have inaugurated the serious study of design and popular culture in Britain. In the late seventies he moved to the United States.
Bibliography Reyner Banham *Design By Choice* Rizzoli, New York, 1981; Academy Editions, London, 1982

Oscar Barnack

1879–1936

Oscar Barnack was the designer of the first effective 35mm camera. Put into production by Leitz, it became known as the Leica (*Leitz camera*). The prototype appeared in 1913, the production model twelve years later. Using film in a rigid cassette, it was light and portable. Max Berck's 'Elmar' lenses made it optically superb, and all subsequent developments in photography depended on the standard he established. In the design of the camera Barnack made no concessions to aesthetics, but his scrupulous attention to detail and his engineer's reluctance to indulge in meretricious ornament made the Leica a symbol of the Machine Age. Furthermore, the camera's ingenuity and precision construction made it the model for all cameras of its type.

Leica Camera, 1925

Barnsley Brothers

Sidney (1865–1926) and Ernest (1863–1926) Barnsley were craftsmen-designers of furniture who set up a Cotswold workshop with **Ernest Gimson** in 1895. They represented the most vernacular end of the British **Arts and Crafts** movement, self-consciously using traditional materials, techniques and furniture types in their work.

Alfred H. Barr

1902–81

Alfred H. Barr was born in Detroit, the son of a Presbyterian minister. As director of New York's **Museum of Modern Art** from 1929 to 1943 he played an important role in the drama of unveiling European modern art and design to the American people. He set up the architecture and design department in 1932 (split, in 1940, into its two halves). It was Barr who was chiefly responsible for MoMA's 'Machine Art' exhibition of 1934 (see p. 46), which looked at the design of anonymous machine parts, and he was behind the movement towards collecting and exhibiting 'good design' for which the museum was known in the forties and fifties. Under Barr the museum also put on two other highly important shows. He gave **Philip Johnson** the chance to introduce European modern architecture to America with the 'International Style' show in 1932, whose title is the origin of the label; and in 1940 **Eliot Noyes** organized the exhibition 'Organic Design in Home Furnishings', with chairs by **Charles Eames** and **Eero Saarinen** that have since become classics (see p. 74).

Barr's museum was greeted in the American press as 'that whorehouse on 53rd Street', but became vital in introducing new art to American society.

Barron and Larcher

Phyllis Barron (1890–1964) and Dorothy Larcher (1884–1952) were designers and printers of hand-block textiles between the Wars. Their distinctive geometric and floral designs were often in restrained colours printed on natural materials.

Roland Barthes

1915–80

The French academic and writer Roland Barthes was one of the creators and popularizers of structuralism and of **semiology**, the study of signs. His essays on popular culture and consumerism, collected in his anthology *Mythologies* (1957), raised writing about design to new, high levels and did a huge amount to increase intelligent awareness of the nature of the modern world and the forces which help create it.

Barthes had studied French literature in Paris and then taught at universities in Romania and Egypt before returning to Paris with a job at the Centre Nationale de la Recherche Scientifique. At the time of his death in 1980 (when he was run over by a laundry truck in Paris) Barthes was working at the pinnacle of French academe, the Ecole Pratique des Hautes Etudes. *Mythologies* contains essays about detergents, steak and chips and margarine, but is best remembered as far as design is concerned for Barthes' evocative account of 'The New **Citroën**'.

Not without irony, Barthes took up **Boulanger**'s car and made a modern monument out of it: 'I think that cars today are almost the exact equivalents of the great Gothic cathedrals: I mean the supreme creation of an era, conceived with passion by unknown artists, and consumed in image if not in usage by a whole population

which appropriates them as a purely magical object.'
Bibliography Barthes *Mythologies* Editions du Seuil, Paris, 1957; *Système de la Mode* Editions du Seuil, Paris, 1967

Saul Bass

b. 1920

American graphic designer and film-maker Saul Bass was born in New York, but runs his office in Los Angeles. Bass brought 'art' into film credits which, before his innovations with *Carmen Jones* and *The Man with the Golden Arm*, employing adventurous graphics in each, had been nothing more than banal, processional lists done by lettering artists. For *Around the World in Eighty Days* and *West Side Story* Bass made the credits into animated or live-action features in their own right.

For blue-chip America, Bass has assembled an impressive range of logotypes whose crisp, clean lines say more attractive things about the corporations than mere facts ever can. He did the bell for 'Ma Bell' (AT&T); for the Aluminum Corporation of America he produced a clean logo with a novel typeface which had curves like those of an extruded aluminium beer can; he produced a scientific, optical and oriental look for Minolta, curlicues for Celanese and Lawry's, and the blobby W for Warner Communications. But it has been for airlines that his work has achieved its most singular handwriting: Continental, United and Frontier all have Saul Bass colour schemes and logos to unite them in appearances of freshness, efficiency and credibility. When asked what he'd do with a free year, Bass replied 'create projects with terrible deadlines'. His *curriculum vitae* looks like the Fortune 500 and the Academy Awards of 1963; he is a very professional designer.

Walk on the Wild Side, 1962
Saul Bass' career began with film credits. For Walk on the Wild Side *Bass devised a dramatic sub plot for the opening titles which has proved more memorable than the film itself.*

United Airlines Corporate Identity, 1974
The area of a plane's tail fin provides a tight discipline for the designer.

Warner Communications Logo, 1974
Here Bass made a logogram and a logotype.

American Telephone & Telegraph Logo, 1984
For the old 'Ma Bell' Bass made the happy coincidence of the name work twice.

Girl Scouts' Logo, 1978
Bass made play with a visual pun.

A
B
C
D
E
F
G
H
I
J
K
L
M
N
O
P
Q
R
S
T
U
V
W
X
Y
Z

Bauhaus

'Bauhaus' is an untranslatable word, coined by **Walter Gropius**, which combines the root of the German verb *bauen*, to build, with *Haus*, house. It is the name given to an art school founded by Gropius under the original title of the Staatliches Bauhaus Weimar, when he combined the Grossherzogliche Sächsische Kunstgewerbeschule and Grossherzogliche Sächsische Hochschule für Bildende Kunst.

The Bauhaus, which lasted from 1919 to 1933, has come to represent the distillation of the **Modern Movement** and the Fundamentalist design ethic. Yet its intellectual origins lay with the **Arts and Crafts** (as well as with the distinctly German traditions of **Biedermeier** and neo-classicism) and its early years, before Gropius moved the school to his purpose designed building in Dessau when it became known simply as the Bauhaus, were dominated by Expressionist art, thought and behaviour.

Under Gropius the Bauhaus became an art school of immense creativity and influence. The curriculum was a broadly based foundation year, followed by craft specializations. Gropius injected a medieval flavour, calling staff 'masters' and 'journeymen'. His approach to design was to stress aesthetic fundamentals and strive for geometrically pure forms, but unlike the practitioners of the Arts and Crafts he did not disdain machines. He hired some of the greatest painters, graphic designers, thinkers and architects of his day, and a roll-call of his staff looks like an index to a comprehensive volume on twentieth-century art and design, including people like Wassily Kandinsky, **Johannes Itten** and Paul Klee (see also pp. 36–8). The building itself was a remarkable monument in its own right, and a vindication of Gropius' educational philosophy: its entire fittings and decorations were produced by staff and students of the school.

Yet, despite its prestige and its reputation, the immediate achievements of the Bauhaus were slight, and throughout its entire fourteen-year life it had a mere 1250 students and only thirty-five full-time staff. Although it was at the Bauhaus that **Marcel Breuer** and **Mies van der Rohe** established some of the canons of modern furniture design in their experiments with tubular steel, very little of the art-into-industry process which Gropius promulgated was actually achieved there, and most of the production of the school's workshops was, in fact, crafts based. Perhaps sensing the irony and futility of his mission, at least in Europe, Gropius resigned in 1928, leaving the direction of the school to the Swiss Marxist architect **Hannes Meyer**. Meyer's politics alienated the school from the local government, whose ruling Social Democrat party dismissed him to placate conservative opposition. Meyer was replaced by **Mies van der Rohe**, who moved the school into a disused telephone factory in Berlin until it closed under the Nazis in 1933.

In a sense, the greatest effect of the Bauhaus was in America, where Gropius realized some of his finest buildings, and where, as professor of architecture at Harvard University, his teaching influenced an entire generation of students with ideas that fascism had driven out of Europe (see also p. 48).

Cover for 'Staatliches Bauhaus in Weimar 1919–1923' by Herbert Bayer
Produced for the Bauhaus exhibition of 1923, Bayer's booklet design was among the first statements of 'classic' Bauhaus graphics.

Bauhaus Building, Dessau, 1926
Walter Gropius' legendary Bauhaus building at Dessau was opened in 1926. With its angular forms and interpenetrating spaces it was a monument not only to Gropius' personal theory of architectural form but also to the Modern Movement in general. Gropius' architecture provided a fittingly heroic symbol for so influential an institution. After the Second World War Dessau became a part of the German Democratic Republic and the Bauhaus building, after some years of neglect, was restored as a Scientific-Cultural Centre.

Poster Design for 'Europaisches Kunstgewerbe 1927' exhibition by Herbert Bayer
Bayer used the typography both as text and as pattern, making form and content one in this masterpiece of information design.

Similarly, Mies van der Rohe and **Moholy-Nagy** settled in Chicago, one establishing the New Bauhaus (now the Institute of Design), the other becoming a teacher at Illinois Institute of Technology. But recently, with the failure of pseudo-Modern Movement housing policies and the rise in popularity of **Post-Modernism**, the achievements of the Bauhaus have come to be viewed with scepticism. In Milan, the avant-garde group **Studio Alchymia** ironically named two of its bizarre collections of furniture 'Bauhaus'. Journalists tend to use 'Bauhaus' as the label for a style while, in fact, the Bauhaus was an educational institution with a sophisticated pedagogic programme, whose main contribution to design has been its educational theory. As it flourished in the twenties, that pedagogic programme was often expressed in metaphors which drew on cars and aeroplanes, and so the Bauhaus has come to stand for the machine culture in art.

Its head of typography, **Herbert Bayer**, looking back on the Bauhaus, wrote in verse form:
'The Bauhaus existed for a short span of time
but the potentials
inherent in its principles
have only begun to be realized
its sources of design remain forever full
of changing possibilities . . .'

Bibliography Hans Maria Wingler *Bauhaus* MIT, Cambridge, Mass., 1969; Hans Maria Wingler *Kunstschulreform 1900–1933* Gebrüder Mann, Berlin, 1977; Frank Whitford *The Bauhaus* Thames & Hudson, London, 1984; Klaus Herdeg *The Decorated Diagram* MIT, Cambridge, Mass., 1984

Brochure for Verkehrsbüro, Dessau, by Joost Schmidt, 1930
The seat of the Bauhaus, Dessau, was also the home of the Junkers aircraft factory. For the brochure for the city's Transport Office the authorities wanted an image which suggested both Dessau's cultural inheritance and its industrial future. (See also p. 35.)

Poster for the Bauhaus 'Art and Technology' exhibition by Joost Schmidt, 1923
Schmidt's design was one of the first Constructivist statements to come from the Bauhaus, after its early Expressionist period. (See also p. 36.)

'Tea-Machine', 1927
Wolfgang Tumpel's 'Teemaschine' of 1927 is a typical product of the Bauhaus' metal workshops.

A
B
C
D
E
F
G
H
I
J
K
L
M
N
O
P
Q
R
S
T
U
V
W
X
Y
Z

A
B
C
D
E
F
G
H
I
J
K
L
M
N
O
P
Q
R
S
T
U
V
W
X
Y
Z

Herbert Bayer

b. 1900

Herbert Bayer was born at Haag, Austria. His first jobs were as an architectural assistant, but in 1921 he went as a student to the **Bauhaus** in Weimar where he studied painting under the Russian abstract artist Wassily Kandinsky. From 1925 to 1928 he taught typography at the Bauhaus in its new premises at Dessau, but by 1938 was in the United States, where he has done much to propagate Bauhaus principles. From 1946 to 1976 he was a consultant to Walter Paepcke's Container Corporation of America in **Aspen**, Colorado. Since 1966 Bayer has been retained by the Atlantic Richfield Oil Company as a visual consultant.

Bayer's best work was the brilliant, fresh, tightly organized yet irreverent typography on Bauhaus posters. He invented his own typefaces, using in the 'Universal' of 1925 (which he revised in 1927) the standardized geometrical forms characteristic of the Bauhaus ethic.

Bibliography 'Herbert Bayer' exhibition catalogue, Bauhaus-Archiv, Berlin, 1983

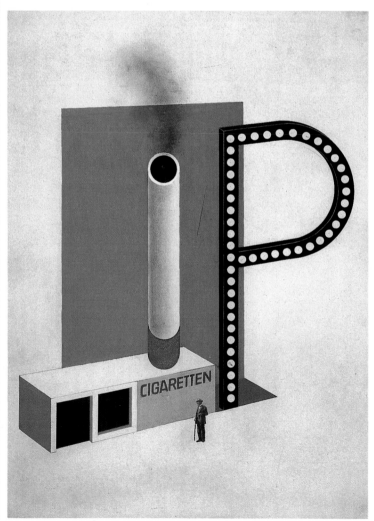

Designs in Collage for Cigarette and Newspaper Kiosks, 1924
Two architectural projects that were never realized. Bayer's cigarette kiosk, in particular, is a witty design in which strong graphics vie for effect and a cigarette motif doubles as a chimney.

BBPR

The letters in this abbreviation stand for Gianluigi Banfi (1910–45), Lodovico Barbiano di Belgiojoso (b. 1909), Enrico Peressutti (1908–76) and **Ernesto Rogers** (1909–69). Banfi died in a Nazi concentration camp.

All four graduated in 1932 and joined **CIAM** in 1935. Belgiojoso wrote poetry and Rogers wrote books about architecture, including *Esperienze dell'architettura* (1958) and *L'Utopia della realtà* (1965). The architectural work of BBPR is the quintessence in building form of the Milanese design culture, especially the Torre Velasca (1958), a building in the centre of Milan which, while uncompromisingly modern in technique, purpose and appearance, has some traditional and historically minded elements.

Peter Behrens

1869–1940

The German architect Peter Behrens was the most outstanding industrial designer of the early twentieth century. He pioneered what is now called **corporate identity**.

Born in Hamburg, he trained at the Karlsruhe and Düsseldorf Art Schools before joining the Munich Secession in 1893. There he mixed with the artistic radicals of his day.

He moved from Munich to Darmstadt at the request of Prince Albert's grandson, Grand Duke Ernst Ludwig, who was building an artists' colony in Hesse's state capital. In Darmstadt Behrens built his own house in which he designed every component, from the structure down to the cutlery. From 1906 he was in charge of graphics and then factory building, workers' housing and industrial design for Emil Rathenau's huge **AEG**. As artistic adviser his brief was to transform the entire image

of the sprawling company. It was like an industrial version of Richard Wagner's *Gesamtkunstwerk*: as one of the first architect-designers to be given such scope by a large industrial concern, Behrens designed buildings, appliances and graphics, establishing a unified identity for the company, in a macrocosm of what he had done in Darmstadt. In 1907 he helped found the **Deutsche Werkbund**. His achievement in the design of every aspect of AEG was the most complete example of what it set out to achieve. Behrens' pupils included **Walter Gropius**, **Mies van der Rohe** and, very briefly, **Le Corbusier**. He was director of architecture at the Vienna Academy in 1932 and director of the department of architecture at the Prussian Academy in Berlin from 1936 until his death. Behrens summarized his views about design in *Kunst und Technik* (1910): 'We have become used to some modern forms of construction, but I do not believe that mathematical solutions will be visually satisfying. Otherwise it would mean a purely intellectual type of art, which is a contradiction in terms.'

Behrens was also a passionate contributor to the Werkbund journal, *Die Form*, where he

Turbine Hall, Berlin, 1909
For AEG Peter Behrens designed a vast shed for assembling industrial turbines, adapting classical architecture to a modern purpose.

wrote in 1922, 'We have no choice but to make our lives more simple, more practical, more organized and wide ranging. Only through industry have we any hope of fulfilling our aims.' Yet the intuitive side of design remained strong with him: commenting on something Rathenau had once said Behrens wrote, 'Don't think that even an engineer, when he buys a motor, takes it to bits in order to scrutinize it. Even he . . . buys from the external appearance. A motor ought to look like a birthday present.' (See also pp. 17 and 81.)
Bibliography Tilmann Buddensieg & Henning Rogge *Industriekultur: Peter Behrens and the AEG 1907–1914* MIT, Cambridge, Mass., 1984; Fritz Hoeber *Peter Behrens* Georg Muller & Eugen Rentsch, Munich, 1913; Alan Windsor *Peter Behrens – architect and designer* Architectural Press, London, 1981; Watson-Guptill, New York, 1982; 'Peter Behrens und Nürnberg' exhibition catalogue, Germanisches National-museum, Nuremberg, 1980

Norman Bel Geddes
1893–1958

Norman Bel Geddes once said that theatre was his 'fickle mistress', and throughout his riotous life dramatic effect dominated his work.

As a theatre set designer, painter, illustrator, self-publicist, author, architect and sometime industrial designer, Norman Bel Geddes was always interested in the total effect. Among his projects were scales for the Toledo Scale Factory, an automobile for Graham Page, and radio cabinets for RCA, but his importance lies not in his completed projects (of which there were very, very few), but in his profoundly felt conviction that design was one of the great driving forces of the age. He became an influential prophet, predicting in his books *Horizons* (1934) and *Magic Motorways* (1940) everything from the freeway system to air conditioning. In the **General Motors** Futurama at the New York World's Fair of 1939 he put flesh on the bones of some of these visionary ideas.

Bel Geddes had met the German Expressionist architect Erich Mendelssohn in 1924, but although he was no doubt an inspiration, Bel Geddes' vision was very much his own. He employed the techniques of an impresario and was the first of the pioneer consultant designers to come to public

notice when a profile of him appeared in *Fortune* magazine in 1930, even though he did not actually have a single finished project or implemented design to show to the journalist who interviewed him. The apocalyptic *Horizons* maintained the pace. In it Bel Geddes wrote, 'The few artists who have devoted themselves to industrial design have done so with condescension, regarding it as a surrender to Mammon. . . . On the other hand, I was drawn to industry by the great opportunities it offered *creatively*.'

After the Second World War Bel Geddes continued to run an office and was briefly retained by **IBM**, but he had become disenchanted by not having enough ideas realized and died in 1958. (See also pp. 43 and 46.)
Bibliography Norman Bel Geddes (edited by William Kelley) *Miracle in the Evening* Doubleday, New York, 1960; Jeffrey L. Meikle *Twentieth Century Limited* Temple University Press, Philadelphia, 1979

Model for Streamlined Bus, 1939
A streamlined bus was designed by Bel Geddes for 'Futurama' at the 1939 New York World's Fair, but was never manufactured. Streamlining offered him an exciting repertoire of forms and motifs.

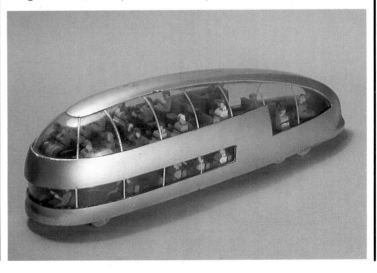

A
B
C
D
E
F
G
H
I
J
K
L
M
N
O
P
Q
R
S
T
U
V
W
X
Y
Z

Mario Bellini

b. 1935

Mario Bellini was born in Milan and studied architecture there, graduating in 1959. He has collaborated continuously with **Olivetti** since 1963, working on their entire product range, but has also worked for **Cassina**, **BrionVega**, Yamaha, Ideal Standard, Marcatre, **Artemide**, **Flos**, FIAT, Lancia and Renault. Bellini's chief work for Olivetti has been the 'Programma' microcomputer (1965), the 'Logos' and 'Divisumma' calculators (1973, p. 56), the 'Lexikon 83' typewriter (1976), the TES 401 text editing system and the ET101 series of electronic typewriters.

Bellini is a highly professional consultant industrial designer. He eschews philosophy, but that is not to say his designs do not have a metaphorical quality which raises them far above the day-to-day into the realms of art. Everything he designs has a strong sculptural presence and a hint of zoomorphic character: for the revolutionary ET101 electronic typewriter, Bellini claims to have derived his inspiration from a photograph of a shark torn from *National Geographic* magazine. He was among the first designers to realize (and then put into practice) the idea that when all machines are driven by essentially the same electronic circuitry, the old notion of 'form follows function' can have no real meaning. Since the integration of solid-state circuitry into office equipment, the typewriter's appearance has been determined solely by a mixture of tradition, aesthetics and **ergonomics**. Bellini has extended an understanding of this further than anyone, so much so that his ET101 has become as much a stereotype for the electronic typewriter as was **Henry Dreyfuss'** Bell telephone for the telephone forty or fifty years ago, and is as widely imitated. With **Giorgio Giugiaro** Bellini is the most practical of contemporary Italian designers, but puts a limit on the value of practicality alone: 'Ergonomics is nothing but a starting point: man is much more complex than an animal or a gadget that can be measured with a rule. He can be read and decoded through many other standards, such as culture, psychology, human relationships. Our needs cannot be reduced to the functional ones. Acting from this starting point I try to give things a value, a content beyond simple appearance . . .'

Bellini does not sketch the designs himself, but has his model-maker, **Giovanni Sacchi**, contrive them in wood and 'only after I touch it, feel it, look at it, can I really tell what I have . . . then I have an artist render it on paper'. (See also pp. 54, 56 and 161.)

J.H. Belter

1804–63

Johan Heinrich Belter was born in Hanover, Germany, and emigrated to New York in 1833 after training as a cabinet-maker. He started up a cabinet-making business in Manhattan in 1844. Belter came from the same artisan tradition as his contemporary **Michael Thonet**, but his translation to the United States changed the course of his career mightily. He was perhaps as ingenious as Thonet, but the demands of American taste forced him into some strange creative manoeuvres. In 1847 he took out a patent for 'Machinery for Sawing Arabesque Chairs', and another in 1858 for the 'Improvement in the Method of Manufacturing Furniture'. This second patent was primarily concerned with the technique of manufacturing laminated furniture, whose industrial application Belter pioneered at the same time as Thonet.

Belter normally used seven laminations of wood, but disguised his technique with grotesque and exaggerated carvings, sometimes politely known as the Rococo Revival, but more nearly comparable to the furnishings familiar in New Orleans bordellos. Belter's furniture and his 'parlor sets' became so popular that 'Belter' became a generic term for a style of elaborately carved and upholstered furniture. When he died he left an estate of $83,218, and countless imitators (although his business fell into the hands of his brother-in-law, J.H. Springmeyer, and went bankrupt in 1867).

___

Model of 'Praxis' Electronic Typewriter for Olivetti, early 1980s
The solid state electronic typewriter series was designed by Mario Bellini and inspired by the angled lecterns used by Roman scribes.

Benetton

The Benetton company was founded just outside Venice in 1965, and began a programme of international expansion in 1978 which was so successful that in a few years it became the world's largest producer of knitwear. It is run by Giuliana Benetton (b. 1938) and her three brothers, who handle marketing, manufacturing and administration.

Giuliana Benetton's simple concept was that young people will inevitably be attracted to bright colours and interesting pastel shades. She has said, 'You never discover a new design, you simply make small changes in the old ones.' There is another fundamental principle which has helped Benetton grow to a chain of 2,500 shops worldwide, with a turnover of $400 million, and that is the store design with dramatic colour-blocking and all the merchandise placed on accessible shelves. The standardization of the shops and their goods on an international basis make it the 'Fast-Food' chain of clothing. Moreover, the Benettons have applied high technology to fashion. The company installed its first computer in 1969 and has been automating all its processes since 1978. Computer models cut bolts of cloth with the least possible amount of waste, while advanced terminals capture check-out details from their stores. At their Castrette warehouse in northern Italy, FIAT-Comau robots administer the company's stock. Benetton also owns 50 per cent of **Fiorucci**.

Walter Benjamin

1892–1940

Walter Benjamin was a member of the Marxist Frankfurt School of sociologists. His contribution to design is one highly intelligent and influential essay, 'The Work of Art in an Age of

Mechanical Reproduction', one of the first attempts to reconcile traditional aesthetics with the industrial world.
Bibliography Walter Benjamin *Das Kunstwerk im Zeitalten seinen technischen Reproduzierbarkeit* Suhrkamp Verlag, Frankfurt, 1968

Ward Bennett

b. 1917

Ward Bennett, an American sculptor and designer, studied in New York with Hans Hoffmann and in Paris with the Romanian avant-garde primitive Constantin Brancusi, who taught him that 'the important thing is not to be clever'. In 1938 he became an apprentice of **Le Corbusier**. These two great men profoundly influenced him.

After the War he began to concentrate on interior design, and his notable works include a concrete beach house at Southampton, Long Island, a vacation house in Easthampton made entirely of telegraph poles, and his own eyrie perched on top of New York's Dakota apartment building. Bennett, who has frequently used industrial waste like an inspired scavenger as the basis of new products, once remarked: 'You can be sure Toscanini and Einstein had great houses. You have to *be* something first. The insecurity of being nobody – that's what starts people buying pseudo-Baroque and pseudo-Spanish. . .'. But Bennett has also been an eclectic and as such has been an influence on the contemporary interest in mixing materials and styles. In the early eighties Bennett became celebrated as the high priest of **High-Tech**.

Berliner Metallgewerbe

Berliner Metallgewerbe was a furniture manufacturer whose proprietor, Joseph Muller, put **Mies van der Rohe**'s first chair design – the 'MR' – into production in 1928.

Harry Bertoia

1915–78

Harry Bertoia was born near Venice and emigrated to the United States in 1930, inspired, he said, by the American Dream. From Cass Technical College in Detroit he entered the new **Cranbrook Academy** where he was a contemporary of **Charles Eames**. In 1942 he joined Eames in Santa Monica, California, where he helped develop his moulded **plywood** furniture which was exhibited at the **Museum of Modern Art** in 1946. In 1950 he went to the East Coast to work on his own furniture designs for **Hans Knoll**. Just as Eames used plywood, an industrial material, in his designs, so Bertoia's most famous chair used steel rod, worked into a grid. His education at Cranbrook left him very aware of sculptural concerns and he said of his chair, 'Like the body in Duchamp's "Nude Descending a Staircase", I wanted my chair to rotate, change with movement.' Later he devoted himself entirely to sculpture in

Steel Wire Chair, 1952
Harry Bertoia produced this welded steel wire chair for Knoll in 1952, after working with Charles Eames in California. A masterpiece of the contemporary style, it has remained in continuous production ever since.

a lonely rural community just outside the Knoll plant at East Greenville.
Bibliography Clement Meadmore *The Modern Chair – Classics in Production* Studio Vista, London, 1974; Van Nostrand Reinhold, New York, 1974

Alfa Romeo, Giulietta Sprint, 1954
This is a typical example of Bertone's style. The car body suggests elegance under tension, and the details are subordinated to an overall effect of seductive beauty.

Nuccio Bertone

b. 1914

Giuseppe 'Nuccio' Bertone was born in Turin, where his father had established a body shop. He joined the firm in 1934 and eventually became its manager, changing it from an artisan tin-bashing business to a studio full of inspired designers, making cars, some fantastic, some real, that were the envy of the world. After **Pininfarina**, Bertone is perhaps the most celebrated Torinese consultant car designer. Apprentices have included **Giovanni Michelotti** and **Giorgio Giugiaro**. Bertone's great designs, characterized by their quirky angularity, include: **Alfa Romeo** Giulietta Sprint (1954), **Lamborghini** Miura (1966), Ferrari Dino 308 (1973), British Leyland Innocenti Mini (1974).

Bertone's designs have a self-consciously avant-garde character. This has always attracted eager apprentices to work at the Bertone Style Centre, established in new premises at Caprie, just outside Turin. Since 1950 Bertone has produced almost sixty influential prototypes and forty production cars, including the Lamborghini Bravo of 1974 and the **Citroën** BX of 1982.
Bibliography Angelo Titi Anselmi *La Carrozzeria italiana – cultura e progetto* Alfieri, Turin, 1978

A B C D E F G H I J K L M N O P Q R S T U V W X Y Z

Flaminio Bertoni

b. 1903

Flaminio Bertoni is the least known genius of automobile design. It was he who was responsible for the appearance of the **Citroën** Traction Avant, the 2CV and the DS. The difference between the 2CV and the DS, one highly functional, the other highly stylized, shows Bertoni's ability to conceptualize the nature of an automobile in a highly abstract way, rather than simply to follow trends in **styling**. Until the sixties, when he was joined by Robert Opron (now head of design at Renault), Bertoni worked alone and had a reputation for working very rapidly, without corrections. His concepts for the Citroëns were said to have taken him only a matter of hours to finalize.

Biedermeier

Biedermeier is a term used to describe petty-bourgeois German and Austrian furniture and interior design style in the period of late neo-classicism. It is a Teutonic equivalent of the Regency. The word derives from *bieder*, which means inoffensive, and Meier, a common German surname.

Max Bill

b. 1908

Max Bill is a Swiss architect who has worked as a painter, designer and increasingly as a sculptor. His work is often identified with the austere minimalism of the Swiss Style, although his first influences came from the **Bauhaus**, where he was a student. From 1949 he promoted the *Gute Form* competitions for the Swiss Werkbund and from 1951 to 1956 he was director of the **Hochschule für Gestaltung** in Ulm, whose buildings he also designed. Bill's product designs

include a wall clock for Junghans (1957) and some electrical fittings (1958). His contribution to modern design has been less through his own creativity than through his continuing international presence as a supporter of Bauhaus principles.
Bibliography 'Max Bill: Oeuvre 1928–1979' exhibition catalogue, Paris-Grenoble, 1969–70

Misha Black

1910–77

Misha Black founded the Design Research Unit (**DRU**) with **Milner Gray** in 1944. It was Britain's first design consultancy. Black was born in Russia and died in London, a 'radical beneath his subfusc suitings', according to **Paul Reilly**. His main area of interest was in exhibition design, often for the Ministry of Information. He was active in both the 'Britain Can Make It' (1946) and Festival of Britain (1951) exhibitions, but his chief contribution was as professor of Industrial Design at the **Royal College of Art**, where his commitment to the practicalities of industrial design did much to break down the barriers between design and engineering in education.
Bibliography John and Avril Blake *The Practical Idealists* Lund Humphries, London, 1969

BMW

The company that became BMW (Bayerische Motoren Werke – Bavarian Motor Works) was founded in Munich in 1916 as the Bayerische Flugzeug Werke, manufacturing aero engines. Consumer products began in 1923 with motor bicycles and five years later it manufactured its first car when it took over the Fahrzeugfabrik of Eisenach, which was producing the Austin 7 under licence (known as the Dixi). The BMW 328 of 1937 was the most celebrated sports car of the pre-War era, but in the fifties the economic conditions within a Germany that was rebuilding itself called for *Kleinwagen*, and BMW, together with less respected names, produced a series of bubble cars. Since then, under Eberhard von Kuenheim, BMW has rebuilt itself completely. Using conservative but refined engineering, and conservative but aggressive design (which made up in presence what it lacked in flair) BMW established a firm market position. Forceful, even aggressive, marketing enhanced the excellence of the actual products by making a BMW car seem to be more than just an agreeable and efficient machine, but the very token of crisp, youthful, worldly success. The design of the cars, under Claus Luthe and latterly under the

Englishman Martin Smith, enforced this; BMW is a company conscious of its own traditions and, like **Anatole Lapine** at **Porsche**, the BMW designers are keen to maintain a family resemblance between successive models. A crease at the beltline, a questing snout, a kidney-shaped air-intake, but most of all the satisfying appearance of looking as if they have been machined from a solid billet of steel, characterize the appearance of all recent BMW cars. In the whole motor industry, BMW is one of the best instances of visual appeal contributing to commercial success.

Detail of BMW, K 100 RS Motorbike, 1984
(See also p. 134.)
Advertisement by Wight, Collins Rutherford Scott, 1984
BMW's success has been helped by slick and aggressive advertising. The British campaign of the eighties has stressed subtle but perhaps insidious sentiments.

THE TRUE TEST OF A FAST CAR
IS HOW WELL IT PERFORMS SLOWLY.

THE ULTIMATE DRIVING MACHINE

Cini Boeri

b. 1924

Cini Boeri graduated in architecture from Milan Polytechnic in 1951. Her first job was as an apprentice to **Marco Zanuso**, in whose studio she worked until 1963. She has designed furniture for Arflex and **Knoll**, and lighting for Stilnovo and **Arteluce**. Her 'Strips' seating system won a **Compasso d'Oro** award in 1979.

'Malibu' Table, 1960s or 70s
Boeri's 'Malibu' table is a mild-mannered classic of modern Italian taste.

Rodolfo Bonetto

b. 1929

Rodolfo Bonetto's first job was in **Pininfarina's** car-design studio in Turin. He founded his own firm in 1958 and includes **BrionVega**, Driade, Borletti, **Olivetti** and FIAT among his clients. His 'Sfericlock' won a **Compasso d'Oro** award in 1964, while he was teaching at the **Hochschule für Gestaltung** in Ulm. With Veglia-Borletti, Bonetto has specialized in the design of instruments for cars, and this developed in 1977 into his completely redesigning the interior of the FIAT 131 Super Mirafiori, where he used single-piece plastic mouldings in a more sophisticated and satisfying way than ever before (or since).
Bibliography Anty Pansera & Alfonso Grassi *Atlante del design italiano* Fabbri, Milan, 1980

Borax

Borax is a contemptuous name given to a popular design style that appeared on certain American consumer products in the years either side of the Second World War. It is characterized by a markedly unfunctional, expressive aesthetic which derived from a watered-down **Art Deco** and **streamlining**. It was most frequently used on cheap furniture, and other domestic objects.
Bibliography Edgar Kaufmann 'Borax, or the chromium-plated calf' *Architectural Review* London, August 1948, pp. 88–93

Michel Boué

1936–71

Michel Boué is identified with one phenomenally successful car design. His Renault 5 appeared in 1972 and became the best-selling French car ever, and the only successful one, ever, with only two doors. There was little radical about the mechanics: the 5 was based on the ancient, agricultural Renault 4, but Boué gave it a superbly packaged and elegant body. Just as the BMC Mini car created a type, so Boué's 5 advanced it, creating a market segment for the 'Supermini' in which every manufacturer had to compete.

The 5 story is one of inspired management as much as of inspired design (where the two are not the same thing). Boué received a brief in 1967 to design a hatch-back car which would create new volume for Renault by appealing to market segments which disdained the Régie's products, namely young people and women. It took Boué just two days to sketch the 5 and it was accepted immediately: Renault's engineering chief, Yves Georges, has said: 'It was amazing. Normally the management of any major car company ask for changes and then for more changes, with styling advice coming from all sorts of different people. Most times this ends up damaging the look of a car. But that did not happen with the R5. It is a pure design. And that is why it looks good and has never needed a facelift. Leonardo da Vinci or Picasso would not have wanted people playing around with their work. A car designer . . . is no different.'

By 1984 Renault had sold 4.5 million R5s, but Boué did not live to see its introduction. He died at thirty-five of cancer of the spine in 1971.

First model of the Renault 5, 1972
Boué's design hardly changed from concept sketches through to production car.

Michel Boué with Prototype Renault 5, 1972
The Renault 5 was a French interpretation of the concept proposed by Issigonis in his BMC Mini: a sophisticated small car with technology and body engineering which took advantage of its size instead of being inhibited by it. Michel Boué provided an inspired interpretation of the idea. His body design for the new Renault small car was so right in performance, proportion and effect that no changes in sheet metal were made from its introduction in 1972 to its demise in 1984.

Designer's Rendering of the First Production Renault 5, 1972

Renault 5, 1984
When in 1984 Renault wanted to replace the '5' they continued to draw on Michel Boué's original design. Although all the sheet metal was different, the new 5 deliberately evoked the appearance of the old car.

A B C D E F G H I J K L M N O P Q R S T U V W X Y Z

Pierre Boulanger

1886–1950

A French automotive engineer, Pierre Boulanger worked for Michelin until the tyre company assumed responsibility for the debt-ridden car manufacturer **Citroën** in 1935, when he embarked on a programme which led to the creation of the highly influential 2CV, the Traction Avant, and ultimately the DS.

Marianne Brandt

b. 1893

Born in Germany, Marianne Brandt, with **Wilhelm Wagenfeld**, was the most famous product of the **Bauhaus'** metalwork studio, run by **Moholy-Nagy**. Although she was in no sense an industrial designer (because all her work was craft prototypes), Brandt's designs for domestic metalware laid the basis for a design aesthetic based on uncompromising geometric purity. A Brandt teapot reflects the inheritance of the Bauhaus in its ostentatious use of pure forms.
Bibliography Hans Maria Wingler *The Bauhaus* MIT, Cambridge, Mass., 1969

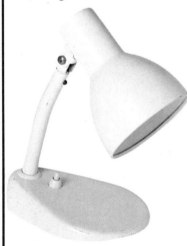

Kandem Night Light, 1928
The night light was designed by Marianne Brandt and Hin Bredensieck while they were students in Moholy-Nagy's classes at the Bauhaus.

Andrea Branzi

b. 1938

A Florentine architect, Andrea Branzi was a member of **Archizoom** in the sixties and went to Milan after the decline of interest in radical design. He worked with **Studio Alchymia** in 1979 and has contributed furniture designs to **Memphis**.
Bibliography Andrea Branzi *The Hot House* MIT, Cambridge, Mass., 1984

Braun

Braun was a small, family-run radio company based in Frankfurt when Artur Braun (b. 1925) took it over in 1951. In the rebuilding programme after the War the company had begun to diversify into household appliances and, with an interest in design shared with his brother Erwin, this presented Artur Braun with a wonderful opportunity to give form to Germany's 'economic miracle'. He hired **Fritz Eichler**, **Hans Gugelot** and **Otl Aicher**, who all came from the **Hochschule für Gestaltung** in Ulm, and later **Dieter Rams**, to achieve this.

Working on Braun's hi-fi, razors and kitchen machines these designers quickly developed an image of visual sophistication, based on attention to detail and geometrical simplicity — a formal and stylized image which created a sensation when it was shown to the public at the 1955 Radio Show in Düsseldorf. While the **Bauhaus** masters had spoken of integrating art with industry and achieving rational, modern products, the fact was that virtually all Bauhaus production was crafts-based. Here, though, was a Frankfurt electrical company achieving the goal of rational, undecorated design. Braun became a synonym for '*Gute Form*' in Germany and for 'good design' in Britain.

However, Braun's excellence in **design management** did not lead to commercial success. Braun engineers spoke of the 'Rams surcharge', or the extra cost of design in the controlled, mystical austerity of mature Braun products. As a result Braun was taken over by the American Gillette concern in 1967 and since then there has been a progressive dilution of the company's standards and identity, although the influence of the Braun style continues to be profound and far-reaching, especially in Japan. Richard Moss, an American journalist, best summed up Braun's achievement. In an article in *Industrial Design* (November 1962) he wrote: 'All Braun products, from desk fan to kitchen mixer, belong unmistakably to the same family. . . . Three general rules seem to govern every Braun design – a rule of order, a rule of harmony, and a rule of economy.' (See also pp. 62–3 and **German design**.)
Bibliography Wolfgang Schmittel *Design: Concept, Form, Realisation* ABC, Zürich, 1977; Inez Franksen et al. 'Design: Dieter Rams &' exhibition catalogue, IDZ-Berlin, 1982

Braun 'dl' Electric Toothbrush by Reinhold Weiss and Robert Oberheim, 1978
Weiss and Oberheim are Dieter Rams' assistants.

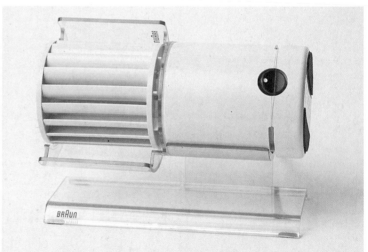

'HLI' Desk Fan by Reinhold Weiss, 1961
German designers' taste for clarity is somewhat paradoxical. The Fan's mechanism is hidden, but its form elegantly expresses the way it functions.

Carl Breer

Carl Breer was chief engineer at Chrysler when **Walter Percy Chrysler** decided to try to take the company from tenth largest US car manufacturer further up the Fortune 500. Chrysler had in mind a radical new car called the Airflow, innovative in many ways but most of all in its **styling**. Early models had marbled vinyl floor-covering, moulded roof panels, tubular steel seats and tripartite bumpers blended into a streamlined shape that was a decade ahead of its time. The American public hated it. Production ceased in 1937, just three years after it had begun. But the influence of Breer's Airflow was immense, and it donated forms to both **Ford** and **General Motors** and ideas to Ferdinand **Porsche**. (See also **aerodynamics**.)
Bibliography Howard S. Irvin 'The History of the Airflow Car' *Scientific American* August 1977, pp. 98–106

Chrysler Airflow, 1935
The Airflow was the result of Breer's experiments in streamlining. A heroic attempt to bring advanced design to the American public, it was too far in advance of popular taste to be successful and production ceased in 1937.

Marcel Breuer

1902–81

Marcel Breuer was born in Pecs, Hungary, and trained at the Vienna Academy of Art. Like many architects and designers from the undeveloped east of Europe, Breuer was attracted by the new German art school, the **Bauhaus**, and became **Walter Gropius'** star pupil at Dessau.
    Breuer's most celebrated designs, **cantilever** tubular steel chairs of 1925–28, emerged from studies made for furniture intended for the Bauhaus' experimental house, a staff and student project. The story is that Breuer got the idea of using tubular steel from the handlebars of his bicycle (although it is more likely that the Junkers aircraft factory, adjacent to the Bauhaus, was more of an influence).
    After the Bauhaus was closed by the Nazis Breuer came to England, where he worked for **Jack Pritchard's Isokon**

company, designing an elegant bent **plywood** chair, based on an earlier Bauhaus project, which went into production in 1936. Breuer briefly worked with the **Maxwell Fry** architectural practice and the pair built some celebrated houses in the **International Style**, but just as the Bauhaus had drawn him from the east, the allure of the United States drew Breuer from Britain. In 1937 Gropius invited him to join the teaching staff at Harvard University School of Architecture, where his pupils became the leading American architects and designers of the next generation: I.M. Pei, Paul Rudolph, **Philip Johnson** and **Eliot Noyes**. Once in the USA it was architecture rather than furniture design that occupied Breuer, but the latest version of his steel Bauhaus chair, known as the 'Cesca' after his daughter Francesca, became a classic produced by **Knoll** (see p. 171). In retrospect, Breuer's contribution to design was to invent aesthetic solutions to the problems of new materials. (See also pp. 37–8 and 48 and **Dino Gavina**.)
Bibliography Marcel Breuer *Marcel Breuer 1921–1962* Gerd Hatje, Stuttgart, 1962; 'Marcel Breuer' exhibition catalogue, Museum of Modern Art, New York, 1981

B5 Chair, 1926
Marcel Breuer experimented continuously with tubular steel as a medium for chair design. The B5 was manufactured first by Standard Möbel of Berlin and then by Thonet.

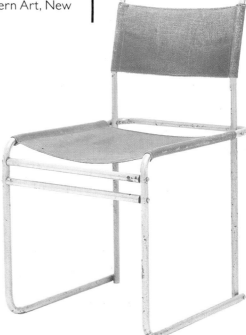

BrionVega

A manufacturer of hi-fi, radios and televisions, BrionVega was established in Milan by the Brion family in the mid-1940s. By commissioning some of Italy's outstanding designers to create his products, Ennio Brion has championed the highest standards in product design. BrionVega's most celebrated products have been a record-player in a **Pop** style by **Achille Castiglioni** in 1966, and the 'Doney 14' television of 1962, the 'Black-12' television of 1969 and a hinged radio of 1965 (p. 60), all by **Richard Sapper** and **Marco Zanuso**. BrionVega's house style is to produce technical purism with a high finish, and much of the effect of the company's products is created by the quality of their plastic shells.

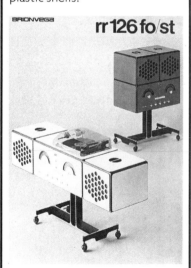

'126' Record Player, 1966
Achille Castiglioni's ingenious design uses the speakers, which can be variously disposed on the top or the sides, as sculptural elements – a facility amply exploited by the stylists of photographs for Italian fashion magazines during the sixties. Before the annihilation of the European hi-fi industry by Japan, the BrionVega '126' was one of the last attempts to find a novel, evolutionary form for a familiar domestic appliance.

British design

Internationally, British design is most often associated with **William Morris** and the **Arts and Crafts** movement. The dual emphases on 'right making' and 'fitness for purpose' have remained evident in British mainstream design from the Design and Industries Association in the twenties to the **Council of Industrial Design** in the post-War period. Although these are worthy principles in themselves, the tradition of Morris and the consequential 'Cotswold effect' (which is anti-urban and anti-industrial) has meant that Britain has not kept pace with the rest of the world when it comes to applying design to industry.

Modern Movement ideas had very little real influence in

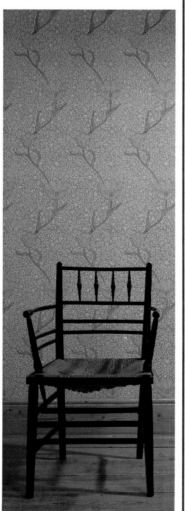

Britain, except in maverick products such as the radios designed for E.K. Cole by **Wells Coates**, and while the Festival of Britain encouraged some experimentation and activity (in the work of **Robin Day** and **Ernest Race**), the best work of the mid-century was really little more than a synthesis of Italian, Scandinavian and American ideas. The dominant mood was reactionary.

The development of mass travel in the fifties was to produce the first breakthrough in changing British taste, and hence design. An important influence in this change was the cookery writer Elizabeth David, whose first book, *Mediterranean Food* (1950), expanded the area of choice to the British consumer nurtured on traditional ideas of food attenuated by the War and

rationing. (Its illustrations, by John Minton, also anticipated fashions in restaurant design that were to erupt in coffee bars, bistros and *trattorie* over the next decade.) A distinguished series of other cookery books followed from Mrs David, and from the availability of *salade niçoise* and *ratatouille* it was only a short step to the wholesale adoption of the Provençal kitchen and French provincial cookware in the repertoire of interior design.

However, it was only with the advent of the **Pop** revolution of the sixties that Britain was able to establish a position of international significance in the world of design. In the liberal atmosphere of the decade Terence Conran and **Mary Quant** became famous and were

'Garden Tulip' Wallpaper, 1885, and Chair by William Morris (far left)

Durabeam Torch by Nick Butler, 1982 (left)
This torch was designed as a promotional tool for the battery manufacturer, but Nick Butler's ingenious solution has made it into an object of virtue in its own right.

'Flotilla' Fabric by Lucienne Day, 1952 (below)

immensely successful in establishing 'design' as a subject of legitimate popular concern. Although Conran and Quant have both gone on to head large retail empires, in recent years British design has, once again, lost direction. A large number of design consultancies sprang up in the sixties, but the majority of their work is with graphics and retail interiors. There is, however, evidence of more energetic activity in the craft area. Sponsored by government funds, the **Crafts Revival** is, perhaps, the inevitable conclusion to a story that began with William Morris detesting industry.

Bibliography Fiona MacCarthy *A History of British Design 1830–1970* Routledge & Kegan Paul, London, 1979; Allen & Unwin, Winchester, Mass., 1979

Corporate Identity for the Royal Bank of Scotland by Lewis Woudhuysen, 1970s

British graphics are perhaps stronger than British product design. Woudhuysen's corporate identity for the Royal Bank of Scotland took a staid institution one step beyond the careful roman script normally favoured by banks.

Telephone by DCA, 1981

David Carter's DCA consultancy specializes in a characteristically British form of pragmatic design engineering. With electronic engineers and ergonomists in his studios, Carter undertakes designs concerned with telecommunications and the working environment.

'Advanced Engineering Bicycle' by Alex Moulton, 1983

Alex Moulton launched his first small-wheeled bicycle in 1962 and revised the concept in 1983. The new version is the ultimate expression of bicycling technology, providing the rider with outstanding comfort and control, together with compactness and portability.

EVERYWHERE YOU GO

THE GREAT GLOBE. SWANAGE.

BY GRAHAM SUTHERLAND

YOU CAN BE SURE OF SHELL

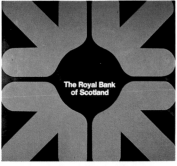

The Royal Bank of Scotland

'Everywhere You Go You Can Be Sure of Shell', Poster by Graham Sutherland, mid-1930s

During the thirties a number of British artists and writers worked for large corporations. Graham Sutherland, who produced a series of posters for Shell, was one example.

Kettle, Russell Hobbs, 1980

The kettle is a British example of 'design without designers'. Understated yet handsome, it is both efficient and durable and has been imitated throughout the world.

A B C D E F G H I J K L M N O P Q R S T U V W X Y Z

C

CAD-CAM
Cantilever
Pierre **Cardin**
David **Carter**
Cassandre
Cassina
Achille **Castiglioni**
CCI
**Central School of Arts
and Crafts (Art and
Design**
Gabrielle **Chanel**
Colin **Chapman**
Pierre **Chareau**
**Chermayeff &
Geismar**
Fede **Cheti**
Chiavari
Walter Percy **Chrysler**
CIAM
Aldo **Cibic**
Citroën
Clarice **Cliff**
Stafford **Cliff**
Wells **Coates**
Luigi **Colani**
Henry **Cole**
Colefax & Fowler
Collier Campbell
Gino **Colombini**
Joe **Colombo**
Compasso d'Oro
Constructivism
Contemporary
**Cooper-Hewitt
Museum**
Hans **Coray**
Corporate identity
**Council of Industrial
Design (CoID)**
Crafts revival
Cranbrook Academy
Walter **Crane**

CAD-CAM

CAD-CAM stands for Computer Aided Design-Computer Aided Manufacture. CAD uses computers so that designs can be generated on a visual display unit (VDU), rather than on paper. As designs can be modified and visualized from any angle, it allows enormous flexibility and speeds the development process, particularly in the design of complex three-dimensional shapes, such as car and aeroplane bodies.

Cantilever

A cantilever is an engineering term used to describe the principle where a projecting bracket supports a load. When applied to tubular steel, the cantilever has produced some of the most radical and influential chair designs of the twentieth century. Tubular metal furniture was known in England in the mid-nineteenth century, when Winfield & Company of Birmingham exhibited tubular brass bedsteads and rocking chairs. But Winfield used the tubular brass under very light loads. With the arrival of high-tensile tubular steel, developed by Mannesmann for use in the aircraft industry, a real breakthrough was possible. In 1925 and 1926 **Marcel Breuer** and **Mies van der Rohe** produced designs for cantilevered tubular steel chairs which proved to be durable in function and in style.
Bibliography Jan van Geest & Otakar Macel *Stühle aus Stahl* Walter König, Cologne, 1980

Pierre Cardin

b. 1922

Pierre Cardin was working as a young man in **Dior**'s couture house when the 'New Look' was produced in 1947. The experience was fundamental to his development: inspired by the range of opportunities which Dior's success suggested was ready to be tapped, he opened his own house in 1953, and became the first couturier fully to exploit the mass-market opportunities of Paris fashion. In 1959 he produced the first line of *prêt-à-porter* clothes for women, quickly moving into licensing operations which covered menswear, bedlinen, lingerie, perfumes and stockings. This also made him one of the first couturiers to turn his signature into an instantly recognizable logotype on all sorts of merchandise. In 1966 the Chambre Syndicale, the watchdog of French couture, forced him to resign because his activities were becoming so diversified that the very concept of couture was being undermined. Since then he has designed aeroplane interiors, theatres and restaurants.

Obsessed with ideas about space, technology and the environment, Cardin can infuriate or bore with his monomania, while his taste rises to the inspired or plunges to the catastrophic.

Button, 1970s
The entrepreneur of French fashion, Cardin used his logo on blazer buttons thereby putting the designer label on the outside of his clothes.

David Carter

b. 1927

David Carter trained at the **Central School of Art and Design** and is one of the few English consultant designers to run a successful practice outside London. DCA Design Consultants specializes in engineering design and **ergonomics**, and its clients include Stanley – for whom he has designed a full range of tools – British Telecom (see p. 99) and the Austin-Rover group.

Tools for Stanley, 1970s
Carter has a great interest in hand tools, as a successful series of products for the Stanley company demonstrates. He is concerned with the principles of man's relationship with machines, even with ones as simple as these planes. Carter is aware that the shape of a tool handle is often determined as much by economical use of the milling machine which cuts the die for the mould as by the actual character of the plastic from which it has been created.

Cassandre

1901–68

Cassandre was the pseudonym of Adolphe Jean-Marie Mouron, a French graphic designer and poster artist. He was born in the Ukraine of a Russian mother and a French father, and moved to Paris in 1915 to study at the Ecole des Beaux Arts and the Académie Julien. Between 1923 and 1936 he designed an astonishingly powerful range of posters for the Compagnie des Wagons-Lits and other clients. He reduced his motifs to silhouettes or to exaggerated pictograms, but always treated his subjects with elegance. Typography and imagery are synthesized in Cassandre's posters, as in **McKnight-Kauffer**'s, to enhance the total effect. He also worked for the Deberny and Peignot type foundry.

'Speed, Luxury, Comfort',
Poster for the Chemin de Fer du Nord, 1930
The wit, elegance and sense of style in Cassandre's posters lent dignity to the Art Deco.

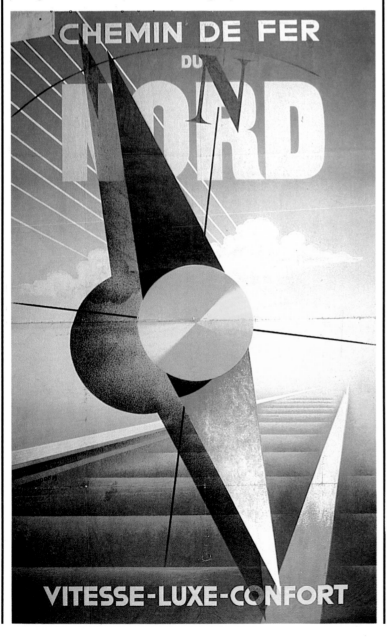

CHEMIN DE FER
DU NORD

VITESSE-LUXE-CONFORT

Cassina

b. 1909

Cesare Cassina was born into a Milanese family that had traditions in the furniture industry going back to the eighteenth century. He trained as an upholsterer and set up his own business with his brother in 1927, on Milan's via Solferino. In 1935 it became Figli di Amedeo Cassina. Whereas before the Second World War Cassina made only customized furniture for particular clients, during Italy's post-War *ricostruzione* the firm pioneered a more progressive approach to design, hiring **Franco Albini**, **Gio Ponti**, **Vico Magistretti**, **Mario Bellini** and many other leading Italian furniture designers to contribute to its catalogue. But in the mid-sixties the firm returned to its origins in reproduction furniture, with the 'Maestri' series of classics by **Le Corbusier**, **Gerrit Rietveld** and **Charles Rennie Mackintosh**. Cassina's reputation is none-theless as one of Italy's most forward-thinking furniture companies. (See also p. 161.)
Bibliography Pier Carlo Santini *Gli anni del design italiano – Ritratto di Cesare Cassina* Editrice Electa, Milan, 1981

'Wink' Chair by Toshiyika Kita, 1980
Toshiyika Kita's 'Wink' chair for Cassina became a familiar component in many chic interiors during the early eighties. Kita is a rare example of an independent Japanese designer working in Europe.

'Sindbad' armchair for Cassina by Vico Magistretti, 1982
For his 'Sindbad' armchair Magistretti was inspired by a traditional horse blanket he saw in a London shop. Slung over a metal frame, it created a remarkable, novel design.

A B C D E F G H I J K L M N O P Q R S T U V W X Y Z

A
B
C
D
E
F
G
H
I
J
K
L
M
N
O
P
Q
R
S
T
U
V
W
X
Y
Z

Achille Castiglioni

b. 1918

Achille Castiglioni is one of three Milanese brothers who have all been designers. Achille's interest in design was first inspired by his elder brothers, Pier Giacomo and Livio, who designed a dramatic plastic-cased radio receiver for Phonola in 1938 with the help of Caccia Dominioni. Achille read architecture at Milan Polytechnic, graduating in 1944, and was one of the founders of the Associazione per il Disegno Industriale in 1956. He designs furniture, lighting and appliances, and his products have won **Compasso d'Oro** awards in 1955, 1960, 1962, 1964, 1967, 1979 and 1984. Six of his pieces are in the permanent collection of New York's **Museum of Modern Art**. Among his best known pieces are a kneeling stool for **Zanotta** and his 'Arco' light for **Flos**. Since the War, Achille Castiglioni has been one of the most prolific of all Italian designers, and he has evolved a unique philosophy which derives from the 'ready-made' concept of Marcel Duchamp, like his chair inspired by a tractor seat. His clients include **BrionVega**, **Flos**, **Gavina**, **Knoll**, **Kartell**, **Zanotta**, B&B, Ideal Standard, Siemens and Lancia, and he contributes to design magazines and the Italian national press. His philosophy of design is that it is an 'attitude arising out of critical habit . . . an art insofar as it invents a function and translates it into a form'. Wit is the central element in his designs; sometimes incongruous materials, such as found objects, are bound together in pursuit of functional elegance. His 'Arco' lamp for Flos uses a marble base weighing about a hundred pounds to support a thin arc of pressed aluminium and a light, spun aluminium reflector; his 'Toio' lamp for the same company uses a car headlamp. (See also p. 111.)
Bibliography Anty Pansera & Alfonso Grassi *Atlante del design italiano* Fabbri, Milan, 1980

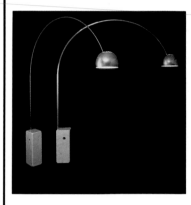

'Arco' Lamp, 1962
Another aspect of Castiglioni's approach to design is his juxtaposition of contrasting materials; his 'Arco' lamp for Flos became a classic of many self-conscious modern interiors. The spun aluminium reflector and the light pressed-aluminium support (which acts as a channel for the cable) arch out from a monumental marble base.

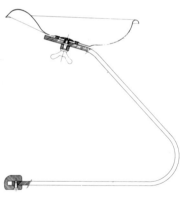

'Mezzadro' Stool for Zanotta, 1957
Achille Castiglioni's studio in Milan includes a surreal collection of objects – toys, junk and ephemera. These are sometimes the inspiration for his witty furniture designs. A stool made from a bicycle seat (p. 247) or one from a tractor seat are typical of his 'ready-made' (almost surreal) attitude to design.

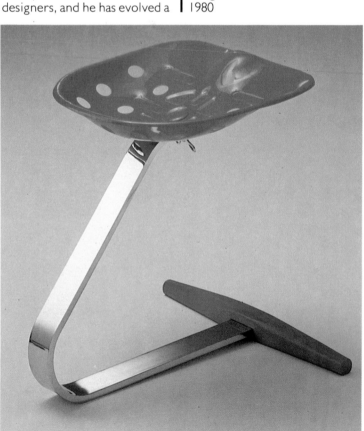

CCI

CCI stands for the Centre de Création Industrielle, the design showplace in Paris' Pompidou Centre, intended to educate the public about its material environment. Its head is François Burckhardt, who once ran the **IDZ-Berlin**.

Central School of Arts and Crafts (Art and Design)

London's Central School of Art and Design was founded as the Central School of Arts and Crafts in 1896 with the brief of displaying design, encouraging manufacturers and, in particular, educating the public about the material environment in general. Its first director was W.R. Lethaby, under whom its first courses were very much crafts-based. In 1946 it established Britain's first course in industrial design. Its distinguished pupils have included **David Carter** and **Tom Karen**. It remains one of Britain's leading industrial design schools.
Bibliography *Central to Design – Central to Industry* Central School of Art and Design, London, 1983

Gabrielle Chanel

1883–1971

'Coco' Chanel's career as a couturier began during the First World War in fashionable Deauville, on the Normandy coast. Her first essay in style was to assemble an outfit composed of a man's sweater pulled over her pleated skirt, tied at the waist by an artfully careless handkerchief. This daring assemblage won her a reputation for chic. The Duke of Westminster helped her start a Paris boutique, and while cruising the Mediterranean in the Duke's yacht Chanel developed a suntan and, practically single-handed,

Suit, House of Chanel, 1977
From the time her salon was reopened in 1954, the classic 'little' Chanel suit has remained virtually unchanged: perfectly cut to allow freedom of movement, lined in silk with a matching blouse, and worn with lots of costume jewellery.

turned *bronzage*, hitherto considered the mark of a peasant labourer, into an international status symbol. Her style was established in the twenties: a neat, tailored suit, matching silk shirt and two-toned shoes that went with anything. Chanel's boutique closed during the Second World War but reopened in 1954, and such was the classic nature of her style that it sold virtually the same lines as it had during the thirties. Her achievement was to introduce simplicity into women's clothes and her designs were adaptable for the ready-to-wear market. Today her house is run by **Karl Lagerfeld**.

Colin Chapman

1928–83

Colin Chapman was a British automotive designer who pioneered the successful use of lightweight structures, **aerodynamics** and other aerospace techniques in the design of racing and road cars.

The Lotus company was set up in Hornsey, North London, in 1952, and was originally run from Chapman's garage. Chapman produced a series of highly competitive sports and racing cars throughout the fifties, then, with the 'Elite' in 1959, Lotus made a passenger car available to the public. The Elite was a sensation, and with its lightweight, aerodynamic shape and highly efficient, small-volume engine predicted by twenty years the general concerns of the automotive industry.

But it was with racing cars that Colin Chapman applied his aeronautical experience most thoroughly. The Formula 1 Lotus 25 of 1962 was the first car to use an aircraft-style stressed monocoque, and its successor, the 33, became one of the most successful racing cars of all time. Throughout the sixties and seventies Chapman pursued the technical limits of racing car design, using wedge shapes, 'ground effect' and advanced materials. He was so successful that only Ferrari has won more Grands Prix.

Chapman's road cars were admired for their elegance of conception but were often let down by reliability and finish. Nevertheless, the Mark 26 or 'Elan' of 1963 and the 'Europa' of 1966, both using fibreglass bodies elegantly designed by Chapman's associate John Frayling, created new standards in the performance of light cars. After the sixties Lotus' performances were mixed. Chapman ran the company in a headstrong way and frequently over-extended himself and his associates. There were a number of radical innovations

in racing car design, but the production cars were affected by the oil crisis. Chapman had **Giorgio Giugiaro** design the body for the Lotus 'Esprit' of 1976, but an association with John De Lorean brought the hitherto unimpeachable company into some disrepute, and Chapman's premature death from a heart attack was blamed on tensions arising out of the De Lorean scandal.

Lotus Climax 33, 1965

Pierre Chareau

1883–1950

Born in Bordeaux, Pierre Chareau dallied between painting, music, furniture design and architecture. In 1930 he was one of the founders of the Union des Artistes Modernes. He emigrated in 1939 to the United States. Chareau made some exceptional and eccentric designs for furniture in wood and metal, some of them for the Compagnie Parisienne d'ameublement, which can loosely be described as **Art Deco**. These were always exclusive rather than popular. Chareau also designed remarkable houses for the Parisian Doctor Dalsace and the American painter Robert Motherwell.
Bibliography René Herbst *Pierre Chareau* Editions du Salon des Arts Ménagers, Paris, 1954

Chermayeff & Geismar

Ivan Chermayeff (b. 1932), the son of the Russian émigré architect of the **International Style** Serge Chermayeff (b. 1900), and Thomas Geismar (b. 1931) opened a graphic design office with Robert Brownjohn in 1957. They were given the job of designing a **corporate identity** for the Chase Manhattan Bank, and then **Eliot Noyes** commissioned them in 1964 to do the graphics for Mobil. Their solution to this task was very simple: the 'o' in the name was made red, both to symbolize the wheel and to give the logotype a special character which reflected the circular, mushroom-like motifs which Noyes used throughout the filling stations. They were fiercely proud of their elegant, unpretentious simplicity, and Tom Geismar once said, 'We get clients who don't want to pay a lot to find answers to easy questions.'

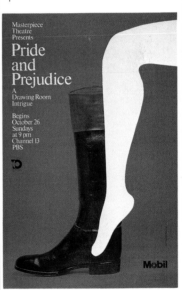

'Pride and Prejudice' Poster, 1981
Besides major corporate identity schemes for clients such as the Chase Manhattan Bank and Mobil, Chermayeff & Geismar have also designed theatre posters in the same hard-edge, colour-field style.

Fede Cheti

1905–78

Fede Cheti established her own textile firm in 1930 and caught the attention of **Gio Ponti** with her exhibits at the Monza Biennale of 1930 and the Milan **Triennale** of 1933. She printed chintz, silk and velvet with strong, though subtle, motifs derived from nature which expressed the **Surrealist** mood then fashionable in Italy. Her upholstery fabrics, sold from her Milanese showroom, were particularly popular in the fifties.

'Moon & Stars' Textile, 1952
Cheti's printed textiles, which echo Surrealist paintings, were popular as furnishing fabrics during the fifties.

Chiavari

Chiavari is, with Brianza, one of the homes of traditional furniture manufacture in Italy. A fishing village near Genoa, its ship-building traditions were passed on into furniture workshops. The modern industry of Chiavari was founded in the early nineteenth century by Gaetano Descalzi, known as 'il Camponino'. He started production by imitating a chair brought from Paris, refining the traditional design and perfecting a new technique of weaving the seat, as well as rounding off wooden details. His objective was to make these chairs, known as 'Camponino' chairs, lighter and lighter. **Gio**

Ponti adopted this element of the traditional Chiavari chair in his 'Superleggera' design of the fifties which **Cassina** manufactured.
Bibliography G. Brignardello *G.G. Descalzi* 1870

A view of Chiavari

Walter Percy Chrysler

1875–1938

Born in Kansas, Walter Percy Chrysler's first job was as a sweeper in the Union Pacific Railroad. When promoted to machinist's apprentice he forged his own tools out of scraps of metal. From there he worked his way through the American railway industry and became superintendent of motive power at the Chicago Great Western Railroad in 1908. In the same year he bought his first car, a Locomobile. His work as a railroad engineer attracted the attention of the founders of **General Motors** and in 1912 Chrysler was made manager of the Buick plant. By 1916 he had become first vice-president of General Motors in charge of operations. He resigned in 1919 and, after flirting in management jobs with some other manufacturers, formed the Chrysler Corporation in 1925.

Walter P. Chrysler's reputation is as a builder of soundly engineered cars, ones which often employed advanced design principles: his company was responsible for the Airflow (p. 97), one of the most radical and influential cars of the thirties.

CIAM

The Congrès internationaux d'architecture moderne was an international organization formed to bring together all the architects and spokesmen of the **Modern Movement** in a campaigning body which would give public relations force to the architectural monument which they had already created at the **Deutsche Werkbund**'s exhibition at Weissenhof in 1927.

Its first meeting was held in 1928 at the château of La Sarraz, outside Lausanne in Switzerland. Organized by **Sigfried Giedion**, the delegates included **Josef Frank**, **Le Corbusier** and **Mart Stam**. The meeting was a symbol of the unity of purpose which the Modern Movement architects and designers felt was expressed in the **International Style**. A series of conferences followed – Frankfurt in 1929, Brussels in 1930 and Athens in 1933 – where the major items of Modern Movement policy were debated and established.
Bibliography Jacques Gubler *Nationalisme et Internationalisme dans l'architecture moderne de la Suisse* L'Age d'Homme, Lausanne, 1975

Aldo Cibic

b. 1955

Aldo Cibic was born in Schio and studied at Milan Polytechnic. He practised interior design in Vicenza, working on shops, offices and apartments, before returning to Milan in 1980, where he made furniture designs for **Memphis**.

Citroën

The French car manufacturer Citroën was founded by André Citroën as an arms factory at the beginning of the First World War. Citröen's father was a Jew whose original name was Limoenmann, but he changed it to a phonic near-miss of the French word for 'lemon' in order to escape the anti-semitic prejudice which was rife in France well into the early years of the twentieth century. Citröen's reputation as a firm of car manufacturers has rested upon a richly deserved reputation for ingenuity.

When the demand for arms declined after 1918 Citroën set up a car factory in order to take advantage of the gear-cutting machines he had to hand for his munitions. His first designer was Jules Saloman, and their Type A of 1919 was Europe's first mass-produced car. With disc wheels, fitted hood, electric lights and on-board starter it raised the standard of automotive engineering overnight; on the day it was announced a vast number of orders was received. But the first Citroën to become a classic was the Type C, a primitive design made interesting by its simple, but adventurous, chassis and suspension: with a flexible frame, no shock absorbers and no bump-stops. This 5CV established Citröen's reputation as a mass-market manufacturer. It was followed by the Traction Avant (front-wheel drive) of 1934, engineered by André Lefebvre, and **Pierre Boulanger**'s 2CV of 1939. The 2CV was conceived as basic transportation that could carry 50kg of luggage at 50km/h, which Boulanger saw as a rival to the **Volkswagen**, although ironically its use of simple materials and geometric forms betrays the influence of **Bauhaus** thought in France. André Citroën himself overinvested in retooling for the Traction Avant and died broke after his major creditor,

Michelin, had taken over the company in 1935.

The Traction Avant was introduced as the 7A. It was a car whose appearance and engineering were so advanced that twenty years after its introduction it was still ahead of its rivals in both respects. By using front-wheel drive, Citroën was able to produce a car which had a wheel at each corner, allowing a free use of passenger space, and the immensely long wheelbase which this system afforded gave passengers greatly enhanced comfort. Citroën's policy when launching new cars was for them to be radically new designs, and to produce and mature them over an extended period. Thus, the successor to the Traction Avant did not go on sale until 1957, but was to be the now legendary DS19.

The DS19 first appeared at the Turin Motor Show of 1955, where it was displayed without wheels on a pylon, so that the startling shape drawn by **Flaminio Bertoni** could be better admired. It was the most advanced popular car of all time, the vehicle celebrated by **Roland Barthes** in a rhapsodic essay. DS is an abbreviation of *voiture de grande diffusion*, but because of the way the letters sound in French the car became known as the *Déesse*, 'Goddess'. It featured a unique oleo-pneumatic suspension system, and its full-width body, large glass area, plastic roof and almost total lack of ornament made the DS, like the 7A, twenty years ahead of its time.

Citroën products became tokens of educated, design-conscious taste. Yet the company rarely made a profit. In 1975 it was taken over by the ultra-conservative Peugeot Group, PSA, and design direction wavered. An Englishman called Trevor Fiore, appointed chief designer in 1979, achieved very little and, to the horror of the purists, the Citröen BX of 1982 used styling consultancy provided by **Bertone**.

In 1982 Citroën's design department was taken over by Carl Olsen (b. 1933), an American who had worked at **General Motors** and taught at the **Royal College of Art**. *Bibliography* Jacques Borge & Nicolas Viasnoff *L'Album de la DS* Editions EPA, Paris, 1983; 'Modellfall Citroën – Produktgestaltung und Werbung' exhibition catalogue, Kunstgewerbemuseum, Zürich, 1967

Citroën 2CV, 1939
The Citroën Deux Chevaux was the French Volkswagen. It appeared in 1939, the brainchild of Pierre Boulanger. Intended to carry 50 kg of luggage at 50km/h, the prototype Deux Chevaux employed materials and geometric shapes in a way that suggests the influence of the Bauhaus.

Poster for Citroen Type A, 1919
The Type 'A' was Europe's first mass-produced car.

Citröen DS 19, 1962
The product of a long development programme, this 'Voiture de Grand Diffusion' employed many technically advanced features including front wheel drive and oleo-pneumatic suspension.

Clarice Cliff

1899–1972

Clarice Cliff trained at Burslem School of Art in the British Potteries area. She worked for the local manufacturer A.J. Wilkinson for whom she designed her 'Bizarre' service, now a collector's piece for those interested in **Art Deco**. Cliff also painted patterns designed by painters Laura Knight and Graham Sutherland on to domestic ceramics manufactured by Royal Staffordshire Pottery. She was typical of the small-scale designer-entrepreneurs of the thirties, producing exclusive work which ultimately had a popular influence.
Bibliography Martin Battersby *The Decorative Thirties* Studio Vista, London, 1971; Clarkson Potter, New York, 1971

Ceramic Plate from 'Bizarre' Series, mid-1930s
From the mid-twenties Clarice Cliff was in artistic control of the Newport Pottery, and in 1928 she introduced her series of hand-painted 'Bizarre' patterns. Their jazz-modern style suggests the influence of French Art Deco.

Stafford Cliff

b. 1946

Stafford Cliff was born and educated in South Australia, and came to London in 1966. Here he joined the Conran Design Group, working on graphics and textile design for **Habitat** and creating corporate identities for Peter Robinson, Peter Dominic, Mowlem and Bulmers. In 1972 he became a director of Conran Associates and subsequently creative director, and has been responsible for the design of the Habitat catalogue almost from inception, turning it into one of the most interesting examples of modern graphics. Stafford Cliff has been the consistent esoteric influence on the visual character of the Habitat chain.

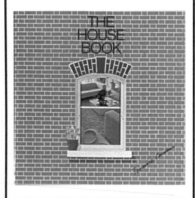

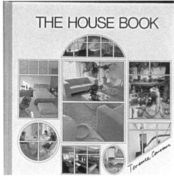

The House Book, 1974
One of the most familiar of Stafford Cliff's graphic exercises was the design of The House Book *which has sold more than a million copies worldwide.*

Wells Coates

1895–1958

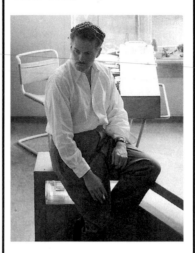

Wells Wintemute Coates was, perhaps, the outstanding English architect of the **International Style**, as well as being a product designer of considerable originality.

He was born in Tokyo, the son of a professor of comparative religion, and left Japan when he was eighteen to attend Canada's McGill University. After the First World War he worked as a journalist and as a lumberjack in Canada, then arrived in London in 1929 and designed some elegant, **moderne** shops whose sparseness reminded some critics that he had, after all, been educated in the Orient.

He founded the Modern Architecture Research Group (**Mars**) in 1933, having the previous year set up the **Isokon** company with **Jack Pritchard**, for which he designed the Lawn Road flats. This building was the first essay in England of the International Style. Another of his major buildings was Embassy Court in Brighton. In 1932 Coates designed a radio set for Eric Kirkham Cole (1901–65), who founded the Ekco company in 1921. It was the first authentic expression in Britain of modern design applied to a domestic appliance.

A polymath, Coates researched a PhD thesis at London University on the gas flow in diesel engines. He also designed the most daring of the studio interiors for the BBC's new Broadcasting House. Coates was a skilled Japanese cook and an impassioned conversationalist on all aspects of art and science. In his work he expressed his sense of the drama of the modern age and, as the London *Times* obituarist remarked, 'For him modern design was not a fashion but a cause demanding unquestioning devotion.'
Bibliography Sherban Cantacuzino *Wells Coates* Gordon Fraser, London, 1978

Ekco AD65 Radio, 1934
Coates' circular bakelite radio was a radical departure from conventional radio design.

Luigi Colani

b. 1928

Luigi Colani was educated in Paris and Berlin. He produces fantastic, 'organic' designs for cars and other consumer products which have frequently been published in popular magazines, but his implemented designs have been few. One of his clients is **Rosenthal**, for whom his 'Drop' porcelain service of 1972 won a Gute Industrieform prize at the Hanover Fair. He is a cult figure among students.

'Drop' Porcelain Service for Rosenthal, 1971
Designed by Colani and characteristically 'organic'.

Henry Cole

1808–82

In 1846 Henry Cole became a member of the Society of Arts, and in the same year the Society awarded him a medal, under his pseudonym of Felix Summerley, for a tea service design of astonishing simplicity. The following year the Society was given a royal charter and became the **Royal Society of Arts**; Cole joined the council and began working on the plans that led to the **Great Exhibition** in 1851.

Cole was the central figure in the establishment of design in Britain, founding the **Journal of Design** in 1849. Institutions he created and reforms he proposed helped build what has become the **Victoria and Albert Museum**, and his idea for an 'Albert University' as a memorial to his mentor, Prince Albert, eventually found form in the **Royal College of Art**. He also invented the *adhesive* postage stamp. He was made a KCB in 1875.

The obituary in the *Journal of the Royal Society of Arts*, another magazine which he helped to found, remarked: 'In his energetic pursuit of what he deemed useful public objects, it cannot be denied that he made many enemies . . . . He possessed, to a large degree, that greatest of all powers – the power of subduing other wills to his own; and this, in the opinion of many who knew him best, was the great secret of his success.' (See also pp. 20–4.)
Bibliography Elizabeth Bonython *King Cole* H.M.S.O., London, n.d.; *Victoria & Albert Museum*, H.M.S.O., London, n.d.

Colefax & Fowler

Colefax & Fowler is a firm of interior decorators founded in London in 1935 by Sybil Colefax, a widowed society figure and a close acquaintance of another decorator, **Syrie Maugham**. John Fowler joined her firm in 1938. Colefax had the right connections and Fowler, through his assiduous studies at the **Victoria and Albert Museum** and elsewhere, the right knowledge to start the most enduring of all firms of decorators. Their style was influenced by Fowler's particular taste for 'pleasing decay', which he nurtured by doing oil paintings in the manner of the Italian architectural *capriccios* of the eighteenth century. The result has been described as 'unpretentious grandeur', although the clients were often the owners of the grandest country houses (as well as the National Trust). The Colefax & Fowler style is the *locus classicus* of that understated, faded gentility which suggests 'Englishness'. John Fowler died in 1977, but the firm still operates from the premises in London's Brook Street which it acquired in the mid-fifties.

Collier Campbell

Susan Collier (b. 1938) trained in hotel management, but was seduced by painting. She turned her interest in painting towards fabric design and worked with **Liberty's** before establishing Collier Campbell in 1979, a business run with her sister, Sarah Campbell (b, 1946). Collier's fabric designs have the power and immediacy of the Fauvist painters she admires, but they also have subtleties too: although the sophistication of the colour is very great and the patterns entirely original, any one Collier Campbell fabric from a given collection works with any other. The designs have been applied across a wide range of fabrics, from upholstery to dress cottons.

'Havanna' and 'Cote d'Azur' from 'Six Views', 1984
Collier Campbell's textiles are inspired by the sisters' conviction that design for fabric is an application of their painterly obsessions. Foreign travel is also a contributory source. 'Six Views', their first licensed range of furnishing fabrics, won the Duke of Edinburgh's Designer's prize in the 1984 Design Council Awards.

A
B
C
D
E
F
G
H
I
J
K
L
M
N
O
P
Q
R
S
T
U
V
W
X
Y
Z

A
B
C
D
E
F
G
H
I
J
K
L
M
N
O
P
Q
R
S
T
U
V
W
X
Y
Z

Gino Colombini

b. 1915

Gino Colombini has been the technical director of **Kartell** since the foundation of this specialized injection-moulding company in 1949. Through Kartell, Colombini was responsible for bringing genuine technical and aesthetic quality to objects made of **plastics**, whether in the design of a colander, a bucket or a chair. He won **Compasso d'Oro** awards in 1955, 1957, 1959 and 1960, for a range of small domestic products.

Baskets for Kartell
Under Colombini, Kartell's sophisticated techniques of injection moulding allowed designers to make mundane products, such as vegetable baskets, of a quality that transcended normal concepts about the limitations of plastics for domestic use.

'Cabriolet' Bed, 1970
Colombo's most dramatic designs were always for miniature environments which extended the definition of 'furniture'. His second 'Cabriolet' bed for Sormani is almost a room in itself.

Joe Colombo

1930–71

Joe Cesare Colombo, an Italian designer who became a cult figure among design cognoscenti during the sixties, died of a heart attack in the 'arms' of his lover in 1971 and was immediately turned into a hero of modern design.

Colombo studied painting at the Brera in Milan and architecture at Milan Polytechnic, and while still a student in his early twenties erected his first building. He experimented with avant-garde painting and sculpture until 1962, when he set up his own architectural office in Milan. As his interest was mainly in interior design, he was led to thinking about the design of furniture and fittings. He soon designed his 'Elda' chair and lights for O-Luce.

All Colombo's designs have a very strong formal value. Nevertheless, he denied that his work had simply a visual character, even speaking in favour of 'anti-design'. This theory about furniture and products was modishly followed by self-styled Italian radicals for a while in the late sixties and seventies, and proposed that the purpose and meaning of a chair or any product should be considered as more important than its appearance. Although he linked himself with this 'radical' posture, with the perspective of time Colombo's work, excellent as it was, seems only to be an evanescent, if perhaps perfect expression of sixties taste.

Bibliography 'The New Domestic Landscape' exhibition catalogue, Museum of Modern Art, New York, 1972; Anty Pansera & Alfonso Grassi *Atlante del design Italiano* Fabbri, Milan, 1981

4801 'Jigsaw' Chair, 1963
Since 1949 Kartell has been Italy's leading manufacturer of high-quality injection-moulded plastics, but has also occasionally used other materials. Colombo's '4801' chair was made out of three slip-jointed pieces of plywood.

Plastic Storage Trolley, 1964
After his experimental mini-kitchen on castors of 1963, it was Colombo's intention to produce mobile units with many possible functions. This is a popularization of the idea.

Compasso d'Oro

Compasso d'Oro is the name of a series of design awards established by the Italian stores **La Rinascente**. First offered as a one-off in 1954, the awards were so popular that they became annual events from 1956. Like the awards offered by the British **Council of Industrial Design**, the aim was to isolate those qualities that made products both attractive and a commercial success.

Constructivism

Constructivism is a term which covers a loose federation of meanings, and eludes precise definition. In Russia Constructivism was the art of the years immediately following the Revolution of 1917, although 'art' is itself a misnomer because the Constructivists wanted to do away with *fine* art. They believed that art should take on the quality of the machine, and that industry could transform life. The most important 'artistic' expressions in the post-Revolutionary years were architecture, town planning, agitprop (posters and propaganda) and **industrial design**. In the Soviet Union Constructivism is at least easy to define historically because it has precise limits: the heroic age of experimentation that started with the Revolution ended with the introduction of the New Economic Policy in 1921. For a brief moment, avant-garde art was totally identified with popular needs.

In the rest of Europe Constructivism is less susceptible of definition. The Dutch **De Stijl** group of architects and painters, the middle years of the **Bauhaus** in Germany, and **Moholy-Nagy** in England are all examples. If it means anything at all here, it means a form of artistic expression that relies not on the traditional materials of oil and canvas and marble but on 'modern' ones – say, **plastics** and steel and film. It is concerned, not with the traditional aims of art (to delight and to exalt), but with the unemotional advancement of social purpose.

Despite its utopian, democratic intentions, Constructivism was nonetheless a rarefied phenomenon, much the same in its exclusivity as any other 'movement' in the fine arts. There was actually little Constructivist design, but the dramatic, austere graphics and paintings of Kasimir Malevich and El Lissitsky have been frequently imitated in the mass-market.

Bibliography Stephen Bann *The Tradition of Constructivism* Thames & Hudson, London, 1974

Contemporary

The term 'Contemporary' came to be used in Britain in the years immediately after the Second World War to describe an expressive, sculptural style in furniture and interior design which began to replace the more austere forms of the **Modern Movement**. Contemporary designs were inspired by the **Surrealist** forms of the sculptors Alexander Calder and Hans Arp, and made possible by new materials and techniques such as steel rod and moulded **plastics**.

The new style was made public at the Festival of Britain. Inspired by technical drawings of the structure of the atom, Lucienne **Day**, for example, designed abstract textile patterns (p. 98). There was a taste for experimentation and variety and the new fabrics, as well as **Ernest Race**'s 'Springbok' and 'Antelope' chairs, soon became widespread (especially in the new towns of the fifties, Harlow and Stevenage). Although 'Contemporary' started out as an exclusive style with encouragement from the **COID**, it soon became exaggerated and debased so that boomerang coffee tables and coat racks made out of black enamelled steel rods with coloured plastic balls were widely sold.

British 'Contemporary' was an expression of an international style. It synthesized features that had appeared in Italy, Scandinavia and the United States. The style itself, somewhat modified in accordance with national preferences, appeared throughout the world. It was a mass style, encouraged by mass taste, driven by popular rather than by establishment values, and emphasizing fantasy rather than function in interior design. (See also **Ercol** and **G-Plan**.)

Bibliography Cara Greenberg *Mid-Century Modern: Furniture of the Fifties*, Harmony, New York, 1984

Festival of Britain Souvenir Kit, 1951
The Festival of Britain was the showplace of the British Contemporary style. The Skylon became its emblem.

Cooper-Hewitt Museum

New York's Cooper-Hewitt Museum is the Smithsonian Institution's museum of design. Its origins are with the City's Cooper Union School. The museum's aim is to collect and display decorative art and design.

Hans Coray

b. 1907

Hans Coray's aluminium 'Landi' chair was the sensation of the 1939 Schweizerischen Landesausstellung (Swiss National Exhibition). It originated in an approach made to a metal plate processor by Hans Fischli, architect of the exhibition. Coray's subsequent design used drop-forging to mould the seat and the latest heat-treatment processes to make it durable. It is light, strong and ingenious, and has been in continuous production for almost fifty years. It was the chief influence on the British designer **Rodney Kinsman**, in the design of his own OMK stacking chair.

'Landi' Chair, 1938
Coray's chair is a remarkable fusion of rational design and the inventive application of materials technology. Aluminium is light but relatively weak and Coray's design exploits its advantages without suffering from its drawbacks.

Corporate identity

Corporate identity is the informal name for the visual character of a company. Its practitioners maintain that it is not only products and services that help their clients become successful, but also their visible character, from the letterhead to the livery of the trucks.

Peter Behrens, with his work for **AEG** at the beginning of the century, was a pioneer, but it is in the United States that corporate identity has really flourished. **Eliot Noyes**, who undertook a vastly successful corporate identity programme for **IBM** in the fifties, described the business when he said: 'Clothes may not make the man, but they do tell you something about him.'

Most American design consultancies specialize in corporate identity as opposed to product design. Among the leaders are Anspach Grossman Portugal, **Lippincott & Margulies** and Landor Associates. (See also **American design, Saul Bass, British design, DRU, Henri Henrion** and **Wolff Olins**.)
Bibliography Wally Olins *The Corporate Personality* Design Council, London, 1978

Bowyer's Packaging by Wolff Olins, 1970

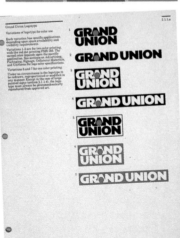

Grand Union Supermarket by Milton Glaser, 1980
As American tastes changed, the traditional supermarket ceased in the seventies to be the symbol of democratic affluence which it had been in the fifties, and instead too often came to represent squalor. Recognizing this problem as one of corporate identity, the English financier Sir James Goldsmith hired Milton Glaser to redesign every aspect of his Grand Union chain of stores in the north-eastern Unites States. Glaser—who believes that sayings such as 'it looks good enough to eat' reveal a fundamental association between food and design—entirely rethought the stores for a corporate identity manual, and designed everything in them from the graphics to the fittings.

ICI Corporate Schemes, by the Design Research Unit, 1968
Britain's DRU was amongst the first firms anywhere to give serious corporate identity advice to its clients.

P & O Ferries by Wolff Olins, 1975–6

Texaco by Anspach Grossman Portugal, 1982

Minolta by Saul Bass, 1980

SAS by Landor Associates, 1983

Alitalia by Landor Associates, 1970

Council of Industrial Design (CoID)

A Council for Art and Industry was established in London under the auspices of the Board of Trade in 1934. This was the basis for the Council of Industrial Design, founded in 1944. The Council was set up to encourage manufacturers to use designers and to raise the level of popular taste. To these ends it organized an exhibition called 'Britain Can Make It' at the **Victoria and Albert Museum** in 1946, and the Council acquired a public face when the Design Centre was opened in the Council's Haymarket premises in 1956. **Gordon Russell** was director from 1947 to 1960, when it became the Design Council under his successor, **Paul Reilly**.

Crafts Revival

The Crafts Revival is a cultural phenomenon, most apparent in Britain, the United States and Scandinavia, which has united a number of different traditions of thought. At its core is the view that a return to some mythical ideal of pre-industrial production is the sole method of redressing the social and economic failings of the modern age, but the more positive aspects of the Revival include a concentration by its exponents on quality and individuality.

In the twentieth century the hero of the Crafts Revival in Britain has been the potter **Bernard Leach**, who was all too aware that those who are nowadays attracted to the handicrafts are self-conscious rather than innocent.

The agent in Britain of the Crafts Revival has been the Crafts Advisory Committee, established in 1971, which became the Crafts Council in 1975. The Council has advanced the cause of the artist-craftsman; but, under increasing pressure to broaden the Council's terms of reference to include artisan crafts, the director, Victor Margrie, announced his resignation to return to potting at the beginning of 1984.

In Britain artist-craftsmen work in a number of traditional media, while in the USA new aesthetic ideas have been applied to the materials of glass, wood and iron.
Bibliography Howard Becker 'Arts and Crafts' *American Journal of Sociology* January 1978, pp. 862–88

Jug by Alison Britton, 1979
The mannered form and disdain for function of this jug are characteristic of the contemporary Crafts Revival.

Cranbrook Academy

The Cranbrook Academy was an educational community, founded in the early twenties by George C. Booth, a British-born newspaper publisher, on his estate twenty miles outside Detroit. Part of Booth's motivation was to create a balance to the increasingly commerical and mercantile character of **American design**. Cranbrook was a re-invention of a cherished American ideal: a dedicated, utopian community. In 1923 Booth met Eliel Saarinen, a Finnish **Arts and Crafts** designer teaching at the University of Michigan, who had come to the United States as a consequence of taking part in the 1922 architectural competition to design a new building for the *Chicago Tribune*. Astonishingly, Saarinen had made his skyscraper designs while living in a forest outside Helsinki. That degree of independent vision helped him to become both the leading creative force behind the Cranbrook Academy and the architect of its buildings.

Cranbrook's influence on American design was in inverse relation to its degree of isolation in the Mid-West, and its teachers and graduates included **Eero Saarinen**, **Niels Diffrient**, **Charles Eames**, Florence **Knoll**, **Jack Lenor Larsen** and **David Rowland**. It has been compared to the **Bauhaus** in its influence, but if the Bauhaus was Germanic in spirit, then Cranbrook was Anglo-Saxon and Nordic. Eliel Saarinen described its philosophy in a speech in 1931: '[Cranbrook] is not an art school in the ordinary meaning. It is a working place for creative art: creative art cannot be taught by others. Each one has to be his own teacher. But [contact] with other artists and discussions with them provide sources for inspiration.'

George Booth died in 1949 and Eliel Saarinen (who had anyway become preoccupied elsewhere) died the year after. Without the presence of its two creators, Cranbrook lost its novelty and its special significance.
Bibliography 'Design in America: the Cranbrook Vision 1925–1950' exhibition catalogue, Detroit Institute of Arts/Metropolitan Museum, New York, 1984

Walter Crane
1845–1915

Walter Crane was a painter, illustrator and wallpaper and textile designer of no particular distinction, but was an administrator and polemicist of some influence. Awed by **William Morris**, he became the chief spokesman for the **Arts and Crafts** movement in his roles as president of the Arts and Crafts Exhibition Society and Master of the **Art Workers' Guild**. He published a book, *The Claims of Decorative Art*, in 1892, and he was principal of the **Royal College of Art** in 1898.

Crane's illustrations helped popularize the Arts and Crafts.
Bibliography Elizabeth Aslin *The Aesthetic Movement* Paul Elek, London, 1969; Praeger, New York, 1969; Isobel Spencer *Walter Crane* Studio Vista, London, 1975; Macmillan, New York, 1976

A
B
C
D
E
F
G
H
I
J
K
L
M
N
O
P
Q
R
S
T
U
V
W
X
Y
Z

D

Danese
Danish
Corradino **d'Ascanio**
Robin **Day**
Michele **de Lucchi**
De Pas, D'Urbino,
    Lomazzi
De Stijl
Elsie **de Wolfe**
Paolo **Deganello**
Design Council
Design management
Design theory
Donald **Deskey**
Deutsche Werkbund
Niels **Diffrient**
Christian **Dior**
Walt **Disney**
Nana **Ditzel**
Jay **Doblin**
Domus
Gillo **Dorfles**
Lou **Dorfsman**
Donald Wills **Douglas**
Jan **Dranger**
Christopher **Dresser**
Henry **Dreyfuss**
DRU

Danese

Bruno Danese founded his company in Milan in 1957. It specializes in what the French call '*le petit design*' – small, exquisite objects in metal and ceramic, and glasses, bowls and vases. Danese's production is characterized by elegance and quality. From the beginning he used **Enzo Mari** and **Bruno Munari** who, since 1964, have been joined by **Angelo Mangiarotti**.

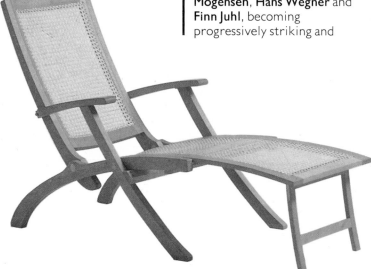

Danish design

The term 'Danish Modern' was coined in the fifties to describe a style of furniture and interior design that depended on spare, sculptural forms and natural finishes (particularly teak).

There is a very strong tradition of furniture design in twentieth-century Denmark. It begins with **Kaare Klint**, who reworked the deck chair, continues with **Mogens Koch** and his version of the campaign chair, and moves through the post-War years with **Børge Mogensen**, **Hans Wegner** and **Finn Juhl**, becoming progressively striking and sculptural. By the fifties Danish furniture had established an international reputation for impeccable craftsmanship and meticulous attention to detail.

While furniture is the most important component of Danish design, as with the other Scandinavian countries, there has been a strong interest in the applied arts (particularly those associated with the kitchen and the table). The Royal Copenhagen Porcelain Company has followed the Swedish model and employs artists to work actually in its factories. Flatware is most readily associated with **Georg Jensen** and with Kay Bojesen,

Deck Chair by Kaare Klint, 1933
Kaare Klint redesigned the form of the traditional deck chair along lines more appropriate to the early twentieth century.

Dining Room by Nana and Jorgen Ditzel, mid-1950s
Made by the Copenhagen firm Magasin du Nord, this room-set emphasizes the urbane quality characteristic of much Danish interior design of this period.

who established **Den Permanente** in 1934 – a continuous exhibition of Danish products which was very influential in maintaining high standards in design.

Although there is a revival of interest in craftsman furniture in Denmark and an **industrial design** movement that has produced many elegant and ingenious products, Danish design has in recent years lost that special identity which throughout the fifties made it synonymous with 'good taste'.
Bibliography 'Design: the problem comes first' exhibition catalogue, Danish Design Council, 1982

Chair by Børge Mogensen, 1950
Mogensen's expressive but elegant chair in beech and leather was inspired by African tribal sculpture.

'F78' Telephone, by Henning Andreasen, 1978
Henning Andreasen's 'F 78' telephone was the Danish response to the international demand for push button telephones which arose in the mid-seventies.

Corradino d'Ascanio

1891–1981

The Italian aviation pioneer Corradino d'Ascanio studied mechanical engineering at Turin Polytechnic and became technical director of Società d'Aviazione Pomilio. Soon after the First World War he left the Pomilio company to found a firm of his own with Veniero d'Annunzio, the son of the poet Gabriele. In 1926, under the patronage of Pietro Trojani, he set up another company dedicated to realizing Leonardo da Vinci's concept of a helicopter. His first model appeared at Pescara in 1926, but was a failure because its rotor blades were rigidly attached to its mast. However, in 1930 he achieved his goal and produced a helicopter which established records for height and duration of flight.

The Italian establishment not being interested in the military potential of the helicopter, d'Ascanio joined the Genoese engineering firm of **Piaggio** in 1934, for whom he designed a range of aircraft components, which included variable pitch propellers. He persuaded Piaggio to work on helicopters in 1939, but it was on a completely new project that he made the greatest impact. At the end of the War Enrico Piaggio asked him to collaborate on a radical two-wheeled motor vehicle aimed at the mass-market. D'Ascanio had had little experience with the design of ground transportation, but he took up the challenge as a task in pure engineering. The result was the **Vespa** motor scooter of 1946, a consumer product designed mainly on aeronautical principles. Not only was its shape streamlined, but its construction in drawn steel was based on aircraft 'monocoque' principles. Eighteen thousand Vespas were produced during its first year of production. It was followed by the 'Ape' car of 1946, a three-wheeled light truck, using scooter components, and by the unsuccessful Vespa 400 car of 1955.

The PD.3 and PD.4 helicopters by d'Ascanio first flew in 1949–52. His last design was for an agricultural helicopter in 1961. D'Ascanio's work demonstrates the influence of **Futurism** on Italian engineering and, in turn, demonstrates the influence that engineering had on popular culture. The Vespa, inspired by d'Annunzio's poetry and the thrill of flight, became a symbol of mobility and affluence for the Italian generation of the *ricostruzione*.
Bibliography 'Veicoli, 1909–1947' *Rassegna* VI, 18/2, June 1984

Polypropylene Chair, 1962
Day's polypropylene chair went into production for Hille in 1962 and became the most successful modern British chair, being produced in greater numbers than any of its rivals. It has subsequently been modified several times but is still in production.

Robin Day

b. 1915

Robin Day studied at a local art school in High Wycombe, then at the **Royal College of Art**. He came to international attention when a chair he designed won first prize in the **Museum of Modern Art**'s 'International Competition for Low Cost Furniture Design' in 1948. In 1949 he started working for the furniture manufacturer **Hille**, and produced for them a variety of chair designs in **plastic** and **plywood** culminating in his 'Polypropylene' chair of 1962, one of the great successes in modern chair design which can be compared to pieces by **Thonet**, **Breuer** and **David Rowland**. Day's wife Lucienne (b.1917) became his partner in 1948. She has achieved success as a fabric designer, working for **Heal**'s and Edinburgh Weavers (see p. 98 and **Contemporary**).
Bibliography 'Hille: 75 Years of British Furniture' exhibition catalogue, Victoria & Albert Museum, London, 1981; Fiona MacCarthy *British Design since 1880* Lund Humphries, London, 1982

ABCDEFGHIJKLMNOPQRSTUVWXYZ

Michele de Lucchi

b. 1952

Michele de Lucchi studied first at Padua and then at Florence, where he got a degree in architecture in 1975. While at Florence he experimented with avant-garde art and film, and even held a seminar on 'Culturally Impossible Architecture' in the Monselice quarries, just outside Padua. Between 1975 and 1977 he was a teaching assistant at Florence University's faculty of architecture, but moved to Milan in 1978. Here he contributed to **Studio Alchymia** and later to **Memphis**, for whom he has created some of their most memorable pieces. In 1979 he became a consultant to the office furniture manufacturer **Olivetti** Synthesis in Massa, and in 1984 to Olivetti SpA in Ivrea. De Lucchi has designed, with **Ettore Sottsass**, Olivetti '45CR' and 'Icarus' office furniture, as well as more than fifty **Fiorucci** shops. His aesthetic is influenced by his philosophy – to render domestic appliances and furniture less hostile and alienating by making them look more like toys.

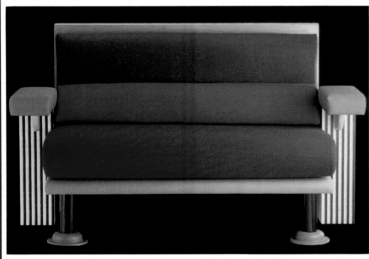

'Lido' Sofa for Memphis, 1981
Since Memphis' first show in 1981, de Lucchi has consistently produced some of its most memorable and striking furniture designs.

De Pas, D'Urbino, Lomazzi

The De Pas, D'Urbino, Lomazzi team was founded in Milan in 1966, in the middle of the decade in which their work is forever located. They are best known for a **Pop**-inspired inflatable 'Blow' chair of 1967 and their 'Joe' chair of 1970, which is in the shape of a stuffed baseball glove. These were succeeded by less memorable designs for other Italian manufacturers.

Inflatable Divan, 1967
This inflatable divan by Jonathan De Pas and colleagues Carla Solari, Paolo Lomazzi and Donato D'Urbino was a novel, if indulgent, essay in sixties style. Electronic welding was used to seal the vinyl.

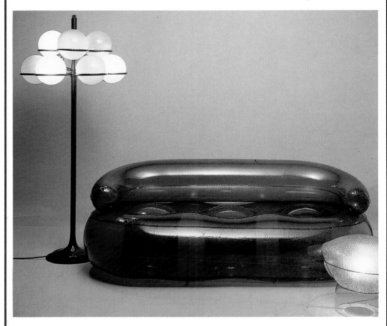

De Stijl

'De Stijl' is Dutch for 'the Style' and is the name of a group of artists and architects who gathered around the (largely theoretical) architect Theo van Doesburg. He founded the group in Leyden in 1917 and published the magazine *De Stijl*, which ran from 1917 to 1928.

De Stijl was one of the European expressions of **Constructivism**. Van Doesburg believed that modern life required a revolutionary, new art for which he coined the term 'Neo-Plasticism'. De Stijl intended to radicalize the public into an appreciation of this art, but it was not an easy job. With his requirement that

Neo-Plastic art should reject any form of overt representation and that it should be restricted to flat planes of colour (either the primaries, or white, black and grey) orchestrated with straight lines, van Doesburg, ironically, took the 'new art' a long way from the taste of the public, which seemed to prefer the old sort.

De Stijl reached its poetic peak in the paintings of Piet Mondrian (1872–1944). Mondrian's status and authority (to say nothing of his ambition to reform human mentality through his art) made De Stijl one of the most influential of the oddball radical groups which flourished in the early twentieth century, and as a result many of the aesthetic assumptions of the **Modern Movement** can be traced back to Theo van Doesburg's aesthetic theories. Similarly, Mondrian's inspired pattern-making has been a consistent stimulus (and source) for graphic designers. The architect and furniture designer **Gerrit Rietveld** became a member of the group in 1918.

Bibliography H.L.C. Jaffe *De Stijl 1917–1931 – the Dutch Contribution to Modern Art* Meulenhoff, Amsterdam, 1956; Joost Baljeu, *Theo van Doesburg* Studio Vista, London, 1974; Macmillan, New York,1974

Paolo Deganello

b. 1940

Paolo Deganello was, with **Andrea Branzi**, one of the founders of the **Archizoom** group of radical designers who came together in Florence in 1966. When Archizoom petered out, Deganello founded the Colletivo Technici Progettisti to continue his campaign for furniture design which appeals to the imagination. His 'Torso' lounge chair of 1982 for **Cassina** rivalled the collections of **Memphis** in perversity, but was also a serious re-working of furniture ideas and forms from the fifties.

Elsie de Wolfe

1865–1950

Elsie de Wolfe, a professional interior designer, invented the term 'good taste' in her book, *The House in Good Taste* of 1915. Although she ushered into American homes a form of brightness with her motto 'plenty of optimism and white paint', her devotion to antiques produced an inertia in upper-class taste in America. Russell Lynes characterized her global achievement as 'defeatism in high places'.

Design Council see Council of Industrial Design

Design management

Design management is the process, now studied at an academic level, in which design activities in commercial bodies are rationalized and organized. It includes the study of the relationship of design to other management functions, but is also being extended to mean how designers can be more effectively used in business.

Chairs for Driade, 1981
Deganello turned fifties revivalist with his 1981 range.

Design theory

Although there has been very little theoretical writing devoted to design in this century, nonetheless many attempts have been made to reconcile the design process with various areas of philosophical speculation.

In the nineteenth century **John Ruskin** and Gottfried Semper related design to architecture, while **William Morris** related it to social theory. At the same time, **Christopher Dresser**, a botanist, and **Owen Jones**, an architect, tried to draw up vocabularies of visual ideas according to the categorizations of their particular disciplines.

The first years of the twentieth century were dominated by **Functionalism** in its various versions. The German **Hermann Muthesius** campaigned for standardization in contrast to the Belgian **Henry van de Velde**'s theories for artistic individualism. The most profound and far-reaching declarations of a design theory for the twentieth century were made by **Walter Gropius** and **Le Corbusier**. Both men were devotees of the machine aesthetic, and each was in his individual way influenced by the ideals of the **Deutsche Werkbund**. Le Corbusier developed a theory about the '*objets-types*' (standardized objects), but it was little more than a poetic re-working of Muthesius' standardization. Although presenting them as the inevitable end to the quest for a relevant design theory for the century, Le Corbusier was, in fact, only offering subjective opinions based on his own preferred aesthetic. Many other **Modern Movement** theorists claimed to ground their thoughts in the objective discipline of engineering, but their motivation was, nevertheless, more poetic than scientific.

After the Second World War

design theory developed strongly in favour of a systematic approach so as to ally design with the governing principles of mass-production and business management. A considerable amount of effort was expended to determine the rules of **ergonomics**, while a movement called 'design methods' attempted to systematize the creative parts of the design process so that (at least in principle) anybody bright enough to read could design a new product. This application of pseudo-rational (and always obfuscatory) thinking was a reaction against the commercial success of **styling**. While **Raymond Loewy** said his only conception of beauty was an upwardly rising sales curve, **Bruce Archer**, Christopher Alexander and Geoffrey Broadbent wrote unreadable tomes on systematic method.

Meanwhile, an alliance in the real world between popular culture and taste meant that design was shifting its base from Functionalism. This was noticed by **Reyner Banham**, **Robert Venturi**, **Gillo Dorfles** and **Roland Barthes**, who all set out to analyse, not so much the *process* of design, as the *meaning* of the object used. This entailed a much less systematic and a more intuitive approach, borrowing methods and techniques from art history, anthropology and sociology. Design theory, like design practice, has in recent years become eclectic. It is no longer concerned to advance a monolithic theory about either an aesthetic or a process, but simply aims to understand design in its social context.

A B C D E F G H I J K L M N O P Q R S T U V W X Y Z

A
B
C
D
E
F
G
H
I
J
K
L
M
N
O
P
Q
R
S
T
U
V
W
X
Y
Z

Donald Deskey

b. 1894

Donald Deskey was, with **Raymond Loewy** and **Henry Dreyfuss**, one of the pioneer consultant designers in the United States. He was also one of the most outstanding figures in **Art Deco** in the thirties. His career as a designer began in 1920 with a job in a Chicago advertising agency, and he was very much influenced by his visit to the Paris exhibition of 1925. Like many of his contemporaries, Deskey was responsible for only a few realized products, but he did design the interior of Radio City Music Hall in New York's Rockefeller Center, and a number of other interiors and pieces of furniture. His work was characterized by experimentation with new materials, such as **aluminium**, cork and linoleum.
Bibliography Carol Herselle Krinsky *Rockefeller Center* Oxford University Press, New York, 1978; David A. Hanks *Donald Deskey* E.P. Dutton, New York, 1985

Interior of Mezzanine Lounge, in Radio City Music Hall, 1930–32
Deskey's Radio City Music Hall in New York's Rockefeller Center was a tour de force *of glamorous American Art Deco. The murals are by Witold Gordon.*

Deutsche Werkbund

The Deutsche Werkbund was an association founded for educational and propaganda purposes, intended to unite business, arts, crafts and industry. It was loosely modelled on the English guilds that sprang up in the second half of the nineteenth century, but was more practical. It was founded in 1907, but, as **Reyner Banham** has said, its 'golden legend' depends on what happened in a few months around 1914. This was when the Werkbund held its first major exhibition, an enormous festival of German art and industry for which **Walter Gropius** designed exhibition buildings.
    The year 1914 also saw a public debate between **Hermann Muthesius** and **Henry van de Velde** over whether the Werkbund should promote standardization and machine-manufacture of products, or free and independent artistic expression. Muthesius prevailed, and his views had a profound influence on the **Modern Movement**.
    During the peaceful Weimar years, to use Banham's words, 'the sense of involvement in the manifest destiny of the German *Volk* persisted . . . in . . . the emphasis on standardization', a sentiment which can trace its origins far back into German culture, and even to the Prussian military ideal which, in 1911, Muthesius had said was an example to German industry. The Werkbund's exhibition of housing at Weissenhof in 1927, the **Weissenhof Siedlung**, organized by **Mies van der Rohe**, was a vindication of Muthesius' beliefs.
    The Werkbund was dissolved in 1934 (see **Hermann Gretsch**), but revived again in 1947.
Bibliography Joan Campbell *The German Werkbund – the politics of reform in the applied arts* Princeton University Press, Princeton, New Jersey and Guildford, 1980

Poster for 1914 Werkbund Exhibition in Cologne
The poster for the crucial 1914 exhibition reveals that not everything about the Werkbund was austerely industrial: many of the elements of the organization's work were reflections of older forms of German culture.

Niels Diffrient

b. 1928

Niels Diffrient was born at Star, Mississippi and graduated from the **Cranbrook Academy**. He worked with **Eero Saarinen** for five years and with **Henry Dreyfuss** for twenty-five. In 1955 he designed a sewing machine with **Marco Zanuso**. With Dreyfuss, Diffrient designed Lockheed, Learjet and Hughes aircraft interiors, as well as instruments, X-ray and diagnostic equipment for Litton Industries and Honeywell. Diffrient has a profound concern for **ergonomics** and left his partnership with Dreyfuss to develop office furniture for **Knoll** and seating for Sunar. Although, or perhaps because, he was responsible for so many aircraft interiors, Diffrient is acutely aware of the shortcomings of most popular seating, and now runs his own consultancy in Ridgefield, Connecticut, intent on bringing rational planning into chair design.

'Jefferson' Office Chair for Sunar, 1983

Diffrient learnt about ergonomics with Dreyfuss. When he came to design his own chair for Sunar-Hausermann he had his first opportunity to define exactly what a chair should be. Called the 'Jefferson' (because the American president preferred to work reclining), Diffrient wanted his design to be an exercise in functional comfort, rather than in high fashion. It was human engineering rather than styling. The chair pivots on a central axis and adjusts to fit all bodies. Accompanied by task accessories to hold telephones and computer terminals, the 'Jefferson' suggests the work environment of the future.

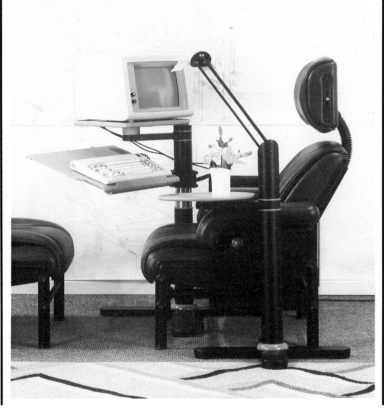

Christian Dior

1905–58

Christian Dior's 'New Look' of 1947 captured the post-War mood and established him as the master of international fashion. European and American women shared a keen appetite for the style and enthusiastically accepted what he offered: a wasp waist with a slim bodice and bouffant skirt, accompanied by stiletto heel shoes which usually emphasized the exaggeratedly feminine shape. Dior studied traditional tailoring techniques and researched historical costume; he was modest and self-effacing, in spite of his influence. Each year he introduced new lines which were immediately pirated by international ready-to-wear merchants: the 'H' line of 1954, the 'Y' line of 1955 and the famous 'A' line of 1956 being the best known. The house of Dior was run for a brief time by his protégé **Yves St Laurent**, who was succeeded by Marc Bohan.

'New Look' Coat, 1947
It is rare for any change of fashion to be given an exact date, but in his very first collection Dior launched a completely new look that swept across Europe and America. His feminine line with its long full skirts ousted the austere, rather mannish styles of the forties and brought him instant success and international fame.

Walt Disney

1901–66

Walter Elias Disney's best-known creation, Mickey Mouse, was called by the Russian film director, Eisenstein, 'America's most original contribution to culture'. Born in Chicago, Disney first set up a cartoon company called Laugh-o-Gram at Kansas City, Missouri, then moved to Hollywood. He conceived the animated beast that made him famous on a journey to New York and introduced him to the world in 1928. He opened Disneyland in 1955 in Anaheim, California, to provide 'a nice clean place to take the kids'. Before he died Disney had created a leisure empire that incorporated all American cultural fantasies into a sugar-glazed system for making money.

Disney was stubbornly un-intellectual. According to the writer Russell Davies, this was probably because 'he shared with most self-made men a dislike of the thought that he might in some ways be a product of forces outside the range of his own initiative'.

His one-time animator, Art Babbit, said of Disney that he had 'the innate bad taste of the American public', and the writer Ray Bradbury said, 'He is the faucet through which the American Dream runs . . . Well . . . maybe he is. Dreams are always in bad taste. It's part of what they're for.'

Disney made the cartoon into a popular medium, and the success of his features added a new element to the repertoire of graphic designers working in mass communication.

Mickey Mouse
Disney's most famous cartoon character made his first appearance in 1928 in two silent films, 'Plain Crazy' and 'Gallopin' Gaucho'. 'Steamboat Willie' followed, using sound. Mickey's success spawned a series of animal characters, including Minnie Mouse.

A B C D E F G H I J K L M N O P Q R S T U V W X Y Z

A
B
C
D
E
F
G
H
I
J
K
L
M
N
O
P
Q
R
S
T
U
V
W
X
Y
Z

Nana Ditzel

b. 1923

Nana Ditzel studied at the Kunsthandvaerkskolen (Crafts school) in Copenhagen and opened her first design office in partnership with her first husband, Jorgen Ditzel (1921–61), in 1946. With their combination of natural materials and simple, elegant forms, her designs for jewellery, textiles, tableware and furniture epitomized what was meant by **Danish design**. Since 1954 she has worked for **Georg Jensen** and from 1970 onwards in London.

Child's High Chair, 1955
Nana Ditzel's design incorporates a bar to restrain the child. (See also p. 112.)

Jay Doblin

b. 1920

Jay Doblin studied at Brooklyn's Pratt Institute and worked as a designer both in government service and in private practice (for **Raymond Loewy**) before becoming the director of the Illinois Institute of Technology, one of America's premier design schools, from 1949 to 1959. He has also been a design consultant to **General Motors**, Shell and Coca-Cola. In 1966 he was one of the founders of the **Unimark** consultancy which specialized in **corporate identity**, and he has remained a significant figure in the American design and educational establishment.

Domus

Domus is a Milanese architecture and design magazine founded by **Gio Ponti** in 1927. It has consistently projected progressive Italian architecture and design to the rest of the world. Under the editorship of the communist **Ernesto Rogers**, *Domus* argued the importance of prefabrication and other architectural solutions to social problems. However, Ponti then restored himself to the editorship and returned *Domus* to its glossy presentation of *la dolce vita*. Since 1979 *Domus* has been edited by **Alessandro Mendini**, an architect who has contributed furniture designs to **Studio Alchymia**, but it has become self-consciously and clumsily avant-garde. (See also pp. 51–2.)

Gillo Dorfles

b. 1910

Gillo Dorfles is professor of aesthetics at Bologna University, with special interests in semantics, **semiology** and anthropology. His central role in the formation of Milanese design after the Second World War is a testament to the eclecticism and the taste for intellectual analysis that has made Milan the centre of Italy's industrial renaissance. He was a key figure in the organization of the **Compasso d'Oro** awards and in the Milan **Triennales**. He was the first Italian to write a book on **industrial design**, and his titles include: *Nuovo riti, nuovo miti, Simbolo comunicazione consumo, Introduzione al disegno industriale, Le oscillazione del gusto* and *Dal significato alle scelte*. His book on **kitsch** (1969) is the major study of the topic.

Lou Dorfsman

b. 1918

An American graphic designer, Lou Dorfsman studied at New York's Cooper Union, and since the end of the Second World War has worked for CBS where he is now vice-president in charge of design. Dorfsman has been an influence on the institutionalization of design in America because of the organizational role he has played in the annual **Aspen** conferences, rather than through anything especially important he has said, done or designed.

Ad for TV Programme, 'Black America', 1968
Dorfsman's advertisement has a visual force and conceptual novelty which are characteristic of his style.

Donald Wills Douglas

1892–1981

Douglas was one of the great aircraft designers of America, a romantic engineer whose solutions to aeronautical problems were so visually original and had such an impact on culture that his influence extends into the area of design.

Douglas was born in Brooklyn in 1892 and was educated at the US Navy Academy in Annapolis. In 1912 he went to study at the Massachusetts Institute of Technology and between 1915 and 1916 was chief engineer at the Glenn L. Martin Company. After a brief period as chief civilian engineer to the US Signal Corps, he founded the Douglas Company in 1920. The Douglas Cloudster was the first aircraft to carry a payload greater than its own weight, and following this technical success Douglas and his colleagues made a series of innovations which helped make popular civil aviation possible, culminating in the celebrated DC-3 series of civil transports. DC stood for Douglas Commercial and this plane (known in its military guise as the C-47 and the Dakota) made mass air travel a commercial reality. It became the most successful aircraft of all time, celebrated for its technical virtuosity and its clean, streamlined, platonic beauty by **Le Corbusier** and **Walter Dorwin Teague**, who illustrated it in their books, *Aircraft* and *Design This Day*. The DC-3 was followed by a series of larger piston-engined transports, and by jet transports such as the DC-8 and DC-9.

In 1967 Douglas' company merged to become the McDonnell-Douglas Corporation of St Louis, Missouri. Pressure led to corners being cut in the design of the DC-10, the last Douglas airliner, and its spectacular accidents at Paris in 1974 and Chicago in 1979 brought the revered Douglas name into books about product liability legislation. (See also p. 46.)
Bibliography John B. Rae *Climb to Greatness* MIT, Cambridge, Mass., 1968

Jan Dranger

A Swedish furniture designer, Jan Dranger is a partner of **Johan Huldt** in the Stockholm design consultancy, **Innovator AB.** He designs principally for Dux Mobel.

Christopher Dresser

1834–1904

Christopher Dresser was a botanical draughtsman who came to be a metalware designer. His status comes from **Nikolaus Pevsner**, who claimed him as a 'pioneer' of modern design.

In his early career Dresser published some successful books on botany and was awarded a doctorate from the University of Jena in 1860, but when he subsequently failed to get the chair at University College, London, he became disenchanted with plant life and concentrated on design instead.

Dresser's main importance in the history of design lies in his various teapots, which are exceptional in that they were astonishingly early to reject decoration and to allow materials and details to speak for themselves. One part of this inspiration was eccentricity,

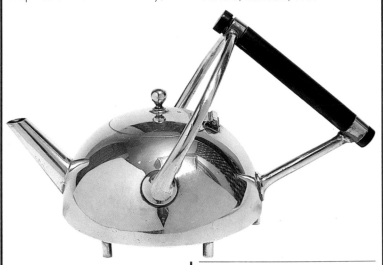

Silver Teapot with Wooden Handle, c. 1881
Basing his 'industrial' designs on metaphors of plant life, Dresser made elegant and minimal designs, such as this silver teapot of about 1881, which historians have subsequently claimed as forerunners of the twentieth-century style.

the other part derived from the simplicity of design in Japan, where he had travelled in 1877. He was also strongly committed to industrial production, and even produced a riveted teapot in 1898.

Although Dresser's best-known work is simple and unfussy, he was not against ornamentation itself, and was considerably influenced by the ideology of **Owen Jones'** *The Grammar of Ornament*. In 1862 he published two books himself, *The Art of Decorative Design* and *The Development of Ornamental Art*, which drew on articles he had published about the relationship of natural forms to design.

Dresser became a buyer for Tiffany of New York, designed carpets and was a manager of the Art Furnishers' Alliance.
Bibliography 'Christopher Dresser 1834–1904' exhibition catalogue, Camden Arts Centre, London, 1979

Henry Dreyfuss

1903–72

Dreyfuss was a contemporary and rival of **Raymond Loewy**, **Walter Dorwin Teague** and **Norman Bel Geddes**.

He was born into a family which dealt in prop and costume hire, and on leaving college at sixteen was drawn to the theatre, where he met Norman Bel Geddes and worked with him on several hit

shows. During the twenties many stage designers and advertising draughtsmen were drawn from the box office and the billboard to the bigger theatre of American industry, which at that time seemed to offer almost unlimited opportunities for ambitious young designers. Dreyfuss was such a man. He set up his own office in 1929 and his first essay in **industrial design** was a re-working of a traditional storage jar, which he modified on space-saving, functional lines. Of the first generation of American designers Dreyfuss was the most proficient 'exponent of cleanliness', according to the journal *American Artist*. Although his crack train for the New York Central Railroad, 'The Twentieth Century Limited', became for many people the very symbol of American design in its most luxurious and expressive years, Dreyfuss generally avoided stylish extravagance, and his commitment to **Functionalism** expressed itself both in a refusal to do pure and simple facelifts of inadequate products, and in his interest in what came to be called in America 'human engineering', or **anthropometrics**. His masterly survey of the concerns of the industrial designer, *Designing for People*, began a tradition of concern with this science which is still maintained in the office he left behind.

Dreyfuss' major clients included Bell (for whom his 1933 telephone design virtually defined a shape which has not been improved in fifty years), RCA television, Hoover vacuum cleaners, Goodyear tyres, Ansco cameras, John Deere agricultural equipment and some plane interiors for Lockheed.

Dreyfuss and his wife committed suicide in 1972. (See also pp. 43–4.)
Bibliography Henry Dreyfuss *Designing for People* Simon & Schuster, New York, 1955

Bell 'Trimline' Telephone, 1965
A little more than thirty years after designing the standard American table telephone for the Bell Company, Dreyfuss produced the compact Trimline in 1965. It was one of the first radical departures from the 'classical' telephone which his work had helped establish.

DRU

DRU stands for the Design Research Unit, a consultancy in London founded by **Misha Black** and **Milner Gray** in 1944. It was the first British consultancy set up on the American model. They were originally artists in two dimensions who also moved into **corporate identity**, exhibition work and packaging. DRU's clients have included several major organizations, such as British Rail, Allied Breweries and ICI (p. 110).
Bibliography John and Avril Blake *The Practical Idealists* Lund Humphries, London, 1969

Corporate Identity Programme for British Rail, 1965
Black's Design Research Unit was responsible for this corporate identity. Although it was a pioneering effort to get 'design' accepted by a state authority, the results all too often lacked sparkle.

E

Charles **Eames**
  Harley **Earl**
    Tom **Eckersley**
    Fritz **Eichler**
  Kenji **Ekuan**
         Electrolux
  Bjorn **Envall**
         Erco
         Ercol
         Ergonomi Design
         Ergonomics
Vuokko **Eskolin-**
         Nurmesniemi
  Virgil **Exner**

Charles Eames

1907–78

Charles Eames was born in St Louis, Missouri, and laboured in a steel mill before becoming a technical draughtsman. He won a scholarship to Washington University's School of Architecture, but did not finish the course and set himself up as an architect and industrial designer (without very much work in hand). He came to prominence when, with **Eero Saarinen**, he won the 'Organic Design in Home Furnishings' competition at New York's **Museum of Modern Art** in 1940 (see p. 74). In 1946 he was the first designer of any nationality to have a one-man show at the museum, with furniture that combined bent **plywood** with steel rods. These designs used the moulded plywood technique first seen in the 'organic' chairs, somewhat refined after he made splints for the US Navy in 1942. Eames' designs were all manufactured by **Herman Miller** of Zeeland, Michigan. Eames' most famous design, the culmination of all his efforts and Herman Miller's most celebrated product, was a rosewood and leather lounge chair and ottoman which was first made in 1955 for the film director Billy Wilder: it became an international symbol of architectural style and, like **Marcel Breuer**'s 'Bauhaus' chair, was widely imitated but never equalled. In 1958 Eames designed the 'Aluminum' chair and at about the same time his tandem seating, using similar constructional principles, was installed at Washington's Dulles and Chicago's O'Hare airports.

The public relations efforts of Herman Miller, together with Eames' decision to become more involved with exhibition design and education (in partnership with his wife, Ray), made him into a more formidable and celebrated spokesman for **American design** than his relatively modest portfolio of mass-produced products would suggest. Some exaggerated claims have been made for Eames and his work, but he is nevertheless a genuinely important and influential figure.

After 1959, when he produced a multi-screen presentation for the US exhibition in Moscow, Eames became progressively more concerned with experimental film, and his *Powers of Ten*, a short about the house he and Ray designed for themselves in Santa Monica, became a cult movie. Before his death, that house (which he had assembled in 1949 out of stock, mass-produced components) became a shrine for student designers all over the world.

In an interview with *Interiors* magazine Eames offered an insight into his philosophy: 'I visited a good toy store this morning . . . It was sick-making. I longed for the desert even though quite a few of the things in other times would have been treasures . . . Affluence offers the kind of freedom I am deeply suspicious

Chair and Ottoman, 1955
Eames' now classic lounge chair and ottoman were inspired by the leather armchairs of English gentlemen's clubs.

of. It offers freedom from restraint, and virtually it is impossible to do something without restraints . . . when somebody is on the ball he eliminates choices and establishes limits for himself . . . We have to rediscover limitations.'
Bibliography 'Connections: the work of Charles and Ray Eames' exhibition catalogue, Frederick S. Wright Gallery, University of California, Los Angeles, 1976–7; Ralph Caplan *The Design of Herman Miller* Whitney Library of Design, New York, 1976

Stacking chairs, early 1960s
Stacking chairs designed by Charles Eames and manufactured by Herman Miller in zinc-coated steel tubes with moulded polyester seats.

Harley Earl

1893–1969

Harley Earl was born in Hollywood into a family of coach-builders. With increasing numbers of orders for customized car bodies coming in from the first generation of film stars, his family set up the Earl Automobile Works in 1908. In 1914 Earl went to Stanford University, while the family firm kept the cash-flow moving by making chariots for epic movies. On being bought out by a local Cadillac dealership in 1919, the company was given over entirely to customized car bodies. At this time Harley Earl developed the now standard technique of using clay models to design car bodies, which gave considerable scope for sculptural expression and enabled car design to become more and more free.

In the early years of the motor industry, as it struggled merely to satisfy the demand from the first generation of car buyers, appearance had not been considered an important factor in an automobile's showroom performance. But in the early twenties the chairman of **General Motors**, Alfred P. Sloan, aware of greater manufacturing capacity, started to suspect that looks might have a beneficial effect on sales performance, and in 1925 invited Earl to Detroit. On 1 January 1928, General Motors' Art and Color section came into existence, under Earl's leadership. His first success for the company was the La Salle of 1927; his first 'dream' car was the 1937 Buick Y Job, and there followed a series of more or less original shapes and motifs. In the year of the Y Job Earl became vice-president of the newly formed Styling Division and his commercial successes with Cadillacs, Chevrolets, Pontiacs, Oldsmobiles and Buicks brought him, by the time of his retirement in 1959, to a position of influence unequalled by any motor designer before or since. However, the inventor of two-tone paint, chromium plating, the tail fin, and designs derived from the shape of jet planes and rockets, never won a design award.

'I like baseball and *love* automobiles,' Earl once said. And by the time he died he had been responsible for the appearance of fifty million of them, and for producing a model of automotive design which was emulated by every other American car manufacturer.
Bibliography Stephen Bayley *Harley Earl and The Dream Machine* Weidenfeld & Nicolson, London, 1983; Knopf, New York, 1983

Cadillac Eldorado, 1959
With the 1959 Cadillac Eldorado, Earl's policy of making cars longer, lower and more ornate reached its peak. (See also p. 46.)

Tom Eckersley

b. 1914

Tom Eckersley was born in Lancashire and studied at Salford College of Art, moving to London in 1934 where he became, along with **Abram Games**, one of the last masters of *drawing* in poster design. Before the Second World War Eckersley worked for those great British mixed-economy patrons, London Transport, Shell-Mex, the BBC and the Post Office. Eckersley's style involves simple, two-dimensional image-making; the messages are simple and the image nicely matches the text. The degree of artifice is slight. From 1957 to 1977 Eckersley was head of graphic design at the London College of Printing, and was an influential teacher of more than two generations of British graphic designers.
Bibliography Tom Eckersley *Poster Design* Studio Publication, London, 1954

Poster for London Transport Museum, 1980

A
B
C
D
E
F
G
H
I
J
K
L
M
N
O
P
Q
R
S
T
U
V
W
X
Y
Z

A
B
C
D
E
F
G
H
I
J
K
L
M
N
O
P
Q
R
S
T
U
V
W
X
Y
Z

Fritz Eichler

b. 1911

Fritz Eichler studied art history and drama before working as a theatre designer from 1945. In 1954 he met Artur **Braun** at just the time when the new image for his company was being prepared for its launch at the 1955 Radio Show in Düsseldorf. Eichler coordinated the company's design policies and first suggested that Artur and Erwin Braun commission designs from teachers at the **Hochschule für Gestaltung** in Ulm.

Kenji Ekuan

b. 1929

Kenji Ekuan has been described as 'the **Raymond Loewy** of Japan'. After graduating from Tokyo's National University of Fine Arts and Music, where he majored in design, he went to Los Angeles for a time, then returned to Tokyo to found a practice called **GK Industrial Design Associates** in 1957, one of the rare examples of a modern Japanese independent design consultancy. His clients include Yamaha motorbikes (p. 163) and Olympus Optical, for whom he designed a much-admired compact camera. He was also responsible for street furniture at Expo 70 in Osaka. Ekuan's frequent appearances at international conferences have done much to establish an identity for Japanese **industrial design**. He has published books on tools, kitchen equipment and **design theory**.

Electrolux

The Swedish electric appliance manufacturer Electrolux was founded in Stockholm as AB Lux in 1901, to manufacture paraffin gas mantles. Its present name dates from 1919 and signifies the concern's increasing reliance on electrical products. An English subsidiary was set up in 1921.

In the thirties, when Swedish industry was becoming more confident, Electrolux began to employ designers to help give its products like vacuum cleaners and refrigerators some special identity. From the United States both Carl Otto and **Raymond Loewy** were commissioned to submit proposals, but Electrolux's most exciting designs came from the Swedish designer of the SAAB car and the Hasselblad camera, **Sixten Sason**, who styled their products using the streamlined aesthetic. By the eighties Electrolux had become, with Siemens, Philips and Zanussi, one of the big four European manufacturers of 'white goods'.

Streamlined Refrigerator, 1948
Electrolux was one of the first Swedish concerns to become conscious of its image. Sixten Sason designed this refrigerator in a streamlined, modern style.

Bjorn Envall

b. 1942

Since 1969 Bjorn Envall has been chief designer of the Swedish car manufacturer, SAAB. He was responsible under his mentor **Sixten Sason** for the SAAB 99 and all of the company's subsequent production. His main concern is with the safety and environmental aspects of the car. His redesign of the 99, creating the 900 series in 1979–80, was responsible for a turn-around in SAAB's sales.

Drawings for SAAB 9000, early 1980s
Envall is only the second designer employed by SAAB. He helped develop the SAAB 99, successor to Sason's epochal 92 (later 96). After Sason's retirement, Envall became chief designer and began development of the 900, a stretched version of the 99. Envall has said that his aim is to produce cars with fine ergonomics and with looks which, if not beautiful, have a subtle, long-term fascination. The successor to the 900 was the 9000, and for this design Envall called upon Giorgio Giugiaro for advice.

Erco

The German firm Erco is one of the leading international suppliers of high-quality architectural lighting. It was founded in 1934 by Arnold Reininghaus, Paul Buschhaus and Karl Reeber as Reininghaus & Co., but is now known as Erco Leuchten GmbH.

Erco's fortune was made in the years of reconstruction after the Second World War, when demand from new home builders during the 'economic miracle' helped many medium-sized manufacturers to flourish. Although Erco has always stressed the priority of technical characteristics in its product development, the company started to use designers to help in creating the corporate character as long ago as the late fifties: Terence Conran, **Ettore Sottsass**, **Roger Tallon** and **Emilio Ambasz** all have products in the current Erco range. The company's logogram was designed by **Otl Aicher**, and he also designed a complete sign system for the firm which was marketed in 1976. Since 1963 Erco has been run by Klaus-Jurgen Maack.

The company's policy has been to promote a modern, elegant image for lighting and hence to attract a market that would appreciate such qualities.

Ercol

Ercol was founded in 1920 in High Wycombe by Lucian Ercolani, an Italian who came to England at the age of seven in 1887. His business specialized in the traditional Windsor chair and in simple, solid elm furniture. Ercol became one of the best-known British furniture companies in the fifties, producing work in the **Contemporary** style.

'Contemporary' Windsor Chair, early 1950s (top), and Traditional Windsor Chair
Ercol produced a good deal of furniture in the Contemporary style during the fifties, but has latterly assumed the role of traditional pasticheur. *This example lacks the guts and integrity of the original.*

Ergonomi Design

Ergonomi Design Gruppen was founded in Sweden in 1979, after the merger of Ergonomi Design with Designgruppen. Its name is derived from **'ergonomics'**, and as this would suggest, the design consultancy is specially concerned with the practical problems of designing everyday tools which work in all circumstances and respects. In particular, Ergonomi's Maria Benktzon (b. 1946) has been involved with the design of cutlery and other manual equipment for the disabled, which has been produced by RFSU Rehab (with aid from the Swedish Government) and by **Gustavsberg**.

Ergonomi Design is a cooperative, its fourteen partners sharing responsibilities and decisions. The company's ethic is: 'The need and desires of the user shall form the basis of the project,' and 'It is vital to work in areas where there are unsolved problems or where the solutions that exist do not satisfy the demands that the user is entitled to make'.

Bread Knife for Physically Handicapped, 1979
The Ergonomi Design Group produced a range of tools and utensils, including this breadknife for people with impaired wrist action, but found that this highly functional design was also liked by people with perfectly healthy wrists.

Ergonomics

Ergonomics is an interdisciplinary science, established during the Second World War, concerned with the relationship of man to machine in the fullest sense. Its main subject is the machine in human work.

In particular, ergonomists study the most comfortable and efficient methods of designing controls and dials, according to the performance of the human hand, eye and brain. Where the hand is concerned an important element is the different types of grip which, in fact, number only four. The first two, the power grip and the precision grip, are the most important because they are the only two which involve fingers and thumb in opposable action. The other two are subsidiary: the hook grip, as used when holding the handle of a suitcase, and the scissors grip, as when holding a cigar. With the eye, ergonomists examine the layout of instruments to find the best way of arranging them so that the operator can work the machine efficiently – any kind of machine is relevant, whether a supersonic jet, a domestic food-mixer, or a hi-fi.

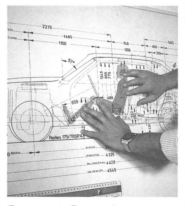

Ergonomic Research at Mercedes-Benz, Stuttgart, early 1980s
As people spend more time in car seats than any other piece of furniture apart from beds, the science of ergonomics has become ever more important to sophisticated car manufacturers.

Vuokko Eskolin-Nurmesniemi

b. 1930

The textile designer Vuokko was born in Helsinki and worked for **Marimekko** before setting up her own firm in 1964. She is married to **Antii Nurmesniemi**, a furniture designer, and is known for bold striped patterns printed on fine, robust cottons. (See also **Finnish design**.)

'Huuto' Fabric, 1964 (left) and 'Iso Tasaraita' Fabric, 1981
The harsh Finnish climate encourages designers to use warm colours for interiors, and Vuokko's fabrics use strong colour fields, as here on these two lounge chairs. Both designs are printed on heavy cotton. The chairs themselves were designed by Antii Nurmesniemi in 1968.

Virgil Exner

Virgil Exner was an office junior in the **General Motors** Styling Studio under **Harley Earl**, but fled to **Chrysler** Corporation in 1957 and donated to the ailing US automobile company some of the glitter, glare and ideas of Harley Earl's Detroit Byzantium.

F

FIAT
Finnish design
Leonardo **Fioravanti**
Elio **Fiorucci**
Richard **Fischer**
Alan **Fletcher**
Flos
Paul **Follot**
Henry **Ford**
Ford of Europe
Fordism
Foreningen
  SvenskForm
Piero **Fornasetti**
Mariano **Fortuny**
Kaj **Franck**
Josef **Frank**
Berndt **Friberg**
Frogdesign
Adrian **Frutiger**
Maxwell **Fry**
Roger **Fry**
Shigeo **Fukuda**
Buckminster **Fuller**
Functionalism
Funkis
Futurism

FIAT

FIAT stands for 'Fabbrica Italiana Automobili Torino'. It is Europe's leading vehicle manufacturer and the largest industrial undertaking in Italy. From its inception FIAT has taken a positive attitude to design: its Lingotto factory outside Turin was heavily influenced by the **Futurists**: Giovanni Agnelli, the founder, asked his architect, Matte-Trusco, to build a race track on the roof (p. 52). Since 1928 FIAT has employed the brilliant designer **Dante Giacosa** as its chief engineer. Under him FIAT has also employed **Ghia**, **Pininfarina** and **Giorgio Giugiaro** as consultant designers, and has produced some of the best-designed cars to come from any of the large international companies. In particular the original 500 of the thirties, the Nuova 500 of the fifties (p. 52), the 127 of the seventies and the Uno of the eighties have led the field in small-car design.

Poster for FIAT Ballila by Marcello Dudovich, 1936
FIAT has a tradition of encouraging the arts and paying careful attention to design in all aspects of its operations.

FIAT 1100, 1953 (centre); FIAT 1100 and 500 B at the Mirafiori factory, Turin, 1948 (below)
The 1100 was one of the first cars to be designed in Italy after the Second World War, and, like the Vespa scooter, its stylish cheapness made it a symbol of the ricostruzione.

Finnish design

Unlike its neighbours, Sweden and Denmark, Finland was late to establish an international design identity. One finally appeared when **Tapio Wirkkala** and **Timo Sarpaneva** exhibited highly expressive art glass at the Milan **Triennales** during the early fifties.

Finnish design since then has tended to be both more sculptural and more exclusive than its other Scandinavian counterparts, and an efficient design publicity machine has evolved to sustain that special image.

In addition to glass, Finnish furniture, ceramics and textiles also have special qualities. From **Aalto** to **Kukkapuro** Finnish furniture combines respect for the nature of materials with a subtle sense of proportion and a feeling for quality, while in ceramics **Arabia** has followed the Swedish model of employing artists to work in its factories. But it is with printed cotton textiles that Finland probably excels: both **Marimekko** and **Vuokko** are well known abroad for their bright, bold fabrics. These very individual contributions have given Finnish design a unique character.

'Plaano' Chair by Yro Kukkapuro, 1978
Kukkapuro's personal style evolved away from the expressive sculptural forms of the sixties towards a leaner and harder aesthetic, in keeping with the more technical terms of the next decade. The 'Plaano' chair has a seat made of pressed birch shavings, supported on an aluminium alloy structure.

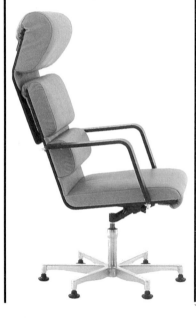

Decanter and Glasses by Timo Sarpaneva, 1979
These show Sarpaneva's preference for slightly mannered, sculptural forms.

'Blue Weed' Tureen by Thure Oberg, 1900; 'Ruska' Tureen by Ulla Procopé, 1960
The Arabia company has a distinguished tradition of ceramic design. Oberg's tureen was shown at the Paris exhibition of 1900; sixty years later Procopé's 'Ruska' had established another stereotype for the table top.

Stacking Stool by Alvar Aalto for Artek, 1933
The beech plywood is laminated in a novel and daring way, but Aalto's now classic design is nevertheless understated.

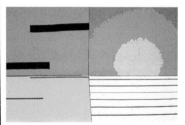

Fabrics by Vuokko (above): 'Iso Sana', 1981 (top left), 'Aurinko', 1964 (top right), 'Sana', 1981 (bottom left), 'Usi Raita', 1981 (bottom right)

'Maisema' Fabric from Marimekko, 1983 (left)

Leonardo Fioravanti

b. 1938

Leonardo Fioravanti joined **Pininfarina** in 1964 after studying mechanical engineering at Milan Polytechnic. His graduate project was for a six-seater **aerodynamic** car, an idea ahead of its time. He is now head of Research and Design at Pininfarina's Cambiano headquarters, where he effectively makes the decisions about what this, the most celebrated of the Torinese coachbuilders, designs.

Fioravanti has created shapes for cars which have been universally celebrated for their beauty and voluptuous elegance. His designs include the experimental BMC 1800 of 1967 (which became the **Citroën** CX and drew on ideas which he had developed while a student), the Ferrari Daytona of 1968, the Ferrari Mondial of 1980 and the Peugeot 205 of 1983. Among the most remarkable cars which Fioravanti has designed is the CNR (for Consiglio Nazionale delle Ricerche) experimental vehicle for aerodynamic research.
Bibliography Vittorio Gregotti *Carrozzeria italiana – cultura e progetto* Alfieri, Turin, 1979

Elio Fiorucci

b. 1935

Elio Fiorucci trained as a shoemaker. He set up his first clothes shop in Milan's Galleria Passarella in 1967 with the aim of bringing the King's Road to Italy. It was designed by **Ettore Sottsass**. Since then Fiorucci shops have become synonymous with **Pop**, Punk and every passing brazen fashion, including what author Eve Babitz called 'junky chic'. Nevertheless, 'Fiorucci' has come to symbolize the avant-garde end of mass-consumed Pop and has been a huge stylistic influence on many areas of production aimed at youthful markets.

In 1974 it was taken over by the major Italian trading company, Montedison, and **Benetton** took a 50 per cent interest in 1981.
Bibliography Eve Babitz *Fiorucci – the Book* Harlin Quist, New York, 1980

Fabric, 1970s
Fiorucci fabrics used a sophisticated refinement of Pop art and cartoon imagery in the seventies.

Richard Fischer

b. 1935

Richard Fischer is of the same generation of German designers as **Dieter Rams** – too young to have participated in the War, but old enough to be imbued with the German tradition in engineering. He first studied mechanical engineering, then went to Ulm to read product design at the **Hochschule für Gestaltung**. Working for **Braun** in Frankfurt from 1960 to 1968, he designed a distinguished series of electric razors. In 1968 he went freelance; perhaps his most successful design of recent years has been the ingenious Minox '35EL' camera of 1972, a marvel of precision engineering, but also a marvel of careful and harmonious design which takes the values of Ulm into the eighties. Since 1972 Fischer has been professor of product design at the Hochschule für Gestaltung in Offenbach.

Alan Fletcher

b. 1931

The British graphic designer Alan Fletcher was trained at the **Royal College of Art** in London and at Yale University's School of Architecture and Design. His career began in New York in the mid-fifties, with jobs for the Container Corporation of America, for *Fortune* magazine and for **IBM**. Back in London in 1959 he formed Fletcher, Forbes & Gill, a firm which did for graphics what **Mary Quant** did for clothes, that is, gave it stylish mass appeal. In 1972 Fletcher, Forbes & Gill became three fifths of the design group **Pentagram**.

Fletcher says he is interested in visual ambiguity and adds 'Function is fine, but solving the problem is not the problem. The problem is adding value, investing solutions with visual surprise and above all with wit. To misquote: "A smile is worth a thousand pictures."'

Flos

Flos was founded in 1960 at Merano in northern Italy, and was intended to pursue research into the use and value of lighting in the home. Its factory moved to Brescia in 1963. Flos is most often associated with the designs of **Achille Castiglioni**, the Milanese architect who has best sensed the possibilities which playing with light offers the designer. Since the Castiglioni-designed shop and showroom opened on the corso Monforte Flos has become an established part of the Milanese design community. A great deal of its reputation has come from Castiglioni's restless inventiveness in lighting design. Flos has acquired **Arteluce** and has associated companies in Germany, France, Switzerland and the United Kingdom.

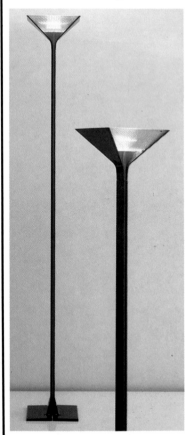

'Papillona' Light by Tobia Scarpa, early 1980s
An up-lighter designed for Flos.

Paul Follot

1877–1941

The decorator Paul Follot's first interior designs were **Art Nouveau**. He matured then into the Frenchified Modernist mode of **Art Deco**, a style whose exclusiveness he can make some claim to have invented. In 1923 Follot became design director of the Bon Marché store and exhibited regularly at the Parisian 'Salon des artistes décorateurs', producing interior designs for the Paris exhibition of 1925, the *annus mirabilis* of Art Deco. His market demanded extravagant materials, fine craftsmanship and the symbolism of luxury. These are what he produced.
Bibliography 'Les Années 25' exhibition catalogue, Musée des Arts Décoratifs, Paris, 1966

Henry Ford

1863–1947

It is unjust that Henry Ford's two pronouncements, about colour and the nature of history, should have become so famous. Ford was not anti-intellectual: he was a friend to Thomas Alva Edison, the inventor, and, when he founded his own museum at Greenfield Village, near Detroit, he said that 'an object can be read like a book . . . if only you know how'. Nor was he contemptuous of the customer: his perfection of series production on assembly lines opened up greater choice to the ordinary customer than ever before. Ford's achievement was an influence on **Walter Gropius** and he was also well acquainted with **Gordon Russell** and Ferdinand **Porsche**.

Henry Ford was born in Springwells township, Michigan, of Irish Protestant stock. It was a remote, rural community and he was struck early in life by the nature of labour there: 'My earliest recollection was that, considering the results, there was too much work on the place.' He started work as a machinist's apprentice and by 1893 had become chief engineer of the Edison Illuminating Company, supplying electric light to urban Detroit. He resigned in 1899 and established the Ford Motor Company in 1903. Success was phenomenally rapid. Between 1908 and 1927 sixteen million Ford Model Ts were produced, and in 1919 it cost Ford $106 million to buy out the minority stock holders. In 1913 he perfected the moving production line, and in 1932 he launched his second most celebrated car, the V8. His son, Edsel, was president of the company from 1919 until he died in 1943. Henry Ford then resumed that role himself until his own death, when his grandson Henry Ford II took over.

Henry Ford's main contribution to design was to translate the methods and ideals of standardization, both aesthetic and practical, into the manufacture of consumer products.

It was in response to Henry Ford's achievements in creating the popular car that Alfred P. Sloan organized **General Motors** and hired **Harley Earl** to give his vehicles style, so that they might be differentiated in the marketplace from the utilitarian products of Ford.

Despite Ford's toughness, he had a strong streak of sentimentality. He named the Fairlane after his grandmother's birthplace and Edsel after his son.
Bibliography Henry Ford *My Life and Work* Doubleday, New York, 1923; Heinemann, London, 1924

Model T, 1909 (above); *Model T Roadster 1926* (left)
The Model T went through nearly twenty years of consistent development. From the early 1909 model to the 1926 Roadster you can trace the evolution of the mass-produced car. The year Model T production ended styling began.

A B C D E F G H I J K L M N O P Q R S T U V W X Y Z

A
B
C
D
E
F
G
H
I
J
K
L
M
N
O
P
Q
R
S
T
U
V
W
X
Y
Z

Ford of Europe

In 1903 the first Ford cars were imported privately into Britain; the Model T arrived in 1909; and separate production began at Dagenham in 1931. With the introduction of the post-War Consul, Zephyr and Zodiac range in 1950, Ford brought a revolution in **styling** to the British market: these were the first cars to introduce the glitter of America to a country just emerging from rationing. In 1962 Ford of Britain produced the Cortina, an extraordinarily successful car, which was drawn by Roy Brown. Brown was a Canadian designer who had been responsible for the disastrous Edsel of 1958. In exile in Dagenham, however, he produced the car that was Britain's Model T. It was a typical Ford product – conservatively engineered, but shrewdly marketed. The name itself was an astute choice, responding to the changing taste of a British public discovering the delights of the Mediterranean. Whereas Ford's previous range had names taken from the classical world, and the Cortina's rivals had the tweedy associations of the university towns, Oxford and Cambridge, after which they were named, the Cortina and its stable-mate the Capri were called after smart but accessible Italian resorts.

Ford's other main European operation was in Germany, where it first imported cars from America in 1907. In 1926 Ford started to produce cars in Germany, having incorporated a factory in 1925 in Berlin. A plant followed in Cologne in 1931, and Henry Ford himself got on well with the leaders of the Nazi regime.

In 1967 Ford of Britain joined with Ford-Werke to become Ford of Europe and the strategy began to change: Ford became more and more conscious of design, and with the launch of **Uwe Bahnsen**'s Sierra in 1982 it established a new standard for design, engineering and packaging for popular cars. (See also pp. 63–4.)
Bibliography 'The Car Programme: 52 Weeks to Job One or how they designed the Ford Sierra' exhibition catalogue, The Boilerhouse Project, Victoria & Albert Museum, London, 1982

Sierra, 1982
The Ford Sierra replaced the old Ford Cortina. Its sophisticated design and engineering signalled a new direction for the hitherto conservative company. (See also p. 64.)

Fordism

Henry Ford is best remembered for his rationalization of the industrial process by the introduction of the moving assembly line in 1913. In this he was influenced by **Taylorism** – Frederick Winslow Taylor's *The Principles of Scientific Management* which proposed that efficient industrial production should entail men working as an analogue of the machine. Ford took the idea a step further and actually replaced men by machines. In fact, the assembly line was not so much an invention of Ford's as the culmination of a tradition of American industrial experiments. However, his system revolutionized the structure of the work process and, in turn, the way industrial products were conceived and designed. Fordism became for architects like **Walter Gropius** an exemplar of what rational industrial society could achieve, and in Europe it became Gropius' ambition to apply Ford's techniques to the construction and design of dwellings (with similar influence, but less happy results).
Bibliography Judith A. Merkle *Management and Ideology* University of California Press, Berkeley and London, 1980

Foreningen SvenskForm see Svenska Sljödföreningen

Piero Fornasetti

b. 1913

Plate from the 'Tema e Variazioni' series. c. 1950
Inspired by Surrealism, Fornasetti makes irreverent use of the art of the past in his individual designs. The effect is both charming and disruptive.

Piero Fornasetti is one of the great independents of Italian design. He is best known for decoration, often Surreal in inspiration, applied to mass-produced furniture and ceramics. Not part of the chic circle which dictates fashions in injection-moulding from the smart salons of central Milan, he comes from a background in the theatre and Surrealist painting, and has said that his greatest fortune was to know the works of the painters Carlo Carrà and Ardengo Soffici, and the Italian school of the nineteenth century, as they have influenced his own idiosyncratic style.

After being expelled from the Liceo Artistico he studied at the Accademia di Belle Arte di Brera and came to notice at a competition sponsored by the Cassa di Risparmio. At the Fifth Milan **Triennale** Fornasetti met

the architect **Gio Ponti**, and the two men worked together on interior designs and *trompe l'oeil* furniture for which Fornasetti designed surface patterns (see p. 160). Fornasetti began to establish a personal character with decorative designs for a set of dinner plates which he called 'Tema e Variazioni'.

Considered an eccentric throughout the fifties, sixties and seventies, now that decoration is being reconsidered Fornasetti's strange and complex pattern-making is accessible to contemporary taste. (See also p. 55.)
Bibliography 'Mobile e oggetti anni '50 di Piero Fornasetti' exhibition leaflet, Mercanteinfiera, Parma, 1983

Mariano Fortuny

1871–1949

Mariano Fortuny y Madrazo was born in Granada, Spain, but was brought up in Rome and Paris, and moved to Venice in 1889. He dabbled in music and stage design, and at the beginning of the century developed his own patent theatrical lights which were eventually manufactured under an arrangement with **AEG**. He was a subtle and distinguished photographer, but is best known as a fashion designer. Fortuny began this aspect of his career by experimenting in 1907 with processes to print and pleat silk, and opened a factory to manufacture it in 1919. From 1907 he also took to producing fashion designs, combining his printed silks with his own versions of classical Greek designs. These dresses became *de rigueur* for a certain species of fashionable, artistic lady during the twenties. He also enjoyed some success as an interior designer.
Bibliography Silvio Fusco et al. *Immagini e materiali del laboratorio Fortuny* Marsilio Editori, Venice, 1978

Kaj Franck

b. 1911

Having trained at Helsinki's Institute of Industrial Art, Kaj Franck worked as an independent designer of lighting, furniture and textiles until 1946, when he joined the **Arabia** ceramic factory as its art director. He retired in 1978. Franck has been one of the most influential and imitated designers of everyday ceramics, and one of the creators of the image of Scandinavian Modern. He injected 'artistic' qualities into Arabia's mass-produced utility wares and his 'Ruska' (p. 125) and 'Kilta' ranges are witnesses of his dedication to quality in the everyday. Franck won a **Compasso d'Oro** award in 1957.

'Teema' Ceramic Dinner Service for Arabia, 1981
Throughout his association with Arabia Kaj Franck has developed a sophisticated language of form for the company's tableware. Never assertive, always practical, Franck's work is characteristic of Finnish design.

Josef Frank

1885–1967

'Primavera' Fabric, 1930s
Frank's fabric was inspired by African and other primitive designs.

The Austrian designer Josef Frank was the main contributing force to the concept dubbed 'Swedish grace' by the English writer P. Morton Shand, to describe a refined, bourgeois, **moderne** style that dominated Swedish taste between the wars.

Frank studied at the Viennese Institute of Technology. He worked in interior design in Germany and became a professor at the Kunstgewerbeschule (school of applied art) in Vienna in 1919. Here he knew and worked with **Peter Behrens** and **Josef Hoffmann**, ran his own interior design firm called Haus und Garten, and designed some bentwood furniture for **Thonet**.

Although Frank had been firmly entrenched in the **Modern Movement** he changed direction when he was

introduced to Sweden by his Swedish-born wife. He began what was to become a life-long association with that country when he first worked for Estrid Ericson's **Svenskt Tenn** store in 1932, and settled in Stockholm in 1934. Apart from 1941–6, when he was professor of architecture at the New School for Social Research in New York, he lived there for the rest of his life.

In Sweden he was able to develop an individual style of interior design, which respected the principles of the Modern Movement, but which was also genuinely responsive to popular taste. He had already expressed reservations about ▶

A
B
C
D
E
F
G
H
I
J
K
L
M
N
O
P
Q
R
S
T
U
V
W
X
Y
Z

too thoroughgoing an interpretation of **Functionalism** in a book, *Architektur als Symbol*, in 1931. In it he quoted Goethe in claiming that architecture was not just about building structures, but about creating sentiment, and he scorned the austere aestheticism of, say, **Mies van der Rohe**, only permitting tubular steel chairs in the garden.

Frank designed furniture, wallpaper, fabrics and lamps. His fabrics used bright, floral patterns, reflecting his conviction that 'a plain surface is tiring; the more pattern the more peaceful the effect'. His furniture expressed (and delivered) comfort, and his lamps, often employing brass, possess what his friend Eva von Zweigbergk called a 'refined neutrality'. Frank wanted his chairs to be complementary to the human body, so that any comfortable chair would necessarily have a complicated shape, and he thought that 'those who choose chairs with square seats harbour totalitarian thoughts in some corner of their hearts'. He considered orderliness to be deathly.

Today Frank's work has high social status in Sweden and is much sought after.
Bibliography 'Josef Frank' exhibition catalogue, National Museum, Stockholm, 1968

Berndt Friberg

1899–1981

The ceramic designer Berndt Friberg was born in Sweden. From 1934 he worked at **Gustavsberg** as a craftsman whose job was to make unique pieces intended not for mass-production but to act as an inspiration for the other designers. His work is characterized by sophisticated glazes and subtle surface colouring.

Frogdesign

Frogdesign is based in Altensteig and is one of Germany's most egregious independent design consultancies. It was founded in 1969 by Hartmut Esslinger (b. 1945), who studied electrical engineering at the University of Stuttgart and the Fachhochschule für Design in Gmund.

Clients include **AEG**, the luxury baggage-maker Louis Vuitton, **Erco** and Apple Computer. Esslinger became associated with **Sony** when the Japanese firm bought out his client, Wega Radio of Stuttgart. Frogdesign's house style is recognizably German, in the tradition of **Dieter Rams**, but adds more colourful and more organic elements to Rams' austere repertoire.

'Concept 51K' Hi-Fi for Wega Radio, 1978
Frogdesign worked for Stuttgart's Wega Radio, before the company was taken over by Sony. Its designs, such as the 'Concept 51', were a slick and commercial version of Dieter Rams' more austere style.

Adrian Frutiger

b. 1928

As a young man Adrian Frutiger was apprenticed to a typographer, and at the Beaux-Arts school in Zürich he specialized in drawing letter-forms. He then became a typographer himself.

Frutiger is one of the inventors of the 'Swiss style' of sans serif faces which became identified with 'modern' during the later fifties and sixties. In 1952 he joined the Fonderie Deberny-Peignot in Paris, and it was while working there that he developed the 'Univers' typeface in 1954.

'Univers' is a sophisticated and much used family of founts in seven different weights, each one capable of being used with the next.

In 1960 he joined with Bruno Pfaffli (b. 1935) to form the Atelier Frutiger & Pfaffli in Paris.
Bibliography Philip B. Meggs *A History of Graphic Design* Allen Lane, London, 1983

Maxwell Fry

b. 1899

The English architect E. Maxwell Fry was born in Wallasey, Cheshire, and studied at Liverpool School of Architecture. From Sir Charles Reilly and Patrick Abercrombie, professors of architecture and town planning respectively, he received a disciplined, classical training. However, Fry became disenchanted with the traditional architectural styles, which he felt to be irrelevant to

the twentieth century, and, after a short period working in New York and in a London town planning office, he joined the group surrounding **Wells Coates** and **Jack Pritchard**. In 1931 he was one of the founders of the Modern Architecture Research Group (**MARS**), a dedicated group of professionals determined to introduce modern architecture into Britain. Troughout the decade before the War Fry built more or less distinguished houses and flats in and around London in the **International Style**, but perhaps his greatest influence on British taste was not his buildings themselves but his achievement in luring **Walter Gropius** and **Marcel Breuer** to England after the Nazis created an atmosphere unsympathetic to their work and ideals in Germany. Fry was also concerned with functional interior planning and with his wife, Jane Drew, he designed fitted kitchens which made early use of modern materials and electrical appliances. They exhibited a compact kitchen at the **Victoria and Albert Museum**'s 'Britain Can Make It' exhibition of 1946.

Roger Fry

1866–1934

Roger Fry studied at Cambridge, and then studied dilettantism. He was a so-so painter and art critic of, among other publications, *The Burlington Magazine*. His main contribution to design was to found the **Omega** workshop in 1913.

Shigeo Fukuda

b. 1932

Shigeo Fukuda is a Japanese graphic designer who has specialized in posters and commercial graphics, and also designed the signing systems for the Winter Olympics at Sapporo in 1972.

Buckminster Fuller

1895–1983

Richard Buckminster Fuller was one of the most ardent and prolix supporters of high technology. Although his actual material creations were relatively few, the apocalyptic, prophetic character of his writings and thought have in recent years made him the darling of **High-Tech** architects and of all designers who are concerned with the earth's resources.

Fuller was born at Milton, Massachusetts. He never had any formal architectural training; in fact he never had much formal training of any sort. Traditional building techniques came to antagonize him, and in 1927 he created the concept of a 'Dymaxion' house – a name he coined by combining 'dynamic' with 'maximum'. It was not to use bricks and mortar, timber and lath, but was to be a tensile, domed structure where the fabric would be used as a grid to supply the services man needed for survival. A 'Dymaxion' car followed in 1932. Ironically, when the house was tested in 1940 in Wichita, it in fact proved expensive and ill-suited to either mass-production or to housing. The car was equally ill-considered. However, his Geodesic dome, an extension of the principle, was used as the US Pavilion at Expo 67 in Montreal, and much influenced those interested in alternative technology.

Fuller's books are his best memorial: *Nine Chains to the Moon* (1938), *No More Second Hand God* (1963) and *Operating Manual for Spaceship Earth* (1969). Fuller was called 'the first poet of technology'. He was an idealist who viewed the world as a single entity, without national boundaries, and who was committed to the idea that design should serve the needs of man, not of industry.

Functionalism

Functionalism is often confused with the **Modern Movement**, although it is in fact two hundred years older, having been a philosophy before it was a movement in architecture and design. At its most simple, Functionalism proposes that the beauty and value of an object or an edifice depends on its fitness for its purpose. This view is even older than eighteenth-century Rationalism: in his *Memorabilia* Xenophon makes the philosopher Socrates say that a dung basket is superior to a golden shield if the one is better made than the other.

This point of view was somewhat modified by **Walter Gropius** and others, who wholly identified Functionalism with the form and spirit of the machine. However, as **Reyner Banham** pointed out in his book, *Theory and Design in the First Machine Age*, there was not much that was necessarily 'functional' about sitting on a metal chair, with a bare globe in a white room. Because the Functionalists' understanding of form was determined by the construction and materials of the object rather than by its purpose, it was an introverted philosophy of design which made no reference to the use to which an object was to be put. The American architect Louis Sullivan, who said 'form ever follows function', took *his* inspiration from biological growth, not from any abstract principle.

Bibliography E.R. de Zurko *Origins of Functionalist Theory* Columbia University Press, New York, 1957

'Dymaxion' Car, 1932
Buckminster Fuller applied the structural theories of his 'Dymaxion' house to the design of cars. They were never produced commercially.

Funkis

The Funkis were some Finnish architects and designers who tried to promote **Functionalism** in Finland during the thirties.

Futurism

The Italian Futurist Movement was the first group of artists and writers to celebrate the seductive power of the machine. The leading spirit was the poet Filippo Marinetti, a friend of d'Annunzio, the unseen legislator of Fascism. Marinetti's acoustic poem 'The Raid on Adrianople' celebrated the first use of aircraft in military action. He also wrote *La Cucina Futurista*, whose recipes cited gasoline as a useful ingredient. As well as being inspired by the dynamism of the 'mass' environment, some of the Futurists aimed to contribute to it. Sant'Elia, the architect, was, however, killed in the First World War before his projects for cities could be realized (he anticipated an environment dictated by modes of transport). In the thirties Giacomo Balla and others applied their vision to ceramics and interiors.

Bibliography Raffaele Carrieri *Futurism* Edizioni del Milione, Milan, 1961; Marianne W. Martin *Futurist Art and Theory 1909–1915* Oxford University Press, London, 1968; 'Futurism' exhibition catalogue, Beinecke Rare Book and Manuscript Library, Yale University, 1983

G

Emile **Gallé**
Abram **Games**
Gatti, Paolini, Teodoro
Antoni **Gaudí I Cornet**
Dino **Gavina**
General Motors
German design
Ghia
Dante **Giacosa**
Sigfried **Giedion**
Eric **Gill**
Ernest **Gimson**
Alexander **Girard**
Ernesto **Gismondi**
W.H. **Gispen**
Giorgio **Giugiaro**
GK Industrial Design Associates
Milton **Glaser**
John **Gloag**
G-Plan
Kenneth **Grange**
Michael **Graves**
Eileen **Gray**
Milner **Gray**
Great Exhibition of the Industry of All Nations
Horatio **Greenough**
Eugene **Gregorie**
Vittorio **Gregotti**
Hermann **Gretsch**
Walter **Gropius**
Group of Ten
Gruppo Strum
Gucci
Hans **Gugelot**
Lurelle **Guild**
Hector **Guimard**
Gustavsberg

Emile Gallé

1846–1904

The glass-maker Emile Gallé was educated as a mineralogist and worked at the Meisenthal glassworks before travelling to England in 1871, where he studied the oriental glass in the South Kensington collections. The first important exhibition of his work was in 1884 at the Union Centrale des Art Décoratifs in Paris. By 1890 he was running a factory providing for the tastes of the new consuming class who, rejecting High Victorian bourgeois cut-glass, favoured instead the sensuous, colourful shapes of **Art Nouveau** (to which glass lent itself so readily). Between his death in 1904 and its closure at the beginning of the First World War, Gallé's factory continued to turn out designs which were essays in expressive form and colour. His achievement was to introduce artistic freedom into glassware and to popularize Art Nouveau.
Bibliography Jean-Claude Groussard & Francis Roussel *Nancy Architecture 1900* exhibition catalogue, Secrétariat de l'Etat à la Culture, Nancy, 1976

Glass Ewer Mounted in Silver and Gilt, c. 1870
Gallé thought of himself as an artist working in glass. His early designs, like this one, were influenced by his study of botany.

Abram Games

b. 1914

The British graphic designer Abram Games was the last master of the drawn lithograph before photography almost completely dominated poster design. Like Lewitt & Him and **Henrion**, Games was one of several Jewish graphic designers who gave the British profession its strength at the mid-century (although, unlike the others, Games was not an émigré). In the late thirties he designed posters for Shell, BP and the War Office; the latter were masterful expressions of his philosophy 'maximum meaning, minimum means'. It was his wartime work, however, doing propaganda for the Ministry of Information, that secured his reputation. In 1951 he was put in charge of graphics for the Festival of Britain, whose logogram he designed, and throughout the following decade he made a most distinguished contribution to the quality of British street life with his colourful and visually witty posters for British European Airways, the *Financial Times* and El Al. He was a guest speaker at the 1959 **Aspen** conference and published his book *Over My Shoulder* in 1960.

'Army: The Worthwhile Job' Poster, early 1940s
Abram Games was the last master of the drawn lithograph before photography replaced traditional techniques in poster design.

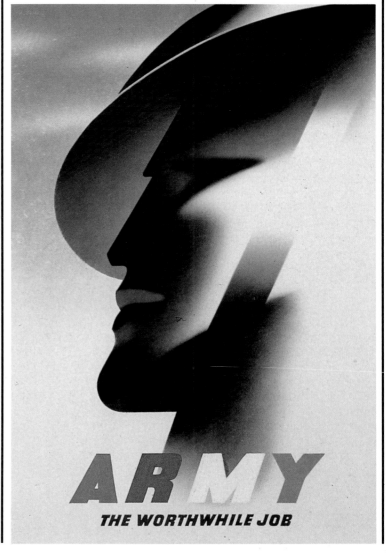

Gatti, Paolini, Teodoro

Piero Gatti (b. 1940), Cesare Paolini (b. 1937) and Franco Teodoro (b. 1939) formed their design group in Turin in 1965, almost a twin to the Milanese **De Pas, D'Urbino and Lomazzi**. They were influenced by current theories of 'radical design' and became famous for the 'Sacco' chair of 1969, produced by **Zanotta** out of polystyrene balls.

'Sacco' Chair, 1969
The 'Sacco' chair was a large, loose, leather (or plastic) bag half-filled with tiny, flexible balls of expanded polystyrene. Designed by Gatti, Paolini and Teodora and manufactured by Zanotta in 1969, it represented the popular face of Italian radical design.

Antoni Gaudí I Cornet

1852–1926

Gaudí was a Spanish Catalan architect who designed no mass-produced consumer products, but who has nonetheless had a remarkable influence on twentieth-century taste.

He was trained in Barcelona during the time when the Gothic Revival was popular amongst leading architects and, in particular, was influenced by Viollet-le-Duc, the great French architectural thinker. A religious man, Gaudí's first commissions were for church furniture and metalwork, but an invitation to design cast iron street lamps for Barcelona in 1879 involved him in civic architecture. Some major houses followed: Casa Vicens (1883–5) and the Palacio Guell (1885–90), where he also designed the furniture. Gaudí's style evolved into a highly personal mixture of Gothic and Moorish, with a large element of his own invention. Although he was an unclassifiable genius, Gaudí's free play in design and his willingness to subjugate all rules (including those of construction) to the god of expression made him an important influence on much of the avant-garde art and design of the twentieth century.

Evelyn Waugh made some typically acute and two-edged remarks about Gaudí's designs in a book about his travels: 'I could easily have employed a happy fortnight at Barcelona tracking down further examples of Gaudism. He designed many things besides houses, I believe, making it his special province to conceive designs for tables and chairs and other objects of common utility which would render them unfit for their ostensible purposes.'

Gaudí was a pioneer of the architectural model as a means of expression, but despite the rationality of the model-maker's technique he was an eccentric at heart: it was said that he conducted the building workers on the church of La Sagrada Familia (which remains uncompleted today) with a conductor's baton. When his body was found after he had been run over and killed by a tram, his shabby clothes led his discoverers to believe that he was a vagrant, not Spain's greatest architect.
Bibliography George Collins *Antoni Gaudí* Mayflower, London, 1960

Dino Gavina

b. 1932

Dino Gavina founded an Italian furniture manufacturing company which was absorbed by **Knoll** in 1968. It was Gavina who made **Marcel Breuer** into a celebrated furniture designer, acquiring the rights to his tubular steel designs and shrewdly marketing them with names instead of Germanic numbers. This acquisition brought Breuer's 'Cesca', 'Wassily' and 'Laccio' chairs and tables into the Knoll catalogue (p. 171). (At the same time and in the same deal, Knoll also acquired the rights to the furniture of **Cini Boeri** and **Tobia Scarpa**, which Gavina also manufactured.)

General Motors

In founding the General Motors Corporation Alfred P. Sloan did for industrial production what Karl Marx had done for political economy: he imposed a whole, new structure upon something that was hitherto indeterminate.

The world's largest industrial undertaking began in 1908 when William C. Durant founded the General Motors Company. Through take-overs, deals, bids, counter-bids, exchanges of stock and other financial machinations, Sloan created a corporation in 1919 which represented the greater part of American vehicle manufacturing interests. Sloan himself wrote, 'No two men better understood the opportunity presented by the automobile . . . than Mr Durant and Mr **Ford**.'

One of Sloan's greater *coups* was in recognizing that appearance would sell cars, and in hiring **Harley Earl** to mastermind their design. From 1925 to 1959 the story of General Motors is really the story of Harley Earl, and from then to his retirement in 1978 it is that of **Bill Mitchell**.

In the early eighties the once impregnable General Motors felt an icy economic wind, and as if to underline America's industrial decline, an extraordinary announcement was made in February 1984. Cadillac, the division that hired Harley Earl to give style to America's master product, entered into a $606 million contract with **Pininfarina** to buy bodies designed and manufactured in Turin for a new Cadillac product to be launched in 1986. Part of the crisis following **Ralph Nader**'s attack on the General was a progressive dilution of the market profile of its most famous products. Cadillac was beginning to lose the identity which Earl and Bill Mitchell had created for it, but now the torch had to be handed to Italians because America had become conscious of 'designer' labels: the generation that bought Armani jeans might now buy a Pininfarina Cadillac.
Bibliography Alfred P. Sloan *My Years at General Motors* Doubleday, New York, 1963; Stephen Bayley *Harley Earl and The Dream Machine* Weidenfeld, London, 1983; Knopf, New York, 1983

Chevrolet Logo, 1950s
Styling motifs developed by General Motors spread a certain image of America across the globe. (See also p. 228.)

A
B
C
D
E
F
G
H
I
J
K
L
M
N
O
P
Q
R
S
T
U
V
W
X
Y
Z

German design

German products have a 'rational' style. Simple shapes, undecorated surfaces, and purity of colour and detail have become the tokens of German design. This approach has its origins in the **Deutsche Werkbund**, an organization which sought to ally art with industry and to impose standardization. This concept of standardization had aesthetic and organizational implications which formed the basis for all subsequent German design.

It was Germany that responded most enthusiastically to the ideas about scientific management established in the United States by F.W. Taylor. The **Bauhaus** (although it had an early phase that was expressionistic) supported rational forms, while companies such as **AEG**, Arzberg, Bosch and **Rosenthal** evolved a simple, rational aesthetic for their products.

In the years after the Second World War Germany was quick to re-establish its industrial supremacy, while sustaining its pre-War design concerns. At the **Hochschule für Gestaltung** in Ulm and with **Braun**, the German ideal always seemed to be reason and purity in front of emotion and complexity. An engineering tradition, exemplified by **Porsche**, has

given esoteric support to this national preference, and has also tended to mean, with the exception of global stars such as **Dieter Rams**, that the designer is an anonymous figure.

The German contribution to the twentieth century has been huge: the most respected products of industry – the **Volkswagen**, Braun appliances, Nixdorf computers, Rosenthal ceramics – as well as the entire Bauhaus tradition, all demonstrate the qualities of integrity and reason on which the reputation of German design is founded. (See also pp. 62–3.)

Full-Size Rendering of Mercedes-Benz 190, c. 1982
The company's design studio produces large-scale drawings for the initial assessment of a new car. The resolution of the design of the radiator grille is said to have taken two years.

'5002E' Drill for Bosch, 1984
Bosch's drills rely on a tradition begun by designer Erich Slany of using a strongly metaphoric style. They are made to look like military equipment, a likeness enhanced by their olive drab plastic shells.

Shaver for Braun by Dieter Rams, 1960
Shavers were the staple in Braun's post-War recovery, the first products to be invested with the company's highly successful 'design' image developed by chief designer Dieter Rams. (See also p. 62.)

BMW K100 RS Motorbike, 1984
Japanese competition forced a change in BMW bike design. The K100 RS had a straight four-cyclinder engine, and epitomized the German taste for refined engineering and exquisite detail. (See also p. 94.)

Ghia

Giacinto Ghia (1887–1944) was born in Turin and learnt production techniques in the workshops of Diatto. Although from a simple background, Ghia soon specialized in luxury sporting cars. Mario Boana continued the tradition when he took over after Ghia's death. Designs coming from Ghia's shop have included the **Volkswagen** Karmann-Ghia (1961), the de Tomaso Mangusta (1966) and the Maserati Ghibli (1968). In 1972, in order to acquire the advantages of an Italian coach-building concern, Ghia was taken over by **Ford**, which now uses the Torinese shop as an experimental station to complement the work done at its own design centres at Dunton in England and Merkenich in Germany.

FIAT 2100S Coupé, 1960
Ghia's design for FIAT's 2100S coupé was first seen at the Turin Motor Show of 1960. Ghia began its business fabricating designs of Bertone, but developed its own styling function. This FIAT coupé shows that while Ghia was able to design cars with personality, it lacked the capacity for elegance so often achieved by its rivals.

Dante Giacosa
b. 1905

'Zero A', 1934
Dante Giacosa, FIAT's chief engineer and designer for almost fifty years, stands next to 'Zero A', the prototype of the 500, on top of the Andrate Pass.

Dante Giacosa was born in Rome and joined FIAT in 1926. He initially designed liquid-cooled aero engines, but was soon to make his name as the greatest of all Italian auto-engineers.

Giacosa transferred to FIAT's car division in the early thirties with the brief to develop a well-engineered, sophisticated, but simple small car, an Italian equivalent to **Boulanger**'s **Citroën** 2CV and **Porsche**'s **Volkswagen**. He responded by producing the 500A in 1936, a car which became known by the affectionate name of 'Topolino' ('Little Mouse'). It was the greatest advance in small car design since the launch of the Austin 7 in 1922, and became the best-selling import in the United States in 1938–9. The 500B introduced in 1948 was a substantial modification and came to be identified world-wide with post-War **Italian design**, like the **Vespa** and the **Olivetti** typewriter. The 500C followed in 1959, and when the line was abandoned (after selling 3.7 million vehicles) in 1955, it was to make way for another Giacosa design, the Nuova 500. Giacosa was also responsible for the conception and execution of the FIAT 124, 128 and 130.
Bibliography Dante Giacosa *I miei quaranti anni alla FIAT* Automobilia, Turin, 1979

A
B
C
D
E
F
G
H
I
J
K
L
M
N
O
P
Q
R
S
T
U
V
W
X
Y
Z

Sigfried Giedion

1888–1968

Sigfried Giedion was a Swiss art-historian whose influence on modern thought equals that of **Nikolaus Pevsner** and, later, **Reyner Banham**.

Giedion studied under Heinrich Wölfflin, who had himself been a pupil of Jakob Burckhardt. He was adept at establishing categories in art history and laying out new areas for research – in fact, his doctoral thesis of 1922 coined the term 'Romantic Classicism'. His second book, *Building in France– Building in Iron– Building in Concrete*, used **Moholy-Nagy** as typographer and was published in 1928. In the same year he was appointed secretary of CIAM, and for more than twelve years Giedion, although a historian, devoted himself to the practical matter of promoting modern architecture. In 1938, via **Gropius**, he was invited to deliver the Charles Eliot Norton lectures at Harvard and these were published in 1941 as *Space, Time and Architecture*. Seven years later his greatest book, *Mechanization Takes Command*, appeared. This was a magnificent work, a fitting contribution to the tradition of all-embracing cultural history established by Burckhardt, whose scriptural presence can be perceived on every page. *Mechanization Takes Command* puts forward the case for technological determinism, arguing that the character of the modern world and its artefacts is continuously moderated by scientific progress. With its analyses of the Yale lock, the Colt revolver (pp. 21–2), the Pullman car, and air-conditioning, this study made the history of art into the history of things. The book emphasized the anonymous, technical aspects of history, instead of the creative individual, and thus reversed the approach of conventional art history.

Bibliography Sigfried Giedion *Bauen in Frankreich* Leipzig and Berlin, 1928; Sigfried Giedion *Space, Time and Architecture* Harvard University Press, Cambridge, Mass., 1941; Oxford University Press, London, 1941; Sigfried Giedion *Mechanization Takes Command: a contribution to anonymous history* Oxford University Press, New York, 1948; *Hommage à Giedion* Birkhauser, Basle & Stuttgart, 1972.

The 'Gill Sans' Typeface, 1928
The typeface was designed for the Monotype Corporation. It is a paradox that Gill's square-cut, sans serif face became a symbol of the Modern Movement (especially after it was adopted by the LNER railway company in 1929), while Gill himself was a reclusive craftsman. The typeface is the one used in the setting of this book.

Eric Gill

1882–1940

Eric Gill was a fantastically prolific engraver, type-designer, sculptor, stone-carver and writer. He produced architectural carvings for Westminster Cathedral and the BBC's Broadcasting House, but he is best remembered for the design of the 'Gill Sans' typeface for the Monotype Corporation. This 'grotesque' (square-cut, sans serif) face became, for many people, the symbol of Modernism in England.

Gill was possessed by a social ideal loosely modelled on the early Christian communities. He also had a mystical approach to the handicrafts, and David Kindersley, a stone-cutting apprentice in Gill's last workshop at Piggotts in Buckinghamshire, recalled that he was taught an 'all-pervading truth in the making of simple objects'. Gill's ideas about life and work, with their romantic anti-capitalism and exaltation of worthy toil, have been crucially influential not only on the recent **Crafts Revival**, but also on an entire generation of students (including Terence Conran) that was exposed to his or his disciples' teaching.

Gill's professional life began with an apprenticeship to the minor Gothic Revival architect, W.H. Caröe. At the same time

he was a student at Lethaby's **Central School of Art** in London, where he studied lettering under **Edward Johnston**. He dallied with the **Arts and Crafts**, but had dissociated himself from it by 1909. Instead, he found what he was looking for in the Church and became a Catholic in 1913. Religion and socialism went hand in hand for Gill, and he set up workshops in Ditchling in Sussex and Capel-y-ffin in Wales, where he taught students much like a medieval master with his apprentices. He left behind a portfolio of ideas which were not merely eccentric but which prefigure recent left-wing thinking about the structure of the economy. Gill knew that the problem was not just that working men should have access to *more* of the wealth, but that the means of producing the wealth should be changed.
Bibliography Brian Keeble *A Holy Tradition of Working: passages from the writings of Eric Gill* Golganooza Press, 1983

Ernest Gimson

1864–1919

The furniture designer and craftsman Ernest Gimson moved with the **Barnsley Brothers** to the Cotswolds in 1895 and, life imitating art, set up a workshop like **William Morris'** at Daneway House in 1902. Gimson is best known for his architecture and furniture designs, which were firmly entrenched in British rural traditions and which were loyal to the **Arts and Crafts** ideals of natural materials and simple forms.

Alexander Girard

b. 1907

Alexander Girard, American architect and interior designer, came to fame in 1949 when he created the influential 'For Modern Living' exhibition on modern design at the Detroit Institute of Arts. In 1951 he was, with **Eero Saarinen**, a colour consultant to **General Motors**, and from 1952 was working for **Herman Miller** as a designer of furniture, fabrics, showrooms and shops. He introduced colour and pattern into Herman Miller's previously austere range of merchandise. He has run architectural offices in Florence, New York and Detroit and established the Girard Foundation at his home in Santa Fe, New Mexico, where he maintains an international collection of toys and 'objects of whimsy' from all over the world.

Girard won an Architectural League Silver Medal for design and craftsmanship for his 1960 interior design for the Fonda del Sol restaurant in New York's Time-Life Building; the design was colourful and exuberant, using collage techniques and evoking South American folklore, but at the same time was highly disciplined and controlled. His most celebrated commission was to redesign the entire appearance of the Texan airline, Braniff International. Taking his brief as being 'to destroy the monotony', in 1965 Girard created for Braniff a **corporate identity** which had every plane in the fleet a different colour: 'this idea was to make a plane like a racing car – with the fuselage painted a solid colour clearly expressing its shape. Incidentally, it couldn't be a simpler or cheaper method of achieving identity.'
Bibliography Alexander Girard *The Magic of a People* Viking, New York, 1968

La Fonda del Sol Restaurant, Time-Life Building, New York, 1960
Alexander Girard has a long-established interest in Latin American popular culture which he projected in the collage techniques used in this celebrated restaurant design.

Textile Design for Herman Miller
Girard uses strong colours with great control and subtlety.

Ernesto Gismondi

b. 1931

Ernesto Gismondi is professor of rocket technology at Milan Polytechnic and owner of the furniture manufacturer **Artemide**. As Artemide, at the pinnacle of the design establishment, gives practical support to the radical group **Memphis**, Gismondi maintains the Machiavellian position of being the *éminence grise* behind both the Milanese establishment and the Milanese avant-garde which is struggling to undermine it.

W.H. Gispen

b. 1890

A Dutch furniture designer, W.H. Gispen studied at the Academie van Beeldende Kunst in Rotterdam. In 1916 he founded a Werkstätte für Kunstgewerbegegenstande aus Metall (workshop for applied art forms in metal). He began producing lights in 1929 and chairs in 1930; with his countryman **Mart Stam**, Gispen was among the first **Modern Movement** designers to make furniture in metal.
Bibliography Otakar Macel & Jan van Geest *Stühle aus Stahl* Walther König, Cologne, 1980

Giorgio Giugiaro

b. 1938

Giorgio Giugiaro studied at the Academy of Fine Arts in Turin, and at seventeen went to work for **FIAT**. At twenty-one he joined **Nuccio Bertone** and in 1965 became chief executive of the design centre of **Ghia**. He set up his own firm, ItalDesign, in 1968.

Giugiaro is one of the most imitated and innovative of all consultant product designers: his work combines style with a sympathy for technology that is rare in **Italian design**. While still with Bertone he designed the **Alfa Romeo** Giulia GT, a car widely considered to be one of the understated classics of all time. At ItalDesign Giugiaro's esoteric influence was huge before he became known as a cult figure. ItalDesign worked on the Alfa Romeo Alfasud (1971), on the **Volkswagen** Golf (1974) and on the FIAT Panda (1980). The oil crisis of 1973 stimulated a change in Giugiaro's views about design. Having established a particular mode of stylish sporting car, he changed to a more practical, more functional one. He even began to practise a form of **obsolescence**, saying: 'I contributed to making the long, low, sleek car fashionable, and now it is time to change. I have

to eat, you know.' Since the firm has become recognized as *the* leading Italian car design consultancy, more and more effort has gone into producing speculative dream cars, unveiled to the industry of the world at every year's Turin Motor Show. Of these, the Medusa of 1980 and the Capsula of 1983 have, with their respective concerns for **aerodynamics** and modularity, predicted the preoccupations of the major manufacturers.

Giugiaro designs sewing-machines for **Necchi** (p. 56), cameras for Nikon, watches for Seiko, crash-helmets for Shoiei and furniture for Tecno. While his car designs all share a crisp, razor-edged elegance, Giugiaro's product designs can be recognized by a deliberately 'technical' aesthetic.

In all his designs Giugiaro does more than offer his clients dramatic and persuasive renderings of projects-to-be. For instance, with the FIAT Panda the first stage of the presentation included two full-scale models, four alternative solutions for the sides, a buck of the passenger compartment and a comprehensive comparative study putting the Panda-to-be alongside its competitors. When these proposals were approved, ItalDesign was requested to

start production studies, build a master model and design provisional tooling and engineer pre-production prototypes. Within a year ItalDesign had produced twenty rolling chassis.

Bibliography 'Giorgetto Giugiaro: Nascita del progetto' exhibition catalogue, Tecno, Milan, 1983

'Chronograph' for Seiko, early 1980s
The success of the Volkswagen Golf brought Giugiaro's studios a great variety of work. For the Japanese Seiko company he designed electronic watches, rich with the symbolism of high technology.

Volkswagen Golf, 1974
Giugiaro's most influential design was the Volkswagen Golf of 1974. With its razor-edged look Giugiaro created a new metaphor in car body design which produced a whole stream of imitators. It had its critics, such as Ford's Uwe Bahnsen, who called it a product of 'the origami school of design', but Volkswagen was so pleased that when the time came in 1983 to replace the old model the company's own chief designer, Herbert Schäfer, merely refined Giugiaro's original shape.

'Voiello' Pasta, 1983
Giugiaro had become so confident of his powers by 1983 that he even designed some pasta, looking at Italy's traditional food as a problem in industrial design. He claims that his pasta cooks more easily and that the channels allow the sauce to adhere more efficiently.

GK Industrial Design Associates

GK is an independent Japanese design group founded in 1957 and run by **Kenji Ekuan.** (See also **Japanese design**.)

Nikon Camera, late 1970s
Giugiaro produced a subtle re-working of Nikon's single lens reflex camera, making the details better coordinated and using ergonomics to determine the position of the controls.
(See also p. 57.)

Milton Glaser

b. 1929

Milton Glaser is the most celebrated living American graphic designer. He was born in New York and studied at Manhattan's High School of Music and Art until 1946, and at the Cooper Union until 1951. In 1952–3 he won a Fulbright scholarship which took him to Italy where he studied at Bologna and learnt print-making techniques from the artist Giorgio Morandi. On his return to the United States he founded the **Push Pin Studio** (with colleagues Seymour Chwast and Ed Sorel). In 1968 Glaser began an important association with Clay Felker, a publisher, designing the influential *New York* magazine, a resuscitated version of a Sunday supplement from an admired, but defunct, newspaper. *New York* not only established new standards in graphic design but also a specialist category in the publishing market. It was widely imitated.

The popular and critical success enjoyed by *New York*, at least until it was taken over by Rupert Murdoch in 1977, gave Glaser terrific puissance in the field of magazine design. In 1973 he redesigned *Paris Match*, the French weekly news magazine, and *Village Voice; L'Europeo, Le Jardin des modes, New West, L'Express*

and *Esquire* soon followed.

In 1974 Glaser began to undertake major supergraphics for architectural interiors: a fresco for the New Federal Office Building in Indianapolis and the restaurants in New York's World Trade Center. In the same year he designed the whole interior and fittings for the Childcraft store in New York and in 1980 was commissioned to create an entire graphic character for the Grand Union supermarket chain – everything from label and package design to the **corporate identity**, shop-fittings and interiors (p. 110).

Milton Glaser has expanded the role of the graphic designer and openly sees himself as an artist: 'I feel a great personal identification with Piero della Francesca,' he has remarked. He is, however, less reverent about art in his posters: to advertise **Ettore Sottsass'** 'Valentine' typewriter for **Olivetti**, Glaser used a detail from a Piero di Cosimo painting, declaring that 'the whole visual history of the world is my resource'. The most striking thing about Glaser's work seen as a whole is the diversity of styles which he has employed, in order, he says, to obviate boredom: 'anything I did long enough to master was no longer useful to me.' If there is any feature that unites his work in this diversity it is the frequent use of tight, nervy typography together with a taste for images, as in his famous Bob Dylan poster, which can be read in two ways – a technique derived from **Surrealism**.

Glaser has said that being born Jewish in New York has helped him to assume his huge range of reference: it is much the same to him whether he is commissioned to design all the jackets for the Signet Shakespeare or the poster for a Stevie Wonder concert.

Bibliography Peter Mayer *Graphic Design: Milton Glaser* Overlook Press, New York, 1972

Ambler Music Festival / Institute of Temple University

Poster for the Amber Music Festival, 1968
A masterpiece of contemporary graphics and characteristic of Glaser's style. Effective graphic design often depends on visual puns: Glaser makes the treble clef work twice, once as musical notation and then as a flower.

Poster for XIV Olympic Winter Games in Sarajevo, 1980
Glaser's graphic style contains many light-hearted references to fine art, and its inventiveness and wit has influenced an entire generation of students. The imaginative imagery of this poster plays with a common symbol of the classical world.

XIV OLYMPIC WINTER GAMES SARAJEVO 1984 YUGOSLAVIA

A B C D E F G H I J K L M N O P Q R S T U V W X Y Z

John Gloag

1896–1981

John Gloag was a writer of wide-ranging interests who came to architecture and design during the thirties when, under the influence of the BBC's promotion of both the theory and practice of design, the subject became as important a part of popular culture as the movies were to be in the seventies.

Gloag wrote more than eighty books in all, and in researching those on design met many of the pioneers of the consultant design profession, especially in America: he said **Walter Dorwin Teague** had 'an ecclesiastical air', and thought

Raymond Loewy a 'bit of a spiv'. The English in general, he believed, were a 'lot of insensitive clots' and that was why **Industrial design**, as a profession, was slower to catch on in Britain than in the United States. One of Gloag's missions in his writing was to introduce the English to American achievements in the organization of design, as well as to try to persuade his conservative countrymen to adopt new materials, such as **plastics**.

Although an important popularizer, Gloag's books have not stood the test of time and are only really of antiquarian, historiographical value today.

G-Plan

G-Plan is a furniture range launched in 1953 by Donald Gomme's (b. 1916) family firm in High Wycombe. Inspired in part by wartime **Utility**, G-Plan became popular in Britain in the fifties and sixties with its moderately priced and subtly suburbanized versions of the modern style, known as **Contemporary**.

Dining Room with G-Plan Furniture, 1954
G-Plan furniture brought the Contemporary style to domestic Britain. For many people this 1954 room set would have been their first experience of modern design. G-Plan were well known for their room-dividers, shelving systems and light chairs and tables.

Kenneth Grange

b. 1929

Kenneth Grange is Britain's leading 'name' product designer. He received his most important training as a technical illustrator while doing national service in the Royal Engineers. He then worked as an assistant in various minor architectural and design offices until setting up his own consultancy, Kenneth Grange Design, in 1971. Then, with Fletcher, Forbes & Gill and an architect called Theo Crosby, he founded the design consultancy **Pentagram** in 1971.

Grange belongs to the generation of writers, fashion designers, painters and film-makers who created the distinctive flavour of British cultural life after the Second World War, when, despite the practical constraints, there was an air of simple optimism. He was one of the first British designers to recognize the significance of the rational style emerging from Germany in the post-War years, and cheerfully admits to the influence which **Braun** has had on his own attitudes to design. More than any other designer in Britain, Grange has enjoyed the thrill of seeing his visions come into being in the everyday world: the 'Venner' parking meter, Kodak 'Instamatic', the Kenwood mixers, the Parker '25' pen, and a cosmetic job on British Rail's 125 train.
Bibliography 'Kenneth Grange at The Boilerhouse' exhibition catalogue, The Boilerhouse Project, Victoria & Albert Museum, London, 1983

'Chef' Food Mixer for Kenwood, 1960s
Kenneth Grange's designs for the Kenwood food mixers, beginning in the early sixties, brought a version of German rationalism into hundreds of thousands of British homes that had never heard of Braun.

Michael Graves

b. 1934

Michael Graves is an American spokesman of the movement in architecture and design known as **Post-Modernism**.

Graves studied architecture at Harvard, and has taught architecture at Princeton since 1962. He first came to public notice in the seventies, when journalists began to write about the 'New York Five', in whose number he was counted. A gifted draughtsman, until 1982 Graves' only substantial contribution to the history of architecture and design was a series of exquisitely coloured drawings, sold in galleries on New York's 57th Street, a dressing table called 'Plaza' for **Memphis**, a table and chair for the American manufacturer Sunar, and a coffee service for Alessi (p. 57). Graves' only realized architectural project has been the Public Services Building in Portland, Oregon, completed in 1982; nonetheless, by force of character and quality of line, together with a taste for colour and pattern which has caught the contemporary mood, Graves has become an internationally acknowledged spokesman for a certain attitude to architecture.
Bibliography Charles Jencks *Kings of Infinite Space* Academy Editions, London, 1983

Eileen Gray

1878–1976

Eileen Gray was an Irish designer who translated the German **Functionalist** style of tubular steel furniture into a form of French chic. She was born at Enniscorthy, County Wexford, Ireland, into a family that was part Scots-Irish nobility, part *plein air* amateur painters. In 1898 she began to study drawing at London's Slade School and took a personal interest in lacquer-work. This assumed greater importance in her creative life when she moved to Paris in 1902 and started a dedicated study of this oriental craft with Sugawara, a Japanese lacquer master who was enjoying celebrity at the time among artistic circles in the French capital.

Her first jobs included lacquer screens and tables, and she began to get noticed in magazines such as **Vogue**, which published an article about her in 1917, but already she was tending toward a different sort of design, personal but more restrained. It was Eileen Gray's achievement to see in the architecture of **Gropius** and **Le Corbusier** a new *style* for the twentieth century which its proprietors' revolutionary zeal had disguised as functional purposiveness. In 1924 she began dabbling in architecture. With Jean Badovici, the editor of *L'Architecture vivante*, she designed in the mid-twenties a house called E-1027 at Roquebrune in the south of France. For all her chic and lack of revolutionary fervour this house was, at the time it was built, as aggressively modern a statement about the new architecture as anything built by **Rietveld** in Holland or Le Corbusier in France. It was from this house that Le Corbusier swam to his death in 1965.

She also designed the 'Transat' chair in leather, wood and lacquer, as well as a tubular steel side table, numerous chests of drawers, and some striking lacquered screens.
Bibliography Stewart Johnson *Eileen Gray: designer 1879–1976* Debrett, London, 1979

Dressing Table, 1928
Eileen Gray's designs, like this dressing table in steel and wood, were the intermediaries between the stern formalism of the Modern Movement and wealthy patrons' taste for exclusivity and luxury.

Milner Gray

b. 1899

The English graphic designer Milner Gray was trained in the days when the calling was more usually known as 'commercial artist'. In 1930 he helped found what became SIAD, one of the world's first professional organizations for designers. During the Second World War he worked with his partner **Misha Black**, doing propaganda exhibitions for the Ministry of Information. It was during the War that he established the principles and ambitions of DRU, the design consultancy he was to set up in 1944. 'The final aim is to present a service so complete that it could undertake any design case which might confront the State, Municipal Authorities, Industry or Commerce' (see also p. 110). Milner Gray has lectured and written extensively on exhibition and packaging design.
Bibliography John and Avril Blake *The Practical Idealists* Lund Humphries, London, 1969

Living Room at Roquebrune, 1926–9
Eileen Gray built her own villa, E-1027, between 1926 and 1929, at Roquebrune. With its openness, rectilinearity and use of textiles it was a masterpiece of the International Style. E-1027 became her home.

Great Exhibition of the Industry of All Nations

Queen Victoria's husband, Prince Albert of Saxe-Coburg Gotha, and **Henry Cole**, an official at the Public Record Office who had dabbled in ceramic design for Minton's, shared a missionary zeal about design in industry. Having unsuccessfully tried to revivify the (**Royal**) **Society of Arts** through a series of exhibitions of industrial design, they decided to organize a better one themselves. Their planning began in 1848; it was originally for a national exhibition, but Cole and Prince Albert decided it should also embrace foreign products. Cole used his colleagues, who helped him with his short-lived **Journal of Design**. The exhibition took place in London's Hyde Park in 1851, in a huge glass structure by Joseph Paxton, a greenhouse designer. Its contents were the applied arts and machinery; the emphasis was on the commercial impact of applied decoration and the excitement of mass-production. This

excitement was felt nowhere more strongly than by the organizers: Prince Albert claimed, 'Man is approaching a more complete fulfilment of that great and sacred mission he has to perform in this world.'

Although the exhibition was a popular triumph, its results shocked its organizers, demonstrating to the officials what they had already known since the 1836 Select Committee *Report on Arts and Manufactures*: that Britain was far behind its continental rivals in matters of design. Cole regarded this as a vindication of his idea and, with renewed zeal, used the Great Exhibition and the surplus of its exhibits and profits to create the series of institutions which eventually became the **Victoria and Albert Museum**. (See also pp. 20–3.)

Garrett & Son Stand: Interior of Crystal Palace, 1851
This stand had some of the less extravagant items on display at the Great Exhibition. (See also pp. 20–2.)

Horatio Greenough

1805–52

Horatio Greenough was an obscure and mediocre American sculptor who has assumed more prominence in this century than in his own on account of thoughts contained in his book, *The Travels, Observations and Experiences of a Yankee Stonecutter*.

After studying at Harvard he travelled around Italy in pursuit of his vocation as sculptor. Although his appreciation that architecture had a *moral* character predates **Ruskin**'s, Greenough did not share the Englishman's tastes: he admired the Greeks and was impatient with the Gothic. When in 1843 there was a public commotion about Greenough's semi-nude statue of George Washington, he began to question American taste. Although his observations all fall within the cultural tradition of the Greek Revival, Greenough's vision was admirably clear: he was, essentially, a machine romantic and admired machines for their elegance and simplicity, being

amongst the first ever to do so. His book was published under the pseudonym of Horace Bender, in the year of his death. Some writers have seen in it the basis for the twentieth-century ideology of **Functionalism**. (See also p. 22.)
Bibliography E.R. de Zurko *Origins of Functionalist Theory* Columbia University Press, New York, 1957

Statue of George Washington, 1832–41
Greenough's pseudo-classical statue of George Washington caused a furore because the President was shown half-naked. Greenough's achievements as a sculptor were, in fact, mediocre, but his book, The Travels, Observations and Experiences of a Yankee Stonecutter, 1852, *contained early Functionalist ideas and became a minor cult among designers and writers.*

Eugene Gregorie

b. 1908

Eugene Turenne Gregorie, a yacht designer by training, joined the **Ford** Motor Company in 1931. In 1935 he became head of the **styling** department, after Edsel Ford had been impressed by the success of his Model 40, advertised on account of its elegant appearance as 'The Car Without a Price Class'. The Thunderbird was produced under his supervision. Gregorie's work for Ford is said to have influenced André **Citroën** in his design of the Traction Avant of 1936.

Thunderbird, 1954

When Ford directors saw the prototype Chevrolet Corvette at the 1952 Paris Auto Show they were shocked into making their own sports car. The Ford Thunderbird, which appeared on the market two years later, exploited as many American myths as General Motors' Corvette and, in turn, passed perhaps even deeper into the traditions of American popular culture. It was this car that was immortalized in The Beach Boys' lyric 'We'll have fun, fun, fun / Till her daddy takes the T'bird away . . .'

Vittorio Gregotti

b. 1927

Vittorio Gregotti was born in Novara in northern Italy. An architect, designer, author, academic and impresario, he has become one of the most articulate and energetic spokesmen for contemporary **Italian design**. He has been editor of *Casabella* and *Edilizia Moderna* and presently edits *Rassegna* and *Lotus*, two of the most luxurious and influential of Italian design journals. Gregotti has been able to use his position in publishing, as well as his academic post in Venice (where he is professor of architectural composition), to secure a central role in the phenomenon of modern design from Milan: Gregotti Associati organize and design exhibitions and interiors (including **Missoni**'s shop in Milan's via Montenapoleone), but have also produced designs for architectural ironmongery made by Fusital.

Door Handles for Fusital, 1981

Gregotti Associati's designs for door furniture for Fusital are based on ergonomic principles.

Hermann Gretsch

b. 1895

After the dissolution of the **Deutsche Werkbund** in the early years of Nazism, Hermann Gretsch headed its successor, Der Bund deutscher Entwurfer (the association of German designers). His Model 1382 tableware, which he designed for the Arzberg Porzellanfabrik in 1931, was a realization of the standards in mass-produced consumer design which the Werkbund had been promoting for two decades. Gretsch was, with **Wilhelm Wagenfeld**, one of the few designers who worked prolifically and successfully throughout the Nazi regime.

Walter Gropius

1883–1969

When Walter Gropius arrived at Harvard he put an end to the Beaux-Arts tradition of architectural education and changed the face of **American design**, forever. He was, indeed, one of the most influential figures of the twentieth century, a man idolized by three generations of students from the **Bauhaus** in Germany to Harvard University School of Architecture in the United States, and eventually satirized by **Tom Wolfe** as an austere and unworldly 'Silver Prince'.

Gropius was born in Berlin into a family of architects whose experience of building went back to at least the beginning of the nineteenth century. He studied architecture in Berlin and Munich, and worked as an assistant to **Peter Behrens** before establishing his own office, in partnership with Adolf Meyer, in 1910. A series of remarkable buildings came out of it, many of which – like the Fagus factory at Alfeld in 1911 and the **Deutsche Werkbund** exhibition building of 1914 – have, despite their smallness and remoteness, become some of the most published and familiar of all modern buildings.

During service as an air observer in the First World War Gropius was granted leave to discuss with the Grand Duke of Saxe-Weimar the possibility of his taking over the Saxon

Academy of Arts and Crafts from the Belgian **Henry van de Velde** (who had recommended him). This was the beginning of the **Bauhaus**, whose influence in the world of art and design can be compared with the influence of the theory of relativity in physics. When conservative local politicians, as well as representatives of craft groups and trade unions, felt threatened by the Bauhaus, Gropius handed over the directorship to **Hannes Meyer** in 1928. This left him free to resume his own architectural practice: his largest project was *Existenzminimum* housing at Siemensstadt, outside Berlin. His life in Weimar and Dessau was colourfully described by his ex-wife, Alma Mahler Werfel, in a memoir, *And the Bridge Was Love* (1957).

Gropius left Germany because he felt his ideas would never gain official recognition under the Nazis and went to England, where he formed a partnership with the English architect **Maxwell Fry**. In 1937 he took up an appointment as a professor of architecture at Harvard and founded The Architects' Collaborative (TAC) in 1945. The title of this architectural practice emphasized Gropius' belief in the importance of teamwork, which had been one of the fundamental principles of Bauhaus education.

Gropius thought that all building should be defined in terms of its (supposed) function, and that the different architectural elements which

TAC I Tea Service for Rosenthal, 1969
In later life Walter Gropius and his architectural practice, TAC (The Architects' Collaborative, a sort of private enterprise Bauhaus), undertook the design of some ceramics for Rosenthal. The 'TAC I' teaset appeared in Rosenthal's 'Studio-Linie' in 1969. It was clean, elegant and functional.

Interior: Walter Gropius' Room at the Weimar Bauhaus, 1923
Gropius' room had furniture by Marcel Breuer and items by other members of the Bauhaus staff. (See also p. 30.)

were inevitably created by this rule should be arranged into a pleasing compositional effect. While **Le Corbusier**'s intention was to make his buildings into elegantly simple sculptural forms (with complex and subtle interior spaces), and **Mies van der Rohe** aimed at perfection of detail and discretion of shape, Gropius sought to create a dynamic interpenetration of forms and spaces. When he taught at Harvard he embodied his principles of functional subdivision in the curriculum.

Even without his architecture, and despite a somewhat narrow interpretation of **Functionalism**, Gropius would be remembered as the most persuasive and sophisticated of all the theoreticians, educators and critics who struggled to accommodate civilized, humane values into a mechanized world. The great influences on his thought were **William Morris**, from whom he took the ideal of the unity of art and life, and **Henry Ford**, from whom he took the concept of standardization of machine-made products.

Bibliography Walter Gropius *Idee und Aufbau des Staatlichen Bauhauses* 1923; *Internationale Architektur* 1925; *Bauhaus Bauten* 1933; *The New Architecture and the Bauhaus* New York, 1936; *Bauhaus 1919–1928* 1939 (with Ilse Frank and Herbert Bayer); Sigfried Giedion *Walter Gropius* London, 1954; Hans Maria Wingler *Bauhaus* MIT, Cambridge, Mass., 1969; James Marston Fitch & Ise Gropius 'Walter Gropius – buildings, plans, projects 1906–1969' exhibition catalogue, International Exhibitions Foundation, 1972–4; Klaus Herdeg *The Decorated Diagram – Harvard architecture and the failure of the Bauhaus legacy* MIT, Cambridge, Mass., 1983

Group of Ten

The Group of Ten is a group of textile designers founded in Stockholm in 1970. Their motivation was to replace the client/designer relationship with one where they were able to oversee the entire process from concept through to sales. The first collection, with one design from each of the ten designers, appeared in 1972. Its Stockholm showroom opened the following year. Now reduced to six, it aims to make collections of textiles and wallpapers of a lasting rather than a fashionable nature.

Design Samples
Sweden's Group of Ten specialize in fabric designs employing bold patterns and strong colours.

Gruppo Strum

Gruppo Strum was a late starter among the Italian radical design groups which briefly flourished in the later sixties. It was motivated by naive ideas about the political possibilities of architecture. In 1972 Gruppo Strum reached its greatest prominence with an exhibition, 'Mediatory City', at the **Museum of Modern Art**'s 'New Domestic Landscape' exhibition in New York. Then its leaders sank back into the comfortable obscurity of provincial Italian academic life.

Gucci

Guccio Gucci opened a saddler's shop in 1904 in Florence, a city famed, among other things, for its leatherware. He added luggage to his range, and his sons Aldo, Vasco and Rodolfo went over to industrial production and began to turn Florentine craftsmanship into an international phenomenon. A shop opened in Rome in 1939, followed by others in Paris, London, New York, Beverly Hills and Chicago.

Gucci stores sell only their own products in their own stores and their franchised outlets. The firm's advertising once proudly claimed that 10 per cent of its product was in the latest styles, 90 per cent classical. This mix is having to be adjusted now that more aggressively marketed Italian couturiers are forcing the pace in the market.

Gucci products are characterized by an emphasis on quality, 'good taste' and social status, signified by the 'G-G' logo that appears on all of them. It represents the opposite end of the spectrum of Italian taste from **Fiorucci**'s 'junky chic'.

Wallet, 1980s
Design is occasionally debased into being little more than an exclusive brand or trademark. Gucci's leatherware has achieved celebrity by expense and rarity alone: the green and red stripe and the gilt motif are internationally recognizable symbols of large disposable incomes.

A
B
C
D
E
F
G
H
I
J
K
L
M
N
O
P
Q
R
S
T
U
V
W
X
Y
Z

Hans Gugelot

1920–65

The Dutch-Swiss architect and designer Hans Gugelot was head of the product design department at the **Hochschule für Gestaltung** in Ulm from 1955 until his death.

Gugelot was born in Indonesia and studied at the Eidgenossischen Technische Hochschule (federal technical college) in Zürich and worked with **Max Bill** from 1948 to 1950 when he designed his first furniture for the Horgen-Glarus stores. He met Erwin **Braun** in 1954, the same year that he started teaching at the Hochschule für Gestaltung, and was to produce several designs for him.

Gugelot was one of the great influences on the forms adopted by the post-War Western manufacturing industry (and those imitated elsewhere). With his pupil and later colleague **Dieter Rams**, he was the most ardent and austere exponent of the **Functionalist** style, which became associated with **German design** of that period. He persuaded himself and his clients that his own preference for muted greys, right angles and the complete eradication of decorative detail produced the inevitably correct and timeless appearance of machines. The 'Phonosuper' record player of 1950 (p. 212), designed with Dieter Rams,

known in Germany as the 'Schneewitchens Sarg' (Snow White's Coffin), was the perfect expression of this style. Gugelot was consultant to the Hamburg U-bahn (1959–62) and was also responsible for the design of the Kodak 'Carousel' slide projector (1962), a machine whose timelessness supports the validity of his taste. However, the electro-mechanical hearts of the machines he designed had been replaced by solid state circuitry, making the attitude to design which he had championed on the basis of 'logic' no more than another preferred style. (See also p. 62.)

Bibliography Alison and Peter Smithson 'Concealment and Display: Meditations on Braun' *Architectural Design* vol. 36, July, 1966, pp. 362–3; 'System-Design Bahnbrecher: Hans Gugelot 1920–1965' exhibition catalogue, Die Neue Sammlung, Munich, 1984

'Carousel S' Projector for Kodak, 1962

Gugelot's projector brought the American Kodak formula of the round slide magazine to Germany, where manufacturers had hitherto used only linear magazines. The 'Carousel S' was developed jointly by the Gugelot Institut and Kodak's Stuttgart factory, a happy marriage of German systematic design and American production technology.

Lurelle Guild

b. 1898

Like **Norman Bel Geddes** and **Henry Dreyfuss**, Lurelle Guild was a pioneer American consultant designer who had his training in the theatre. By 1920 he was selling cover artwork to **House & Garden** and the *Ladies' Home Journal*, and he soon found that the advertisers for whom he designed layouts actually wanted him to design their products too. As a result he produced a range of spun-aluminium kitchen ware and other small objects in the fashionable streamlined style, and also some textured linoleum.

Doorway, Castel Béranger, Paris, 1894–8

Guimard saw this apartment block as a total artistic statement which he amplified in his book Le Castel Béranger – L'Art dans l'habitation moderne *(1898).*

Hector Guimard

1867–1942

Hector Guimard is best known for his contributions to the vocabulary of **Art Nouveau**. His Castel Béranger flats in Paris of 1894–8 announced the characteristics of his style: ostentatious applied architectural ornament and cast-iron stairways and balconies with sinuous, asymmetric, tendril-like forms, as if derived from over-cooked vegetables. Guimard also designed the Métro entrances, where wrought iron is worked into organic curves, topped by electric globes looking as if they are the buds of the plant. Guimard's combination of structure with decorative form was typical of the attempts by Art Nouveau designers to replace nineteenth-century historicism with stylistic novelty.

Bibliography 'Hector Guimard' exhibition catalogue, Museum of Modern Art, New York, 1970

Gustavsberg

Gustavsberg is a small town fifteen miles outside Stockholm which, since 1825, has given its name to Sweden's leading ceramics factory. The first products to appear were earthenware, following current German technical practice, but printed patterns began to appear around 1830 under the influence of England.

In the late nineteenth century the predominant style of domestic ceramics was Nordic National Romantic, an overbearing decorative manner heavy with folklore and light on art. But a great structural change overcame the company in the 1890s with the appointment of the painter **Gunnar Wennerberg** as artist-in-residence. Wennerberg's much more refined designs were first seen at the 1897 Art and Industry exhibition in Stockholm: he chose as motifs freshly observed paintings of wild flowers, in effect offering the Swedish consumer a version of the principles of **Art Nouveau**.

Wennerberg's appointment created a precedent which Gustavsberg readily augmented by a series of further distinguished appointments: **Wilhelm Kåge** joined the company in 1917 and promptly designed a working man's service (as if in direct response to **Gregor Paulsson**'s appeal for 'more beautiful everyday things'). This 'Praktika' service was a direct response to the international **Modern Movement**, although the majority of his work manifested more obviously decorative qualities. **Stig Lindberg** joined in 1937 and in 1949 he succeeded Kåge as artistic director of the company. Under Lindberg's direction Gustavsberg produced the first acceptable oven-to-table earthenware, which did much to characterize 'Swedish Modern' to consumers throughout the world.

Lindberg hired other artists to work for Gustavsberg, Karin Bjorquist and Lisa Larson joining during the fifties.

In 1937 Gustavsberg had passed from the private control of the Odelberg family into that of the Swedish Cooperative Society, and its commercial interests broadened into sanitary ware and plastics. Gustavsberg now uses its new plastics expertise to manufacture intelligent tools for the disabled, and in employing the Stockholm human factors consultancy, **Ergonomi Design**, continues the inspired tradition it began nearly one hundred years ago with the job it gave to the academic painter Gunnar Wennerberg.

Bibliography 'Gustavsberg 150 ar' exhibition catalogue, Nationalmuseum, Stockholm, 1975

'Praktika' 1930, and 'Pyro' 1933, ceramic ware by Wilhelm Kåge
By a designer who made Gustavsberg famous, the services show the two poles of Swedish thirties design: one traditional and successful, the other adventurous, and a commercial flop.

Gustavsberg Workshops, 1896
The Gustavsberg ceramic factory began to employ practising artists at the end of the nineteenth century to work in its factories to improve the aesthetic standard of the goods produced. This was perhaps the first appearance of the authentic modern designer.

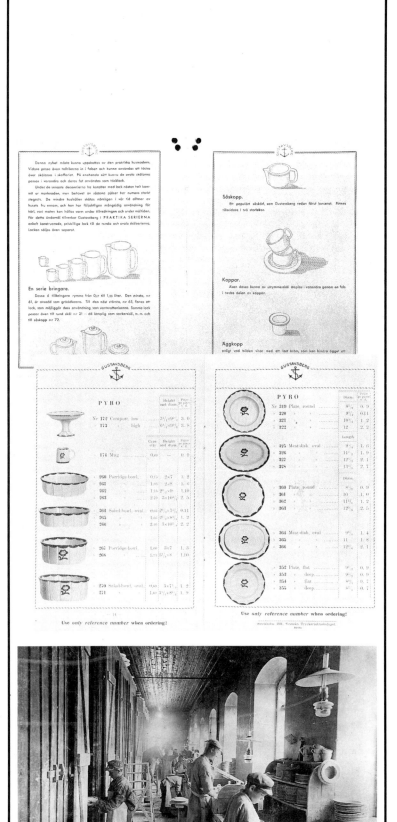

H

Habitat
Edward **Hald**
Katherine **Hamnett**
Ambrose **Heal**
Deryck **Healey**
Jean **Heiberg**
Piet **Hein**
Poul **Henningsen**
Henri Kay
Frederick **Henrion**
René **Herbst**
Robert **Heritage**
Erik **Herlow**
David **Hicks**
High-Tech
Oliver **Hill**
Hille
**Hochschule für
Gestaltung**
Josef **Hoffmann**
Hans **Hollein**
Knud **Holscher**
Honda
House & Garden
Johan **Huldt**

Habitat

The Habitat chain of stores brought design to the public's notice in Britain. The first store opened in London's Fulham Road in 1964, a furniture shop to meet the needs of the new **Pop** culture. The founder was Terence Conran (b. 1931), who has remained its head and guiding force ever since. Conran trained as a textile designer at London's **Central School of Art and Design**, and when he left set up a studio with the sculptor and print-maker Eduardo Paolozzi, making modern metal furniture and designing fabrics and ceramics. Conran had opened his own bistro, the Soup Kitchen, in 1955, the same year that his consultancy, The Conran Design Group (now Conran Associates), was founded. Two years later he designed the Bazaar boutique for his friend **Mary Quant**, but despite these local successes he was consistently frustrated by the conservative buyers in the big department stores who refused to consider stocking his bright, modern furniture.

The first Habitat was a response to this and its impact was immediate: it was the first shop to offer a complete range of stylish and sensible goods at reasonable prices. It was not only merchandise that Habitat offered for sale, but a whole way of life (or, at least, the vision of it): furniture, cookware, glass, crockery, cutlery, rugs, tiles, fabrics and lights, stacked floor-to-ceiling as if in a warehouse. In some quarters Habitat won itself a reputation for being a sort of commercialization of the **Bauhaus**, but the merchandise is very much more eclectic: on its opening, the first store stocked not only **Braun** appliances, but also French professional cookware and Polish enamel. As one store has evolved into an international chain, Habitat is necessarily less the expression of one man's taste and more the product of sophisticated, professional retailing, but it still has a fundamental philosophy. Terence Conran expressed it in a 1967 interview with **House &** **Garden**: 'I am not interested in "pure" design, which designers do for other designers . . . I am interested in selling good design to the mass market.' The validity of Conran's interpretation of the modern shop has been proved by Habitat's growth; there are now branches in France, Belgium, Iceland, the United States and Japan. In 1981 Habitat took over Mothercare, a major retailer of clothes and equipment for mothers and children, and in 1983 the company acquired **Heal**'s, bringing a phenomenon that was a child of the sixties directly into the established tradition of British furniture design and manufacture.
Bibliography Barty Phillips *Conran and the Habitat Story* Weidenfeld & Nicolson, London, 1984

'Country' Kitchen, 1977
Every year the Habitat way of life is projected to the millions of people who buy its catalogue. This illustration shows a kitchen from its 'Country' range of 1977.

Edward Hald

1883–1980

A Swedish glass and ceramics designer, Edward Niels Tove Hald once studied painting under Henri Matisse. With the help of the **Svenska Sljödföreningen** he worked at **Rörstrand** and then at the **Orrefors** glassworks, where he started as designer in 1917, rising to become managing director from 1933 to 1944. With Simon Gate, Hald was one of the founders of modernism in Sweden, designing simple, decorative forms which were made by the company's craftsmen. His son Arthur was artistic director of **Gustavsberg** until 1981.

Both father and son contributed fine-art talents to the applied arts, designing ceramics and glass characterized by the application of light, often figurative decoration, which caused 'Swedish Modern' to be perceived as being more humanistic than the style emerging from Germany at the same period.

Bibliography 'Edward Hald – Malare, Konstindustripionjar' exhibition catalogue, Nationalmuseum, Stockholm, 1983

Katharine Hamnett

b. 1947

The British fashion designer Katharine Hamnett studied at London's St Martin's School of Art and became the couturier of Britain's second **Pop** phase in the early eighties. Having initially run a company called Tuttabankem (1964–9), she freelanced in London, Paris and New York, and set up in business again in 1979. Her adventurous clothes in pre-washed cotton (1979) and crushed silk (1980) brought immediate success. In 1983 she began producing gigantic T-shirts with supergraphic political slogans. In 1984 she was nominated as the most influential designer by the British Fashion Industry's Awards panel.

T-Shirt, 1984
Katharine Hamnett's slogan T-Shirts gave fashion a much-copied idea.

Ambrose Heal

1872–1959

Ambrose Heal's family had been involved in furniture since his great-grandfather, also Ambrose Heal, had established a London furniture business in 1810. After an education at Marlborough and apprenticeship to a cabinet-maker in Warwick, Heal joined the family firm in 1893. His cousin, Cecil Brewer (an architect who was to design the new Heal's store just before the First World War, in which he was killed), had introduced him to W.R. Lethaby, **C.F.A. Voysey** and the **Arts and Crafts** Exhibition Society, where Heal began showing his furniture designs in 1896. The great achievement of Heal's early career was to get his simple designs into the stores. Tottenham Court Road, where the family store had moved in 1840, was a centre for the manufacture of reproduction furniture, for which the public had a keen appetite, and Heal's own salesmen asked him how on earth they were expected to sell 'prison furniture', so stark did his designs seem in contrast to the vulgar and gross ▶

Poster for Heal's, 1928
The graphic design combines quaintness with certain modernistic gestures, including the pseudo-Bauhaus banderolles. Like the store itself, the poster projects a mixture of ancient and modern.

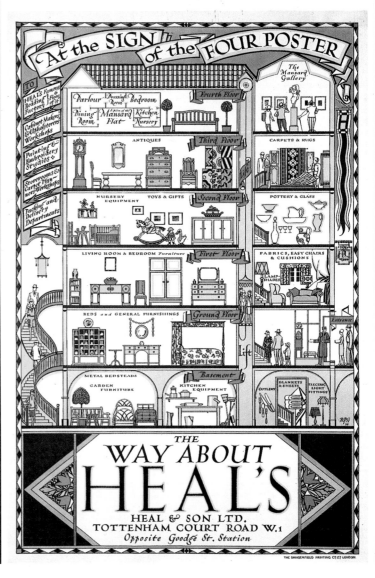

ABCDEFGHIJKLMNOPQRSTUVWXYZ

ornamentation of the popular 'Queen Anne' cabinets. The turning-point in Heal's search for recognition amongst the London furniture trade came when **C.R. Ashbee**'s foreman joined the company rather than move with the respected Guild of Handicrafts from London to Chipping Campden.

Ambrose Heal became chairman of the business in 1913, helped to found the Design and Industries Association (DIA) in 1915 and was knighted in 1933.

As a craftsman-designer Heal was influenced both by the ethics and idealism of **William Morris**, and also by the standards of craftsmanship of the great English furniture designers of the eighteenth century: the quality of the wood itself and a respect for the tools and the materials (learnt at the bench) were fundamental to his own work as a cabinet-maker, winning him a silver medal at the Paris Exhibition of 1900. His influence extended far: as chairman of Heal's he expanded the business to include a comprehensive range of household merchandise, while continuing the tradition of bed-making which had been the foundation of the firm. Antique furniture, textiles and studio pottery were added to the stock, and when the Tottenham Court Road building was

Living and Dining Room Exhibited at British Industries Fair, 1953, Furnished by Heal's
Heal's consistently promoted the latest in 'good' design. This room of 1953 contains only furniture and furnishings in the Contemporary style.

enlarged in 1929 a gallery for exhibitions was added. During the fifties Heal's introduced a discriminating English public to Scandinavian design, and at the same time sold a successful range of fabrics designed by Lucienne **Day** and others . In 1983 Heal & Son was taken over by **Habitat** Mothercare.
Bibliography Susanna Goodden *At the Sign of the Four Poster – A History of Heal's* Lund Humphries, London, 1983

Deryck Healey

b. 1937

Deryck Healey was born in South Africa and studied at Manchester College of Art and Design. He founded Deryck Healey International in 1966 and it became a leading international colour consultant, offering a total package to the fashion industry.
Bibliography Deryck Healey *Living With Colour* Macmillan, London, 1982; Random House, New York, 1982

Jean Heiberg

1884–1976

Jean Heiberg was a Norwegian painter who studied in Munich and in Paris, latterly under Matisse, and became the designer of arguably the first 'modern' telephone, and certainly the most familiar one to British eyes.

About 1930 the Swedish Ericsson company was developing a new technology for telephones, replacing cranks with dials, and the search went out for a designer to provide them with a new, marketable shape. Initially the job was given to a company engineer of Oslo's Elektrisk Bureau, an Ericsson subsidiary, called Johan Christian Bjerknes. His brief was to develop a machine that

would have universal appeal, as Ericsson considered that its market was no less than the entire world. Bjerknes decided to use **Bakelite**, but then discovered that he needed help with the design. Norway's leading artist of the day, Alf Rolfson, was too busy with a hospital mural so the job was given to Jean Heiberg, who had just returned from the ateliers of Paris to take up a post as professor in Oslo's National Academy of Fine Art. Production of Heiberg's design, which still retains elements of the neo-classical stylobate which dominated his first plaster drafts, went into production in 1932 as the 'DBH1001'. By 1937 there were six presses in England alone, stamping out the Norwegian painter's designs.

Plaster Prototype for the Ericsson 'DBH1001' Telephone, c. 1930
The painter Heiberg modelled this design for his telephone on neo-classical architecture.

***Three Versions of the Ericsson 'DBH1001' Telephone** (from left to right) 1932, a perspex novelty, 1937*

Piet Hein

b. 1905

The Danish mathematician, cartoonist and designer Piet Hein became a popular figure in the sixties when his mathematically determined 'super-ellipse' was applied both to urban roundabouts and to a table manufactured by **Bruno Mathsson** from 1964.

Bibliography 'Design: the problem comes first' exhibition catalogue, Danish Design Council, 1982–3

'Super-Ellipse' Table, 1968

Hein's 'Super-Ellipse' table is characteristic of the Danish use of natural materials and clean, sculptured forms. It was designed to a formula which combines the advantages of the square and of the circle. The legs click into a fitting without the use of tools.

Poul Henningsen

1895–1967

The Dane Poul Henningsen became famous for the 'PH' lamp he designed in 1925, which is still manufactured by the Copenhagen factory of Louis Poulsen.

Henningsen was an articulate spokesman for the integration of artists into manufacturing industry, and condemned the pretentious solipsism of painters locked in their studios. He was a significant contributor to 'Scandinavian Modern' design, and the long-lived 'PH' lamp is a symbol of that achievement.

With **Kaare Klint** in the later twenties Henningsen edited the journal *Kritisk Revy*. This architectural magazine was Denmark's most influential publication as far as increasing popular awareness of standards in design is concerned, Henningsen using it to harangue both manufacturers and artists to become more responsive to the twentieth century. He once wrote: 'Throw away your artists' berets and bow ties and get into overalls. Down with artistic pretentiousness! Simply make things which are fit for use: that is enough to keep you busy and you will sell vast quantities and make lots of money.'

Bibliography 'Design: the problem comes first' exhibition catalogue, Danish Design Council, 1982–3

'PH5' Light Fitting, 1958

Designed by Poul Henningsen for Louis Poulson in Copenhagen, the PH5 was intended to provide friendly, diffused light and has become a classic of Danish design, familiar from countless interiors.

Cover of Kritisk Revy, *1928*

A B C D E F G H I J K L M N O P Q R S T U V W X Y Z

A
B
C
D
E
F
G
H
I
J
K
L
M
N
O
P
Q
R
S
T
U
V
W
X
Y
Z

Henri Kay Frederick Henrion

b. 1914

Henri Henrion studied textiles in Paris and went to Palestine in 1936 to work as a poster artist. He came to England during the Second World War and was a consultant designer to the Exhibitions Division of the Ministry of Information, for whom he designed many distinguished propaganda posters which mixed the concepts of **Surrealism** with those of commercial art.

Henrion settled in London and became a major figure in both national and international design bodies, while simultaneously developing his graphic design practice. He began to find that his work was extending beyond commercial art, and in the fifties began to offer his clients – who included Blue Circle Cement, BEA and KLM – a total design package which integrated all aspects of a company's visual character. Henrion can thus be seen as a pioneer of **corporate identity**. *Bibliography* H.K.F. Henrion & Alan Parkin *Design Coordination and Corporate Image* Studio Vista, London, 1968

'Stub it Out', Poster, 1943
Henrion's wartime posters for the Ministry of Information were often startling in their boldness.

René Herbst

b. 1891

A Parisian, René Herbst was one of the founders of the Union des Artistes Modernes in 1930, and his designs, mostly formal exercises in new materials, are characteristic examples of French modernism. A nickel-plated tubular steel chair he designed in 1930–2 and manufactured in his own Etablissements René Herbst has become a modern classic, and since 1979 has been reproduced by Ecart International. *Bibliography* René Herbst *25 années UAM* Edition du Salon des Arts Ménagers, Paris, 1956

Robert Heritage

b. 1927

The British furniture and lighting designer Robert Heritage was taught at London's **Royal College of Art** by R.D. 'Dick' Russell, brother of Sir Gordon. In 1953 he set up his own design office. He designed the furniture which **Ernest Race** fitted into the liner *Queen Elizabeth II* in 1968, but is best known for his work on behalf of Concord, an architectural lighting manufacturer. Heritage has won more **Design Council** awards than any other individual. Since 1974 he has taught at the Royal College of Art, where he is now professor of furniture design.

Erik Herlow

b. 1913

Head of the department of industrial design at the Royal Academy of Denmark, and consultant to the Royal Copenhagen porcelain factory, Erik Herlow has been instrumental amongst those who have been responsible for getting **Danish design** recognized throughout the world.

Herlow's clients in the consultant design practice he opened in 1945 include **Georg Jensen** and Dansk Aluminium. His designs are mostly in steel, a medium to which he has brought the sophisticated, sculptural forms which have also dominated other areas of Danish design. Herlow's achievement in promoting Danish work was such that when Cyra McFadden published her satire about Californian lifestyle, *The Serial*, in 1976 she only had to mention 'Dansk stainless' to evoke a whole concept of modern taste.

Quartet Major Spotlight for Concord Lighting, 1965
Heritage's ranges of architectural lighting for Concord have been widely imitated. The internationally adopted concept of a domestic 'spotlight' is largely his invention.

David Hicks

b. 1929

David Hicks' career as an interior decorator began during the austere post-War years in Britain. By the late fifties he had established a distinctive personal style: a Hicks interior would often use uncompromising contrasts of colour with pinks and oranges juxtaposed. With his crisp clarity of detailing and his flair in the arrangement of objects, Hicks' style became the quintessence of chic for London town houses. For country houses he evolved a style which re-interpreted eighteenth-century design in terms of strong colours and geometric patterns. Modern elements such as light fittings would often be used in traditional rooms. Hicks' own house, Britwell Salome, was the perfect expression of this simplified grand style in that it combined old and new ('the mix'), and featured precious groupings of objects which the decorator christened 'tablescapes'.

Today Hicks runs a large international practice of interior decorators. Its emphasis has turned to the marketing of fabrics, carpets, furniture and accessories, with a growing interest in garden design.

Bibliography David Hicks *On Living – With Taste* Leslie Frewin, London 1968

High-Tech

Like **Post-Modernism**, High-Tech was a style label invented by journalists. It therefore had more influence on newspapers and magazines than it did on real life.

The basis of the style was the idea that utilitarian products, originally designed for use in factories and laboratories, could provide the raw material for interior design. As a result, objects like surgeons' trolleys, metal shelving and rubber flooring suddenly invaded some homes.

Bibliography Joan Kron & Suzanne Slesin *High-Tech – the industrial style and source book for the home* Clarkson Potter, New York, 1978

Shop Interior, Astrohome, London, 1981
High-Tech is one of a number of consumer styles which have vied for attention after the Modern Movement fell into disfavour. The High-Tech 'ethic' requires that objects for home and interior decoration are selected from the catalogues of industrial and commercial manufacturers. This hard, glittery style was marketed by stores such as London's Astrohome.

Oliver Hill

1887–1968

Oliver Hill contributed brilliantly to that stylized vision of architecture as entertainment which was the **moderne** world of Britain in the thirties. However, as Sir James Richards saw him, he was little more than a skilled eclectic, 'a man of taste rather than conviction who liked to try his hand at every style in turn'. He did not discriminate between historicism and modernism as either furniture designer or as architect, but would build in any style which suited his purposes.

Hill was educated at Uppingham, and before joining the architectural practice of William Flockhart was apprenticed to a firm of builders. After exhibiting a drawing of a country house at the Royal Academy in 1930 Hill became a frequent exhibitor there and many commissions followed.

Hill's major works included the decoration of the Midland Hotel, Morecambe, where **Eric Gill** was among the artists commissioned to work on the interior, and a house called Holtshanger at Wentworth in Surrey (1933–5). He was a member of the Council for Art and Industry (1933–8) and designed the exhibition of 'British Industrial Art' which was held at Dorland Hall in 1933.

Bibliography 'The Thirties' exhibition catalogue, Hayward Gallery, London, 1979; David Dean *The Thirties: recalling the English architectural scene* Trefoil, London, 1983

A
B
C
D
E
F
G
H
I
J
K
L
M
N
O
P
Q
R
S
T
U
V
W
X
Y
Z

ABCDEFGHIJKLMNOPQRSTUVWXYZ

Hille

Hille was the outstanding manufacturer of Modern furniture in Britain from the Second World War to 1983 when its directors merged the company with Ergonom. In a conservative market Hille has been the one contract furniture manufacturer consistently to speak up for modern design and to risk new materials and new designers.

The business was established in London by a Russian émigré, Salamon Hille, who started a workshop which restored eighteenth-century furniture in Whitechapel just after 1900. In 1906 he set up a business to manufacture high-quality reproduction furniture (much of which found its way into

'Supporto' Chair by Fred Scott, 1979
Scott's piece is a systems chair. It is an example of a British design that competed favourably with foreign rivals.

some of London's livery halls). The Hille firm did not become involved in modern furniture until after the Second World War, when Leslie Julius (who had married the founder's grand-daughter) joined the company. Julius took specific responsibility for product design and it was he who managed **Robin Day**'s distinguished contributions to Hille's product lines during the twenty-five years when 'Hille', 'Day' and 'modern British furniture' became synonymous. Since the sixties Hille has worked with a number of distinguished designers, including Fred Scott.
Bibliography Sutherland Lyall *Hille – 75 Years of British Furniture* Elron Press, London, 1981

Cocktail Cabinet, 1928
Hille was the first British manufacturer to make Modern furniture, but before that it produced reproduction furniture, and then Art Deco, such as this bizarre cabinet.

Hochschule für Gestaltung

The Hochschule für Gestaltung (College for Design) in Ulm has often been called the new **Bauhaus**. In purpose, form and practice it was inspired by and imitated its legendary pre-War predecessor.

The Hochschule was founded after the war by Grete and Inge Scholl, whose family had been persecuted by the Nazis, with the Swiss architect-sculptor **Max Bill** as its first director and designer of its buildings. He was succeeded by the Argentinian theoretician **Tomas Maldonado**. The purpose of the Hochschule was to revive the ideals of cooperative endeavour which had been Gropius' inspiration (if not his practice) and its aim was to humanize a mechanistic civilization as well as to make the process of design a systematic one. The curriculum at Ulm included a great deal of contextual study, including psychology, games theory, **semiotics** and anthropology. Every effort was made to move away from design as a purely *formal* exercise.

Perhaps paradoxically, the most famous products to emerge from the Hochschule seem to modern eyes to be highly formal, stylized symbols of that very mechanized civilization which the school's fathers were trying to ameliorate. The school's spirit was the influence behind the work of **Hans Gugelot** and **Dieter Rams** and, therefore, was the inspiration for the design of **Braun** electrical products.

The Hochschule was closed down in 1968 by local authorities who thought its policies were too avant-garde.

Josef Hoffmann
1870–1956

The Austrian architect Josef Hoffmann was born in Pirnitz, Moravia, and studied under **Otto Wagner**. In 1899 he was one of the founders of a Viennese group of architects and designers who styled themselves the 'Secession' in order to identify their avant-garde and anti-establishment motivation. Hoffmann wrote in the Viennese journal *Das Interieur* that the purpose of all architects and designers should be to break away from the historicist stranglehold of the museums and to create a new style.

In 1903, with Kolo Moser and Fritz Waerndorfer, he founded the **Wiener Werkstätte** (Viennese workshop), which executed some of his metalware designs. One of Hoffmann's direct sources of inspiration for the Werkstätte was **C.R. Ashbee**'s Guild of Handicrafts. He was to design for the Werkstätte for nearly thirty years, but all of his greatest work was done before

Metal and Glass Vase, 1905
This displays Hoffmann's characteristic geometrical style: square-cut apertures make a rhythmic pattern which creates the structure and animates the surface of the design.

the First World War, his masterpiece being the Palais Stoclet in Brussels, which was completed in 1911.

Hoffmann's achievement was to create a style of interior and furniture design that, under the influence of the British **Arts and Crafts**, as well as the simple peasant architecture he had seen on his Prix de Rome trip to Italy in 1895, was more minimal and elegant than anything created heretofore. His style is characterized by grid patterns, a sort of rectilinear **Art Nouveau**. He wrote in the Werkstätte's manifesto: 'An incredible disaster has come upon us – mass production and thoughtless imitations of bygone styles. This sickening influence infiltrates the entire arts and craft production of the world . . . our workshop . . . should become a centre of gravity surrounded by the happy noise of handicraft production and welcomed by everybody who truly believes in **Ruskin** and **Morris**.' Hoffmann and his contemporary **Adolf Loos** made fine British thoughts into fine Viennese furniture and decorative objects. They and their contemporaries waited avidly for copies of *The Studio* to arrive in their Viennese coffee houses, and designed furniture, tea-sets, fruit-bowls and many small domestic objects from its inspiration. However, as the historian Edward F. Sekler has pointed out, 'Hoffmann was incompletely informed about British architecture and design, but what he knew was sufficient to provide him with guiding principles and to activate his imagination towards the invention of forms that were unmistakably his own.'

Hoffmann's designs have recently enjoyed a sort of bastardized revival, as the inspiration for some New York designers of **Post-Modernism**. *Bibliography* '*Josef Hoffmann*' exhibition catalogue, Fischer Fine Art, London, 1977

Hans Hollein
b. 1934

An Austrian architect, Hollein graduated from the University of California in 1960 and has been consistently involved with architectural experiments designed to reverse the supposed domination of the **Modern Movement**. He became a professor at the Staatlichen Kunstakademie, Düsseldorf, in 1967, and designed the new museum in Mönchengladbach (1981). Hollein has been associated with **Memphis**, the avant-garde Italian design group, and his frequent use of historical reference in his drawings and designs has identified him with **Post-Modernism**.

Knud Holscher
b. 1930

The Danish architect Knud Holscher worked early in his career with **Arne Jacobsen**, but is best known for his partnership with the English designer Alan Tye. They have designed architectural ironmongery for Modric and the 'Meridian One' ceramic bathroom fittings for Adamsez. Each is characterized by quality of execution and an elegant minimalism.

Honda

The Honda Motor Cycle Company was founded by Soichiro Honda in Hamamatsu, Japan, in 1948. Honda's idea was to use army surplus engines and harness them to bicycles. The eventual result was the Honda '50' (known as the C-100 Super Cub in Japan), which, since its introduction in 1958, has become the world's most popular motorcycle. Honda cleverly exploited European standards of design and by 1983 had diversified into power appliances and motor cars to such an extent that motorbikes accounted for only 29 per cent of the firm's business.

The head of Honda's Research and Development Department is Shinya Iwakura, who trained as a fine artist. Honda was the last of the Japanese automotive companies to start producing passenger cars (in 1964) and Iwakura says, 'The fact that Honda was such a new company meant that there were no old influences to overcome. We could establish our own independent ideas.' Under Iwakura, Honda, like **Sony**, has designed sophisticated products which employ technology transfer and symbolism (as well as advanced engineering) to achieve an effect which is highly seductive to the consumer mentality.

House & Garden

House & Garden is an interior design magazine, created by **Condé Nast** in 1915 after taking over the original title and amalgamating it with *American Homes and Gardens*. With this publication Nast took architecture and interior design to a level of popular chic similar to that achieved in fashion, manners and style by his other magazines, **Vogue** and *Vanity Fair*.

Johan Huldt
b. 1942

Johan Huldt is the son of Ake Huldt, one time director of the **Svenska Sljödföreningen**. He studied at Gothenburg Military Naval College and then at the Enskede Trade School, where he learnt industrial woodworking. From 1964 he was a student at the Swedish State School of Arts and Design and founded **Innovator AB** on his departure in 1968. With his partner **Jan Dranger** Huldt has produced many fine pieces of furniture which have advanced the concept of 'Swedish Modern' from its fifties image by abandoning the traditional interest in natural materials and finishes in favour of a more **Pop** aesthetic.

100cc Super Cub Motorcycle, 1958
Small-engined Hondas arose out of necessity and expedience. The 50, of which the 100 was a development, became the most successful motor vehicle of all time.

IBM
ICOGRADA and
  ICSID
IDZ-Berlin
IKEA
Industrial design
Innovator AB
Institute of Design,
  Chicago
International Style
Iron
Isokon
Alec **Issigonis**
Italian design
Johannes **Itten**

IBM

In the world of office automation and data processing, one of the oldest tropes is the one that says 'IBM isn't the competition; it's the *environment*.' This remarkable state of affairs has come about not only through technical excellence, but also through a commitment to **design management** which was unique in American industry. Through the work of **Eliot Noyes** in the fifties and sixties IBM has created an international stereotype for the appearance of modern office machines. It is a measure of IBM's success that much radical thinking in product design is directed towards breaking that very stereotype.

Typewriter, 1948
In the years immediately after the Second World War IBM had the technology to produce advanced electric typewriters, but had no design identity with which to project its image to the public. Norman Bel Geddes was retained briefly as a design consultant, but failed to create a recognizable look for the corporation. This typewriter, manufactured in about 1948, was typical of IBM's production before Eliot Noyes took charge of the manufacturer's corporate identity.

'Selectric' Typewriter by Eliot Noyes 1961
The IBM 'Selectric I' typewriter of 1961 was Eliot Noyes' greatest single product design. While IBM achieved a major advance in typewriter technology with its moving 'golfball' typing head, and its stationary 'carriage', Noyes gave the machine an entirely new shape to distinguish it from conventional typebar machines. The keyboard was designed on ergonomic principles, disposed at angles to suit the ways the fingers strike the keys.

ICOGRADA and ICSID

ICOGRADA stands for the International Council of Graphic Design Associations, ICSID for International Council of Societies of Industrial Design. Both bodies arrange bi-annual conferences around the world, bringing designers into contact with one another for the exchange of ideas on graphic and industrial design. (See also **Peter Muller-Munk**.)

IDZ-Berlin

The Internationales Design Zentrum in Berlin was Germany's major show place for exhibitions about design. Because of its geographical location the IDZ was used as a 'show window' for the West and it received funding both from the city of Berlin and from the Federal Government. This did not, however, compromise its political position, which was consistently radical. Like the **Hochschule für Gestaltung**, the IDZ's activities were restrained by pressure from the Government.

IKEA

IKEA is a Swedish furniture company, founded by Ingmar Kamprad in 1943, which now sells widely throughout Europe, the Far East and North America. Its simple, knocked-down furniture is designed to appeal to a large section of the market.

Industrial design

The term 'industrial design' came into use in Britain in the thirties, but not into general use until after the Second World War. In the United States the expression was known a little earlier. Characteristically, it was **Norman Bel Geddes** who claimed, in 1927, to be the first 'industrial designer', but Joseph Sinel (1889–1975), who set up a studio in 1919, has priority. Until the thirties the term 'industrial art' was in more general use, as in Britain's first professional association of designers, the Society for Industrial Artists (now the SIAD), which was founded in 1930. Of this, **Milner Gray** recalled: 'It is noteworthy that only one of the signatories of the original Memorandum . . . listed himself as a "designer" and none as an "industrial designer" '; but in 1944 the Board of Trade in Britain established a Council of Industrial Design.

These English terms, 'industrial design' and the more familiar ellipsis 'design', have become international currency. No other language has a viable synonym, and the Italian *Migliorini* dictionary of 1963 included the term under its *Parole Nuove* (new words) section, even though the English word derives from the *disegno* described by Vasari and other Renaissance writers.

The first generation of industrial designers was anxious to map out the limits of its territory. **Henry Dreyfuss**, **Walter Dorwin Teague** and **Harold van Doren** all made some extravagant claims about the degree of 'science' involved in their design studios. Certainly, each of these pioneers had a primitive understanding that their work should pay attention to **ergonomics**, to efficient function and to cost-effectiveness, but with the perspective of history we can see that they were really most concerned to blend aesthetics with morals in order to create a 'style' all of their own. Although **styling**, which is often held to be inferior to industrial design, was reviled as meretricious, it is merely an approach to industrial design which uses visual tricks and effects in order to stimulate sales. Therefore, any industrial designer at work in a commercial economy has to devote himself, at least to an extent, to styling.

Innovator AB

The Innovator Design Studios are a Swedish design consultancy founded in Stockholm by **Johan Huldt** and **Jan Dranger** in 1968. Innovator has done interior and exhibition design for the Swedish Government, but is best known for its colourful furniture design for Dux Mobel, and lately for mass-market furniture in a **High-Tech** style.

Bislet Pine Bunk Bed, 1970s
IKEA has popularized Swedish design in its hugely successful stores, selling furniture which is all designed to be knocked-down and sold flat. The 'Bislet' bed was designed by Rutger Andersson.

'Slim' Chair and Table by Innovator, 1983
Huldt's designs are strong, durable, brightly coloured and practical, without whimsy. He designed this chair and table for Innovator, the company he founded.

A B C D E F G H I J K L M N O P Q R S T U V W X Y Z

Institute of Design, Chicago

The Institute of Design in Chicago was founded in 1937 by **Laszlo Moholy-Nagy** after his 'New Bauhaus', also in the city, failed. In 1940 it was absorbed, with the Armour Institute of Technology, into the Illinois Institute of Technology. The original curriculum included not only design, but also contextual studies such as literature and psychology. Like the original **Bauhaus** before it, very little real designing for industry went on there and some of the Institute's most famous students were to become craftsmen.

International Style

The International Style was a name invented by **Philip Johnson** for an exhibition he arranged at New York's **Museum of Modern Art** in 1932. The exhibition took its name from **Walter Gropius'** book, *Internationale Architektur*, of 1925.

The first buildings of note were French, Dutch and German, designed by **Le Corbusier**, J.J.P. Oud and Gropius. These architects did not at first refer to their efforts as 'The International Style', but after Johnson's exhibition the label tended to stick. The name refers to the supposed international validity of the **Modern Movement**, but, as Johnson's own later career demonstrated, the International Style *was* just a fashion and its claims to timelessness or permanence proved to be false.
Bibliography Henry-Russell Hitchcock & Philip Johnson *The International Style* W.W. Norton, New York, 1966

Exterior, Villa Savoie, 1929–31
Le Corbusier's Villa Savoie, at Poissy, outside Paris, was the chief monument of the International Style. The apparently simple, yet really very complex, building appears to float effortlessly above the grass, as if to justify its alternative name, 'Les Heures Claires'.

Iron

Iron was, perhaps, the most important structural material of the first industrial era. In its cast form it appeared in Abraham Darby's bridge at Coalbrookdale (1779), as well as in the major engineering structures of the nineteenth century. Wrought iron made the sinuous curves of **Art Nouveau** possible and was used for the decorative balconies and gates which define that style. Steel is an artificially produced type of iron, whose production was made possible by the development of the Bessemer process in the middle of the last century. Steel has superior technical qualities to iron and its manufacture was behind many of the leaps forward in mass-production and the dominant environmental forms which characterize the last hundred years. Steel enabled

Gates of the Philharmonic Public House, Liverpool, 1898–1900

the making of things that had never been seen before, such as huge expanses of riveted sheets, light structural frameworks, or automobile bodies pressed into complex curves. Tubular steel first appeared in bicycle manufacturing at the end of the nineteenth century. It was also used in early aeroplanes, and as the **Bauhaus** was next door to the Junkers aircraft factory some of the teachers there decided that this new material could be used for making furniture. The resulting tubular steel designs of **Marcel Breuer** and **Mies van der Rohe** have become some of the most familiar ikons of the twentieth century. After the Second World War some designers, most notably **Harry Bertoia**, **Charles Eames** and **Ernest Race**, turned to the use of steel rod so as to evolve a lighter, more elegant image for modern furniture.

Isokon

Isokon was a company established by **Jack Pritchard** in the early thirties to manufacture in laminated **plywood** the furniture designs of **Marcel Breuer** and **Wells Coates**.

Alec Issigonis

b. 1906

Born in Smyrna, Turkey, Alec Issigonis became one of the few British automotive engineers to achieve international celebrity. He was educated at Battersea Polytechnic before working as a draughtsman with Rootes Motors in Coventry. He then joined Morris Motors in Oxford and became its chief engineer. In 1961 he was made chief engineer and technical director of the British Motor Corporation.

Issigonis is famous for the conception and execution of three cars: the Morris Minor of 1948, the Morris Mini of 1959 and the Morris 1100 of 1962. Each was pioneering in its own way, but the Mini was undoubtedly the most influential. It was the first car to become classless, and it symbolized the aspirations of an entire generation. It also created an international demand for sophisticated, small, front-wheel-drive cars which **Michel Boué**'s Renault 5 and **Giorgio Giugiaro**'s **Volkswagen** Golf also satisfied, perhaps more efficiently.

Drawing for Morris Mini Minor
Issigonis' design for the Mini was emphatically unstyled. Its appearance was dictated almost entirely by the engineering and the passenger space (although it did also owe something to BMC's own Austin A35). The Mini was perhaps the most radical departure from conventional design ever to appear. Its tiny ten-inch wheels, transverse engine, front-wheel drive, rubber suspension, uniquely functional interior bins and original window slides all introduced advanced design to the general public.

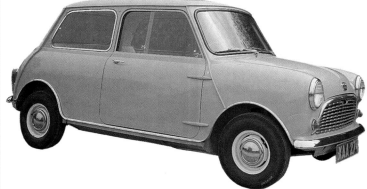

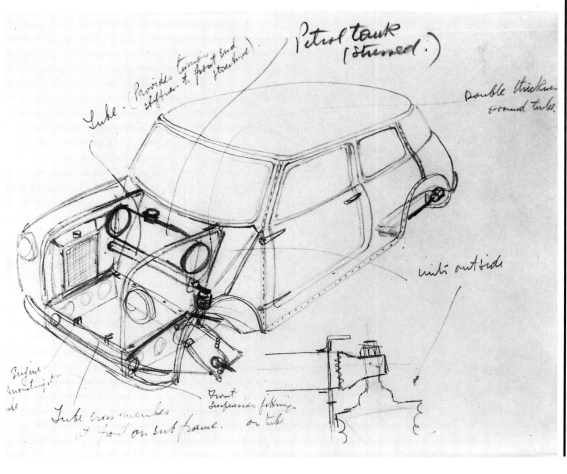

Morris Minor, 1949 model
The Morris Minor appeared in 1948. Its engineering was revolutionary: Issigonis chose unitary construction and torsion bar suspension which made the Minor Britain's first modern car. Its body styling aped Packards and other American cars of the late thirties and early forties, but the Minor's smaller scale made it lovable, rather than impressive. The car remained in production for more than twenty years.

Morris Mini Minor, 1959
The BMC Mini was a development of engineering ideas which Issigonis had sketched in the Morris Minor. It became one of the symbols of an entire generation. The Mini is still in production after more than twenty-five years, and is the most successful British car of all time; it influenced European car production for at least two decades.

A
B
C
D
E
F
G
H
I
J
K
L
M
N
O
P
Q
R
S
T
U
V
W
X
Y
Z

Italian design

Since the Second World War Italy has been the pre-eminent nation in design. There it is a complex activity encompassing exclusive, stylized furniture, sophisticated electronic products, and more traditional trades such as *carrozzerie* (coach building, or, in modern times, car body design).

During the period of *ricostruzione* after the War, design was seen as an important element in Italy's industrial regeneration. From the outset it was associated with the names of certain architects – including the **Castiglioni** brothers, **Ettore Sottsass** and **Marco Zanuso** – who had trained during the thirties and who were employed on a consultancy basis by the newly founded or reorganized firms based around Milan and Turin: **Olivetti**, **Cassina**, **BrionVega** and **Artemide**.

In the forties and fifties the visual source for Italian design was contemporary 'organic' sculpture and this, combined with new production techniques used for the new metals and **plastics**, created a unique aesthetic. Design emerged as an element in marketing policies which emphasized exclusiveness and the 'good life' in products aimed at a wealthy, international market. This bid for a share of world trade was supported by Milan's **Triennale** exhibitions, a vast variety of magazines and **La Rinascente**'s **Compasso d'Oro** awards.

By the mid-fifties Italian chic had been accepted as an international style by the wealthy, while a watered-down version became fashionable at a popular level with espresso coffee and the **Vespa**. However, by the sixties there was a growing dissatisfaction with the chic national image, and some architect-designers who wanted a stronger social base for their work proposed a protest movement called anti-design. Ettore Sottsass was a principal influence in this, together with **Superstudio** and **Archizoom**, and his **Pop** furniture and ceramics were an inspiration to many young Italian designers keen to work outside the constraints of manufacturing industry. Recently, in an apparently deliberate counterpoint to the industrial success of Olivetti and the fashionable success of the middle-of-the-road furniture manufacturers, an irreverent spirit has again emerged in the form of the **Memphis** group of designers, who have reclaimed for Italy the avant-garde.

Bibliography Anty Pansera & Alfonso Grassi *Atlante del design italiano 1940–1980* Fabbri, Milan, 1981

La Rinascente Store, Rome, by Franco Albini and Franca Helg, 1957–1961
Like Milan's Torre Velasca, Rome's La Rinascente store became an architectural symbol of Italy's ricostruzione.

Alfa Romeo 1750 6c Gran Sport by Touring, 1933; Cabinet by Gio Ponti and Piero Fornasetti, 1950
Touring's bodywork for the Alfa Romeo Gran Sport established a norm of beauty and elegant proportion for sports car design. Gio Ponti's cabinet, decorated by Piero Fornasetti, makes use of a renaissance architectural perspective in trompe l'oeil *in order to play with our sense of propriety. The Alfa Romeo is proper, taut and exquisite in its detail; the cabinet is a sophisticated joke. Both elements remain continuously influential in forming the character of Italian design.*

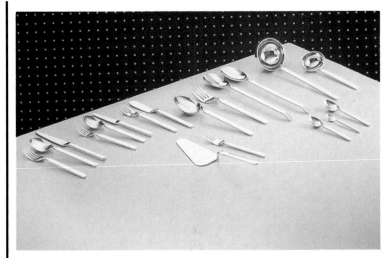

**'DRY' Cutlery by Achille
Castiglioni for Alessi, 1984**
*Castiglioni's cutlery won him a
Compasso d'Oro award.*

**'Il Colonnato' Table by Mario
Bellini for Cassina, 1977**
*Bellini is Italy's leading product
designer. This table's massive
and organic shapes share some
of his products' formal
characteristics.*

**Running Shoe for Kappa by
ItalDesign, early 1980s;
Espresso Percolator for Alessi
by Richard Sapper, 1979**
*Since the Second World War
Italian designers have made
objects to celebrate the 'good
life'. High style and high finish
are essential components.*

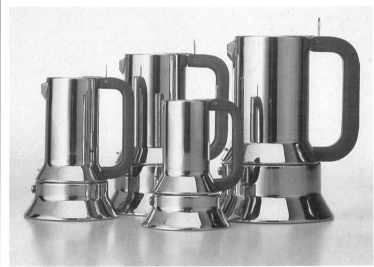

Johannes Itten
1888–1967

Johannes Itten was a Swiss
pedagogue, mystic and designer
who developed the Foundation
course at the **Bauhaus**, after
being introduced to **Walter
Gropius** by Alma Mahler,
Gropius' adventurous wife.
Itten was a disciple of the bogus
pseudo-Iranian religion
Mazdaznan and when he left the
Bauhaus he studied oriental
philosophy. However, his
influence on art education has
been profound. He insisted that
students should 'learn by
doing', and this stipulation has
affected all subsequent art
education.

Itten left the Bauhaus in 1923,
after a disagreement over
policy with Gropius. He
founded his own school in
Berlin in 1926, and later became
director of the art schools in
Zürich and Krefeld.
Bibliography Johannes Itten
*Mein Vorkurs am Bauhaus:
Gestaltung und Formlehre*
Ravensburg, 1963

Plan for a Newspaper, 1920s
*Design for a newspaper
published by the Utopia Press
by Itten and Friedl Dicker. The
idiosyncrasies of this piece
show Itten's preference for
artistic self-expression. This led
him into conflict with Walter
Gropius, who wanted to
concentrate on industrial
design, and when in 1923
Gropius attempted to restore a
technical character to the
Bauhaus curriculum, Itten left.*

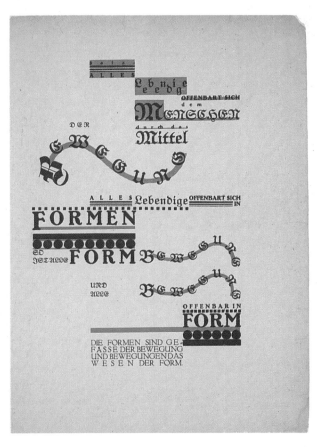

A
B
C
D
E
F
G
H
I
J
K
L
M
N
O
P
Q
R
S
T
U
V
W
X
Y
Z

J

Arne **Jacobsen**
Japanese design
Paul **Jaray**
Charles-
Edouard **Jeanneret**
Jeep
Jenaer Glasverein
Georg **Jensen**
Jakob **Jensen**
Betty **Joel**
Clarence L.
'Kelly' **Johnson**
Philip **Johnson**
Edward **Johnston**
Owen **Jones**
**Journal of Design
and Manufactures**
Jugendstil
Finn **Juhl**
Dora **Jung**

Arne Jacobsen

1902–71

Arne Jacobsen designed both chairs and buildings. He studied architecture in Copenhagen, graduating from the Royal Academy of Fine Arts in 1927, but only came to prominence in the fifties. It was Arne Jacobsen's achievement to turn the austerity of **Functionalism** into refinement and elegance, as was characteristic of **Danish design**. As a contemporary wrote, 'A distinctive feature of Arne Jacobsen's work is the care with which every detail is designed to support the whole. He saw a building as a physical setting for the life to be lived there, and he considered furniture and fittings, floor and wall materials, lighting and window details to be just as important as the building's general design and outward appearance.' Jacobsen designed three important chairs for Fritz Hansen: a stacking chair in 1952 and the 'Egg' and the 'Swan', both of which first appeared in his SAS Hotel in Copenhagen of 1958. Like all his work, they combine sculptural elegance with technical sophistication.

'Egg' Chair, 1958
The 'Egg' Chair was made for Copenhagen's SAS Hotel which Jacobsen also designed.

'Ant' Chair for Fritz Hansen, 1953
Jacobsen's 'Ant' chair was originally designed for the canteen of a pharmaceutical factory in Copenhagen. It has a moulded double shell of plywood and steel rod legs. Jacobsen said that he despised 'good taste' in furniture design and thought that industrial techniques could satisfy all functional and aesthetic requirements.

Japanese design

To a Western observer Japanese design evokes two simultaneous images: one is of traditional craft objects such as lacquerwork and ceramics, the other is of mass-produced high-technology artefacts such as hi-fi, cameras and motorbikes. Each is an expression of the same tradition.

The modern Western concept of design was introduced to Japan in the second half of the nineteenth century, when individuals like **Otto Wagner** and **Christopher Dresser** travelled to the East. This began an interchange of ideas between East and West which has continued throughout this century.

After the Second World War, with the restructuring of the economy under the Marshall Plan, art and industry were deliberately integrated, and great Japanese manufacturers, **Sony** and **Honda** for instance, arose out of the desolation of war to dominate world markets. At first the emphasis was on cheap high-volume production, and manufacturers simply aped European or American rivals, but when the markets for these goods were saturated the Japanese began to explore higher-margin territory. On top of this, pressure from government bodies in the later fifties forced the major manufacturers to develop design policies for their goods. Although Nissan used American and Italian designers (including **Giovanni Michelotti**), the first expression of Japanese design was unique to the country, comprising, in the early sixties, a messy aesthetic which relied for its strength on a symbolic expression of technological supremacy: thus, hi-fi sets were covered with knobs and dials and motorbikes were made to look deliberately complex and aggressive. An important development was an exhibition in Tokyo in 1965 organized by the Japanese Council of Industrial Design, followed by an **ICSID** exhibition in Kyoto in 1973. At these Japanese designers were exposed to **Braun** products, and picked up their stylistic features, pursuing them further than the Germans ever did. Nevertheless, Japanese product design remained, and still is, deficient in **ergonomics** and emphatic in expression and in emotive appeals to consumer psychology.

With the exception of **GK Industrial Design Associates**, the designer's role in Japan is an essentially anonymous one. Just as in other aspects of Japanese life, the self is subordinated to the will of the group; the corporations have their own huge design studios, which are usually subsidiaries of research and development or marketing departments.

The Japanese contribution to contemporary design has been abstract and organizational rather than merely visual. It is a total attitude which many Western companies are now struggling to imitate. While the Japanese began by copying the West, the signs are that the relationship is beginning to be reversed. (See also pp. 58–63.)

Toyota Corolla, 1.3GL, 4 door Saloon, 1984

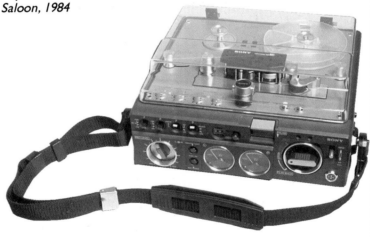

Olympus 'OM10', 1978 (left, top) and 'XA', 1980 Cameras
After Japanese manufacturers had flooded world markets with conventional single lens reflex cameras such as the Olympus 'OM10' new markets were needed. The Olympus designers exploited a niche for a high quality, compact, range-finder camera, with the 'XA' of 1980, which includes many ingenious details including a sliding barrier which acts as shutter lock, lens cap and carrying case.

'TC-5550–2' Tape-Recorder, 1982
Sony has a well-justified reputation as one of Japan's most design-conscious manufacturers. Its 'TC-5550–2' of 1982 imitated the Swiss Nagra tape-recorder used by professionals in broadcasting, but is intended for domestic use. This is typical of Japanese commercial psychology, which aims to project the mystique of professionalism in its products.

Toyota A1, 1935
Japanese design has consistently imitated Western models, but with remarkable innovations in production engineering. Toyota's first passenger vehicle was the self-developed A1 of 1935, which imitated American cars in its styling – but with less commercial success, for only three A1s were ever built. Half a century later, the same company's Corolla became one of the world's best-selling cars. Its body styling was derived from more refined European cars.

Sony 'Trinitron' Television, 1982
Like Braun before them, Sony's electrical and electronic products confer dignity on their surroundings whether they are switched on or not.

Yamaha RD 350 Motorbike by GK Industrial Design Associates, 1973
GK Industrial Design Associates mixes a Buddhist care for perfection with a commercial attention to detail. This bike is typical of its work: GK created the aggressive, sporting image, made each part interesting, and the whole fascinating.

A B C D E F G H I J K L M N O P Q R S T U V W X Y Z

Paul Jaray

1889–1974

Paul Jaray was a Swiss engineer who pioneered the study of **aerodynamics** as applied to motor vehicles. His career began as an engineer in the Zeppelin airship works, where he helped refine the airship into a tear-drop-shaped tube with the aid of mathematical models. In 1922 he won a patent for an aerodynamic car, using many of the principles he had established as sound on the Zeppelin. Jaray's vocabulary of form – which included faired-in headlights, wraparound windscreens, flush door handles – was eventually to pass into the language of car design, although not before he and his solicitors had tried to sue almost all his imitators. Jaray's ideas about the shape of cars were a profound influence on Ferdinand **Porsche** and his **Volkswagen** project engineers.

Charles-Edouard Jeanneret see Le Corbusier

Jeep

Since its appearance at the beginning of the Second World War, the Jeep has been admired as a masterpiece of utilitarian form and proportion.

It was designed by Army Captain Robert G. Howie, in cooperation with Colonel Arthur W.S. Hetherington, the co-founder of a company intended to manufacture four-wheel-drive utility vehicles. The prototype appeared at Fort Benning, Georgia, in 1940. Production was taken over by Willys-Overland and **Ford**. More than 600,000 were built during the War.

Its name is a contraction of the Army usage, 'General Purpose' vehicle, or 'Gee Pee'.

Georg Jensen

1866–1935

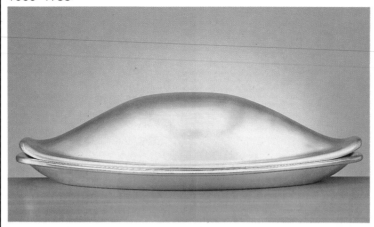

Georg Jensen was a Danish silversmith who evolved an elegant, simple style for tableware. He opened his Copenhagen workshop in the early years of the century, inspired by the British **Arts and Crafts** movement. At first Jensen's style was highly decorative, but gradually became more simplified. Most of the leading Danish silversmiths, including Kay Bojesen and **Erik Herlow** have done work for his company.

Fish Platter in Sterling Silver, 1954
Georg Jensen has consistently offered high standards of craftsmanship in its silverware, and has frequently attracted artists, such as the sculptor Henning Koppel, whose fish dish of 1954 is typical of his mannered style. Koppel gave everyday objects a monumental character which was frequently imitated by manufacturers with less demanding standards than Jensen.

Jakob Jensen

b. 1926

Jakob Jensen is the chief designer of Bang & Olufsen, the Danish audio manufacturer whose elegant rosewood and satin steel products were the last words in consumerist chic before Japanese technology overtook Danish taste. Jensen studied at Copenhagen's Kunsthandvaerkskolen (applied arts school) and then worked with Sigvard Bernadotte before going to the United States and working at the University of Illinois from 1959 to 1961. Although his achievement is very much that of **styling**, Jensen has been responsible for some technical innovations, including the tangential pick-up arm, which was introduced on the 'Beogram 4000' in 1972.

'Beogram 4000' Record Deck, 1972
As much as Hans Wegner's 'The Chair' (1949), Jacob Jensen's elegantly minimal designs for hi-fi manufacturer Bang & Olufsen have come to symbolize Danish design. However, the 'language' and efficacy of Jensen's design is now played out. Bang & Olufsen relies more and more on Japanese components in its struggle to stay financially afloat.

Betty Joel

1894–1985

For a short period during the twenties and thirties, Betty Joel was one of the outstanding designer-decorators in London working in the Modern style. But the shortness of her career underlines how evanescent the influence of the **Modern Movement** was on **British design**.

In 1921 Joel set up a furniture workshop on Hayling Island, with a showroom on London's Sloane Street. She used the skills available at the nearby Portsmouth Dockyards to have yacht fitters make her furniture. At first this was an austere version of the **Arts and Crafts**, but it later turned into an exuberant form of Modernism. This transformation did not come about through a commitment to the socialistic aims of **Walter Gropius**, but purely for stylistic expression. There was very little that was austere in her designs: although she favoured simple, uncluttered, curved forms (which she felt to be 'feminine'), her flamboyant use of luxury woods and decorative veneers led to criticism from the then hard-line **Architectural Review**, although it also brought commissions to design interiors for the Savoy Group hotels, as well as for Winston Churchill and Lord Mountbatten. She went into retirement in 1937 after her divorce.

Bibliography David Joel *The Adventure of British Furniture* 1953

Clarence L. Johnson

b. 1910

'Kelly' Johnson studied **aerodynamics** and structures at the University of Michigan, joining Lockheed as a tool designer in 1933. He became chief engineer in 1938.

Johnson was a second generation romantic engineer, a man able to impose his vision of how machines might be on to the production lines of mighty corporations. His first remarkable design was for the Lockheed P-38 pursuit plane of 1941, a remarkable creation with dramatic twin tail booms which influenced **Harley Earl** to introduce decorative tail fins on to his line of **General Motors** cars. The P-38 proved that even within the strict rules of military aerodynamics there was enough room for personal expression. At Lockheed's 'Skunk Works' in Burbank, California, Johnson's team brought science fiction to reality with the P-80 'Shooting Star', America's first jet fighter, which was designed and built in just 143 days during 1943. He was appointed Lockheed's chief designer in 1952 and was responsible for the overall layout and, no doubt, the appearance of the U-2 spy plane, the C-130 ('Hercules') transport and the 'Jetstar' liaison aircraft. As vice-president of advanced development from 1958, Johnson was responsible for the SR-71 'Blackbird', the most technologically advanced aircraft in the world. Kelly Johnson became a senior vice-president of Lockheed in 1969.

Johnson has been given every civilian award available to an American citizen. Perhaps his greatest achievement transcends his actual products and his designs and lies in his ability to integrate theoretical insights with solid, hard-won practical skills. He deplores specialization and was proud that he had a very high proportion of non-graduates working for him.

Although none of Johnson's aircraft designs is a 'consumer' product in the strictest sense, they are widely admired by designers and architects as symbols of high technology allied to imagination. A plane like the SR-71, although at the summit of modern technology, is also a powerful expression of a will-to-form. Because his dramatic shapes have fascinated designers, Johnson could claim to be one of the important hidden influences on modern taste.

He became an Honorary Royal Designer for Industry in 1984.

Clarence 'Kelly' Johnson with his U-2 Spy Plane, early 1960s
As chief engineer of California's Lockheed Corporation, Johnson designed dramatic aircraft shapes which donated a new language of form to designers and architects.

Philip Johnson

b. 1906

Philip Cortelyou Johnson, an American socialite who became an architect and a creator of styles, was born into a wealthy family in Cleveland. As his family became even wealthier he did not need to graduate from Harvard's architecture school until he was thirty-six. **Walter Gropius** was among his teachers, but Johnson had already made his name with an exhibition he organized at New York's **Museum of Modern Art** with the architectural historian Henry-Russell Hitchcock in 1932. This was the first major American exhibition on the **International Style**, a movement which it introduced to American art-lovers looking for a new fashion. He returned to the Museum of Modern Art as director of the architecture and design department from 1946 to 1954, when he left to concentrate on architecture.

Johnson has remained an influential figure in American taste. A right-wing anarchist, he recently said, 'What good does it do to believe in good things?' Although he still works in Park Avenue's Seagram Building, a **Mies van der Rohe** tower block on which he was the job architect, Johnson soon tired of the purity of the European Modernism he had introduced to America and began, on his own admission, to work like an architectural whore and design anything for anyone who paid him. In 1961, at a speech in London, Johnson said 'You cannot *not* know history,' and this opened up a whole vista of more-or-less witty historicism which would have been antithetical to his hero, **Le Corbusier**.

In 1975 Johnson was approached by AT&T Corporation to design their corporate headquarters in New York. Johnson produced a monumental tower block with a Chippendale open pediment about a thousand storeys off the ground. It was one of the first expressions of **Post-Modernism** in architecture. Johnson said of himself that he wanted to be remembered as the man who introduced the glass box and fifty years later . . . broke it.
Bibliography Charles Jencks *The Language of Post-Modern Architecture* Academy Editions, London, 4th edn, 1984

Glass Covered Arcade of AT&T Building, New York, 1978–1984
In the forties when the Modern Movement was fashionable, Johnson built himself a summer house in suburban New Canaan, Connecticut, which openly imitated the architecture of Mies van der Rohe. Forty years later, Johnson (who had never been very greatly moved by the social purposes of the Modern Movement) had tired of copying Mies and became one of the chief spokesmen for Post-Modernism. His AT&T Building on New York's Madison Avenue, with its historical references and expensive materials, has been greeted as the first 'masterpiece' of that movement.

A B C D E F G H I J K L M N O P Q R S T U V W X Y Z

Edward Johnston

1872–1944

Edward Johnston had intended to become a doctor, but poor health prevented him and he became a calligrapher instead, carrying on **Eric Gill**'s principles of simplifying lettering. In 1899 he was invited to teach writing at the **Central School of Arts and Crafts** by W.R. Lethaby. He published two books, *Writing and Illuminating, and Lettering* (1906) and *Manuscript and Inscription Letters* (1909), which were important contributions to the revival of calligraphy in the twentieth century. Although much of Johnston's work was handicraft, he became famous for a commission given him in 1916 by **Frank Pick** to design a sans serif typeface for London Transport, which is still in use today.

London Transport Underground Station
London Transport still uses the signs which Johnston designed for it seventy years ago.

Owen Jones

1809–74

A Welsh architect, Owen Jones formed part of the circle around **Henry Cole** and was, therefore, in a position to influence modern taste. His great work was *The Grammar of Ornament* (1856), in which he illustrated architectural decoration he had seen on his tours of the Middle East and Spain. The *Grammar* was not just another book of architectural details, but was a polemical tract (and, incidentally, an early monument to the skills of the colour lithographer). Jones assembled all the ornaments he could, not so that designers might copy them, but so that they might be inspired by their underlying principles, such as made, say, Jacobean linenfold and Greek meander, each successful in its way. The book was prefaced by thirty-seven propositions about design in which Jones attacked historicism and slavish fidelity to the past, and encouraged designers to create new, rational, formalized patterns, long before **William Morris** had the same idea. Proposition 37, for example, says, 'The principles discoverable in the works of the past belong to us; not so the results. It is taking the end for the means.' Jones was a profound influence on **Christopher Dresser**.
Bibliography Nikolaus Pevsner *Some Architectural Writers of the Nineteenth Century* Oxford University Press, Oxford and New York, 1973

Journal of Design and Manufactures

The *Journal of Design* was founded by **Henry Cole** in 1849. Earlier than the **Great Exhibition** and the **Victoria and Albert Museum**, it was the first vehicle to bring his ideas to the British nation. It was short-lived, but succeeded in communicating to a wide audience many of the central ideas about design reform and the relation of art to industry in those years.

Jugendstil

Jugendstil, literally 'Youth Style', is the term used in the German-speaking and Scandinavian countries for **Art Nouveau**.

Finn Juhl

b.1912

A designer of eloquently sculptural chairs, Finn Juhl studied architecture under **Kaare Klint.** With **Erik Herlow**, **Arne Jacobsen** and **Hans Wegner**, Juhl was one of the individuals who made **Danish design** into a phenomenon in international taste. By showing in his designs from the fifties – including the 'Chief Chair' – the influence of primitive African sculpture, he was influential in moving Danish designers away from their indigenous craft traditions towards a more expressive, even modern, aesthetic.

Leather Chair, early 1950s
Juhl has designed the most expressive Danish furniture, strongly influenced by primitive, especially African, sculpture.

Dora Jung

1906–8

A Finnish textile designer, Dora Jung was trained at Helsinki's Taideteollisuuskeskuskoulu (applied arts school) and set up her own weaving shed in 1932. She won prizes at the Milan **Triennales** of 1951, 1954 and 1957. Her work is characterized by simple, geometric patterns, inspired by folk weaves.

Wilhelm Kåge

1889–1960

Wilhelm Kåge's name is inseparable from that of his employer, the Swedish ceramics manufacturer **Gustavsberg**.

He trained as a painter, but like **Gunnar Wennerberg** and **Jean Heiberg** found the appeal of industry irresistible. Kåge once remarked, 'From the old, provincial handicrafts to the modern industrial worker's taste there are no pathways.' During his forty-three years at Gustavsberg he was responsible for many formal and practical innovations: oven-to-table ware, stacking china and attractive services designed for low-income families, known as 'KG' in the Gustavsberg catalogue. For the Stockholm Exhibition of 1930 he experimented with **Functionalism**, producing an abstract dinner service called the 'Pyro' service (p. 147). It was intended for volume production and was designed to be rational: it was stackable, dishes could double as lids, there was no applied decoration apart from some simple banding, and there were no inaccessible recesses. It was a commercial failure, but a great critical success. As a result of that failure he introduced a softer and less stylized version called 'Praktika' (p. 147), which remained in production for thirty years.

In the later thirties Kåge continued with his restless inventiveness; his 'Set of Soft Forms' appeared just before the New York World's Fair of 1939 and gave rise to the expression 'Swedish Modern'. It was to establish the aesthetic standards of the fifties. Kåge left Gustavsberg to return to painting in 1949.

Bibliography Nils Palmgren *Wilhelm Kåge* Nordisk Rotogravyr, Stockholm, 1953

'Home Exhibition' Poster, 1917
The 'Home Exhibition' of 1917 was crucial to the development of Swedish design. This poster, designed by Kåge, evoked the domestic and natural concerns characteristic of Swedish culture.

Wunibald Kamm

1893–1966

With **Paul Jaray**, Kamm is one of the great automotive engineers. His name is not well known, but his theories about **aerodynamics** have had a pervasive effect on our assumptions about how cars should be designed.

Kamm was born in Basle and graduated from Stuttgart's technical college in 1922. His first job was also in Stuttgart, working for Daimler-Benz. He went on to become head of the Forschungsintitut für Kraftfahrwesen und Fahrzeugmotoren Stuttgart (FKFS, or Research Institute for Motor Transport and Motor Vehicle Engines), where he had the opportunity to develop theories outlined in an undergraduate thesis on aerodynamics. In fact, he was the first engineer to make aerodynamics an exact science rather than an empirical one, and as part of this process he developed the first commercial wind tunnel. Kamm promulgated the so-called 'K-Heck', or Kamm tail, a device where a car's bodywork is dramatically truncated just to the rear of the passenger area, as his research indicated that this enhanced a vehicle's aerodynamic effectiveness by ▶

Wilhelm **Kåge**
Wunibald **Kamm**
Tom **Karen**
       Kartell
Masura **Katsumie**
Edward
McKnight **Kauffer**
       Kenzo
Frederick **Kiesler**
Perry **King**
Rodney **Kinsman**
       Kitsch
Poul **Kjaerholm**
Calvin **Klein**
Kare **Klint**
Hans **Knoll**
Mogens **Koch**
Erwin **Komenda**
Henning **Koppel**
       Kosta
Friso **Kramer**
Yrjo **Kukkapuro**
Shiro **Kuramata**

improving the behaviour of 'boundary layer' air.

In 1935 Kamm set up the automobile department in Munich's Deutsches Museum. For ten years after 1945 he worked at the Stevens Institute of Technology at Hoboken, New Jersey, returning to Germany in 1955 to head the Department of Mechanical Engineering at Frankfurt's Battelle Institut.
Bibliography Ralf J.F. Kieselbach *Stromlinienautos in Deutschland – Aerodynamik im PKW-Bau 1900 bis 1945* Kohlhammer, Stuttgart, 1982

Bar Stool in High-Specification Plastic by Anna Castelli Ferrieri, 1979

Nursery School System, 1978
This colourful system combines the functions of furniture and plaything. It is made of PVC and melamine, and has rubber feet to minimize noise.

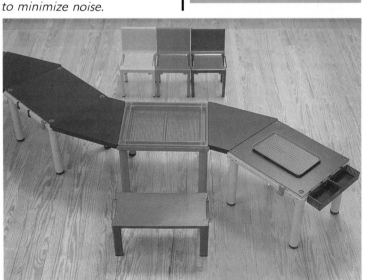

Tom Karen see **Ogle**

Kartell

Kartell is a Milanese furniture manufacturer, founded in 1949. It specializes in high-quality **plastic** injection mouldings, and in the early fifties was innovative in producing plastic objects designed by **Gino Colombini**. His aesthetic was aggressively modern and his use of plastics not imitative of other materials. Since then Kartell has made furniture to the designs of **Joe Colombo** and **Marco Zanuso**.

Masura Katsumie

1904–83

Masura Katsumie founded Tokyo Zokei Art and Design University and established the journal, *Graphic Design*. He was design director of the 1964 Tokyo Olympics, Expo 70 in Osaka and the 1972 Winter Olympics at Sapporo.

Edward McKnight Kauffer

1890–1954

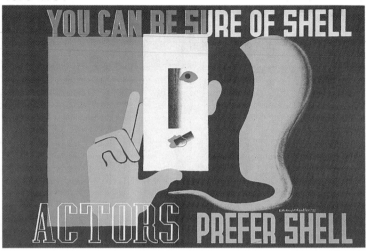

Edward McKnight Kauffer was born in Great Falls, Montana, and, after a series of dead-end jobs, arrived at the Art Institute of Chicago and then went to study in Munich and Paris. On his way back to the United States on the outbreak of the First World War he stopped in London and decided to stay. His first commission came in 1915 from London Underground to design a poster; so successful was this and subsequent posters that he gave up painting in 1920. McKnight Kauffer's reputation continued to rise in the early twenties and in 1926 he was given an exhibition at Oxford's Ashmolean Museum, a rare honour for a 'commercial artist'. In 1937 he had a retrospective show at New York's **Museum of Modern Art**.

Kauffer's poster technique was one of dramatic stylization, rather comparable to Henri Gaudier-Brzeska's sculpture or Wyndham Lewis' illustrations. It suited posters very well, but worked less happily when contained by the edges of a page. He returned to the United States in 1941.
Bibliography Mark Haworth-Booth *Edward Mcknight Kauffer* Gordon Fraser, London, 1968

'Actors Prefer Shell', Poster, 1934
During the thirties Shell Petroleum was one of the great patrons of design in Britain. In 1932 it combined its publicity efforts with BP under Jack Beddington who, with his patronage of John Betjeman (who wrote some of the Shell Guides) and McKnight Kauffer, became a private sector equivalent of London Transport's Frank Pick.

Kenzo

b. 1939

Kenzo Takada was the first Japanese fashion designer after **Hanae Mori** to establish a reputation in the West, although having his head-quarters in Paris has cut him off from the native influence which still inspires his contemporary, **Issey Miyake**, and his younger followers, Yohji Yamamoto and Rei Kawakubo.

Kenzo started the 'Jap' label for his own boutique Jungle Jap after a series of Paris collections, beginning in 1971, where he showed big skirts and broad-shouldered jackets in a mixture of modern Western and oriental styles. After an early hiatus produced by the pirating of his revolutionary shapes and exacerbated by his own primitive production systems, Kenzo has now established chains of boutiques across Europe and the United States.

Knit ensemble, 1982–3
The oversize jacket and interesting silhouette are characteristic of Kenzo's youthful, innovative style.

Frederick Kiesler

1892–1965

Frederick Kiesler was born in Vienna and studied there at the Technische Hochschule and at the Akademie der Bildenden Kunst. He worked on a slum clearance project with **Adolf Loos**. In the early twenties he began to work on stage design, providing the *mise-en-scène* for the first production of Karel Čapek's *R.U.R.* (1922), using motion pictures instead of painted backdrops. For the 1925 Paris Exposition Internationale des Arts Décoratifs Kiesler designed a sensational 'floating city'. He moved to the United States in 1926 and wrote an influential book about shop design in 1930. From 1933 to 1957 Kiesler was Scenic Director in the Design Laboratory of New York's Columbia University's School of Architecture.
Bibliography F. Kiesler *Contemporary Art Applied to the Store and its Display* Pitman, London, 1930

Perry King

b. 1938

Perry King was born in London and studied at Birmingham College of Art. He went to Italy in 1965 and worked with **Ettore Sottsass** until 1970 on various projects for **Olivetti**, including the abortive Valentine typewriter and the more successful 'Synthesis 45' office furniture. In 1972 he became design coordinator in the **corporate identity** department of Olivetti, under **Hans von Klier**. In 1977 he formed a partnership with Santiago Miranda, with whom he has designed, amongst other things, a series of lights for **Flos**.

Olivetti 'Valentine', 1969
Perry King designed Olivetti's 'Valentine' typewriter in partnership with his early mentor, Ettore Sottsass. Conceived by Sottsass as a machine that could help demolish popular prejudices about office equipment with its Pop styling, the 'Valentine' was promoted in a distinguished series of posters by Milton Glaser, but it was technically mediocre and failed to sell. Nevertheless, stylistically it is one of the more remarkable artefacts of the sixties.

Rodney Kinsman

b. 1943

Rodney Kinsman is the 'K' in **OMK**, which he set up in 1966 with two furniture designers who graduated with him from London's **Central School of Art and Design** in 1962. Kinsman's first chair was the T1, in bent tubular steel and suede. It did not achieve success, but that came in 1971 with Omkstack chair, a fusion of **Hans Coray**'s pre-War design and **David Rowland**'s GF/40. During the seventies OMK licensed some of its designs to Bieffe in Italy.

Kitsch

The word Kitsch is derived from the German '*verkitschen etwas*', which means to knock something off. Its meaning is complex and subtle, but can broadly be said to imply the deliberate confrontation of accepted standards in design and manners. In an essay of 1939 'Kitsch and the avant-garde', Clement Greenberg, the veteran American critic of modern art, gave one of the best explanations of Kitsch, saying that it was an attitude to art and design which preyed on mature cultures, raiding them for tricks and effects, in order to achieve a facile and superficial result which betrays the consumer because it is undemanding and ultimately unsatisfying.

The term was first current in the German-speaking countries, particularly in Vienna, around the turn of the century, and as early as 1909 Gustav Pazaurek had opened a 'Museum of Bad Taste' in Stuttgart's Industrial Museum. The word was enshrined in the title of a book of 1924 by Fritz Karpfen, but the key work is an anthology of essays edited by **Gillo Dorfles** in 1969.

Since **Post-Modernism** became fashionable it has become acceptable in some quarters to celebrate Kitsch as the populist expression of a taste which is opposite to that of the **Modern Movement**. The veteran American critic, James Marston Fitch, described thus, disapprovingly, the work of **Michael Graves**, a leader of Post-Modernism. Some people see Kitsch as a means of re-establishing expression and symbolism as parts of the designer's concern. But as the critic Peter Dormer has explained, 'Kitsch relies on duping the purchaser . . . It does not need and will not survive more than a first glance in order to deliver all it has to offer.'
Bibliography Clement Greenberg *Art and Culture* Beacon Press, Boston, 1961; Gillo Dorfles *Kitsch* Thames & Hudson, London, 1969; Gustav Pazaurek *Guter und schlechter Geschmack im Kunstgewerbe* Deutsche Verlags-Anstalt, Stuttgart & Berlin, 1912; 'Taste' exhibition catalogue, The Boilerhouse Project, Victoria & Albert Museum, London, 1983

Cocktail Shaker, late 1960s
Kitsch is a constant force in modern industrial culture. When industry has made an abundance of choice available it is inevitable that some manufacturers and consumers will consciously elect to have things which violate norms of good taste. This motorized cocktail shaker, in the form of a bikini-clad girl, was produced in Japan.

Poul Kjaerholm

1929–80

Poul Kjaerholm studied at Copenhagen's Kunsthandvaerkskolen (applied arts school) and then became a furniture designer. His speciality is a pure and elegant form of minimalism, using striking combinations of stainless steel with cane and African goat skin, so that the variety and contrast of textures is a complement to the austerity of the form. The ikon of his career is a chaise-longue manufactured by E. Kold Christensen, which has been described as 'a diagram of relaxation'. Other important designs of his include a marble coffee table.

The 'Hammond' Chair, 1965
It is traditional in Denmark to use wood for furniture, but Poul Kjaerholm's chaise-longue used cane and tempered steel instead. The strength of the steel allowed him to achieve an elegant minimalism.

Kaare Klint

1888–1954

Perhaps more than any other individual, Kaare Klint can claim to have been responsible for the Danish tradition in modern furniture. Although Klint did not identify himself with **Functionalism** and regarded the **Bauhaus'** curriculum as unhelpfully narrow, his early studies in design were concerned with standardization, modular construction and with actual need, rather than being self-conscious essays in style. He was amongst the first furniture designers seriously to study

anthropometrics. He regarded the famous English cabinet-makers of the eighteenth century as models of excellence. Furthermore, he expanded the vocabulary of **Danish design** by making it possible for furniture manufacturers to use unvarnished woods, undyed leathers and plain fabrics. Klint's principal designs date from the thirties when he reworked the safari chair and the deck chair (p. 112), two classics of functional seating. **Bibliography** Erik Zahle *Scandinavian Domestic Design* Methuen, London, 1963

Calvin Klein

b. 1942

It was in the US fashion industry that the term 'designer' first became a bankable and desirable epithet for merchandise, when, in 1977, Warren Hirsh of Murjani International persuaded socialite Gloria Vanderbilt to add her name to a line of jeans. In 1980 Hirsh joined Murjani's rival, Puritan, and conjured the same magical formula, this time using the name of fashion designer Calvin Klein.

Klein had been in business since 1968, specializing in simple classic designs in quality natural fabrics, clothes that

were plain and well cut, big but not heavy. He was influenced by **Yves St Laurent**, but produced designs that were more American in colouring and more showy. After the extraordinary, if temporary, success of his 'designer' jeans, Klein was tempted into a whole range of design activity, including furs, shoes, bags and bed linen, and in 1984 he began marketing men's 'Y' front underpants for women. He maintains tight creative control on all activities that bear his name, including the television commercials. He is the first American designer to win the Coty award for five consecutive years.

Jeans and Leather Jacket, 1979
Klein here combines the casual look with status-filled luxury, using fine fabrics, soft leathers and glamorous colours.

'Safari' Chair, 1933
Kaare Klint's 'Safari' chair was manufactured by Rasmussens of Copenhagen. Klint's interest in exotic furniture led him to the 'safari' chairs of the nineteenth-century explorers. These light, compact chairs, which were easy to store, although they had been derived from century-old models, proved socially appropriate to spare, modern interiors. The 'Safari' was among the first chairs to be sold 'knocked-down' for ease of distribution.

Hans Knoll

1914–55

Hans Knoll was born in Stuttgart, the son of a cabinet-maker. He was educated in Switzerland and in England, where he first attempted to set up a business, but the British market was slow to accept modern furniture design. Moreover, a cousin, Willi Knoll, had already established a business in Britain, based on a new system of springing chairs which he had devised. Parker-Knoll was the partnership he formed with Tom Parker; it specialized in well-sprung chintz and plush, tailored for middle-class British taste.

Hans Knoll went instead to America, in 1937, and established the Hans G. Knoll Furniture Company in New York. With his second wife, Florence Schust, who had studied at **Cranbrook Academy** and was a friend of **Eero Saarinen**'s, he established Knoll Associates in 1946. Hans Knoll's idea was to promote designers by name and to pay them royalties on furniture sold from his 'collection', and thus he reached a unique accommodation between European design and American business practice. The moment was absolutely right: from its shop on Madison Avenue Knoll Associates was able to supply corporate America with the modern furniture which was to dominate US building for the twenty-five years after the Second World War. As merchant and manufacturer Hans Knoll introduced Danish furniture into America and made **Marcel Breuer** and **Mies van der Rohe** famous: **Isamu Noguchi** compared the achievement to that of the **Bauhaus** itself (see also p. 48 and **Dino Gavina**). It is the only company allowed by Breuer's family to manufacture his furniture.

Hans Knoll was killed in a car crash in Havana, Cuba, in 1955, but Florence Knoll carried on running the company and attempted to sustain high design standards by working with other leading designers through the following decades.

Although continuously maintaining a high critical reputation, Knoll Associates was never wholly successful in financial terms. In 1968 it was taken over by Art Metal, and in 1977 was sold to General Felt. **Bibliography** Eric Larrabee & Massimo Vignelli *Knoll Design* Abrams, New York, 1981

Knoll Fabrics, mid-1970s
A trade magazine advertisement designed by Massimo Vignelli in 1977.

Furniture by Marcel Breuer
Virtually every individual design by Marcel Breuer was being manufactured by Knoll during the seventies. From left to right: 'Cesca', with and without arms, 'Wassily', and Breuer's chaise-longue.

Furniture by Gae Aulenti, 1975
This advertisement for Gae Aulenti's 1975 range of furniture was designed by Massimo Vignelli in 1976. The contrast between the modern furniture and its classical setting is characteristic of Knoll's self-consciousness as a manufacturer of furniture whose appeal is in part based on a knowledge of traditions in the fine arts and architecture.

Mogens Koch

b. 1898

The Danish furniture designer Mogens Koch is known for one great design, the 'Mk 16' chair of 1933. Like **Kaare Klint**, Koch helped revive traditional chair forms in natural materials, and he was an important influence on the development of **Danish design**.

Erwin Komenda

1904–66

Erwin Komenda was a body engineer who worked for Ferdinand **Porsche** and was responsible for the physical appearance of the original **Volkswagen** and also the series of Porsche cars which began with the Type 356 of 1949 and ended with the Type 901 of 1963. (The Type 901 has been marketed, for copyright reasons, as the Type 911.)

Komenda joined Porsche's Stuttgart office from Daimler-Benz where he had been chief designer for body development. His first assignment at Porsche was the body design for the astonishing Auto-Union racing car. Komenda's body design for the Volkswagen was a perfect consolidation of the ideas around at the time. It combined advanced **aerodynamic** qualities together with a sophisticated integrated appearance. There is no welded seam on the Volkswagen which has to be covered by leading, all the body panels fitting together organically. Although Komenda's interpretation of aerodynamics betrays the fashions of thirties **streamlining**, he would never have accepted that **styling** had any part to play in car body design; he would, instead, have seen it as a question of engineering responsibility. In all its essentials the Volkswagen body which Komenda designed remained in production in Europe for more than forty years (and is still being produced in Mexico, Brazil, South Africa and Nigeria).
Bibliography Ferry Porsche & John Bentley *We At Porsche* Haynes, Yeovil, 1976; Doubleday, New York, 1976

Henning Koppel

1918–81

Koppel was a Danish designer of silverware and glass, which was often sculptural and attenuated in form. After 1945 he worked mostly for **Georg Jensen** in Copenhagen, but also became a freelance designer for **Orrefors** in 1971. Koppel's treatment of his medium is characterized by a strong sense of organic form, but without recourse to literal representation. Thus, a platter he designed for Jensen in 1954 *suggests* that it should hold a fish, but does not actually imitate one. Koppel's designs, whether in silver, glass or stainless steel, evoke the refined yet democratic mood of the Scandinavian interior of the fifties.
Bibliography David Revere McFadden *Scandinavian Modern Design 1880–1980* Abrams, New York, 1982

Kosta

Swedish glassworks, founded in Smaland in 1742.

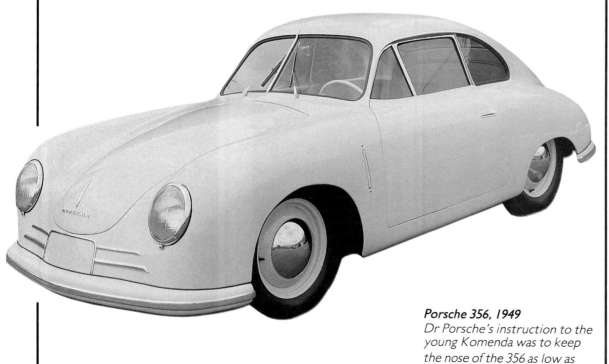

Porsche 356, 1949
Dr Porsche's instruction to the young Komenda was to keep the nose of the 356 as low as possible. The shape he produced became the inspiration of a whole tradition in car design.

Friso Kramer

b. 1922

The Dutch furniture designer Friso Kramer studied electrical engineering in Amsterdam and only became directly involved with the creative side of design when in 1962 he founded **Total Design**.

Poster for the Stedelijk Museum, Amsterdam, showing Kramer's Office Chair, 1977

Yrjo Kukkapuro

b. 1933

Yrjo Kukkapuro was born in rural Finland and studied **industrial design** in Helsinki. He opened his own practice in 1959, producing designs almost exclusively for the Haimi Oy company. His 'Karuselli 412' chair of 1965 was one of the classics of the sixties. The design employs a steel reinforced glass-fibre shell, thinly padded with leather; the shape of the shell is sufficiently organic for only slight upholstery to be necessary, while the cradle, which allows swivelling and rocking, means that the sitter can change his posture without shifting his body. Kukkapuro now designs chairs for Vivero Oy which are ergonomically efficient while supremely elegant in form. (See also **Finnish design**.)

'Karuselli 412' Chair, 1965
Yrjo Kukkapuro began experimenting with metal chairs and glass-fibre chairs in the sixties. His 'Karuselli' chair for Haimi Oy was an elegant reduction of the structural ideas he had been developing for more than a decade: a careful blend of modern materials, a certain formalism in the design, and an interest in ergonomics. After Haimi ceased production, all the rights to Kukkapuro's furniture designs were bought by Avarte.

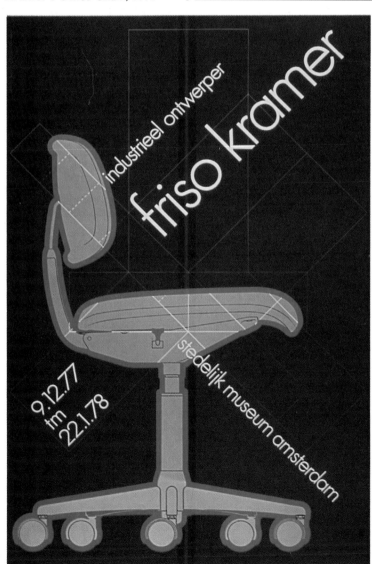

Shiro Kuramata

b. 1934

Shiro Kuramata was born in Tokyo and studied woodworking before joining the Teikokukizai furniture factory. He then worked in the interior design departments of some major Japanese department stores before founding the Kuramata Design Office in 1965.

Kuramata specializes in a highly refined minimalism which blends Western Modernism with the traditional Japanese taste for austerity. Interiors he has designed for the fashion designer **Issey Miyake** and the Seibu store have done a great deal to establish Japan as a leader in design during the seventies and eighties. He has also designed furniture for Ishimaru and Aoshima, although his most publicized pieces have been show pieces of 'Furniture in Irregular Forms' for Fujiko (1970) and a glass armchair for the Mhoya Glass Shop (1976). He has also worked with the radical Italian group **Memphis**.
Bibliography 'The Works of Shiro Kuramata 1967–1981' exhibition catalogue, Aram Designs, London, 1981

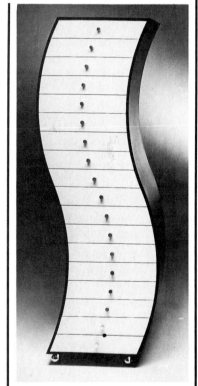

Drawers, 1970s
Kuramata designs furniture and interiors which acknowledge the traditions of both the West and the East. His designs are recognizably modern, in a European sense, but also have an element of particularly Japanese restraint and quality, while having a quirky, surreal humour all of the designer's own.

A
B
C
D
E
F
G
H
I
J
K
L
M
N
O
P
Q
R
S
T
U
V
W
X
Y
Z

L

Karl **Lagerfeld**
René **Lalique**
Lamborghini
Lambretta
Lamination
Allen **Lane**
Anatole **Lapine**
Jack Lenor **Larsen**
Ralph **Lauren**
Bernard **Leach**
Le Corbusier
Liberty's
Stig **Lindberg**
Lippincott &
Margulies
Raymond **Loewy**
Adolf **Loos**
Herb **Lubalin**

Karl Lagerfeld

b. 1939

The fashion designer Karl Lagerfeld was born in Germany, went to live in France when he was fourteen, but feels most at home in Italy. His internationalism is reflected in his work: for the past twenty years he has been chief designer for the French retail fashion firm Chloé, but since 1965 has also been designing clothes, shoes, furs and fragrances for Fendi, an Italian company. In 1983 Lagerfeld became chief designer for the house of **Chanel** and his sophisticated, glamorous clothes are very much in the Chanel tradition, but more aggressive and innovative (as one might expect of so enigmatic and philosophical a man). An early patron of **Memphis**, Lagerfeld is self-consciously at the apex of the European fashion world.

Suit for Chloé, late 1970s
Styled with chic femininity, this Lagerfeld suit displays many of the elements that characterize his work of the late seventies – svelte shape, soft fabric and knitted texture.

René Lalique

1860–1945

René Lalique was a glass-maker and jeweller whose style has become identified with **Art Nouveau**. Jewellery came first: reacting against the formalism of High Victorian or Empire design, Lalique produced jewellery where the semi-precious stones were often actually subordinated to their settings, and these settings usually had the favourite Art Nouveau motifs of wilting vegetables and lissom naked women. His glassware was equally typical of Art Nouveau, and he also designed car mascots. He established small factories at Combes-la-Ville in 1909 and at Wingen-sur-Moder in 1921.

'Suzanne', c. 1925
Lalique's statuette dates from his Art Deco period, and is typical of his later work.

Lamborghini

Ferruccio Lamborghini (b. 1916), a mechanical engineer and entrepreneur, had made a successful business out of manufacturing industrial oil burners and agricultural equipment before he set up a car-manufacturing company at Sant'Agata, just outside Bologna, in 1963. Lamborghini lacked the humility not to challenge Ferrari as the greatest Italian manufacturer of luxury sports cars. He was successful for a decade, but in 1979, despite its superb product line, the company went bankrupt. It was saved by a Franco-Swiss businessman called Patric Mimram who re-established the company. Lamborghini's chief enginéer is Giulio Alfieri, who came from Maserati. His cars have included the Miura, Countach and Jalpa and are the most technically and visually exciting in the world. The bodywork of all Lamborghinis is by **Nuccio Bertone**.

Lambretta

With **Corradino d'Ascanio**'s more famous **Vespa**, the Lambretta was one of Italy's most popular motor scooters. This type of vehicle was one of the first popular, deliberately designed products to emerge from Italian industry. **Ettore Sottsass**, looking back fondly at the post-War years of *ricostruzione*, mused that the scooter seemed the very symbol of the new Italian industrial democracy.

The Lambretta, which was much more utilitarian than the Vespa, appeared in 1947. In its first phase its structure was visible and it lacked the curved body-shell which it soon gained, in imitation of the Vespa. It was designed by Cesare Pallavicino and Pierluigi Torre and was manufactured by Innocenti.
Bibliography Centrokappa (ed.) *Il Design italiano degli anni '50* Editoriale Domus, Milan, 1980

Lamination

Lamination is the technique of gluing together thin strips of material – for example, **plywood** – in order to create a substance that is both strong and light. It has been frequently used in furniture manufacture, from **J.H. Belter** to **Alvar Aalto**, **Marcel Breuer** and **Charles Eames**.

Allen Lane

1902–70

Allen Lane was the founder of **Penguin Books**.

Anatole Lapine

b. 1930

Anatole Lapine was born in Latvia, but emigrated to the United States where he described his education – in Nathaniel West's phrase – as the University of Hard Knocks. He joined **General Motors'** design staff under **Harley Earl**, but moved to Germany in 1965 to work for the General's German subsidiary, Adam Opel. His brief at Opel was to revitalize the character of the marque and much of Opel's improved performance during the sixties and seventies can be directly attributed to the clean, aggressive lines which Lapine bestowed on their cars. In 1969 Lapine left Opel for **Porsche**, where he became head of the studio at the company's research centre at Weissach, just outside Stuttgart. Lapine's brief is to maintain the Porsche character while moving the company ahead into a broader and more widely competitive market position. He was responsible for the design of the Porsche 928.

Jack Lenor Larsen

b. 1927

An American textile designer, Jack Lenor Larsen has specialized in using power looms and man-made fibres, while also developing ethnic resist-dying techniques for luxurious mass consumption. Larsen trained at **Cranbrook Academy** and opened his own studio in New York in 1952. His first major commission was the draperies in Park Avenue's Lever House, a glass-walled skyscraper by Skidmore, Owings and Merrill which has become a landmark of the **Modern Movement** in the USA: when it opened its contents must, as Paul Goldberger has remarked, 'have seemed like a dazzling vision of a new world'. Since that dazzling vision in 1952

Larsen has woven upholstery fabrics for airlines (including Pan-Am and Braniff) and made an upholstery fabrics collection for **Cassina** (1981), but his speciality is large-scale architectural works. His recent major commissions include quilted silk banners for the Sears Bank in Chicago's Sears Tower (1974).

Larsen buys from all over the world and has run workshops in Africa, Haiti and Vietnam. An obsessive collector of textiles, he says, 'We started out as revolutionaries only wanting to make brave new designs for a contemporary society. Today our mission is to maintain the great tradition for luxurious quality as a buffer against mass production.'
Bibliography Jack Lenor Larsen & Mildred Constantine *The Art Fabric* New York, 1981

Ralph Lauren

b. 1939

Ralph Lauren used to be a tie salesman in Brooks Brothers, the Madison Avenue store that has clothed the American upper-middle-class male for more than a hundred and fifty years. The Brooks Brothers style is a highly identifiable American vernacular: blazers, tennis shirts, loafers, button-down collars, 'military' ties (often English) and traditional suits. Lauren realized that it could be successfully merchandised and established a 'Polo' line based on this Ivy League Look in 1967. Women's fashions, in a slightly androgynous mode, followed in 1971. Lauren's 'Polo' clothes have continued to be inspired by the vernacular, but from a wider range of sources – if not Princeton, then the Navajo blankets which were the source of the 1981 knits, or the Prairie/Homestead look which formed the basis of Lauren's assault on international markets. Lauren won the US Coty award for men's fashion in 1976 and for women's the following year.

'Freesia' Fabric, 1984
Jack Lenor Larsen is now big business in carpet, leather, textiles and furniture. The 'Freesia' fabric was designed by Jason Pollen for the Larsen Design Studio.

'Fiandra' Sofa by Vico Magistretti, Textile by Jack Larsen
Larsen has designed textiles for many important post-War American corporate buildings, and has also supplied fabrics for the major furniture manufacturers, including Cassina, as in this photograph. The main influences on his work are primitive cultures from around the world, but he turns these into a form of sophisticated Modernism.

Bernard Leach

1887–1979

Bernard Leach, Britain's most celebrated craft potter and a hero of the **Crafts Revival**, was born in Hong Kong and studied early Chinese and Korean art. His oriental background was fundamental to his later work, and in 1909 he went to study in Japan. On returning to England in 1920 he set up a pottery in the artists' colony at St Ives, Cornwall. Leach was responsible for establishing the pot, rather along the Japanese example, as a work of art. This celebration of individual artisanship ran parallel with other people's, ultimately worthier, attempts in Britain to establish genuinely higher standards in the day-to-day. Leach's works always had a down-to-earth quality.
Bibliography Bernard Leach *A Potter's Book* Faber & Faber, London, 1940; Transatlantic Arts, Levittown, New York, 1965

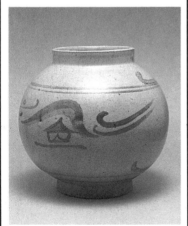

Stoneware Vase, 1926
The simple, brushstroke-like decoration and the muted grey glaze of this vase quite openly display Leach's debt to Japanese ceramics.

Le Corbusier

1887–1965

Le Corbusier was the *nom d'artiste* chosen by the Swiss architect Charles-Edouard Jeanneret. It means nothing, but suggests a meaning which combines the bird 'raven' with the architectural feature 'corbel'. What is perhaps more significant is Jeanneret's choice of the definite article: his *nom d'artiste* was like a *nom de guerre*. He was out to fight a battle.

Jeanneret was born in the Swiss watch-making town of La Chaux-de-Fonds in 1887. It had been burnt down in the eighteenth century and reconstructed on a grid pattern, and it is possible that the severe geometry of his home town had an effect on the young man's creative imagination.

Jeanneret was to become the most inspired and original and inventive of all modern architects. The dimensions of his thought qualify him for the description of genius and the range and quality of his formal inventions qualify him for the description of great artist.

In La Chaux-de-Fonds he was apprenticed to an architect called Charles L'Eplattenier and then travelled to Germany, where he worked in **Peter Behrens'** office. He first came to international prominence at the 1925 Paris Exhibition, where he built the Pavilion de L'Esprit Nouveau and furnished it with **Thonet** bentwood chairs and fitted furniture which he designed himself. In 1927 he began an association with **Charlotte Perriand**, producing a distinguished and elegant set of furniture designs (which are now reproduced by **Cassina**). In each piece traditional luxury and aggressive modernity vie for dominance. All their chair designs were exhibited at the Paris 'Salon d'Automne' of 1929: a chaise-longue, the 'siège grand confort' and the 'basculant' chair. As designers Jeanneret and Perriand were at their strongest working together; after they separated in the late thirties Le Corbusier designed no more significant furniture and Charlotte Perriand never really designed anything very much at all, preferring to take an interest in folk art rather than machine production.

Besides the furniture and the architecture Le Corbusier's ideas were highly influential. He was in love with machines and with beauty; he was passionately concerned with social purpose and with healthy living; he was an architect and propagandist whose every thought was suffused by optimism. His vision was of a world where modern technology allied with a sense of beauty could create an ideal and socially beneficial environment. A one-time employee of the Voisin aircraft company and an enthusiast for fast cars, he understood and sympathized with the beauty often inherent in fine machines. His most famous dictum is usually quoted without the context. In full, it is: 'The aeroplane is the product

'Grand Confort' Armchair, 1928
Le Corbusier's 'grand confort' armchair of 1928 used the tubular steel fashionable at the time, but, unlike many of his contemporaries, he complemented it with luxurious, well-stuffed leather cushions to combine Modernism with French luxury. In its shape it was a deliberate attempt to imitate Thonet's bentwood. Since 1965 Le Corbusier's original design has been produced by Cassina.

of close selection. The lesson of the aeroplane lies in the logic which governed the statement of the problem and its realization. The problem of the house has not been stated. Nevertheless, there do exist standards for the dwelling-house. Machinery contains in itself the factor of economy, which makes the selection. The house is a machine for living in . . . As to beauty, that is always present when you have proportion.'

Le Corbusier made it possible, in theory, at least, for the world to appreciate the beauty of well-made ordinary things, introduced new systems of construction and new, cleaner, brighter, better, ways of living, but his ideas have subsequently often been badly misinterpreted and misapplied.

Le Corbusier swam to his death in 1965, from the pier of **Eileen Gray**'s house, E-1027, at Roquebrune. (See also pp. 34–5 and **Amedée Ozenfant**).
Bibliography Renato de Fusco *Le Corbusier, Designer Furniture, 1929* Barron's, Woodbury, 1977; Le Corbusier *L'Art décoratif d'aujourd'hui* Collection 'L'Esprit Nouveau', Paris, 1925; Stanislaus von Moos *Le Corbusier: Elemente eine Synthesis* Hüber, Zürich, 1968; Peter Serenyi (editor) *Le Corbusier in Perspective* Prentice-Hall, Englewood Cliffs, 1975

Liberty's

Liberty's is a store in London founded by Arthur Lasenby Liberty (1843–1917). Liberty himself was born in Nottingham, the son of a lace manufacturer, and moved to London in 1862 to take up a post as manager of Farmer & Rogers' Oriental Warehouse in Regent Street. The store was a magnet for many of the artists of the day, and between his appointment and its closure in 1874 Liberty added Frederick Leighton, Edward Burne-Jones,

Dante Gabriel Rossetti, **William Morris** and James McNeill Whistler to his list of friends and acquaintances. In the year after the Oriental Warehouse closed Liberty set up his own business near its old premises. Here he experimented with his own peculiar brand of mercantile philanthropy, being a supporter of the early closing movement and taking a passionate interest in the welfare of his employees.

Liberty was one of the first merchants to understand and exploit popular taste. He had realized that oriental merchandise appealed to more than just a narrow circle of artists, and when on his own he manufactured fabrics which had a fineness of quality and a subtlety of pattern and colour that had been hitherto unknown in home-produced goods, but which were present in those he had been selling previously. A trip to Japan in 1888–9 reinforced his oriental expertise. Liberty educated public taste and in doing this forced domestic manufacturers to higher standards of production. He and his successors have had a consistent reputation as patrons of designers, from Edward William Godwin to Susan **Collier**. Liberty was knighted in 1913.

'Ianthe' Fabric
'Ianthe' was designed for Liberty's at the turn of the century and was sold with no designer attribution. First produced on silk, from 1968 it was printed on heavy cotton and is still in production today.

Stig Lindberg
1916–82

The ceramic designer Stig Lindberg was educated at technical school in Stockholm, and studied under **Wilhelm Kåge** in Paris before joining **Gustavsberg** in 1937. He spent two periods, interrupted by the important lectureship in ceramics at Stockholm's Konstfackskolan (applied arts school) and a brief time in Italy, as Gustavsberg's artistic director, from 1949 to 1957 and then from 1970 to 1977.

His first full service was called 'LB' and appeared in 1945; 'Servus' followed in 1950 and a range of flameproof cooking utensils called 'Terma', which summarize Lindberg, Gustavsberg and, indeed, the entire Swedish domestic design ideal, were first seen at the H55 exhibition at Halsingborg in 1955.

Lindberg also designed textiles for Stockholm's leading department store, the Nordiska Kompaniet.
Bibliography Dag Widman & Berndt Klyvare *Stig Lindberg* Raben & Sjogren, Stockholm, 1962

Vase, 1972
Since the 1940s Lindberg's enthusiasm for Italian design has softened the more utilitarian approach characteristic of much Scandinavian ceramic work.

Lippincott & Margulies

Gordon Lippincott (b. 1909) and Walter Margulies (b. 1914) founded their company, Lippincott & Margulies, in 1946. It has specialized in **corporate identity** and clients include Eastern Airlines, Borg-Warner, Esso, **Chrysler**, American Express, Chemical Bank, Uniroyal and Xerox. Gordon Lippincott had strong views about **obsolescence**. He once said: 'Industrial designers today have become commercial artists rearranging a lot of spinach to come up with a new model. If we eliminate yearly models, we put a premium on better design.' Lippincott & Margulies is typical of the way the consultant design profession in America has matured since its creation in the thirties.

American Motors

Logos for American Motors
In American business, design is often concerned with changes in corporate identity. This is one of the specializations of the New York firm, Lippincott & Margulies, who redesigned the original logo for American Motors in 1968 (top), giving the staid car manufacturer a brighter, fresher image.

A
B
C
D
E
F
G
H
I
J
K
L
M
N
O
P
Q
R
S
T
U
V
W
X
Y
Z

A
B
C
D
E
F
G
H
I
J
K
L
M
N
O
P
Q
R
S
T
U
V
W
X
Y
Z

Raymond Loewy

b. 1893

Loewy was born in Paris but went to New York in 1919 as a demobbed captain in the French Army with artistic ambitions. Much of Loewy's career has passed into the region of myth, partly through the popularity of his autobiography *Never Leave Well Enough Alone* (1951).

Loewy was part of the generation of designers who created the consultant design profession in New York during the 1920s. He was the first designer to make a *Life* cover. Loewy's hallmark was the transformation of Gestetner duplicators (p. 45), Coca-Cola dispensers and Coldspot fridges into objects which became familiar ikons of American consumer journalism during the mid-century.

Like his pioneer contemporaries, **Norman Bel Geddes**, **Walter Dorwin Teague**, **Henry Dreyfuss** and **Harold van Doren**, Loewy's reputation is based on his pre-War work, although he did design some notable products after the War, among them the Studebaker car and the Lucky Strike cigarette pack (p. 73). By 1978, although he ran a small office in London and a larger one in Paris, known as the Compagnie de l'Esthétique Industrielle, he no longer did business in his own country.

Although Loewy's flair for style and for publicity did much to bring the design of objects before the public eye, and although his client list looks like a portion of the Fortune 500, his name has always been associated with **styling**, in the pejorative sense which Europeans used to condemn the commercialization of design and designing in America. Nonetheless, Loewy was responsible for many of the symbols and images which characterize, for the later twentieth century, modern America in its 'bourbon Louis

romp', as **Tom Wolfe** described it. At some time during the forties or fifties an average American could have spent his entire day surrounded by products fashioned by Loewy: a Schick razor, Pepsodent toothpaste tube packaging, the Studebaker car, the Lucky Strike cigarette pack, a Coca-Cola dispenser and, at the end of the day, a tin of Carling Black Label beer. For Kennedy Loewy also designed the colour scheme for 'Air Force One', the President's personal Boeing 707, and began the association with NASA that led to him making proposals, very largely unimplemented, for habitability systems in the Skylab series of spaceships.

Loewy once remarked of his career: 'I found it difficult to reconcile success with humility. I tried it at first, but it meant avoiding the very essence of my career – a total exhilaration and the ecstasy of creativity.' (See also pp. 44–6 and **American design**.)

Bibiography Raymond Loewy *Never Leave Well Enough Alone* Simon & Schuster, New York, 1951; 'The Designs of Raymond Loewy' exhibition catalogue, Renwick Gallery, Smithsonian, Washington, 1976; Peter Mayer *Industrial Design* Overlook Press, New York, 1978

Vacuum Cleaner Attachments for Electrolux, 1939
Loewy was the first American industrial design consultant to open up shop in Europe. These are typical examples of his use of streamlining.

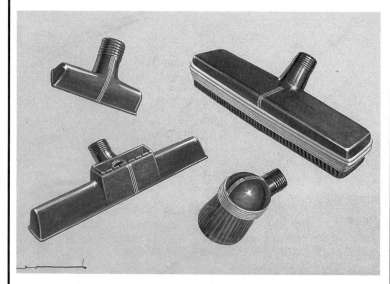

Coca-Cola Dispenser, c. 1948 (left)
Loewy's streamlined packaging for the bar top Coca-Cola dispenser became a symbol of American culture across the world.

Rendering of Electrolux Appliance, c. 1939
The high finish was an important part of the sales pitch to the client.

Adolf Loos

1870–1938

Adolf Loos was the romantic radical of the Viennese Enlightenment. On reading Loos' numerous polemical, wide-ranging texts it is impossible not to recall that he came from the rich culture of Vienna, the city that produced Freud.

Loos was born in Brno, was in America from 1893 to 1896, and then returned to Vienna to work in the offices of **Otto Wagner**. He built some remarkable houses and shops, but his greatest influence came from his writings on design in *Die Zeit* and *Das Kunstblatt*. His most celebrated article was called '*Ornament und Verbrechen*' (Ornament and Crime), appearing in 1908. In 1912 it was published by the Berlin review *Der Sturm* and the following year **Le Corbusier** published it in his own journal, *L'Esprit nouveau*. The gist of the text was that ornament represents cultural degeneracy, and that modern, civilized society is represented by undecorated form: 'Ornamentation is wasted effort and therefore a waste of health. It has always been so. But today it means a waste of material as well, and the two things together mean a waste of capital.'

Instead of the aromatic vapours of high, decadent art, Loos offered in his architecture and his pamphlets the promise of a systematic evaluation of life. To him architecture was not merely the work of the building trade, but was the tangible expression of a society's culture.

Loos also published his own journal, *Das Andere* (The Outsider), in which he advanced his ideas, including one that the British gentleman was the model of taste. Loos execrated ornament in architecture and design in the same way that Freud excluded from his vision of the soul all those devices which had been used to disguise its essential primitivism.

Loos designed a set of glasses for the Viennese firm, Lobmeyr, which is still in production, and other pieces of applied art, mostly intended for the interiors of his buildings. (See also pp. 29–30.)
Bibliography Benedetto Gravagnuolo *Adolf Loos* Idea Books Edizioni, Milan, 1982; Adolf Loos *Spoken into the Void* MIT, Cambridge, Mass., 1982

Advert in 'Das Andere', 1903
Das Andere was Adolf Loos' own journal, a vehicle for his radical ideas about design, culture, dress and manners. This page from a 1903 edition shows the influence of British taste on early twentieth-century Vienna.

Herb Lubalin

1918–82

The typographer Herb Lubalin was born in New York and graduated from the Cooper Union in 1939. He worked as an art director for Sudler & Hennessey before founding Herb Lubalin, Inc., in 1964, which became Lubalin, Peckolick Associates, Inc. in 1980. After 1973 Lubalin edited his own Journal, *U&LC* (for 'Upper and Lower Case'), an international journal of typographics.

Lubalin worked in advertising, posters, packaging, editorial design and typeface design, but his very distinctive personal style is most of all concerned with typography. He made it his business to break the rules, jamming words together on the page, playing graphic tricks with letter-forms, using words to become images in themselves. When he was invited to design a logo for the magazine *Mother & Child*, in 1967, he inserted the ampersand and the word 'child' into the 'o' of mother, thus creating not only a symbolic image of maternal protection, but also a tight and clever graphic form. Lubalin created the 'Davida' and 'Lincoln Gothic' typefaces during the sixties.

Marriage, 1965, Mother & Child, 1966 and Families, 1980, Logos
Lubalin's logos make effective use of graphic double-entendres.

Moller House, Vienna, 1928
Loos was strongly opposed to ornamentation in architecture; but later owners of the Moller House have not necessarily shared his feelings, as this recent photograph reveals.

A B C D E F G H I J K L M N O P Q R S T U V W X Y Z

M

Charles
Rennie **Mackintosh**
A.H. **Mackmurdo**
Marshall **McLuhan**
Vico **Magistretti**
Louis **Majorelle**
Tomas **Maldonado**
Robert **Mallet-Stevens**
Carl **Malmsten**
Angelo **Mangiarotti**
Enzo **Mari**
Marimekko
Javier **Mariscal**
MARS
Enid **Marx**
Bruno **Mathsson**
Herbert **Matter**
Syrie **Maugham**
David **Mellor**
Memphis
Alessandro **Mendini**
Roberto **Menghi**
Hannes **Meyer**
Giovanni **Michelotti**
Ludwig **Mies van der Rohe**
Herman **Miller**
Missoni
Bill **Mitchell**
Issey **Miyake**
Modern Movement
Moderne/Modernistic
Børge **Mogensen**
Laszlo **Moholy-Nagy**
Hanae **Mori**
Stanley **Morison**
William **Morris**
Motorama
Olivier **Mourgue**
Alfonso **Mucha**
Hermann **Muller-Brockmann**
Peter **Muller-Munk**
Bruno **Munari**
Keith **Murray**
Museum of Modern Art
Hermann **Muthesius**

Charles Rennie Mackintosh

1868–1928

Charles Rennie Mackintosh entered Glasgow School of Art in 1885. He qualified in 1889 and joined the architectural firm of Honeyman & Keppie. As a young man Mackintosh came into contact with the work of Aubrey Beardsley, the Dutch Symbolist artist Jan van Toorop and the English architect **C.F.A. Voysey** through reading *The Studio*. Inspired by them he produced some novel furniture and decoration, and designs which won a competition for a new Glasgow Art School. This work was noticed and published by *The Studio*'s editor, Gleeson White, suddenly giving his ideas prominence and authority, and on the basis of *The Studio*'s articles alone, Mackintosh was invited to exhibit in Vienna at the 1900 Secession exhibition. His success in the Austrian capital made him suddenly a leading figure of an international group of architects and designers so that, with precious little of a back-list, he was thrust into equal status with **Josef Hoffmann** and Koloman Moser. The first stage of the Glasgow School of Art was built between 1897 and 1899. It was his first (and, indeed, only) opportunity to design a total environment from the building down to the ashtrays. In the same year as he completed the Glasgow School of Art designs Mackintosh designed the first of the tea-rooms he was to be commissioned to do by Catherine Cranston, a Glasgow tearoom tycoon. His other major works followed over the next ten years: Hill House, just outside Glasgow, for the publisher Walter Blackie in 1902, further tearooms for Miss Cranston and the interior for a house in Northampton belonging to the model railway magnate J. Bassett-Lowke (who later commissioned **Peter Behrens** to design an entire dwelling).

Mackintosh's furniture is characterized by the use of strikingly emphatic rectilinear patterns, inspired by Japanese design. He often used painted wood, but lightened the severity of his forms with stylized motifs, loosely derived from Celtic ornament. Although he was contemporary with the **Arts and Crafts** movement, Mackintosh's work was much more concerned with visual effect than with either quality of execution or with 'truth to materials'.

Little more was heard of Mackintosh after his work for Bassett-Lowke. He retired to Port Vendres on the Basque coast and painted water-colours, returning to Britain to die in 1928. Some of Mackintosh's furniture designs are now reproduced by **Cassina**.

Bibliography Robert MacLeod *Charles Rennie Mackintosh, Architect and Artist* Collins, London, 1983

Entry for 'House of an Art Lover' Competition, 1901
A room designed by Mackintosh for the 'Haus eines Kunstfreundes' exhibition, organized by the Viennese magazine Zeitschrift für Innen-Dekoration. *Mackintosh's designs were extremely influential in Austria and contributed to the development of the work of the Wiener Werkstätte.*

180

A.H. Mackmurdo

1851–1942

Arthur Heygate Mackmurdo was a friend of **John Ruskin** and **William Morris** and founded the Century Guild in 1882, an **Arts and Crafts** club. Mackmurdo is mainly famous today because the title page he designed in 1883 for his book, *Wren's City Churches*, was singled out by **Nikolaus Pevsner** as a pioneering work of modern design. Mackmurdo worked primarily as an architect, but some furniture designs, although Arts and Crafts in origin, approach the expressiveness of continental **Art Nouveau**.

Wallpaper by Jeffrey & Co for Century Guild, 1884
Mackmurdo's wallpaper design is characteristic of his taste for flowing forms which anticipated Art Nouveau.

Marshall McLuhan

1911–81

Marshall McLuhan was a Canadian professor of English whose books, *The Mechanical Bride* (1951), *The Gutenberg Galaxy* (1962), *Understanding Media* (1964) and *The Medium is the Message* (1967), were among the first serious studies of the impact of the mass media on popular culture. McLuhan saw ephemera such as print, games and mass-produced appliances not just as commercial products but as important aspects of contemporary culture, and thus encouraged a more critical approach towards the area of production. McLuhan coined the term 'global village' and predicted the downfall of printed information in the electronics age.

Vico Magistretti

b. 1920

The Italian furniture designer Vico Magistretti was born in Milan and studied architecture at the Polytechnic there, graduating in 1945. Like many of his contemporaries, he turned from architecture to design in the years of Italy's *ricostruzione* after the War. In 1962 he became the first Italian designer to produce a plastic chair, called 'Selene'. It was chic rather than cheap. His work for **Artemide** and **Cassina** from the sixties on has included simple wooden chairs and padded sofas, as well as the curious 'Sindbad' chair of 1982 which was derived from a horse blanket (p. 101). He works as a consultant, employing a single draughtsman, and dividing his time between Milan and London, where he teaches at the **Royal College of Art**.

'Modello 115' Chair for Cassina, 1964
Vico Magistretti's 'Modello 115' has a red painted wooden frame and rush seating which recalls vernacular Italian chairs of the last century. His best-known work, it has contributed to a popular acceptance of Italian furniture design.

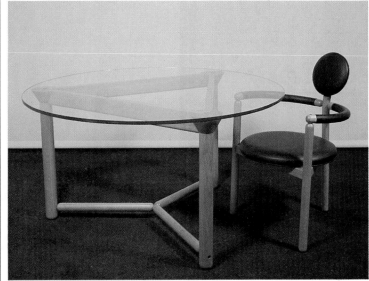

'Pan' Chair and Table
Magistretti produced the 'Pan' chair and table set for Cassina. It exhibits the wilful styling characteristic of some contemporary Italian design.

A
B
C
D
E
F
G
H
I
J
K
L
M
N
O
P
Q
R
S
T
U
V
W
X
Y
Z

Louis Majorelle

1859–1926

Louis Majorelle, a native of Nancy and the son of a manufacturer of reproduction eighteenth-century furniture, was one of the chief beneficiaries of the **Art Nouveau** style and the most flamboyant representative of what has become known as the 'School of Nancy'. He mechanized his workshop so that he could turn out masses of highly decorated furniture at prices the middle classes could afford. His factory was burnt down in 1916; by the time it was possible to rebuild it, Art Nouveau had declined in popularity in favour of the next fashion, **Art Deco**. Majorelle quickly accommodated himself to that style.

'Nenuphars' Side Table, c. 1900
Louis Majorelle's side table was made in mahogany, burr walnut and ormolu. Its exotic name and the expensive materials complement the extravagant style.

Tomas Maldonado

b. 1922

The Argentinian design theoretician Tomas Maldonado was born in Buenos Aires and studied at the Beaux-Arts there. By 1951 he was editing a journal called *Nueva Vision*. This brought him into contact with the Swiss sculptor and designer **Max Bill**, who invited him to join the new **Hochschule für Gestaltung** in Ulm. From 1954 to 1966 Maldonado's cerebral presence dominated the thinking at the Hochschule: his interest lay in systematizing design, both in terms of the process of making, and in terms of the process of analysing, or 'reading', designed objects. Because he thought the automobile was a symbol of 'Detroit Machiavellismus', car design was never taught at the Hochschule. His own design work, however, is pretty desiccated: some medical apparatus in 1962, an interior for a Prisunic store at Le Mans in 1972, and consultancy work for **La Rinascente**. He now lives in Milan and is a professor of design at the University of Bologna.

Robert Mallet-Stevens

1886–1945

Robert Mallet-Stevens was an architect who turned the **Modern Movement** into a chic style for wealthy Parisians. He was the first president of the Union des Artistes Modernes.
Bibliography Yvonne Brunhammer *Le Style 1925* Bascet, Paris

Carl Malmsten

1888–1972

Carl Malmsten achieved fame with a commission to provide furniture for the new Stockholm Town Hall (1916–23) and became an influential teacher and spokesman for the crafts. He disliked twentieth-century styles and, with **Gunnar Asplund**, campaigned to revive interest in vernacular furniture types. They developed a neo-classical style which became very popular in Sweden in the twenties.

Angelo Mangiarotti

b. 1921

Angelo Mangiarotti was born in Milan and graduated from the Polytechnic there in 1948. In 1953–4 he was a visiting professor at the Illinois Institute of Technology's Institute of Design and ran his own office in Ohio. He returned to Italy in 1955. He has designed a clock called 'Secticon' (1962) for the Swiss manufacturer, Portescap. This clock was strongly sculptural and Mangiarotti tends to specialize in emphatic forms, including marble objects for **Knoll** and silverware for Cleto Munari. (See also p. 108.)

'Secticon' Clock, 1962
Mangiarotti's 'Secticon' clock for the Swiss firm, Portescap, is a clear example of how in the sixties the Italians combined sculptural form with a rational approach to the functional elements of their products.

Enzo Mari

b. 1932

Enzo Mari studied at the Accademia di Belle Arte di Brera in Milan between 1952 and 1956. Being interested in **semiology**, he is among the more intellectual of his generation of Italian designers, and has written on design, analysing it as a linguistic system. His aesthetic approach to the practice of design is, however, highly formalist, and he has designed strongly sculptural storage jars and containers in melamine and polypropylene for **Danese**. His book *Funzione della ricerca estetica* was published in 1970.

Sterling Silver Bowl, 1982
Mari's silver bowl was made by hand for Danese.

Marimekko

Marimekko (which means 'Mary's little dress') is a Helsinki fabric store founded by **Armi Ratia**. In 1951 Ratia joined an oil cloth company called Printex. Her first job, it is said, was to leave the oil out. The next thing she did was to ask some designer friends to come up with patterns that could be used on the cloth. In the grisaille austerity of the post-War years the colourful, monumental shapes caused a sensation and Marimekko became a cult. The colours and patterns of Marimekko combine subtle adaptations of the Finnish rustic tradition with a very fresh and uninhibited sort of Modernism (some of which comes from its Japanese designers). Since 1968 Marimekko has licensed its products worldwide.

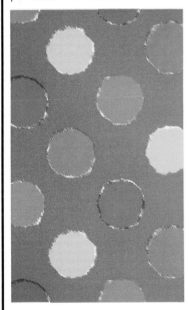

'Jäävvoret' Fabric by Fujiwa Ishimoto, 1983
Marimekko's identity is so strong that the styles of individual designers can be easily incorporated without any compromise of the company's character. Ishimoto's design exemplifies Marimekko's debt to Finnish peasant tradition. (See also Finnish design.)

Javier Mariscal

b. 1950

The Spanish designer Javier Mariscal studied at the Escuela de Grafismo Elisava in Barcelona. Known as a cartoonist and textile designer, his 'Hilton' drinks trolley was a part of the first **Memphis** collection in 1981.

MARS

The Modern Architecture Research Group was founded in London in 1933 by a group of architects at the Architectural Association as an English response to **CIAM**. Its members, who included **Wells Coates** and the historian Sir John Summerson, were leaders of the British **Modern Movement**.

Enid Marx

b. 1902

Enid Marx, a British fabric and book jacket designer, studied at the **Central School of Art and Design** and the **Royal College of Art** before setting up her own studio to design and print textiles. On the basis of the reputation established in doing this **Gordon Russell** invited her to join the wartime **Utility** Furniture Design Panel for whom she designed fabrics. The limitations of the brief – four colours, two types of yarn, frequent repeats – suited her style and imagination perfectly, as she was well known for fabrics with minimal pattern and restricted colour. Her designs were used as seating fabrics for London Transport.

Bruno Mathsson

b. 1907

Bruno Mathsson was born at Varnamo in Sweden where his father had a furniture factory. He became a furniture designer at just the moment when the Swedes were becoming conscious of their national design, and he was able to combine his training as a cabinet-maker with his family's expertise and an attitude to his products that pleased the consumer by using natural materials in a sophisticated and graceful way. His most famous design for a chair with a laminated beech frame and hemp webbing has become known as *the* Bruno Mathsson chair. It was designed for Dux Mobel in 1934 and is still in production today. Mathsson has collaborated on furniture design with **Piet Hein** and still runs the family business from Varnamo.

'Eva' Chair, 1941
Mathsson produced his 'Eva' chair in laminated wood and webbing in 1934. An upholstered armchair version appeared in 1941. Later known as the 'Penilla', it was brought back into production by the Swedish firm, Dux Mobel, in 1966.

Fabrics, 1942
Enid Marx's fabrics for the wartime Utility Furniture Design Panel were limited by financial restrictions to a small range of colours, but still achieved an imaginative and pleasing effect.

Herbert Matter

b. 1907

Herbert Matter was born in Engelberg, Switzerland, and studied at the Ecole des Beaux-Arts in Paris from 1923 to 1925, a pupil of **Amedée Ozenfant** and Fernand Léger. At the Beaux-Arts Matter began to take photographs and after graduating worked on **Vogue** before returning to Switzerland to do travel posters for the Swiss Transport Office. Matter's style was photo-montage, employing dramatic contrasts of scale and integrated colour with monochrome photography. Like **Laszlo Moholy-Nagy** he took the medium of the photograph beyond mere photo-chemical recording and created with it a vivid new form of graphic communication.

In 1939 Matter went to the United States, set up his own graphics studio and became professor of photography at Yale University. His best-known work there was to design the original **Knoll** logotype.

Syrie Maugham

1879–1955

Syrie Maugham, the wife for twelve years of writer Somerset Maugham, was one of the most famous interior designers of her day. Her firm, Syrie Ltd, was established in the early twenties and designed rooms in a traditional idiom with the occasional flash of daring. By the end of that decade she had discovered the possibilities of the monochromatic paint schemes with which her name is principally associated: following the success of her own all-white drawing room, she bleached, pickled and painted old French furniture and whitened or silvered picture frames for more than a decade. Her interiors achieved a spare elegance.

David Mellor

b. 1930

A British cutler and industrial designer, David Mellor has been the outstanding British flatware designer of the twentieth century. Born in Sheffield, he established a studio-workshop-factory there in 1954. In his first year as an independent designer he produced a traditional service, known as 'Pride', which won one of the first **Design Council** awards in 1957. Since then he has benefited from many official commissions, principally the 'Embassy' service of 1963, designed for use in British embassies, and two years later the 'Thrift' service, intended for use in Government institutions. He has also designed other objects, including bus shelters. There is something essentially English about the character of Mellor's designs: they are elegant but understated, strong in character, but unobtrusive.

Mellor also has strong views about the designer's role: he sees his designs as very much a way of supporting a view of life. Design, for him, is a far broader issue than even the profession's spokesmen are prepared to admit: 'It is concerned not *just* with making objects . . . but just as importantly with making *choices*, with choosing what we use, choosing how we live.' Since 1969 he has given form to his own particular world view in his exquisite kitchen equipment shops in London and Manchester, where a huge range of refined working implements are offered for sale in a totally designed environment. Mellor was chairman of a Design Council committee which reported on the state of product design in Britain in 1983 and in the same year he became a Trustee of the **Victoria and Albert Museum**. He has a substantial influence on British institutional awareness of design, although his attempts to reform the Crafts Council were unsuccessful, leading to his resignation from its chairmanship only months after he was appointed.

'Provençal' Cutlery, 1973
The original was made in rosewood, but this version is manufactured from the more efficient and economical black acetal resin. The rivets are of brass.

Memphis

Memphis was the name of a collection of furniture, fabric and ceramics designers who gathered around **Ettore Sottsass** at the 1981 Milan Furniture Fair and caused a sensation in the international media. In fact, the group had grown out of **Studio Alchymia**, another Milanese avant-garde group, which had itself developed from the groups of radical architects and designers which flourished in Italy during the later sixties.

Memphis provided a vehicle for Sottsass after what he described as an extended period of helplessness, and provided a forum for himself and younger designers to express ideas about furniture which he had been nurturing for twenty years. While Studio Alchymia indulged in the wilder extremes of performance art, Memphis got support from **Artemide** and took a showroom on the corso Europa in central Milan. It did not intend to be dangerously radical: it wanted to be a band of guerrillas, but only at the furniture fair. The group used industrial materials and mixed fifties revivalism with an iconography simultaneously derived from ancient art and Pop music. Overlaid on all of this were continuous references to the urban structure of Milan; Sottsass once said he was 'quoting from suburbia . . . Memphis is not new, Memphis is everywhere.' Memphis offended conservative designers like **Vico Magistretti**, who said: 'In my opinion this furniture offers no possibility for development whatsoever. It is only a variant of fashion.' Memphis' designers include Martine Bedin, **Andrea Branzi**, **Aldo Cibic**, **Michele de Lucchi**, George Sowden and **Marco Zanini**, but they are all, in fact or in theory, subordinated to the spirit of the genius of the group, Ettore Sottsass. When asked to explain it, he just said

MEMPHIS
Milano   In London

that 'Memphis' function is to exist,' adding ironically, 'Why *should* homes be static temples?' (See also p. 54).
Bibliography 'Memphis Milano in London' exhibition catalogue, The Boilerhouse Project, Victoria & Albert Museum, London 1982; Barbara Radice *Memphis* Rizzoli, New York, 1984; Andrea Branzi *The Hot House: Italian New Wave Design*, MIT, Cambridge, Mass., 1984

Alessandro Mendini

b. 1931

Alessandro Mendini is one of the bourgeois radicals of Italian design. He was born in Milan, and until 1970 worked as an architect for **Marcello Nizzoli** Associati. From 1970 to 1976 he was editor of *Casabella* and since 1979 has been editor of *Modo* and **Domus**. Mendini is more politically and intellectually orientated than **Ettore Sottsass**, and has contributed furniture designs, which he likes to think of as '*banale*', to **Studio Alchymia** and silverware to Alessi.
Bibliography Barbara Radice *Ologia del banale* Studio Alchymia, Milan, 1980; Andrea Branzi *The Hot House: Italian New Wave Design* MIT, Cambridge, Mass., 1984

Coffee Service for Alessi, 1983
Mendini's coffee service typifies the mannered style of Post-Modernism.

Broadsheet for Memphis Exhibition, The Boilerhouse Project, 1982

Roberto Menghi

b. 1920

With **Gino Colombini**, Roberto Menghi was the Italian designer who developed the most sophisticated technical *and* aesthetic attitudes to **plastics** during the fifties. For Moneta Smalterie Meridionali he produced a superb range of integrated vessels, including an exquisite polyethylene bucket, an example of which is permanently on show in New York's **Museum of Modern Art**. For Pirelli he has designed disposable plastic canisters (1959) and a hot-water bottle (1961): to both of these everyday objects he has brought scientific understanding and Italian style. Since the sixties Menghi has worked almost exclusively on architectural projects, including the Excelsior Hotel on the Venice Lido.
Bibliography 'Il Disegno dei materiali industriali' *Rassegna* 14, June 1983

Hannes Meyer

1889–1954

The Swiss Marxist architect Hannes Meyer was briefly the director of the **Bauhaus**, after **Walter Gropius'** resignation in 1928 and before **Mies van der Rohe**'s takeover in 1931. Although Meyer's political ideals actually meant that he took the school nearer to its declared purpose of being a genuine industrial force than Gropius had ever done, and while he was an intellectual Marxist and not a practising revolutionary, his uncompromising politics accelerated the closure of the Dessau campus by exciting the attention of the conservative local authorities, who put pressure on the governing Social Democrats to close the school.
Bibliography Hans Maria Wingler *The Bauhaus* M.I.T., Cambridge, Mass., 1969

Giovanni Michelotti

1921–80

Giovanni Michelotti was born in Turin and at only sixteen entered the body shop of Farina, before it became known as **Pininfarina**. In 1949 he set up his own practice. Michelotti worked for Triumph and was the first non-Japanese designer to be commissioned by a Japanese manufacturer. His (Datsun) Prince Skyline appeared in 1961 and his Hino Contessa in 1965. Other notable designs include the Daf 44 (1966), the Alpine-Renault (1968) and the Triumph 2000 (1963).

Triumph Herald, 1959
Italian design had a very thorough, if often indirect, influence on English taste. The Triumph Herald overtly acknowledged the relationship, as its bodywork was designed by Giovanni Michelotti. However, Standard-Triumph's primitive metal-pressing technology did not enable the manufacturer to reproduce the sumptuous curves which had been intrinsic to Michelotti's original design, and instead the car was angular and slab-sided.

Ludwig Mies van der Rohe

1886–1969

Ludwig Mies was born in Aachen, Germany, the son of a mason. He added his mother's name to his father's to give himself more style. Mies was trained in his father's building yard, but was also apprenticed to Bruno Paul and to **Peter Behrens** so that when he began to work in the field of architectural design he practised in a restrained and severe version of the German classical school of the nineteenth century, whose most famous exemplar was the Prussian architect Karl Friedrich Schinkel, the creator of much of neo-classical Berlin.

The influence of Schinkel on Mies' work was first seen in an unrealized project for a Bismarck monument of 1912. Mies also worked on Behrens' monumental German Embassy in St Petersburg, but first came to international attention as the organizer of an experimental housing estate at Weissenhof, outside Stuttgart, for the **Deutsche Werkbund** in 1927. This was followed by his design for the German national pavilion at the Barcelona international exhibition of 1929. His minimal grid for the building and the fine furniture he designed for it achieved a totemic excellence far beyond the capabilities of the day-to-day architect of Modernism,

constrained by practical briefs. In the same year Mies built the Tugendhat House at Brno in Czechoslovakia, for which he also designed chairs and other furniture (p. 48).

Mies succeeded **Hannes Meyer** as the director of the **Bauhaus** during its last days in Dessau, and, when political pressure from the local government forced the famous school to close down, moved it to an old telephone factory in the Steglitz quarter of Berlin. When he failed to sell the idea that Modernism was authentic German design to the Nazis he was forced to close the Bauhaus completely. Unlike many of his colleagues, such as **Gropius**, **Marcel Breuer** and **Moholy-Nagy**, who chose to escape to England, Mies went straight to the United States, where he became professor of architecture at the Armour Institute (which later became the Illinois Institute of Technology). Here American patronage and a national longing for status symbols from European culture gave Mies the opportunity to practise an architecture which, paradoxically, had had little

future in Europe even before the Nazis tried to stamp it out. In a series of buildings for the IIT campus Mies defined the visual character of the modern technological university. It is a tribute to the integrity of his designs that they still evoke the idea of 'Modern', and it is with something of a shock that one sees contemporary photos in which the new buildings butt up against their dated automobile peers, the curvaceous Buicks and Packards of the early fifties, which were an expression of the same culture.

Mies built flats at Lake Shore Drive in Chicago between 1946 and 1959 and a monumental office building for the Seagram Corporation on New York's Park Avenue (1958).

Mies' furniture designs for the Tugendhat House and the Barcelona pavilion were licensed to **Knoll**. Through their marketing efforts his exquisite and expensive chairs, products of the twenties, became the *de rigueur* status ornamentation of corporate lobbies throughout America. Just before his death in 1969 Mies designed an office block

'MR' Chair, 1927
Mies van der Rohe's 'MR' chair is a simple but ingenious use of the cantilever principle.

intended for a new London development to be known as Mansion House Square. The planning battle which developed over this building became a set-piece in the debate about Modernism, **Post-Modernism** and conservation in the early eighties.

Bibliography Arthur Drexler *Ludwig Mies van der Rohe* Braziller, New York, 1960; Mayflower, London, 1960; Hans Maria Wingler *Bauhaus* MIT, Cambridge, Mass., 1969; Werner Blaser *Mies van der Rohe: furniture and interiors* Barron's, New York, 1982

Model of Mansion House Square Building, City of London, 1968
Mies' last project is still the subject of public controversy. Similar in character to his Seagram Building in New York, his unbuilt 'glass stump' was planned for a revered but shoddy part of London, and led to a fierce debate about modern architecture and conservation. It has all the elements of Mies' style: exquisite detail, fine proportions, superb materials and a severe beauty.

'Barcelona' Chair, 1929
Although the Barcelona chair was designed by Mies for the exclusive use of the king of Spain at the Barcelona Exhibition of 1929, it became a familiar status object in many American lobbies. Somehow, a temporary perch for a king became translated into a token of corporate modernity.

Herman Miller

Like **Knoll**, Herman Miller is one of the most respected names in American furniture, but unlike its rival, which was founded by an immigrant in cosmopolitan New York, Herman Miller was established by local businessmen at Zeeland, Michigan, near the traditional centre of American furniture-manufacturing at Grand Rapids. The company's origins date back to the early years of this century, but it did not acquire its reputation until immediately after the Second World War when it began to manufacture designs by **Charles Eames** first seen in exhibitions at the **Museum of Modern Art**.

In 1909 D.J. De Pree joined the company Miller and other local businessmen had established five years earlier. De Pree married Miller's daughter, acquired 51 per cent of the stock and changed the company's name. With De Pree the company concentrated on quality control in its reproduction designs. Modern designs only began to interest them when the cabinet-maker Gilbert Rohde joined them in the thirties, bringing European standards of taste with him.

The company acquired an eloquent spokesman when **George Nelson** was appointed design director in 1946, succeeding Rohde. Nelson designed a 'Storage Wall' for Herman Miller in 1946 (p. 195), a 'Steelframe Group' in 1954 and the 'Action Office' ten years later. Eames' **plywood** and steel chair went into production in 1948.

George Nelson directed Herman Miller more towards the architectural market and away from run-of-the mill commercial clients. He insisted on abandoning the reproduction lines and encouraged Charles Eames to continue producing furniture designs. Under his tutelage Eames' famous lounge chair appeared commercially in 1956 (p. 120), followed by the 'Aluminum' group seating in 1958 and the 'Soft Pad' development of it in 1969. From 1952 **Alexander Girard** introduced more colour and pattern into the company's merchandise.

Herman Miller (UK) was set up in 1970.
Bibliography Ralph Caplan *The Design of Herman Miller* Whitney Library of Design, New York, 1976

Room Setting, 1930s
Gilbert Rohde began to work for Herman Miller in 1931, and was the first designer to persuade the hitherto traditional company to produce modern furniture.

ABCDEFGHIJKLMNOPQRSTUVWXYZ

A
B
C
D
E
F
G
H
I
J
K
L
M
N
O
P
Q
R
S
T
U
V
W
X
Y
Z

Missoni

The Missoni knitwear shop on Milan's via Montenapoleone, with its luxurious, colourful merchandise and an arresting interior design by **Vittorio Gregotti**, is a symbol of the city's rise to the status of the world's fashion and design capital. Its owners are Ottavio and Rosita Missoni. Ottavio was a contender in the 400m hurdles at the Wembley Olympics. His entrée in knitwear was in making the tracksuits for the Italian Olympic team on two knitting machines bought immediately after the War by a friend, another athlete called Giorgio Oberweger. The Missoni aesthetic is derived from primitive people, and from the Duke of Windsor. Ottavio has travelled to Guatemala, Afghanistan, Central America, Kashmir and Africa in pursuit of ideas for his extraordinarily subtle, yet casual, knitwear. Missoni has taken inspiration from the Duke of Windsor's tweed knickerbockers, his jarring tweed jacket and cap, his Fair Isle pullover, Argyle socks and woollens. These inspired Rosita Missoni to remark: 'Only an elite could have taken such liberties – the Duke of Windsor or an Afghan shepherd – resulting in such eloquence.'

Wool Ensemble, 1968

Bill Mitchell

b. 1912

Bill Mitchell was born in Cleveland, Ohio. He was hired by **Harley Earl** in 1935 and soon became head of **General Motors'** Cadillac studio. Mitchell succeeded Harley Earl and became General Motors' vice-president in charge of **styling** from 1958 to his retirement in 1978. Unlike Earl, who based his iconography on the race track and on science fiction, Mitchell wanted to bring to 'The General's' line-up something of the quality of low-production-run cars like the American Duesenberg and the European Mercedes-Benz, but it was his fate to be in charge of General Motors' design during the American motor industry's most blighted years. Despite authoritative designs such as the Chevrolet Corvette, Mitchell's achievement was overshadowed by his predecessor.

Issey Miyake

b. 1939

Hanae Mori was the first Japanese fashion designer to become an international celebrity, **Kenzo** was the second, but the third, Issey Miyake, is probably the most important.

Miyake was born and brought up in Hiroshima, but went to Tokyo to study graphics at Tama Art University. As a student he became interested in the theatre and then in fashion. However, in the early sixties such an interest was not encouraged in Japan and to get training Miyake had to travel to Paris, where he worked with Hubert de Givenchy and Guy Laroche, and to New York, where he worked with Geoffrey Beene. By the time he returned to Tokyo to found the Miyake Design Studio in 1971 he had, for a Japanese, an unusually cosmopolitan background.

Miyake's clothes are all inspired in their cut by traditional Japanese forms, but they have an uncompromisingly modern appearance. His great strength, however, is with materials. He specializes in rich, subtle and complex weaves, which evoke traditional values without recourse to adventitious historicism. He acknowledges that he is interested in exploring the 'limits' of clothing, both in its general sense as well as in particular areas such as pattern, texture and looseness. Although very influenced by youth culture with a sixties flavour – he says he wants people who wear his clothes to know what it is like to be 'free' – Miyake has a shrewd business sense. When in the early eighties he wanted to expand his design studio into larger premises he had no hesitation in taking part in television advertisements for whisky and cars to raise the necessary funds. Miyake has helped turn Tokyo into an international city of design.

Bibliography Issey Miyake *East Meets West* Heibonsha, Tokyo, 1978; *Bodyworks* Shogakukan, Tokyo, 1983

Separates, 1984
Issey Miyake's fluid draped shapes combine oriental disguise and Western style.

Modern Movement

There was never *really* such a thing as the Modern Movement, in the sense of an association of artists and designers. It is a convenient abstraction, used by both its champions and its enemies, to describe the adherents to an attitude to design which did not separate form from moral values and social purpose and which sought to create a new aesthetic for a new technological world.

The 'movement' was strongest in Germany, followed by France, Italy and Austria; its leaders were **Walter Gropius**, **Le Corbusier** and **Mies van der Rohe**. In Britain, despite the efforts of a few pioneers like **Wells Coates** and **Maxwell Fry**, the influence of **William Morris** created a huge obstacle to the acceptance of the Modern Movement, which only tentatively took any root at all in the late twenties.

The chief effect in Britain was due to the wave of emigrants from Hitler's Germany. Of these Gropius, **Marcel Breuer** and **Laszlo Moholy-Nagy** moved to the United States, where at New York's **Museum of Modern Art** and at university campuses in Harvard and Chicago they found a more receptive audience of students and clients. Modern Movement dreams which were never fully realized in Germany or in England became reality on Park Avenue or in the showrooms of **Hans Knoll**.

The architect Berthold Lubetkin wrote in 1947 that the Modern Movement in architecture and design is 'a statement of the social aims of the age. Its compelling geometrical regularities affirm man's hope to understand, to explain and control his surroundings. By asserting itself against subjectivity and equivocation, it discloses a universal, purposeful order and clarity in what appears to be a mental wilderness.'

However, after some catastrophic engineering and social failures by later adherents of the movement during the sixties and seventies, the Modern Movement began to be widely attacked and alternative 'philosophies' such as **Post-Modernism** were proposed. Although the Museum of Modern Art had been at the forefront of promoting the Modern Movement, in the mid-sixties it commissioned what became **Robert Venturi**'s *Complexity and Contradiction in Modern Architecture*, a heterodox book which helped create the atmosphere in which Post-Modernism could flourish.

Seagram Building, New York, 1958
The Seagram Building on New York's Park Avenue quickly came to be seen as the most typical manifestation of the Modern Movement being employed by American corporate capitalism.

Moderne/Modernistic

'Moderne', from the French, is a term usually applied in dismissive tones to the degeneration of the **Modern Movement**'s aesthetic in superficial decorative details. It is sometimes used as an adjectival synonym for **Art Deco**. 'Moderne' became popular and successful in the United States, where the style was mass-produced on a large scale. The term now implies an exaggerated commercialism far removed from the idealism of the Modern Movement.

Dream Office for MGM by Cedric Gibbons, E.B. Williams and William Horning, 1936
The public was fed dandified visions of the 'moderne' by the cinema long before such furniture was ever widely available.

Børge Mogensen

1914–72

Børge Mogensen was a pupil of **Kaare Klint**, the Danish designer whose own study of 'classic' English furniture types fed considerable influence into the **Modern Movement** in Denmark. Mogensen became a certified journeyman cabinet-maker in 1934 before studying at the Furniture School of the Royal Academy of Fine Arts in Copenhagen. His reputation is based on work as head of the design department of the Danish Cooperative Society (1942–50) where his objective was to make quality of conception and execution available to the consumer at a reasonable price by employing the most advanced production techniques. His most celebrated design is of a sofa which folds into a simple bed. (See also **Danish design**.)

Leather-Backed Armchair, 1950s
From the early fifties Børge Mogensen developed eclectic furniture designs. Inspired by traditional forms, as in this Spanish leather-backed armchair, they were rich in cultural reference but avoided mere copyism.

A
B
C
D
E
F
G
H
I
J
K
L
M
N
O
P
Q
R
S
T
U
V
W
X
Y
Z

Laszlo Moholy-Nagy

1895–1946

Painter, photographer, typographer, educationalist and film-maker, Laszlo Moholy-Nagy never designed anything that went into series production, but became a major influence in the world of design through his books and his teaching. He was born at Bacsborsod in Hungary, and studied law in Budapest. He began sketching while injured during military service in the First World War, and after the War founded an avant-garde group and journal called *Ma* (Tomorrow). By 1920, an ambitious artist, he had moved to Berlin, and joined the **Bauhaus** staff in 1922. At the Bauhaus he ran the metalwork shop, where his students included **Wilhelm Wagenfeld** and **Marianne Brandt**, made abstract and semi-abstract films, and edited the *Bauhausbücher*, a series of books on art and design theory which came out of Weimar and Dessau and whose authors included **Walter Gropius**, Wassily Kandinsky and Kasimir Malevich. Moholy-Nagy was one of the first 'fine' artists to draw attention to the beauty implicit in machines. His *Buch neuer Kunstler* of 1919 used photographs of aeroplanes to advance his novel aesthetic.

After the closure of the Bauhaus, Moholy-Nagy moved to London where he worked as a display designer for the Simpson's department store, while illustrating books for John Betjeman and doing art direction for the **Architectural Review**. In 1936 he left for Chicago and, under the patronage of Walter Paepcke, founder of the Container Corporation of America,

Book Design, 1928
Moholy-Nagy designed all the Bauhaus' books, including Walter Gropius' Bauhaus Bauten Dessau, the twelfth of the series.

established there the New Bauhaus, which became the Chicago Institute of Design. In Chicago Moholy-Nagy attempted to unify his ideas about art and technology into an ambitious pedagogic programme. After his death from leukaemia his books *The New Vision* and *Vision in Motion* remain highly important texts in art education. (See also p. 36.)

Bibliography Laszlo Moholy-Nagy *The New Vision, from Material to Architecture* Brewer Warren/Putnam, New York, 1928; Laszlo Moholy-Nagy *Vision in Motion* Paul Theobald, Chicago, 1946; Richard Kostelanetz *Moholy-Nagy* Allen Lane, 1972; Lucia Moholy *Marginalien zu Moholy-Nagy: dokumentarische Ungereimtheiten* Richard Sherpe, Krefeld, 1972

Hanae Mori

b. 1926

Hanae Mori can claim to be the founder of modern Japanese fashion design. After being educated at Tokyo's Christian Women's College she designed costumes for movies before opening her own shop in Tokyo in 1955. The Japanese are curiously self-effacing about some of their achievements and it required Mori's example in proving that there could be excellence in native fashion design to lay the way open for **Kenzo**, **Issey Miyake** and Yohji Yamamoto to become major international figures.

Her designs are essentially Western in style, but employ specially woven and dyed textiles which follow Japanese traditions. This successful and influential combination of East and West has put paid to the fallacy, often heard in Japan, that 'only blue-eyed people can be creative'. In 1973 Mori opened a showroom in New York and has shown regularly in Paris since 1977.

Bauhaus Verlag Letterhead, 1923
Moholy-Nagy designed the official letterhead for the Bauhaus in his Constructivist style.

190

Stanley Morison

1889–1967

While working for the Monotype Corporation, Stanley Morison persuaded **Eric Gill** to become a modern typographer. Gill's first face for Morison was 'Perpetua', derived from the inscriptions on Trajan's column, and he also designed 'Gill Sans' for him. Morison was himself typographic adviser to the Cambridge University Press. He also designed the face called 'Times New Roman' in 1931 for *The Times*. When it was introduced the following year, even the traditionally conservative *Times* readers considered it a masterpiece of clarity and concision; nor did they object that Morison had changed the newspaper's Gothic masthead for a classical one, so impressed were they by the improvements in legibility he brought to their paper.

Bibliography Stanley Morison & Kenneth Day *The Typographic Book 1435–1935* Ernest Benn, London, 1963

The Times, *October 1932*
In October 1932 The Times' 'Gothic' masthead, in use for 120 years, was replaced by Morison's 'Times New Roman', a serif face that won praise for its legibility and elegance. 'Times New Roman' used ascenders that were slightly more squat than conventional Roman faces, and this gave it a pleasing feeling of robustness.

William Morris

1834–96

William Morris was an influence on virtually everybody in early twentieth-century design. His ideas became widespread, and it is with his ideas rather than his achievements that he has most influenced the history of design, but his prose and poetry were wordy and some of it is now almost unreadable.

Morris was the first to discuss the value of craft principles, such as truth to materials, which were the basis for the **Arts and Crafts** movement. He was a great lover of simplicity, and propagated an ideal of rustic living, writing in 1880, 'Simplicity of life, begetting simplicity of taste, that is a love for sweet and lofty things, is of all matters most necessary for the birth of the new and better art we crave for; simplicity everywhere, in the palace as well as the cottage.' The problem was, Morris had funny ideas about simplicity.

Although **Nikolaus Pevsner** singled him out as a pioneer of the **Modern Movement** in his influential book of 1936, these ideas have, in fact, had a malign influence. Morris' anti-urban, anti-industrial conservatism undermined the basis for the Modern Movement to flourish in Britain. In fits of socialistic agitation (comfortably removed from the city) he would condemn industrialization, once telling a miner 'I should be glad if we could do without coal.'

Morris is not free from the charge of hypocrisy. He wanted his 'revolution' in values to ensure that 'the twentieth century . . . gets its goods wholesome and its ornaments hand-made', but made his own ornaments by machine. He spoke of craft principles, but manufactured reproduction furniture. He looked back to an idealized view of the Middle Ages, but was supported in comfort by a modern age he rigorously condemned.

Morris was, however, a talented designer of carpets, wallpapers and furniture, founding the firm of Morris, Marshall & Faulkner in 1862. He later turned to book design with the Kelmscott Press located in a Cotswold house where he could escape from the civilization which, while sustaining him, he so contumaciously despised. (See also pp. 26–9 and **British design**.)

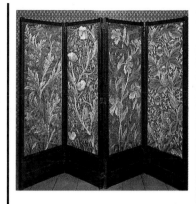

Four-Panel Screen, *1890*
Morris' screen is a coloured silk embroidered on canvas in stem and darning stitch.

Room by William Morris, *1866*
In 1866 Morris and his partners in Morris, Marshall & Faulkner were commissioned to design the West Dining Room in Henry Cole's South Kensington Museum (now the Victoria and Albert Museum). The result is a gloomy masterpiece of Arts and Crafts. The painted panels and stained glass, depicting the months, are by the painter Sir Edward Burne-Jones. With appropriate antiquarianism, the frieze details are adapted from the font of Newcastle Cathedral.

ABCDEFGHIJKLMNOPQRSTUVWXYZ

Motorama

Motoramas were an invention of **Harley Earl**'s as a means of showing off his dream cars to the American public. These fifties' exhibitions were masterly marketing devices where Earl exploited his already hard-pressed designers (getting them to devise ever more extreme fantasies to titillate the public) as well as exploiting the public itself, whom Earl pumped for free opinion research. Although a colleague of Earl's called him a 'nigger driver' for demanding so much creativity from his design team, everyone enjoyed the successes which the Motoramas brought: most of the famous styling motifs of the fifties were tested at a Motorama before they found their way into production.

Olivier Mourgue

b. 1939

Olivier Mourgue, a French furniture and toy designer, studied at the Ecole Nationale Supérieure des Arts Décoratifs. He summarized sixties design five years before the decade finished with his 'Djinn' zoomorphic fantasy chaise-longue and chair. Constructed out of polyurethane foam stretched over a tubular steel armature and upholstered in hard-to-look-at air terminal greens and oranges, they were chosen by film-maker Stanley Kubrick to suggest the future space station in *2001: A Space Odyssey*. Mourgue has recently worked as a colour consultant for Renault and now teaches at the Ecole d'Art in Brest.

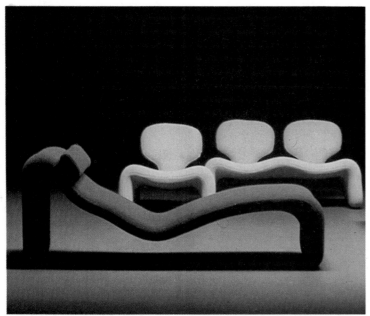

'Djinn' Chaise-Longue, 1965
With polyurethane foam upholstery on a metal frame, Mourgue's chaise-longue was a deliberate essay in the use of modern materials.

Alfonso Mucha

1860–1939

Mucha was born in what is now Czechoslovakia. He became an artistic adviser to the actress Sarah Bernhardt in 1894, and was a minor practitioner of **Art Nouveau**. His strongest work was his graphic design for posters, but he also attempted some jewellery and furniture.

Hermann Muller-Brockmann

b. 1914

The Swiss graphic designer Hermann Muller-Brockmann was born in Zürich and studied at Zürich's Kunstgewerbeschule (school of arts and crafts) before setting up his own practice in 1936. He worked in exhibition design from the thirties to the fifties and became a graphic consultant to **IBM** Europe, an equivalent of **Paul Rand** in the United States. His style is the Swiss school of austere minimalism, which has enjoyed an international influence.

Peter Muller-Munk

Peter Muller-Munk was one of the second generation of American designers, following the example of **Raymond Loewy** and his contemporaries, but with a degree of extra tact and discretion. He inaugurated the first professional course in industrial design at Pittsburgh's Carnegie Institute of Technology in 1936 and established his own consultancy in the steel town in 1945, specializing in corporate and product design for Westinghouse, US Steel and Texaco. He was one of the founders of **ICSID**, whose first president he became in 1957.

Bruno Munari

b. 1907

Bruno Munari was born in 1907, in time to be one of the late Futurists, and worked in Milan in the thirties in the company of Fortunato Depero and Ulrico Prampoline. He was involved in various ambiguous artistic movements until in 1957 he started working seriously for **Danese**. Munari is one of the elder statesmen of post-War **Italian design**, the author of many books and articles including *Design as Art*. His main commitment is to graphic design, although he produced small decorative domestic objects for **Danese**.

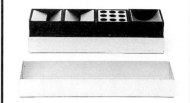

Desk Set, 1958
Munari started his career as a painter, and inspired by the Futurists became fascinated with machines. His product designs show a sophisticated distillation of the machine aesthetic.

Keith Murray

1892–1981

Keith Murray was born in New Zealand and moved to England with his parents in 1906. He studied at the Architectural Association in London, but the depressed condition of the architectural market encouraged him to look for his first job elsewhere, and he chose the minor arts of glass and ceramics, working for Stevens & Williams of Brierly Hill and **Josiah Wedgwood**, respectively. His simple geometric designs were influenced both by what he had seen of Scandinavian design at the Paris exhibition of 1925, as well as by his own architectural training. In 1936 he became one of the first of the Royal Society of Arts' 'Royal Designers for Industry'. He found his way back into architecture in the later thirties and designed Wedgwood's new factory at Barlaston, Staffordshire.
Bibliography 'The Thirties' exhibition catalogue, Arts Council, London, 1979

Jug and Mug for Wedgwood, 1930
The understated, simple forms are typical of Murray's work.

Hermann Muthesius

1861–1927

Hermann Muthesius was one of the *éminences grises* behind the formation of the **Deutsche Werkbund** and the importation of English design ethics into Germany. He can be seen as one of the intellectual originators of the **Modern Movement**.

Muthesius was made superintendent of the Prussian Board of Trade for Schools of Arts and Crafts in 1903. From 1896 to 1903 he had been attached to the German Embassy in London, where he researched English housing, and wrote an article about **C.R. Ashbee** for the German magazine *Dekorative Kunst* in 1898. In 1904–5 he published a three-volume account of English architecture, *Das englishe Haus* in which he particularly praised the work of the late-nineteenth-century architects, and which became a fundamental influence on German taste. Muthesius' ideas on design were widely publicized in 1914 when he was involved in an animated debate with **Henry van de Velde** on the approach to be followed by the Werkbund. Muthesius said that it should support the concept of *Typisierung* (standardization of objects), while Van de Velde supported freedom of artistic expression. Muthesius' main contribution to design was theoretical.
Bibliography Joan Campbell *The Werkbund – Politics and reform in the applied arts* Princeton University Press, Princeton, New Jersey and Guildford, 1980

Museum of Modern Art

The art critic Robert Hughes wrote that 'if America is design-conscious, then the wells of its obsession were dug by the Museum of Modern Art's **Alfred H. Barr**'.

MoMA is a part of the New York way of life. Its staff have included **Philip Johnson** and **Eliot Noyes**, and its governing body **Walter Gropius** and **Marcel Breuer**. Its building, on West 53rd Street, finished in 1939 to the design of Philip L. Goodwin and Edward Durrell Stone, is one of America's first complete essays in the **International Style**, and thus was a rare case of form perfectly matching function. From the beginning the Museum set out to promote the **Modern Movement**, and ran a hugely influential series of exhibitions, 'The International Style' (1932), 'Machine Art' (1934, see p. 46), 'Organic Design in Home Furnishings' (1940, see p. 75) and 'Good Design' exhibitions annually during a period in the fifties. These have firmly established MoMA as a world leader in taste.

The aestheticism of Alfred H. Barr's attitude to modern art was inherited by the Museum's design department, which collects and displays manufactured objects purely on the basis of their appearance. MoMA's architecture department has been more radical. Having done a great deal to establish the character of 'modern' architecture, the Museum then helped reverse the orthodoxy, commissioning the lectures that became **Robert Venturi**'s *Complexity and Contradiction in Modern Architecture* in 1966 and organizing a huge exhibition about the Beaux-Arts in 1975. Ironically, both these ventures contributed to the intellectual atmosphere that encouraged the growth of **Post-Modernism**.

Philip Johnson added a wing to the building in the style of **Mies van der Rohe** in 1951, and in 1983 Cesar Pelli's Museum Tower took advantage of the 'air rights' over Goodwin and Stone's originally modest structure.

Title Page from **Das englishe Haus**, *1905*

Facade of Museum of Modern Art, 1942
The original building, shown here in 1942, was finished in 1939 but has since been remodelled with Pelli's Museum Tower of 1983. The mobile shown hanging from the outside is by Alexander Calder, and was erected to mark the 'Cubism and Abstract Art' Exhibition.

N

Ralph **Nader**
Condé **Nast**
    Necchi
George **Nelson**
Marcello **Nizzoli**
Isamu **Noguchi**
Bob **Noorda**
John K. **Northrop**
Eliot **Noyes**
Antii **Nurmesniemi**

Ralph Nader

b. 1934

Ralph Nader is a lawyer who took legal action against Chevrolet's Corvair and in so doing changed the design perspectives of the American auto industry. To Nader consumer advocacy is a means of preventing the decline of civilization. He has presented American customers with a spectre of their corporations as huge, inhuman, manipulative syndicates. His goal, in his own words, is 'nothing less than the qualitative reform of the Industrial Revolution'. His attack on the Corvair on the grounds of its lack of safety provisions was made in a book, *Unsafe at any Speed*, which grew out of a paper written at Harvard. After its publication in 1965 **General Motors'** staff spied on him, but without being able to discover anything that could undermine its success. Under the influence of the zealous, monkish Nader, Congress passed twenty-five pieces of consumer legislation between 1966 and 1973 which were directly influenced by his activism. A US Senator has said, 'More than anyone else, Nader made the consumer movement a considerable factor in American economic and political life.' After Nader it was impossible for a major corporation to market irresponsible products.

Condé Nast

1873–1942

With his friend, **Elsie de Wolfe**, Condé Nast, the publisher of **Vogue** and many other magazines, was a profound influence on American taste during the first half of the twentieth century by propagating an image of acceptable chic. His publications were targeted at the most affluent and fashionable people in America and Europe, and he flattered his public by commissioning only the best writers and the best photographers to fill not only *Vogue*'s pages, but also those of *Vanity Fair*, **House & Garden** and *Jardin des Modes*. His biographer, Caroline Seebohm, has compared Nast to his contemporary, Scott Fitzgerald: 'Both came from the Mid-West; both were brought up Catholic; both were raised in genteel poverty; and both were preoccupied by, and based their careers on, the implications and consequences of class, money, the East, and sophisticated, unattainable women.'
Bibliography Caroline Seebohm *The Man who was Vogue: the life and times of Condé Nast* Weidenfeld & Nicolson, London, 1982; Viking, New York, 1982

Vogue *Cover, 1909*
Before photography overwhelmed fashion publishing, Vogue *'s covers used modish illustrations.*

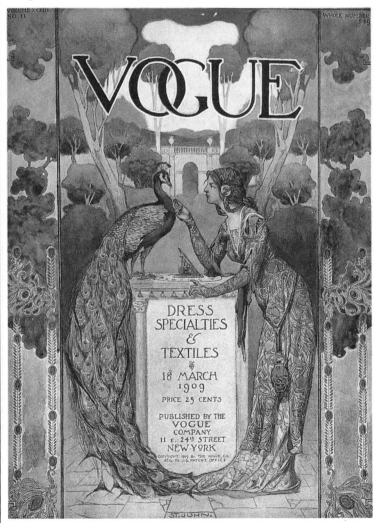

Necchi

Necchi is a Milanese sewing-machine manufacturer, which employed **Marcello Nizzoli** in the early years of Italy's post-War *ricostruzione*. Nizzoli's 'Mirella' of 1956 is a perfect symbol of the formal perfection of recent Italian **industrial design**. Necchi employs **Giorgio Giugiaro**'s ItalDesign to work on its current product line (see p. 56).

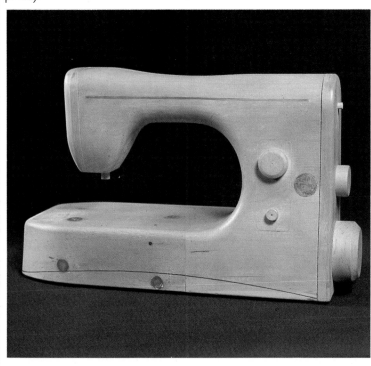

'Mirella' Sewing Machine for Necchi, 1956* (left); *and Wooden Model
The model was made by Giovanni Sacchi to a design by Marcello Nizzoli. With its smoothly flowing lines and elegant shape, the 'Mirella' became a distinguished symbol of the post-War Italian ricostruzione.

'Storage Wall' for Herman Miller, 1946
Nelson's storage system is a masterpiece of responsible design and rational application of functional principles.

George Nelson

b. 1907

George Nelson is perhaps the best-known American designer of what might be called the European School, a group of architects and designers more or less associated with the ideals and the educational programmes of New York's **Museum of Modern Art**, who repudiated the commercialism of **Raymond Loewy** and the other purveyors of **styling**.

Nelson was born in Hartford, Connecticut, and graduated in architecture from Yale University's School of Fine Arts in 1931. The winner of a Prix de Rome, Nelson travelled in Europe from 1931 to 1933 and became one of the first Americans to discover the revolution taking place in European architecture and design. He was instrumental in introducing **Mies van der Rohe** to the United States. On his return from Europe in 1933 Nelson, with colleagues Howard Myers, Henry Wright and Pal Grotz, founded *Architectural Forum*, a journal which, like the **Architectural Review** in England, promoted Modernism, but, unlike its English counterpart, served also as a voice of corporate power, or, at least, one part of it. From 1936 he worked on architecture and interior design projects, pioneering pedestrian malls and designing a 'Storage Wall' system, with which he first made his reputation as a furniture designer. He worked for **Herman Miller** from 1946, to whom he introduced **Charles Eames**. In 1947 Nelson set up his own offices in New York. In 1965 he designed the 'Action Office' for Herman Miller, an early attempt in pre-automation days to find a rational, ergonomic solution to the bureaucratic environment, and in 1968 the Editor 2 typewriter for **Olivetti**.

With his journalism, as well as his work at the International Design Conference at **Aspen**, Colorado, Nelson became one of the most witty and articulate spokesmen for American design. Of patronage he has said: 'It's always the same, you've either got the Church or you've got IBM.' But he is better known perhaps for appearing on committees and conference platforms all over the world, and for his books, than for his design projects themselves.
Bibliography George Nelson *The Problems of Design*, Whitney Library of Design, New York, 1957

Marcello Nizzoli

1887–1969

One of the greatest of all product designers, Marcello Nizzoli was the first and most influential of designers to work for **Olivetti**, the Italian business equipment company.

He was born at Boretto and studied at the School of Fine Arts in nearby Parma. His first calling was that of painter and his first public appearance was when he exhibited two pictures at the '*Nuove Tendenze*' exhibition of 1914. He began to gain a varied reputation as a poster, fabric and exhibition designer, and was hired by Adriano Olivetti in 1938 to work in the advertising office (which the company had established in 1931). He went on from there to design a series of machines which have become 'classics' of modern industrial design: the 'Lexicon 80' (1948), the 'Lettera 22' (1950) and the 'Divisumma 24' (1956). For **Necchi** he designed the 'Mirella' sewing-machine (1956). All shared a sculptural sophistication which found expression in organically curved body shells which hide the mechanical components; Nizzoli also paid great attention to the cut-lines in his products, as well as to the application of graphics.

Isamu Noguchi

b. 1904

Isamu Noguchi is a Japanese–American sculptor who studied in Paris, where he met the sculptors Constantin Brancusi and Alberto Giacometti. He came to notice as a furniture and lighting designer in the forties when both sculpture and furniture design were becoming more organic and more free. He has made designs both for **Knoll** and for **Herman Miller**, but is best known for his wire and paper lampshades whose celebrity created an internationally acknowledged stereotype.

Glass-Topped Coffee Table for Herman Miller, 1945
Having trained as a sculptor in Paris, Noguchi married expressive form with oriental elegance in his furniture designs. This glass-topped coffee table was produced by Herman Miller in 1945, although its design dates back to 1939.

Bob Noorda

b. 1927

A graphic designer, Bob Noorda was born in Amsterdam but since 1952 has lived and worked in Milan. After some distinguished poster campaigns for their tyres, he became art director of Pirelli in 1961. Noorda was one of the founders of **Unimark**, a multi-disciplinary Milanese consultancy, in 1965. He was responsible for all the signs on **Franco Albini**'s Milan subway system, the 'Metropolitana'. Typical of his approach, Noorda conducted serious research into levels of visibility and the legibility of certain letter-forms in subway conditions, but equally typically the result he achieved had a very light touch. (See also p. 50.)

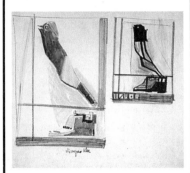

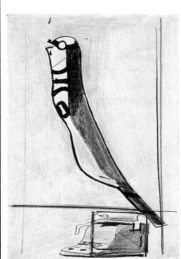

Advertisement for 'Lexicon 80' and Sketches, 1949
As well as designing products for Olivetti, Nizzoli took charge of poster design. The sketches for his 1949 advertisement of the 'Lexicon 80' reveal that he was influenced by bird form in his design of the typewriter.

John K. Northrop

1895–1981

John Knudsen Northrop was a romantic aircraft engineer whose remarkable, visionary designs donated the shapes of **streamlining** to popular culture. A pioneer of all-metal aircraft construction, Northrop was also one of the enthusiasts for the 'flying-wing' concept, in which the wings and fuselage merge (which **Norman Bel Geddes** made popular in his book, *Horizons*). Northrop was co-founder and chief engineer of Lockheed and the designer of the 'Vega' aeroplane which

Amelia Earheart used on her solo Atlantic crossing of 1932. Although his friend **Donald Douglas** once remarked in the 1940s that 'every major aircraft in the sky has some Jack Northrop in it' he retired, demoralized, in 1952, after the armed forces had cancelled two of his 'flying-wing' designs.
Bibliography E.T. Wooldridge *Winged Wonders – The Story of the Flying Wings* National Air and Space Museum, Washington, 1983

Eliot Noyes

1910–77

Eliot Noyes was the son of a Harvard professor of English, and was educated at Andover and later at Harvard's School of Architecture, where he met **Walter Gropius** and **Marcel Breuer**. As an archaeology student at Andover he had first read **Le Corbusier**'s *Vers une architecture*, and Gropius' teaching confirmed his enthusiasm for the European design ethic.

Under Gropius' sponsorship, Noyes became the director of **industrial design** at New York's **Museum of Modern Art**, a post he held both immediately before and immediately after

the Second World War. But it was the War itself which was to have a decisive effect on Noyes' career as a designer. In the Army Glider Program he met Thomas Watson, the son of the founder of **IBM**. He renewed the acquaintance in the later forties while he was briefly working in the office of **Norman Bel Geddes**, who held a consultancy contract with the company, and Watson then employed him as a designer. The work he was to do for IBM, although influenced by the European example of **Olivetti**, became perhaps the most celebrated design exercise in corporate history. Telling Watson that he 'would prefer neatness', Noyes transformed the entire appearance of the

huge corporation. Using **Paul Rand** to develop new graphics and hiring architects like Breuer to design buildings, Noyes himself took charge of the products and, in the words of the American journalist Ursula McHugh, 'brought the **Bauhaus** to big business'. In 1956 Noyes was formally appointed corporate design director of IBM, a role whose guaranteed access to the chief executive gave Noyes as much influence over the face of American manufacturing industry as **Harley Earl** had with his vice-presidency at General Motors. His products for IBM included the 'Selectric' typewriter of 1961 (p. 18) and the 'Executary' dictating machine of 1961. Impressed by the changes which Noyes' **corporate identity** programme had made on IBM's business, similar appointments and briefs followed for Westinghouse in 1960 and Mobil Oil in 1964.

Noyes reshaped entire corporations and established new standards of integrity and efficiency in American design. In order to do this he insisted that his clients should accept the following terms of business: they should agree with his design philosophy, they should allow adequate time for the completion of each project, and they should be prepared to pay for quality. He despised market research and said that the first generation of American designers, men like **Raymond Loewy** and **Norman Bel**

Wooden Model for Cummins Diesel Engine, 1964
Eliot Noyes' adoption of the Bauhaus ethic shows through even in his design for a diesel engine. (See also p. 75.)

Geddes, might have proved that appearance sells, but 'simply were not motivated by a high enough intent'. Noyes' own house at New Canaan, Connecticut, a masterpiece of American Modernism, won *Progressive Architecture's* design award in 1954. (See also pp. 46–8 and **American design**.)
Bibliography 'Art and Industry' exhibition catalogue, The Boilerhouse Project, Victoria & Albert Museum, London, 1982

Antii Nurmesniemi

b. 1927

The Finnish designer Antii Nurmesniemi studied interior design at Helsinki's Taideteollinen oppilaitos (applied art school). He worked in an architect's office, designing banks, hotel and restaurant interiors, before setting up his own studio in 1956. He married **Vuokko Eskolin** (**Marimekko**'s chief designer) in the fifties. His clients include **Artek** and Wartsila, for whom he has designed a number of domestic objects, including cooking utensils and chairs. Nurmesniemi is a frequent visitor to international conferences, where he is an articulate representative of **Finnish design**. (See p. 123.)

'005 Chair', 1982
Nurmesniemi brought a certain type of Pop Modernism to traditional Finnish design. The fabric on this chair was designed by his wife, Vuokko.

Obsolescence
Ogle
Olivetti
Omega
OMK Design
    Workshop
Brian **O'Rorke**
    Orrefors
Amedée **Ozenfant**

Obsolescence

Planned obsolescence was a feature of the American economy in the fifties. There were two views about it. To an industrial designer like **Harley Earl** it was one of the springs of wealth and the greatest possible stimulus to designers; he actually called it the 'dynamic economy'. Similarly enthusiastic, Brooks Stevens said, 'Our whole economy is based on planned obsolescence, and everybody who can read without moving his lips should know it by now. We make good products, we induce people to buy them, and the next year we deliberately introduce something that will make those products old-fashioned, out of date, obsolete . . . It isn't organized waste. It's a sound contribution to the American economy.' But to consumer activists like **Vance Packard** obsolescence was a social evil, providing the opportunity for manipulation as soon as production began to outstrip demand. He identified three types of obsolescence in his book *The Waste Makers* (1960): of function, quality and desirability. The obsolescence of function was when a new product came along to do the job better, of desirability when fashion changed. Of that of quality, this was what made Willy Loman in Arthur Miller's *Death of a Salesman* say, 'Once in my life I would like to own something outright before it's broken! I'm always in a race with the junkyard! I just finish paying for the car and it's on its last legs. The refrigerator consumes belts like a goddam maniac. They time those things. They time them so when you've finally paid for them, they're used up . . .'

Manufacturers still 'life' products: the consequences of an economic system where durability means people out of work have still to be faced.
Bibliography Vance Packard *The Waste Makers* McKay, New York, 1960; Longman, London, 1960

Ogle

David Ogle was a staff designer for Murphy Radio before forming Ogle Associates in the late fifties, a practice intended to cover all aspects of design from exhibitions and packaging through to products. Ogle was killed in a car crash when only forty, but the firm survived and has, under its managing director Tom Karen, successfully specialized in vehicle design, being retained as a consultant to British Leyland, among others. Ogle has been responsible for many vehicles which are familiar to the public under manufacturers' brand names, notably the cab design of the Leyland T45 and MT211 trucks.

Leyland T45 Truck, 1980
It was part of Ogle's intention to make the T45 look less aggressive than its rivals, and its soft curves and unassertive air intake help make the massive vehicle appear more friendly.

Olivetti

The Olivetti company was founded in 1908 by Camillo Olivetti (1868–1943) and brought to greatness by his son, Adriano (1901–60). Adriano was celebrated for cultural, social and political avant-gardism, while in more recent years his heirs have been celebrated for what has become known as **design management**.

Olivetti produced Italy's first typewriter, the 'M1' (using American machine tools), in 1911. In 1932 the portable 'MP1' came on the market. Designed by Aldo Magnelli with his brother, the abstract painter Alberto, this was the first typewriter to be deliberately conceived as a consumer product. That is to say, its body was **styled**. In 1935 the 'Studio 42' appeared, designed by the painter **Xanti Schawinsky** and the architects Figini and Pollini. This extraordinary machine created a stereotype for the form of the modern typewriter that took forty years to change. In 1936 Olivetti commissioned Figini and Pollini to design a new factory in his home town of Ivrea, Piedmont, for the family business machine company. It became one of the landmarks of **Modern Movement** architecture in pre-War Italy, alongside Giuseppe Terragni's Casa del Fascio in Como.

Through the enlightened patronage of artists such as Schawinsky and **Marcello Nizzoli**, Olivetti made his firm's products the symbols of Italian **industrial design**. The influence of art ran through every aspect of the Olivetti company's character and production: painters and sculptors worked in the publicity department, designed exhibitions and decided what typewriters and comptometers should look like. In 1952 New York's **Museum of Modern Art** recognized this by holding an Olivetti show, and the influence of this, together with the dramatic presence of the firm's Park Avenue showroom (designed by Belgiojoso, Perresutti and Rogers), was one of the influences on **IBM** which inspired that company's president, Thomas Watson, Junior, to hire **Eliot Noyes**.

Adriano Olivetti was a pioneer of the Italian industrial revolution, a man consumed by social purpose. Not only was he the impresario of the Olivetti 'style', but he was also an influential thinker. He became a member of the *Movimento Comunità* and wrote or caused to be published many essays and books on social issues. He ▶

'Lexicon 80' Typewriter for Olivetti, 1948
In his products for Olivetti Nizzoli combined a sculptor's sense of form with a designer's immaculate sense of detail. The 'Lexicon' was a model for typewriters for almost a generation and its success made a valuable contribution to Olivetti's status as a distinguished patron of design.

Poster for 'MP1' Typewriter by Xanti Schawinsky, 1935
The Olivetti 'MP1' was the first typewriter to be styled: the ribs on the typebar basket suggest that designer Aldo Magnelli was inspired by the abstract paintings of his brother, Alberto.

Modular Terminal System by Ettore Sottsass and Others, 1974
Olivetti's system is adaptable to individual needs and can be hooked up to a computer either by switched or dedicated lines. Even with this sophisticated equipment, Sottsass' sense of playfulness comes through.

A B C D E F G H I J K L M N O P Q R S T U V W X Y Z

founded the journals *Zodiac* and *Urbanistica*, and was awarded a **Compasso d'Oro** in 1955.

The story of Olivetti is no less than the story of Italian industrial design. At one time or another every great Italian designer has worked in some capacity for the company: **Franco Albini, Gae Aulenti, Mario Bellini, Rodolfo Bonetto, Michele de Lucchi, Vico Magistretti, Marcello Nizzoli, Carlo Scarpa, Ettore Sottsass** and **Marco Zanuso**. However, despite its international reputation for excellence, by the late seventies Olivetti was a debt-laden, moribund company with a stagnant product line of mechanical and electro-mechanical typewriters and some uncompetitive computers. Then in 1978 Carlo De Benedetti (b. 1934) became chairman. He still believed in a central role for design in Olivetti, but that role was now interpreted as 'forward-looking marketing input'. He turned the company around in a dramatic manner; under his guidance Olivetti manufactured the first electronic typewriter and began to establish a position as the major European supplier of office automation equipment, word processors, electronic typing systems and mainframe computers. The

Olivetti Logogram, early 1980s
This Olivetti logogram was redesigned especially for the sales outlets by Hans von Klier, head of the company's corporate identity office. It was intended to give concessionaries a character of their own, while maintaining their visual association with the parent company.

aesthetic excellence of the products continued, particularly with the influence of Bellini, Sottsass and de Lucchi. In 1983 De Benedetti signed an agreement with America's AT&T whereby the American concern acquired 25 per cent of the Italian company in return for Olivetti having access to AT&T's Bell Labs research facility. With this marriage of office automation and telecommunications De Benedetti set out to establish another phase in the Olivetti corporate career as exciting and challenging as the one Adriano Olivetti initiated fifty years before. (See also p. 56.)
Bibliography 'Olivetti' exhibition catalogue, Kunstgewerbemuseum, Zürich, 1960; 'Design Process Olivetti 1908–1978' travelling exhibition, catalogue published in 1979 by Olivetti's Direzione Relazioni Culturali/Disegno Industriale Pubblicità, Milan

Omega

The Omega Workshop was founded by the art critic **Roger Fry** in 1913, much encouraged by a subscription of £250 from George Bernard Shaw. The idea was to reinvent the **Wiener Werkstätte** and **Paul Poiret**'s Studio Martine so that young designers could be encouraged, but Omega was Bloomsbury gone to art. It had none of the social purpose of **John Ruskin** and **William Morris** and their workshop ideals, but was from the start only a Bohemian retreat for decadent demi-mondaines with a taste for the decorative. Omega cared nothing for technique and strived mightily for effects alone.

For Fry, Omega represented Post-Impressionist design, and in July 1914 a room setting showing 'Post Impressionism practically introduced into decoration and furniture' was displayed at the Seventh Salon of the Allied Artists' Association. Omega members also decorated and furnished Roger Fry's own home, Durbin's, near Guildford (1914), and Charleston, near Firle in Sussex, the home of

Duncan Grant and Vanessa Bell (1916). Other members of the Omega Workshop included the architect Frederick Etchells (1886–1973), who translated **Le Corbusier** into English, and even **Edward McKnight Kauffer** showed some of his pictures at the Workshop before he abandoned painting for posters. Omega closed in 1921.

Sir Roy Strong pinpointed the amateurism of Omega when he recalled that 'any visitor to Charleston while Duncan Grant was still alive will remember the utter chaos . . . The Omega Workshops come across as a monument to amateurism and muddle. Running through is that deadly lack of seriousness and professionalism that has been the ruin of so much in this country. It is an attitude which goes straight on down to the Festival of Britain.'
Bibliography 'The Omega Workshops 1913–1919: decorative arts of Bloomsbury' exhibition catalogue, The Crafts Council, London, 1984

Painted Screen, 1913–14
This screen was produced by Vanessa Bell at the Omega Workshop.

OMK Design Workshop

OMK is a British furniture manufacturer, founded by **Rodney Kinsman**, Jerzy Olejinik and Bryan Morrison in 1966.

Omkstack Chair, 1971
Rodney Kinsman's stacking chair is manufactured by Bieffe of Padua.

Orrefors

The Swedish glass manufacturer Orrefors was established at Kalmar in 1898. Among its artistic directors were Simon Gate and **Edward Hald**, who pioneered the cooperation between fine-artists, craftsmen and industry now seen as a characteristic of **Swedish design**. Under Hald, Orrefors produced some of the most refined decorative modern glass.

Glass by Edward Hald
Edward Hald's patterns for Orrefors were often inspired by Matisse, one of his teachers.

Amedée Ozenfant

1886–1966

Amédée Ozenfant was an artist who was acutely aware that in the twentieth century the legitimate concern of his vocation was to deal, in one way or another, with the machine. With his friend **Le Corbusier** he devised the aesthetic philosophy known as Purism, about which they said: 'The picture is a machine for the transmission of sentiments. Science offers us a kind of physiological language that enables us to produce precise physiological sensations to the spectator . . . The mechanical object can in certain cases move us, because manufactured forms are geometrical, and we are sensitive to geometry.'

He and Le Corbusier published from 1920 to 1925 the review *L'Esprit nouveau*, which formed the basis for Le Corbusier's epochal book, *Vers une architecture*. Their ideas were given form in the Pavillon de l'Esprit Nouveau at the Paris Exhibition of 1925.

Brian O'Rorke

1901–74

Brian O'Rorke was a British designer of liner and aircraft interiors. After studying engineering at Cambridge and architecture at the Architectural Association in London, O'Rorke set up his own office in 1929. Besides factories, dwellings and offices he designed three Orient Line ships between 1933 and 1939. Immediately after the Second World War he designed the interior of the Vickers Viking aeroplane.

Interior of Vickers Viking, 1946
The Vickers Viking was one of the first post-War civil planes. In its interior Brian O'Rorke attempted to establish a design which distanced a passenger from a military craft.

A B C D E F G H I J K L M N O P Q R S T U V W X Y Z

P

Vance **Packard**
Verner **Panton**
Victor **Papanek**
    Parker-Knoll
Gregor **Paulsson**
    PEL
    Penguin Books
    Pentagram
den **Permanente**
Charlotte **Perriand**
Gaetano **Pesce**
Michael **Peters**
Nikolaus **Pevsner**
    Piaggio
Frank **Pick**
    Pininfarina
Giancarlo **Piretti**
    Plastics
Warren **Plattner**
    Plywood
Paul **Poiret**
Gio **Ponti**
    Pop
    Porsche
    Post-Modernism
Jack **Pritchard**
Ulla **Procopé**
Jean **Prouvé**
Emilio **Pucci**
A.W.N. **Pugin**
Jean **Puiforcat**
    Push Pin Studio
    Pyrex

Vance Packard

b. 1914

The American writer Vance Packard studied at Pennsylvania State University and at Columbia. His first job was as a journalist on a Boston daily paper and he then moved into magazine feature writing. Before **Ralph Nader** he was the most vocal critic of American consumer society. Packard's study of mass psychology and his motivational research gave his books a special edge. *The Hidden Persuaders*, a book about advertising, was published in 1957, his analysis of the class system, *The Status Seekers*, in 1959, and *The Waste Makers* in 1960 (see p. 48). Packard's target was often the profligacy he saw in **Harley Earl**'s idea of the dynamic economy, or planned **obsolescence** as it is sometimes called. When trying to define a consumer 'durable' Packard suggested it was any product that would outlast the final hire purchase instalment.

Packard lives in New Canaan, Connecticut, where his neighbours have at various times included **Eliot Noyes**, **Marcel Breuer** and **Philip Johnson**.

Verner Panton

b. 1926

The Danish furniture designer Verner Panton trained in Copenhagen as an architect, and worked in **Arne Jacobsen**'s office before starting his own firm in 1955. He has specialized in refining and executing the idea of a one-piece stacking chair, either in **plastic** or in wood. The stacking chair in injection-moulded plastic which he designed in 1960 was manufactured by **Herman Miller** from 1967 to 1975. Recently, Panton has become interested in the expressive possibilities of furniture and has designed some bizarre, organically shaped plastic chairs.

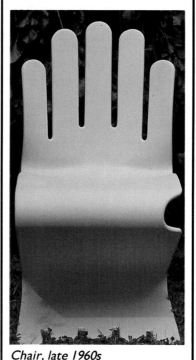

Chair, late 1960s
This chair in the shape of a hand is one of Panton's stranger pieces; he has specialized in making plastic furniture in complex, sculptural forms.

Victor Papanek

b. 1925

Victor Papanek is professor of design at the University of Kansas. His book *Design for the Real World* (1967) called attention to the needs of the Third World. It was written out of a conviction that most industrial design was concerned only with 'concocting trivia', and that real needs were being conscientiously ignored. He has publicized his ideas on strenuous lecture tours on all continents, describing to his audiences the need to consider the under-privileged, as well as diminishing world resources. Papanek was a cult figure while ecology was fashionable during the early seventies.

Parker-Knoll

Parker-Knoll is a furniture-manufacturing company established in Britain by Willi **Knoll** and Tom Parker. When the Knoll family split up both Willi and his cousin Hans left Germany to settle in Britain, but only Willi stayed. His contribution to the development of furniture design was a new method of springing which he submitted to **Heal**'s. Heal's did not take it up, but Willi's innovation was noticed by Tom Parker and the two went into business together producing 'lounge' furniture characteristic of suburban Britain during the thirties. Parker-Knoll produces in its Witney factory a type of furniture more than an ocean distant from Hans' company on Madison Avenue.

Gregor Paulsson

1890–1977

Gordon Russell once wrote of Gregor Paulsson, 'There are few people from whom I have learned more, or more agreeably, than Gregor Paulsson.' Paulsson was born at Halsingborg, Sweden and educated at Lund University. Studying in Germany, he witnessed the foundation of the **Deutsche Werkbund** in 1907 and became acquainted with the work and the ideals of **John Ruskin**, **William Morris** and **C.R. Ashbee**. In 1912 he was appointed keeper at Stockholm's National Museum. In 1925 he was commissioner-general for Sweden at the Paris Exhibition, and in 1930 organized the great **Stockholm Exhibition**. He is perhaps best remembered for two things, one his book, *Vackrare Vardagsvara* (More Beautiful Everyday Things) 1919, the quintessence of the Scandinavian design ethic, and his directorship of the **Svenska Sljödföreningen** (1920–34). Paulsson persuaded the Swedish Cooperative Society to employ Eskil Sundahl as chief architect and from that moment on the standards of design in Sweden were enhanced at a stroke, as the Cooperative Society was a huge patron of architecture, packaging design and shop-fitting. Much of the character of 'Swedish Modern' can be put down to Paulsson's influence.

He also wrote *The New Architecture* (1916), *The Social Dimension of Art* (1955) and *The Study of Cities* (1959).

PEL

PEL stands for Practical Equipment Lìmited, an offshoot of the Accles and Pollock Group which pioneered in England the use of tubular steel for domestic furniture.

In 1929 Accles and Pollock set up a department at their Oldbury works to make steel furniture frames and 'Pel' was first registered as a company in 1931. The first catalogues were issued in 1932, but the fashionable life of tubular steel was a brief one. Pel furniture filled Marshall and Snelgrove's stores, Lyons Corner Houses and the BBC's Broadcasting House, but it never achieved real popularity. Even **John Gloag**, who in other contexts was a defender of Modernism, wrote that 'The metal furniture of the Robot modernist school can claim fitness for purpose, and exemplifies a just and original use of material. It expresses the harsh limitations of the movement to which it belongs.'

By the mid-thirties more and more Finnish **plywood** was coming into Britain and some of the leading architects and designers preferred it to tubular steel as a medium for modern furniture design.

Bibliography 'Pel and Tubular Steel Furniture in the Thirties' exhibition catalogue, Architectural Association, London, 1977

Penguin Books

The publishing imprint founded by **Allen Lane** in 1935 has been a great disseminator of ideas and thought amongst the general population. Lane's obituarist in *Design* magazine asked of her subject's life and work 'What other achievement in enlightenment is comparable?', and Sir Compton Mackenzie once spoke of the 'Penguin University'.

Lane's career in books began in the office of his uncle, John Lane, of the Bodley Head, publishers of the *fin-de-siècle Yellow Book*. He said of Penguin: 'I wanted to put into the hands of people like myself the books they would have read if they had gone to university.' Penguin rose to prominence in the thirties, bringing publications on the fringes of art and culture to the ordinary reader at very modest prices. It was the decade of the mixed economy and of democratic opportunity.

Lane's Penguins, like the BBC's *Listener*, were also at the sharp end of promoting the new modern design in Britain – a strategy which they advanced in spirit by publishing Anthony Bertram's *Design* as a Penguin Special in 1938, and in substance by ensuring their books were as well designed as possible: the original Penguins were proportioned almost exactly on the Golden Section, with all the titles set in **Gill** Sans. Immediately after the Second World War, when restrictions on employing foreigners were lifted, Lane employed the Swiss designer-typographer **Jan Tschichold** as a consultant. His influence was felt until 1961, when Romek Marber provided a new grid for Pelicans and Penguins which took the imprints through the sixties and into the seventies when, after Allen Lane's death, there was speculation about whether the 'noblest list in the history of publishing' would degenerate into just another softback house.

Allen Lane was a close friend of **Nikolaus Pevsner** and published all his most influential books. He was knighted in 1952.

Two Jacket Designs

From their first publication in 1936 Penguin Books used sophisticated typography and layout, introducing successive generations to standards of design which had hitherto been the exclusive domain of a rich and privileged minority. (See also p. 48.)

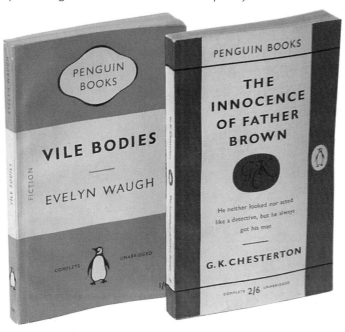

Pentagram

Pentagram is the London design consultancy founded by **Kenneth Grange**, **Fletcher**, Forbes & Gill and Theo Crosby in 1971.

Den Permanente

Den Permanente is a store-cum-exhibition, opened in Copenhagen by the silversmith Kay Bojesen and Christian Grauballe, head of the Holmegaard glassworks, in 1931. The idea was to create a permanent exhibition of **Danish design**, to act as a stimulus and as a means of raising public taste. Rigid quality standards were imposed and these, together with its popularity, made den Permanente into a genuine influence on the progress of design in Denmark.

Charlotte Perriand

b. 1903

Charlotte Perriand trained in Paris at the Ecole de l'Union Centrale des Arts Décoratifs, attending courses run by Paul Follot of Le Printemps department store and Maurice Dufrène of Galeries Lafayette. Her most significant work was done with **Le Corbusier** in a collaboration that began after she exhibited some wooden furniture at the 'Exposition Internationale des Arts Décoratifs' in 1925, and from 1927 to 1937 she was responsible for all the fitting out in Le Corbusier's atelier.

The chaise-longue and armchair that they produced together in 1929 were inspired by Le Corbusier's sketches of bodies in repose. The atelier could not afford to make the chairs, so they were manufactured by **Thonet**. Perriand became fired with the enthusiasm of the atelier for metal furniture, so much so that she overstated its case. In reaction, frequent trips to the mountains made her familiar with the simple tastes and needs of shepherds, and their *ad hoc* furniture became an important stimulus for her after the War, when the team spirit of le Corbusier's atelier began to diminish.

Perriand designed a prototype kitchen for Le Corbusier's 'Unité d'Habitation' in Marseilles (1951), and her other late interiors included designs for the Air France and French Tourist offices in London. But over the last three decades her creative efforts have been directed towards planning for leisure and designing for batch production.

Chalet and Furniture
Perriand has turned in later life to more intimate interior designs, often using elements derived from vernacular architecture. (See also p. 210.)

Gaetano Pesce

b. 1939

Gaetano Pesce was born in Venice and studied at the university there. He was a radical designer from the outset, creating furniture that was conceptual (rather than practical). These concepts were concerned with mortality and alienation, giving his shocking, lumpy chairs and asymmetric bookcases, produced by **Cassina**, an existential quality. He divides his time between Milan and New York.
Bibliography Andrea Branzi *The Hot House: Italian new wave design* MIT, Cambridge, Mass., 1984

'Serie Up' Furniture, 1969
Pesce specializes in furniture designs which are often challengingly amorphous, deliberately rejecting the formal canons of the Modern Movement. His 'Up' series furniture was designed for B&B Italia in 1969. Its polystyrene matrix adapts to the shape of the body.

Michael Peters

b. 1941

Michael Peters studied at the London College of Printing and at Yale, and worked at CBS television and at the advertising agency Collett, Dickenson & Pearce, before founding Michael Peters & Partners in 1970. Michael Peters is a graphic design consultancy which specializes in packaging and has achieved unusual success in its application of eclectic style to jams, scents and yogurts. His major clients include the French tobacco monopoly SEITA, Fine Fare, Elsenham and Thresher's.

Label of Glass Scent Bottle for Penhaligon's, c. 1977
The Peters style is characterized by historicism, expensive finishes and simple ideas meticulously executed.

Nikolaus Pevsner

1902–83

Nikolaus Leon Bernhard Pevsner studied at Leipzig, and became an assistant keeper at the Dresden Gallery and then a lecturer at Göttingen University before being driven to England by the threat of Nazi persecution. His arrival in England changed the shape of the study of art, architecture and design in Britain. While before, such writing as there had been about art was of the *belles lettres* sort – genteel discussion of nice topics – Pevsner brought German academic method to Britain and turned the history of art into more of a science.

His books include *Pioneers of the Modern Movement from William Morris to Walter Gropius* (1936), *An Enquiry into Industrial Art in England* (1937), *Academies of Art Past and Present* (1940), *High Victorian Design* (1951), *Some Architectural Writers of the Nineteenth Century* (1973), *A History of Building Types* (1976) and his mammoth multi-volume survey of *The Buildings of England*. Notwithstanding that he actually invented the history of architecture and design as a serious academic subject, Pevsner's contribution to modern design has been much more than a merely scholarly one. His books have had such a huge structural effect on the common perception of history that his influence can be compared to **John Ruskin**'s in moulding taste. Of the three great historians of architecture of the twentieth century, **Sigfried Giedion**, **Reyner Banham** and Pevsner, it was Pevsner who concentrated most entirely on the matter of *style*: with Hegelian determinism Pevsner saw the achievement of **Walter Gropius** as the necessary, indeed inevitable, conclusion to a series of historical developments which had preceded it.

His *Pioneers of the Modern Movement* was only a moderate success when it was issued by Faber in London in 1936, but when it was reissued by the **Museum of Modern Art** in 1949 it immediately became a classic. Although the arguments seem nowadays a little stilted, it is the Bible of **industrial design** for Modernists. Pevsner was at one time a buyer for **Gordon Russell** and held senior academic posts at Birkbeck College, University of London, and was Slade Professor of Fine Art at Cambridge, 1949–55. He was knighted in 1969. Because of his unfluctuating views about the moral and historical correctness of modern architecture, expressed in his books and during his period on the editorial board of **Architectural Review** during its golden years, Pevsner has come in for some sneering and jeering in recent years from the articulate right wing of the conservationist lobby, in consort with the spokesmen of **Post-Modernism**. In a way the wheel has come full circle; in his early days on the magazine he was known as 'Plebsveneer' and 'Granny' by some of his colleagues who could not get their minds around his 'modern' concern with social purpose.

Bibliography David Watkin *Morality and Architecture* Cambridge University Press, 1978

Piaggio

Rinaldo Piaggio started business at Sestri Ponente, near Genoa, in 1884. His company grew into a huge industrial concern, involving ship-building and railway rolling stock. From 1917 Piaggio became obsessed with flight, and from 1923 to 1935 his company produced no fewer than fourteen original aircraft.

Piaggio's most famous consumer product, however, was the **Vespa** motor scooter, designed by the helicopter engineer **Corradino d'Ascanio**. At the end of the Second World War Rinaldo's son, Enrico, invited d'Ascanio to design a motor scooter which could be manufactured at his factory at Biella, whose production was at the time restricted to aluminium saucepans. Announced in March 1946, the Vespa had an ingenious, but simple, technical specification and all-enveloping bodywork which suggested the influence of aircraft practice. In a sense, it was the Italian equivalent of the **Citroën** 2CV.

Bibliography Centrokappa (ed.) *Il Design italiano degli anni '50* Editoriale Domus, Milan, 1980

Vespa Motor Scooter, 1946
The revolutionary scooter synthesizes aircraft engineering, Italian flair and American streamlining.

Frank Pick

1878–1941

Frank Pick, a solicitor who was one of the founders of the DIA, when commercial manager of London Transport in the twenties instituted one of the most thoroughgoing **corporate identity** schemes ever by employing the architect Charles Holden and the typographer **Edward Johnston** to create a unified appearance for the system. It was a British realization of the theory of 'standardization' for which **Hermann Muthesius** had argued almost two decades before.

London Transport Logo
Pick commissioned the distinguished design of London Transport's corporate identity. It is still in use today, and was the best realization of the aims of the DIA. In recognition of his achievement the Architectural Review's obituary compared Pick to Lorenzo the Magnificent.

Pininfarina

Battista Farina (1893–1966) was born in Turin. He travelled in the United States in 1920 to learn about the new techniques of automobile production, and established his own bodywork shop in his native city in 1930. In 1959 he handed it over to his son, Sergio (b. 1926). Two years later, out of respect to Battista, who was affectionately nicknamed Pinin, its name was changed to Pininfarina.

Of all the great Italian *carrozzerie* (before ItalDesign) Pininfarina has been the most concerned with research into the practical, as well as aesthetic, possibilities of car design. In addition, more than any other Italian firm of designers, it has contributed a language of form. The great cars to bear the badge with the cursive 'f' have established stereotypes it is hard to avoid, and almost impossible to surpass in beauty; the great cars include the Lancia Aurelia B20 (1952), the Austin A40 (1958), the Ferrari 330GT (1964), the Austin 1100 (1963), the Ferrari Daytona (1971), the Peugeot 504 (1968) and the Ferrari 308 GTB4 (1975).

Alfa Romeo 2500 Coupé, 1946 (top); Lancia Aurelia, 1952 (centre); Ferrari 246, GTS, 1969 Pininfarina's bodywork designs achieve a fluid beauty that makes the shop the outstanding carrozzeria *in Italy. Its designs are always refined and elegant.*

Giancarlo Piretti

b. 1940

Giancarlo Piretti studied at the Istituto Statale d'Arte in Bologna. He has worked ever since leaving college as Castelli's director of research and design. Of all the Italian furniture manufacturers Castelli best understands the realities of the industrial process and Piretti's classic 'Plia' folding chair of 1969 is a serious piece of engineering intended for mass-production. Although not daringly experimental, it is a superb piece of design, as Piretti made a chair with harmony and purity out of the most elemental materials and shapes. Recently he has worked with **Emilio Ambasz'** Open Ark, collaborating on the design of the 'Vertebra' chair (see p. 73) and the 'Osiris' light for **Erco**.

'Plia' Chair, 1969
Piretti's stackable folding chair is an example of clarity. The steel tube frame can be chromium-plated or plasticized white, red, green or black. The seat is usually in transparent or smoked Cellidor, but is sometimes seen with solid coloured polypropylene. Another version with cane seat and wooden frame is also available.

Plastics

Of all this century's new synthetic materials, plastics are the ones which have had the most radical effect on the mass environment. In their various forms they have helped create many of the most familiar everyday forms.

The age of plastics began in 1860 when Alexander Parkes produced 'Parkesine', a mixture of gelatine and cotton fibre which reached the market under the brand name 'Celluloid'. Parkes' invention was ingenious but unstable, but it provided a base for development in answer to demand from the international arms industry. Further impetus was provided by the need for anti-static materials in the new electrification schemes in London, New York, Berlin and Brussels. Early plastics were natural materials, or such materials simply modified. A major breakthrough came with the first completely synthetic plastic, which was developed by Leo H. Baekeland in 1907 and marketed as **'Bakelite'**. This led to the profusion of plastics in the twentieth century.

Although the relative cheapness of plastics made them more widely available than natural materials, it was a long time before they were accepted by designers. **Walter Gropius** proscribed them at the **Bauhaus** because he said they had no intrinsic qualities of their own, but were by their very nature imitative and derivative. His antipathy was because the first application of plastics in radio cabinets and small decorative items was as a substitute material, replacing wood, jade and ivory. Only in rare cases, such as **Wells Coates'** designs for Ekco, were plastics treated on their own merits.

It was in the United States that most money was spent on plastics research. Its immense domestic market with homogenous tastes encouraged designers and manufacturers to produce a genuine 'plastics aesthetic', and in 1940 **Harold van Doren** could write in his book, *Industrial Design*, about ways of making edge details in the new material. However, it was not until after the Second World War, and in Europe, that considerable thought was put into the aesthetic implications of plastics products. Firms like BIP and Runcolite in Britain and **Kartell** in Italy employed innovative designers, including David Harman-Powell, Gaby Schreiber, and **Gino Colombini**, to work on the formal and colour properties of the design of goods made of the new materials.

The post-War period also saw further advances made in the development of new plastics. For instance,

polyurethane foam replaced foam-rubber and allowed more flexibility in the design of soft furnishings. Italy took the lead in this direction, and designers like **Vico Magistretti** fully exploited the chromatic and formal qualities of plastic, for instance in his chair designs for **Cassina** and **Artemide**. At the same time in Britain, **Robin Day** designed the best-selling 'Polypropylene' chair for **Hille**. In continuous production since 1963, it uses a softer and cheaper plastic than the high-finish, hard ones favoured by the Italians.

While the techniques of plastics production are complex, and there is a bewildering variety of types available, there is only a limited number of ways in which

plastics can be formed – most commonly by injection moulding, die casting and vacuum forming – and the method determines the aesthetic possibilities. But colour variations are now highly sophisticated and the dull pastels of the fifties are no longer imposed on the designer.

The great achievement of plastics has been to democratize products, but as most plastics are oil-based since 1973 they have become more expensive and metals are again being seen as economical alternatives.
Bibliography 'Plastic Objects, 1860–1960' exhibition catalogue, Folkwang Museum, Essen, 1984; Sylvia Katz *Plastics* Studio Vista, London, 1978

Warren Plattner

b. 1919

Warren Plattner studied architecture at Cornell University in Ithaca, New York. He then worked in the offices of **Raymond Loewy** and **Eero Saarinen**. Throughout the fifties Plattner worked on the design of wire furniture which **Knoll** eventually put into production in 1966. Since setting up his own studio at North Haven, Connecticut in 1967, Plattner has tended to concentrate on big-budget contract interiors, the biggest of which was the glittery 'Windows on the World' restaurant in New York's World Trade Center (where he collaborated with **Milton Glaser**) and Chicago's Water Tower Place.

Plywood

Plywood is a form of structurally laminated wood. It first appeared in the eighteenth century, but was only fully exploited when **Michael Thonet** began to make laminated furniture in Austria in the mid-nineteenth century. A light and flexible material, plywood relies for its strength on the three or more laminations of wood with cross-running grain.

Alvar Aalto used plywood to design furniture that was both technically and aesthetically revolutionary (see also p. 125). His processes and forms were widely imitated – by **Gerrit Rietveld**, **Marcel Breuer** and **Bruno Mathsson** – and to the avant-garde designer in countries that preferred 'natural' materials, plywood became an alternative to tubular steel. Until **Charles Eames** plywood was only bent in two dimensions, but he bent it in three in his furniture designs, as first seen at the **Museum of Modern Art**'s 'Organic Design in Home Furnishings' exhibition in 1940 (see p. 71).

'Crayonne' Range, 1973
The 'Crayonne' range of injection-moulded plastic house accessories was designed by Conran Associates.

Bandalasta Plastics, 1927–32
Early plastics aped the appearance of more traditional and more expensive materials. This catalogue for the Bandalasta company suggests that the market was not yet prepared to accept radical new designs made with the true nature of plastic in mind.

Paul Poiret

1879–1944

The pioneer French couturier Paul Poiret was one of the great entrepreneurs of the fashion industry. He was known as the 'Sultan of Fashion', and the 'Pasha of Paris', both on account of his aggressively masculine admiration of women and because he introduced oriental influences into early twentieth-century clothes. His greatest achievement was to dispose of corsetted Edwardian formalism and replace it with 'Hellenic' dresses in a loose look which fell from the shoulders. In this he was much influenced by the exotic *bizarrerie* of Diaghilev's Ballet Russe when the company first appeared in Paris in 1908, and many critics assumed that his substitution of sombre greys and khakis with jonquils, cherry reds, Delft blues and begonia pinks had been directly lifted from the example set by Leon Bakst's costumes for them.

Poiret was an effective self-publicist, commissioning the artist Georges Lepape to illustrate a vanity publication, *Les Choses de Paul Poiret* (1911–12). He also started his own-brand line of cosmetics and perfumes and ran a craft workshop for poor girls, coyly named 'Martines' after one of his daughters. A genuinely original talent in marketing fashion and design, Poiret was also an egocentric, extravagant man. He failed to adjust to the different Europe that existed after the First World War, and died in poverty after attempting to continue living in unrepentant profligacy in his later years.
Bibliography Paul Poiret *En habillant l'époque* Grasset, Paris, 1930

Evening Coat, 1922
Poiret's loose shape is teamed with bold colours.

Gio Ponti

1891–1979

Gio Ponti founded the leading Italian architecture and design journal **Domus** in 1927. As the moving spirit behind the Monza Biennale and the Milan **Triennale** (as it became), Ponti is a major force behind twentieth-century Italian design.

Throughout the forties and fifties he worked for Arflex, **Cassina** and Nordiska Kompaniet, but is best remembered as architect of the Pirelli Tower, the Milanese office building of 1956 which was to Europe what the Seagram Building was to the United States. Similarly, his 'Superleggera' chair, which Cassina began to manufacture in 1957, has become a true classic and has passed into the international urban culture because of its almost universal use in Italian restaurants of a particular price bracket. Ponti got the idea from vernacular fishermen's chairs seen at **Chiavari** near Genoa. Despite the quality of his own actual furniture and architectural designs, Ponti's real influence has been as a propagandist. He was a moving force behind the establishment of the **Compasso d'Oro** awards and, as professor of architecture at Milan Polytechnic, he was able to train and form the opinions of generations of Italian designers, promoting the importance of tradition and his commitment to 'the good life'. (See also p. 160).

'Superleggera' Chair, 1957
Ponti's celebrated 'Superleggera' chair derived from the vernacular 'Chiavari' chair, but succeeded at the same time in projecting strongly the character of the fifties.

Pop

The British-based Pop movement of the sixties helped break down the autocracy of the **Modern Movement**, introducing in its place more expressive possibilities in design. It began with fine art but embraced hitherto neglected popular culture, making it intellectually respectable. The first response was in fashion, with **Mary Quant**, and then in furniture and interiors, with a spotted paper chair by Peter Murdoch, inflatable furniture, and Zanotta's 'Sacco' chair. At the same time, previously drab shop fronts began to make a colourful impact on the high street.

British Pop was a profound influence on **Ettore Sottsass** and **Elio Fiorucci**. In many ways the sense of liberation created by the Pop movement opened up numerous paths that design has taken in the past generation, from the **Crafts Revival** to **Post-Modernism**. 'Pop' introduced the possibility that design might fill symbolic rather than utilitarian needs, and created wide public interest in design.

Oz Magazine Cover, 1971
London's Pop 'revolution' produced a series of 'underground' magazines whose graphics reflected the indulgent obsessions of the era.

Paper Chair by Peter Murdoch, 1965
Murdoch's chair was a faddish symbol of Swinging London Pop.

Porsche

Ferdinand Porsche (1875–1951) was the designer of the **Volkswagen** and the founder of the Stuttgart company that bears his name. The Porsche itself came into being because Porsche and his son, Ferdinand Porsche II (b. 1909), known as 'Ferry', wanted to make a sports car, but as it was a state-owned firm the enterprise was considered too frivolous for Volkswagen. They decided to set up their own company, mainly using Volkswagen parts for their first car. Taking the design office number 356, this was made in 1949 at Gmund, Carinthia, in Austria. The body was designed by **Erwin Komenda**, who employed the experience he had gained at Auto-Union, and also, significantly, from his work in the wind tunnel at the Zeppelin docks in Friedrichshafen and in the Stuttgart tunnel operated by **Wunibald Kamm**, the great **aerodynamics** pioneer. Ferry Porsche encouraged him to keep the car as low as possible, so that the nose was only just above road level. For the engine Porsche used a flat four, designed by F.X. Reimspiess and derived from the original NSU design which had gone into the Volkswagen.

Since 1969 the Porsche studio has been run from the Porsche Development Centre by **Anatole Lapine**.

Porsche 911
The Porsche 911 is a remarkable piece of engineering and design. The basic concept derives directly from Ferdinand Porsche's Volkswagen design of the thirties, which is deliberately reflected in the body sketched by his grandson Ferdinand-Alexander Porsche. In production since 1964, the Type 911 is a rare example of a product design that appears to have reached stasis.

Post-Modernism

Although the term 'post-modernism' has been familiar in literary criticism for many years (at least since the publication of Ihab Hassan's *The Dismemberment of Orpheus: toward a Postmodern literature* in 1971), it has only more recently been applied in the context of architecture and design. The author of this usage is Charles Jencks (b. 1939), an American academic-journalist living in London. Post-Modernism is the most successful of the many style-labels which Jencks has coined, but has in fact influenced journalists and publishers more than practising architects.

Jencks' idea was to find a name for a cause adopted by a number of architects disillusioned by the failures of modern architecture to redress *all* the ills which its pioneers had established as its legitimate target. Many of these reacted by adopting meretricious ornament and cheap details, or robbed exotic styles and cultures for easy effects, or else produced designs that were meant to be no more than

jokey. In furniture design Post-Modernism appeared in **Studio Alchymia** and **Memphis** (which themselves borrowed from Italian radical design of the 1960s).

The architect Berthold Lubetkin dismissed Post-Modernism as 'Transvestite Architecture' in his 1982 Gold Medal Address at London's RIBA. A year later, Bruno Zevi, the distinguished Italian architectural critic, also speaking at the RIBA, called it 'narcissistic nonsense' and declared it to be a 'minor pseudo-cultural event'. Nevertheless, some eminent architects and designers (in particular, **Robert Venturi** and **Michael Graves**) are content to be identified with Post-Modernism, while others feel it to be a temporary phase only. Despite the radical claims of cheer-leaders like Jencks, Post-Modernism is only an errant child of Modernism. In *Modernism* (1976), Malcolm Bradbury and James McFarlane saw this as true of its literary manifestation: 'The argument around Post-Modernism now adds to the abundance of versions of Modernism.'

Jack Pritchard
b. 1899

Jack Pritchard was a furniture manufacturer and entrepreneur who had a huge influence on the introduction of modern architecture and design into Britain. While still at Cambridge, he designed and made his own chair. His first post-university job was with Michelin, but he soon left to work for Venesta Plywood, a large building materials supplier, which brought him into contact with many architects. In 1930 he was able to commission **Le Corbusier** and his brother, Pierre Jeanneret, to design a stand for Venesta at an exhibition, and soon after **Laszlo Moholy-Nagy** was commissioned to design advertisements for the firm. It was Pritchard who invited **Walter Gropius** to England, and Gropius stayed with him at his flats in Lawn Road, Hampstead, which he had commissioned **Wells Coates** to design. At this time Pritchard set up **Isokon** to make furniture out of moulded **plywood**; Gropius acted as consultant designer and **Marcel Breuer** designed a chaise-longue (see p. 171).
Bibliography Jack Pritchard *View from the Long Chair* Routledge & Kegan Paul, London 1984

'Grandma' Sofa by Robert Venturi for Knoll, 1984
Post-Modernist design apes styles of the past, as in Venturi's overstuffed furniture.

A
B
C
D
E
F
G
H
I
J
K
L
M
N
O
P
Q
R

X
Y
Z

Ulla Procopé

1921–68

Ulla Procopé was one ceramic designer employed by **Kaj Franck** at the **Arabia** factory in Helsinki. She is most celebrated for Arabia's 'Ruska' service (p. 125), a characteristically Finnish design in those rich, apparently natural textures and materials that do not compromise efficient function. In the case of 'Ruska' this means that it looks very folksy, but is oven-to-table serviceable.

Jean Prouvé

b. 1901

The French furniture designer Jean Prouvé was born in Nancy, the son of a painter in the **Art Nouveau** Nancy School. Throughout the twenties and thirties Prouvé made metal furniture which attempted to redefine some of the mechanical aspects of seating. In 1931 he founded the Société des Ateliers Jean Prouvé.

As an architect, Prouvé was concerned to find an authentic method and technique of applying scientific methods of construction to the business of living, although he was not prepared to compromise the individual's demand for variety. In the fifties he experimented with prefabricated buildings.
Bibliography Otakar Macel & Jan van Geest *Stühle aus Stahl* Walther König, Cologne, 1980

Emilio Pucci

b. 1914

Emilio Pucci, a Florentine aristocrat, was thirty-three when he began making sportswear for people in his own social *milieu*. Despite his credentials, Pucci disarmingly claims that 'It doesn't make sense to produce dresses worth as much as a round-the-world air ticket.' His innovations have nevertheless often been concerned with the travel obsessions of his class: in 1954 he began to produce ultra-lightweight silk jersey dresses, patterned with his distinctive abstract designs, which looked as if they had been designed with air travel in mind. Pucci scrawled his signature on the fabrics, as well as on the wide range of accessories he marketed as desirable status symbols. He now combines political interests (he was a Liberal member of the Italian Parliament from 1963 to 1972) with making couture robes (often beaded and embroidered), while at the same time licensing his name to manufacturers of jeans, lingerie and carpets. Pucci has designed uniforms for the stewardesses of Qantas and porcelain for **Rosenthal**.

Salle de Réunion, Pavillon de Tunisia, Paris Exhibition, 1925 The furniture is by Charlotte Perriand and Jean Prouvé.

A.W.N. Pugin

(1812–52)

Augustus Welby Northmore Pugin was a pioneer of the **Gothic Revival**. The first architect to associate buildings with morality and social purpose, he strongly believed that values such as 'good' and 'bad' could attach to architecture and design. In this he was a great influence on **John Ruskin** and thus on one whole strain of thought in the **Modern Movement**. (See also pp. 20–21.)

Wallpaper for the House of Lords, 1847 Pugin's designs evoked the medieval past.

Jean Puiforcat

1897–1945

Jean Puiforcat was an **Art Deco** silversmith. One biographer has said of his silver tableware 'he specialized in costly simplicity'. Throughout the thirties silver tea services that Puiforcat designed were manufactured by both French and English concerns: they are characterized by shiny surfaces and geometrical forms.

Push Pin Studio

The Push Pin Studio was founded in New York in 1954 by the graphic designers **Milton Glaser**, Ed Sorel and Seymour Chwast.
Bibliography 'The Push Pin Style' exhibition catalogue, Paris, Musée des Arts décoratifs, 1970

Pyrex

Pyrex is the trade name of a heat- and chemical-resistant borosilicate glass which was introduced commercially by the Corning Glass Works in America in 1915. Pyrex was developed in response to a demand from American railroads to find glass lenses which were tolerant of a wide range of temperatures, and Corning adapted the results to the needs of international commerce. Corning licensed the manufacture of Pyrex in Britain in 1921, in France, Spain and Italy in 1922, in Germany in 1927, and in Japan in 1930.

Pyrex products are made both by press moulding and by blow moulding. Like traditional glass, Pyrex lends itself to decoration, but not by cutting (which would impair its thermal and mechanical performance), but by transfer printing, banding and spray coating. However, these techniques were all too often used to impose witless, artless derivative patterns on to functionally efficient vessels. In 1934–5 Pyrex used Harold Stabler as a design consultant and from 1952 to 1969 **Milner Gray**. The firm's most distinguished products are the ones which carry least decoration.
Bibliography Don Wallance *Shaping America's Products* Reinhold, New York, 1956; 'Pyrex: 60 Years of Design' exhibition catalogue, Tyne and Wear County Council Museums, 1983

Mary Quant

b. 1934

Mary **Quant**
David **Queensberry**

Mary Quant's fashion design became so much a symbol of London in the sixties that in 1973–4 the London Museum put on an exhibition called 'Mary Quant's London'. Her clothing emphasized youth, play, fun and wit, and being cheap, comfortable and wearable, made high fashion widely available.

Mary Quant opened her first shop, Bazaar, in 1955. She was to do for fashion what Terence Conran did for furnishings, and her revolutionary concept, the mini-skirt, appeared in 1964, the same year that Conran's **Habitat** opened in London's Fulham Road. Both Conran and Quant were inspired by the same circumstances: the drab condition of London in the ten years or so after the Second World War. Just as Conran had abominated the goods in the furniture stores where he wanted to sell his simple modern furniture, so Mary Quant hated everything that she saw going on around her in fashion, and 'disagreed with what women did to themselves'. At the time she started out, it did not occur to her that these needs were very widely felt, but looking back in 1966 she could say, 'Although at the start we made every mistake anybody could, the need was so strong that we couldn't fail.' Shopping was about to become an entertainment, not an ordeal; when Bazaar opened people were six-deep on the pavement outside and the entire stock was sold in ten days. Mary Quant recalled: 'We wanted people to be at ease in the shop, and to be friendly. We employed the sort of girls who would never have sold in shops before . . .' It was more than the beginning of a new fashion in clothes, it was the beginning of the realization that the environment of the store was an essential part of retailing success. Shopping had to be an agreeable experience, not merely the selection of merchandise. Mary Quant was one of the very first modern retailers to be aware of this, and her control over the graphics used in her shops had as much of an influence over her success as her eye for fashion.
Bibliography Mary Quant *Quant by Quant* Cassell, London, 1966

Bazaar, King's Road, London, 1955
Mary Quant's shop, Bazaar, opened in Chelsea's King's Road in 1955. It was the beginning of a revolution both in British fashion and in British retailing.

David **Queensberry**

b. 1929

David Harrington Angus Douglas, the 12th Marquess of Queensberry, is a noted ceramics designer. He was professor of ceramics at the **Royal College of Art** from 1959 to 1983 and has been a consultant to **Rosenthal**. He now works in an independent consultancy with Martin Hunt, another ceramics designer. Over the past two decades Queensberry has designed many simple, sophisticated and practical pieces of tableware.

R

Ernest **Race**
Dieter **Rams**
Paul **Rand**
Rasch Brothers
Armi **Ratia**
Herbert **Read**
Paul **Reilly**
Retro
Richard **Riemerschmid**
Gerrit **Rietveld**
La **Rinascente**
Terence
Harold **Robsjohn-Gibbings**
Ernesto **Rogers**
Rörstrand
Rosenthal
Alberto **Rosselli**
David **Rowland**
Royal College of Art
Royal Society of Arts
John **Ruskin**
Gordon **Russell**

Ernest Race

1913–64

Ernest Race became one of the few English furniture designers of the twentieth century to have acquired an international reputation. He studied architecture at London's Bartlett School and worked in the design department of Troughton & Young, a lighting manufacturer, before going to live in India in the mid-thirties, where he designed textiles to be handwoven there. On his return to London he opened a shop to sell this merchandise, but it closed soon after the beginning of the Second World War. In 1946, with a light engineering manufacturer, Race founded Race Furniture in order to make wholly modern designs. He presented two chairs at the Festival of Britain which have since become famous – the 'Antelope' and 'Gazelle'. Rather like the designs of **Charles Eames**, they make expressive use of the properties of steel rods. In 1954 Race won a gold medal at the Milan **Triennale**.

Paul Reilly said of him: 'Anyone seeking Englishness in modern English furniture would immediately think of Race, for all his work had the directness, logic, economy and sturdy elegance that one associates with the best of our eighteenth-century craftsmanship and the best of our nineteenth-century engineering.'

'Antelope' Chair, 1951
Race's chair is a masterpiece of the spiky Contemporary style.

Dieter Rams

b. 1932

Dieter Rams was born in Wiesbaden and was apprenticed as a joiner, then studied architecture and design at the Wiesbaden Werk-Kunstschule (art and technical school). His first job was with the Otto Apel architectural practice; then he went to **Braun**, soon becoming its chief designer. While **Hans Gugelot** brought the discipline of the Ulm **Hochschule für Gestaltung** to bear on the Frankfurt factory, Rams developed an in-house style that depended in part on the severe training of the craftsman. Rams has been responsible for the major

'SK4' Record Player for Braun, 1956

Designed by Rams and Hans Gugelot, the 'SK4 Phono-super's austere appearance earned it the nickname, 'Schneewittchenssarg' (Snow White's Coffin).

domestic machines that have made the Braun company the aesthetic epitome of Germany's 'economic miracle'. His is an austere, restrained style where graphic purity vies with sculptural presence for effect, and he has said, 'I regard it as one of the most important and most responsible tasks of a designer today to help clear the chaos we are living in.' Rams' projects include his kitchen machine of 1957 and numerous other domestic appliances upon which he bestows the same purity of form and attention to detail. (See also pp. 62–3 and **German design**.)
Bibliography François Burkhardt & Inez Franksen *Design: Dieter Rams &* IDZ Berlin, 1982

'KM 321' Kitchen Machine for Braun, 1957

Harmony of details within a beautiful, platonic form are Rams' trademarks.

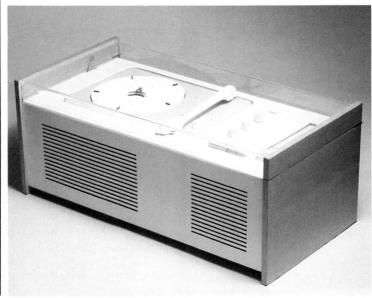

Paul Rand

b. 1914

A graphic designer, Paul Rand studied art at New York's Pratt Institute and at the Parsons School of Art. His first job was as art director of the magazine *Esquire*, and in 1959 he opened his own office. **Eliot Noyes** invited him to be the graphic designer on the new **corporate identity** programmes he was implementing for **IBM** and Westinghouse, and he designed a new logo and new packaging for both.

Rand wrote in 1980, 'Design clichés, so-called Post-Modern (dingbat design), meaningless patterns, trendy illustrations and predetermined solutions are signs of . . . weakness. An understanding of the significance of modernism and familiarity with the history of design, of painting, of architecture and other disciplines, which distinguish the educated designer and make his role more meaningful . . . are not always his strong point.'

Bibliography Paul Rand *Thoughts on Design* Wittenborn, New York, 1946; *Design and Play Instincts* George Braziller, New York, 1966

IBM Packaging, 1960
When Eliot Noyes took charge of corporate identity at IBM he construed his job to be in control of buildings, products and graphics. He commissioned Rand to design the packaging. Rand's graphics perfectly matched Noyes' concept of the corporation.

Rasch Brothers

The two Rasch brothers, Heinz (b. 1902) and Bodo (b. 1903), founded a Workshop for the Manufacture of Domestic Fittings in 1922, and published an influential book, *Der Stuhl*, in 1928. Throughout the twenties and thirties they made furniture designs in metal which were manufactured by L. & C. Arnold of Schorndorf. They also had a contract to design wallpapers for the **Bauhaus** workshops. The quality of their ideas in relation to their designs for mass-production was impressive.

Bibliography Heinz & Bodo Rasch *Der Stuhl* Stuttgart, 1928; Otakar Macel & Jan van Geest *Stühle aus Stahl* Walther König, Cologne, 1980

Armi Ratia

1912–79

Armi Ratia founded **Marimekko** in Helsinki in the mid-fifties. It is a shop, a manufacturer and a consultancy all in one. Ratia drew designers from all over Finland for the store and created a strong, vivid style, part entirely original, part derived directly from Finnish folk culture. Perhaps the best known Marimekko designer is **Vuokko Eskolin**.

Herbert Read

1893–1968

Herbert Read was the most distinguished of the English writers who popularized design in the thirties, the country's most influential and perceptive art critic since **Roger Fry**.

He was born in Yorkshire in 1893, and his first job was as a clerk in a Leeds bank, but he studied at night school to gain a place at Leeds University. Although from a prosperous family background, his personal struggle to gain education encouraged him to a poetic radicalism, inspired by Tolstoy rather than Marx. Like Verdi, he said, 'I am by birth and tradition a peasant,' and added, 'I despise the whole industrial epoch – not only the plutocracy which it has raised to power but also the industrial proletariat which it has drained from the land.' After the First World War Read worked in the **Victoria and Albert Museum**, publishing learned works on glass and ceramics, and in 1931 became professor of fine arts at Edinburgh University. His appointment as director of a planned Museum of Modern Art came to nothing because of the Second World War. He was knighted in 1953.

Although his own enthusiasms were, perhaps, more with poetry and literary criticism, Read became wellknown as a champion of modern art, and his book, *Art and Industry* (1936), was the most persuasive statement by an English author to call for an awareness of the beauty of machines. The main problem it presented was whether everyday objects should be treated as art in the manner he proposed. It has been said that, despite the character and influence of his writings, Read was not, in fact, sympathetic to machine art, yet he was the first director of the Design Research Unit (**DRU**). **Milner Gray** said *Art and Industry* was 'the turning point for most of us in the clearer understanding of machine art' and described Read as 'a man of steel in his convictions, yet wonderfully moderate and gentle in his contact with his fellows . . . the practical poet, the design philosopher and guide'.

Read belongs to the spirit of the thirties in his whole-hearted acceptance of **Walter Gropius'** principles, and is a less popular figure now than he was after the War.

Paul Reilly

b. 1912

Paul Reilly was born the son of an architect, Sir Charles Reilly. He was variously a **plywood** salesman, a leader writer for the *News Chronicle* and technical journalist before becoming chief information officer for the **Council of Industrial Design** in 1947, under **Gordon Russell**. It was Reilly who moved the Council on from the tradition of **C.R. Ashbee** and the **Arts and Crafts** to the wider international context of design. Throughout the fifties and sixties he was the most eloquent British spokesman for responsible attitudes in design and served on many national and international committees, including those on postage stamps and **ICSID**. He became deputy director of the CoID in 1954 and director in 1960, was knighted in 1967 and received a life peerage in 1978.

Through his strong and frequent contacts with the Scandinavian design establishment, Reilly did as much as anyone to influence taste in Britain, although during the explosion of **Pop** in Britain Reilly moved the Council towards pure engineering and away from consumer products, which led the Design Council to become distanced from culture and experience. He once observed: 'There are three kinds of design appreciation. First, the taste of those who like what they know – the one most usually found because based on shop windows. Second, the taste of those who know what they like – a better educated taste which is based on magazines. Third, the taste of those who know what they like so long as it is like nothing that they know – this is the taste of the creative minority and is very important since ideas like water flow down hill.'

Retro

The term 'retro' was first used by French journalists in the mid-seventies to describe a tendency in popular design to look back nostalgically at recently past styles and tastes. From the early sixties Victoriana, **Art Nouveau**, **Art Deco** and **Contemporary** were all revived as if to subvert the **Modern Movement**'s obsession with the future and restore the power of psychological and symbolic meaning in design. In addition to this simple revival, another tendency also emerged which was concerned with the simple, vernacular objects associated with pre-industrial rural life. This was, in turn, associated with the larger 'back to nature' movement which, preferring natural materials to synthetic ones, and naiveté to sophistication, was itself related to the **Crafts Revival**.

Eventually the distinction between the various 'retro' styles became eroded into a joyless, directionless eclecticism which presented the world with the alternative to Modernism sought by 'retro's' various originators.

Richard Riemerschmid

1868–1957

Richard Riemerschmid founded the Vereinigte Werkstätten für Kunst im Handwerk (united workshops for art in craft) in Munich in 1897 and was, with **Peter Behrens** and Bruno Paul, one of the first German designers to adapt himself to the possibilities of machine production and the implications of standardization. Like Bruno Paul, he produced furniture designs for the Werkstätten which were amongst the simplest of their day.

Wood-Framed Chair, 1900
Riemerschmid's chair was designed for a room set in the Paris Exhibition of 1900. His design reflects the preoccupations of the Vereinigte Werkstätten which, like the Wiener Werkstätte, was influenced by British Arts and Crafts ideas, but with somewhat stiffer Teutonic character.

Gerrit Rietveld

1888–1964

Gerrit Thomas Rietveld, a Dutch architect, was born in Utrecht and started his career as an apprentice joiner in his father's shop. He had no contact with the **Modern Movement** until Robert van t'Hoff commissioned him to design furniture in 1916. In 1917 he designed an uncompromisingly geometrical chair, which formed the basis for his 'Red-Blue' chair. From this time contact with the avant-garde Dutch group of painters who called their movement **De Stijl** was crucial. The 'Red-Blue' chair, intended to be made in plain wood, with colour used to emphasize its structure, appeared in 1919, and his 'Zig-Zag' chair in 1934. Both are now reproduced by **Cassina**. Rietveld did relatively little metal furniture, but some awkward tubular steel designs of the late twenties and early thirties were manufactured by the Dutch firm Metz & Co. He also produced chairs of packing-crate wood in the Depression, an upholstered chair, and chairs made of aluminium. His monument was the Schroeder House in Utrecht, which was built in 1925 (p. 37). This house and Rietveld's designs for it were strongly influenced by **Frank Lloyd Wright**, the American architect whose designs were enjoying a vogue in Holland at the time.

Rietveld continued to experiment with chairs all his life, but it is for his early, formalist experiments that he is remembered, even though these are illogical as structures for actually sitting in.
Bibliography D. Baroni *I mobili di Gerrit Thomas Rietveld* Milan, 1977; H.L.C. Jaffe *De Stijl* Amsterdam, 1956

'Red-Blue' Chair, 1918
Rietveld's 'Red-Blue' chair was a programmatic example of the design theories of the avant-garde Dutch group, De Stijl.

La Rinascente

La Rinascente is a chain of department stores in Italy which inaugurated the **Compasso d'Oro** design awards in 1954. It became one of the symbols of the nation's post-war *ricostruzione*.

Terence Harold Robsjohn-Gibbings

1905–76

Cecil Beaton described Robsjohn-Gibbings in 1954 as 'the best designer of modern interiors in America today', and characterized him as 'staunchly set against the mania for antiques, for European imitation and gimcrack period creations'. His was a quest for the timeless, eternal values of the classical style in decoration. Arriving in America from England, Robsjohn-Gibbings first designed furniture of great purity and simplicity, but his most characteristic work came when he went to live in Athens for a time (where he had an apartment enjoying a view of the Parthenon). Here he designed white rooms where antiquities stood next to austere, blanched furniture which he had refined from ancient models into idealized forms almost without substance. Robsjohn-Gibbings saw the home as a place where man confronted himself: 'Consider the alternative to the endless scrambling for ostentation,' he wrote. 'No compulsion from state, society or fashion can force a living soul to be other than himself inside the one toehold he has on this planet – his home. In equipping a house, every individual choice . . . will reveal . . . the likeness of the inhabitants.'
Bibliography T.H. Robsjohn-Gibbings *Goodbye, Mr Chippendale* Knopf, New York, 1944; *Mona Lisa's Moustache* Knopf, New York, 1947; *Homes of the Brave* Knopf, New York, 1954

Ernesto Rogers

1909–69

Ernesto Rogers was one of the partners in **BBPR**, an influential Milanese architectural practice, and the editor of the magazine **Domus** in the years immediately after the Second World War. His studio was a training camp for some of the best-known post-War Milanese designers.

Rörstrand

The Swedish ceramics factory Rörstrand was founded in 1726. In 1874 it established the **Arabia** factory in Helsinki, and in 1964 was itself bought by the conglomerate Upsala-Ekeby. Rörstrand has, like other Swedish ceramics manufacturers, maintained a long tradition of employing designers in independent studios within the factory in pursuit of the characteristic Swedish commitment to democratic values and 'good', simple design. However, in recent years Rörstrand has lost the high standards which it set in the fifties and sixties.

'Ivory' Service by Christian von Sydow, late 1970s/early 1980s

Rosenthal

The Rosenthal Porzellan AG was founded at Selb in Bavaria in 1880, by the grandfather of the present director, Philip Rosenthal, who bears the same name. Rosenthal came to prominence in the early twentieth century, marketing refined versions of **Art Nouveau**, sometimes designed by Rosenthal himself. The present Rosenthal has brought fame to the company in another way. Perhaps more than any other comparable concern anywhere, Rosenthal Porzellan hires consultant designers, and **Raymond Loewy**, **Wilhelm Wagenfeld**, **David Queensberry**, **Walter Gropius** and **Tapio Wirkkala** have all worked for the firm. Perhaps

'Form 2000' Service by Raymond Loewy and Richard Latham, 1954
Loewy's angular designs are in keeping with Rosenthal's post-War work. He later created similar forms when designing the in-flight ceramics for Air France's Concorde.

Rosenthal's single most respected product is the service designed by Walter Gropius which went into production in 1962. It is the most thoroughgoing of all Gropius' designs, and, despite its small scale, exemplifies to the full the principles which the **Bauhaus** sought to establish. Every aspect of the function of the service has been rationally reconsidered and, while formal considerations are secondary to functional requirements, the result is nonetheless aesthetically satisfying.

Like **Wedgwood** two hundred years before, Rosenthal opened a series of shops (in this case, the international 'Studio-House') to bring the firm's wares nearer to the public.

Alberto Rosselli

1921–76

Alberto Rosselli was the first editor of Italy's *Stile industria* magazine. An important symbol of Italy's *ricostruzione*, it was founded in 1953 but closed in 1962. (See p. 52.)

A
B
C
D
E
F
G
H
I
J
K
L
M
N
O
P
Q
R
S
T
U
V
W
X
Y
Z

David Rowland

b. 1924

The chair designer David Rowland was born in Los Angeles. After wartime duty as a combat pilot in Europe he studied physics at a liberal arts college in Illinois, before joining **Cranbrook Academy**. His first job was working with **Norman Bel Geddes** in the last days of his studio, and he opened his own offices in 1955.

Rowland's '40-in-4' chair of 1963, manufactured by General Fireproofing, is one of the great chair designs of the century and won the Grand Prize at the 1964 Milan **Triennale**. Its name refers to the fact that forty of these wire chairs can be stacked in four feet, and it has been praised for having 'all detail refined to a point of near extinction'. This was followed by the 'Sof-Tech' stacking chair of 1979 for **Thonet**. Rowland tells the story that when he was starting out to sell the '40-in-4' he approached the New York representative of a large Japanese trading house. After months of delay with no reply from the head office in Tokyo, Rowland called the office again, to be told, 'I just received cable from Head Office, Tokyo, they are report latest word is that Japanese people still sit on floor.'

Royal College of Art

Like its neighbour the **Victoria and Albert Museum**, the Royal College of Art developed in the atmosphere of zealous reform which surrounded Prince Albert and his circle. At first called the Normal School of Design, the college was among the first products of the new design education system which was formed in Britain during the nineteenth century. However, its progress through the early years of the twentieth century was largely uneventful and the college tended, despite its early idealism, to give priority to fine-artists at the expense of designers for industry.

Robin Darwin, previously professor of fine art at Durham University, became principal in 1948 and began to reorganize the college. Under him it finally acquired its own building

---

'40-in-4' Chair, 1963

Rowland's ingenious stacking chair uses either pressed steel or moulded plywood as seat and back, with the sparest imaginable steel rod frame.

(designed by H.T. Cadbury-Brown and Sir Hugh Casson) in 1962. For the first time since the Commons Select Committee on Arts and Manufactures reported in 1836 that they wanted to extend the principles of design among the people, the premier art school in Britain was at last housed in something more than a collection of huts in South Kensington. The year after the college's new building was opened, Lord Robbins' *Report on Higher Education* declared that the college should have university status and so, in a sense, the ideals of the 1836 Commons Committee, which had hoped to roll back the incursions of foreign imports by providing British industry with rationally trained designers, seemed to have a chance of being realized.

When Darwin arrived the college was, in all essentials, still using the educational methods established just after 1851, which by now were narrow, repetitive, unrealistic and inbred. Of this Darwin once commented, 'Looking back, it may well appear amazing that the college was able, during all those years, to maintain any kind of reputation at all . . . There seemed after the war very little justification indeed for the continued existence of the RCA.' As part of his rationalization of the college he introduced a new qualification, 'Des.RCA', intended to identify designers qualified for work in industry. But since Darwin's day the college has lacked a strong leader, a purpose and an identity, until newspaper magnate Jocelyn Stevens was appointed in 1984. Stevens promised to turn the RCA into a realistic, modern, commercially astute institution.
Bibliography Nikolaus Pevsner *Academies of Art Past and Present* Cambridge University Press, Cambridge, 1940; Quentin Bell *The Schools of Design* Routledge & Kegan Paul, London, 1963

Royal Society of Arts

The Society for the Encouragement of Arts, Sciences, and Manufactures was founded by William Shipley (1715–1803) in 1754. The motivation behind Shipley's remarkable initiative was similar to that of, say, Erasmus Darwin and the provincial Enlightenment, of **Josiah Wedgwood** and of the numerous Literary and Philosophical Societies which sprang up in London and the provinces in the later eighteenth and nineteenth centuries. Before the division of labour took place it was possible for men like Shipley to talk easily of arts and sciences in the same breath, and all knowledge was useful and accessible, whether concerned with archaeology or fisheries. The society was founded on the basis of such catholicity of taste and interest, and maintains it to this day. It was granted a Royal charter in 1908.

Prince Albert used the Society of Arts as a platform for generating interest in his proposed **Great Exhibition**. He acted on Shipley's wish that the Society of Arts 'may prove an effectual means to embolden enterprise, to enlarge Science, to refine Art, to improve Manufactures and extend Commerce: in a word, to render Great Britain the school of instruction, as it is already the centre of traffic, to the greatest part of the known world.' (See also p. 14.)
Bibliography D.G.C. Allan *William Shipley – founder of the Royal Society of Arts* Hutchinson, London, 1968

John Ruskin

1819–1900

John Ruskin was the most influential art critic of the nineteenth century, and his attitudes to art, architecture, design and their relation to society and to morality had a profound effect on British culture.

Like his contemporary **William Morris**, Ruskin despised the industrialized world; he started writing the second volume of *The Stones of Venice* on the day the **Great Exhibition** opened – a display of which he had much adverse criticism to make. Ruskin had much to say about almost every aspect of the man-made world, and was a great champion of the Gothic. He despised the slick artificialities of the day, especially as apparent in the decoration of domestic villas, and railed against wood-graining and all forms of dishonesty in decoration. Every object and every gesture had a moral character for him, as is typified by his description of William Holman-Hunt's painting 'The Awakening Conscience' in his *Academy Notes* for 1854, where he drew particular attention to 'the fatal newness of the furniture' which the painter showed in the philanderer's drawing room. Ruskin's world view was of such breadth that it is not surprising that it became bifurcated. The anti-capitalist, anti-industrial, anti-material branch led to the philosophy of the **Arts and Crafts** movement. The other, moral, element went abroad, particularly to Germany. Travelling via **Hermann Muthesius**, it had a profound effect on **Walter Gropius** in his formulation of the ideology which moved the **Bauhaus**. (But through numerous translations, Ruskin's thought also influenced the German reactionaries who opposed the Bauhaus.)

Ruskin's personal circumstances were a profound influence on his formation as a writer and thinker: he once remarked that he gained a ravenous hunger for visual delight from his strict, non-Conformist upbringing where, at home, the paintings were turned around to face the wall on Sundays, no diversions being allowed. Similarly, the majestic cadences of the authorized version of The Bible influenced his prose style. He died insane. (See also pp. 27 and 29.)
Bibliography Martin J. Wiener *English Culture and the Decline of the Industrial Spirit* Cambridge University Press, Cambridge, 1981

Gordon Russell

1892–1980

Gordon Russell did not actually create the Design Council, but when he became the second director of the **Council of Industrial Design** in 1947 it was only four years old so he was able to formulate a policy which created its character and had a significant influence on English culture during the fifties and sixties.

Russell's father had been a banker who became a rural hotelier, opening the Lygon Arms at Broadway in Worcestershire (p. 29). It was in an antique-restoration shop in Broadway at the end of the First World War that Gordon Russell, just back from the War, became interested in making things. He had his first exhibition of furniture designs in Cheltenham in 1922. The economic necessity of installing machinery in his Broadway workshop brought Russell face to face with the twentieth-century problem of reconciling traditional practice to modern need. While respecting the traditions of the craftsman, Russell was not afraid to use machines if they made a job easier or a shop more efficient. It was these experiences in his country workshop that Russell carried through into public life. He also had no delusions about the division of labour and was very happy simply to be the boss, having teams of toiling craftsmen executing his designs.

During the Second World War Russell became chairman of the Board of Trade's **Utility** furniture panel and was a formative influence in the direction of the Festival of Britain. When he retired as director of the Design Council in 1960 he was succeeded by **Paul Reilly**.

Throughout his life Russell was a fanatical devotee of the concept 'skill', which was the subject of his last public address. The design of Gordon Russell Ltd furniture was, in fact, never very inspired, nor ever in touch with the reality of the popular budget, or even the dreams of advanced taste. Although always fine in quality, in spirit it was a sort of 'repro'. Only with the cabinets designed for Murphy radio in the thirties by his brother, Dick, soon after **Henry Ford** visited the village of Broadway, did the firm design for the mass market.

Gordon Russell's achievement was to bring to public and official attention the idea that making things is a serious, professional business.
Bibliography Ken and Kate Baynes *Gordon Russell* Design Council, 1980; Gordon Russell *A Designer's Trade* John Murray, London, 1968

An 'Ideal' London Flat, 1947
Although socially idealistic, Russell's designs projected an example of mediocrity on to British taste.

A B C D E F G H I J K L M N O P Q R S T U V W X Y Z

S

SAAB
Eero **Saarinen**
Giovanni **Sacchi**
Bruno **Sacco**
Roberto **Sambonet**
Astrid **Sampe**
Richard **Sapper**
Timo **Sarpaneva**
Sixten **Sason**
Ferdinand de **Saussure**
Afra and
Tobia **Scarpa**
Carlo **Scarpa**
Xanti **Schawinsky**
Elsa **Schiaparelli**
The **Schools of Design**
Douglas **Scott**
Semiotics
Peter **Shire**
Joseph **Sinel**
SIAD
Silver Studio
Erich **Slany**
Sony
Ettore **Sottsass**
Yves **St Laurent**
Mart **Stam**
Stockholm Exhibition
Giotto **Stoppino**
Streamlining
Studio Alchymia
Styling
Superstudio
Surrealism
Svenska
 Sljödföreningen
Svenskt Tenn
Swedish design

SAAB

'SAAB' stands for Svenska Aeroplan Aktiebolaget, or 'Swedish Aircraft Company'. It was one of the many Swedish manufacturing concerns established by the banker Marcus Wallenberg. Within a few years of its foundation on the eve of the Second World War it was producing the advanced SAAB 21, the first plane to have an ejector seat. At the end of the War SAAB found itself with a lot of manufacturing plant and no demand whatsoever for warplanes, so the engineers decided to make a car. Chief engineer Gunnar Ljungstrom planned it with no preconceptions – in fact only two of the staff actually had driving licences. The company's technical illustrator Sixten

Sason was called in to advise on the form and the project became the SAAB 92, launched in 1950 (p. 221). It was the basis of later SAAB models, and the 96 remained in production until 1980. Since Sason's death in 1969 SAAB's chief designer has been **Bjorn Envall**.
Bibliography Svensk Form The Design Council, 1980

SAAB 93, 1956

SAAB is extremely conscious of its origins in aerospace. The company's car division even used to describe its staff as 'the craftsmen who made the jets', and many aeroplane constructional principles have been used in its passenger cars. Advertising in the fifties stressed the relationship (as it still does today). This picture shows a SAAB 93 car and a SAAB Lansen jet fighter.

Working Drawing of SAAB 900 by Bjorn Envall, early 1970s
Bjorn Envall had worked as an assistant to his mentor, Sixten Sason, on the design of the SAAB 99 of 1969. His first chance to design a car of his own came with the development of the stretched 900 series. This preliminary rendering shows that SAAB's design policy is an evolutionary one. (See also p. 122.)

Eero Saarinen

1910–61

The son of the famous Finnish architect Eliel Saarinen, Eero Saarinen was born in Finland but moved with his father to the United States in 1923. He studied architecture at Yale. Working with **Charles Eames** he won the **Museum of Modern Art**'s influential 'Organic Design in Home Furnishings' competition (which **Eliot Noyes** had helped organize) in 1940 (see p. 74). Saarinen then became a teacher at the **Cranbrook Academy** and it was through this school that he became acquainted with Hans and Florence **Knoll**, for whose firm he designed the 'Grasshopper' chair in the late forties and the famous moulded plastic 'Tulip' chair in the late fifties. Promoted by Knoll, this chair became as familiar a piece of furnishing in high-style architectural interiors as any piece by **Mies van der Rohe** or **Le Corbusier**. It was the first moulded pedestal chair, a unique sculptural design which blended all the elements of a chair into an integral whole.

Saarinen was invited by **Harley Earl** to be architect of the new General Motors Technical Center at Warren, just outside Detroit, in 1956, a commission which the London *Times* obituary said was 'the most distinguished application of the ideas of Professor Mies van der Rohe to the needs of American industry'. He was also the architect of the Dulles Airport at Washington (1963), the TWA Terminal at New York's Kennedy Airport (1962) and the Gateway Memorial Arch, St Louis (1964), buildings whose stressed, parabolic roofs recall the form of birds in flight and whose wilful symbolism has often led apologists for **Post-Modernism** to claim them and their architect as precursors.

'Tulip' Chair for Knoll, 1957
Saarinen's chair used a glass-reinforced plastic seat on a cast aluminium (aluminum) pedestal.

Giovanni Sacchi

Since 1946 Giovanni Sacchi has been the master model-maker of the Milanese design establishment. From his workshop in central Milan he has realized models of the product designs made by **Marcello Nizzoli**, **Ettore Sottsass**, **Marco Zanuso** and **Mario Bellini**. Almost all of the award-winning products of **Olivetti**, **BrionVega**, **Necchi** and Alessi were first seen in wood in Sacchi's workshop. In 1983 the Milan **Triennale** celebrated his achievements in promoting design by organizing an exhibition of his models.

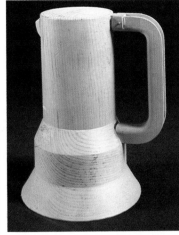

Wooden Model of Espresso Coffee Percolator, 1978
Sacchi conceptualized Richard Sapper's idea for a design for a coffee percolator in this model. (See also p. 161.)

Bruno Sacco

b. 1934

Bruno Sacco is an Italian designer who has been head of design for Mercedes-Benz since 1975. He trained in Turin and went to work in the Stuttgart factory in 1958. One of his first jobs was on the CIII experimental car, and he was project leader for the special class of 1980 and the 'compact' 190 of 1982.

Like **Anatole Lapine** at **Porsche**, Sacco is conscious of his customers' taste for tradition. He insists that it is more of a challenge to create a new generation of car with a tangible relationship to its predecessor than to design something where anything goes (and often nothing does): 'You concentrate very hard on avoiding gimmicks . . . and when you do, it's fairly easy. You act in a normal, straightforward way. There are many examples of long-lasting design in other fields: in architecture and fashion. You can design a suit to last either three months or ten years. It's the same with a car.'

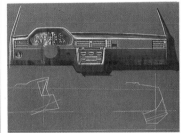

Mercedes-Benz 190/190E, 1982
The Mercedes-Benz 190 was the first 'small' car produced by the revered Stuttgart manufacturer. In the design of the body and interior Sacco made no compromises or improvisations and every detail was moderated either by the demands of engineering or the pull of Mercedes' tradition. The instrument panel is designed to offer visibility and certain functions to the front-seat passenger as well as to the driver. In terms of design the panel is totally integrated into both interior and exterior, and every single element determined according to its function. (See also p. 134.)

A
B
C
D
E
F
G
H
I
J
K
L
M
N
O
P
Q
R
S
T
U
V
W
X
Y
Z

Roberto Sambonet

b. 1924

Roberto Sambonet was born in Vercelli, between Milan and Turin, and graduated in architecture from Milan Polytechnic in 1945. Until 1954, when he joined the family flatware and cooking ware company, he painted and worked at the Museum de Arte in São Paulo, Brazil. His designs for Sambonet show a preference for elegant attenuated sculptural forms. Their elegance was acknowledged when a fish-serving dish he designed in 1954 won a **Compasso d'Oro** award. With **Achille Castiglioni** and **Ettore Sottsass**, Sambonet began work in 1981 for a complete new system of street furniture for the city of Turin.

Astrid Sampe

b. 1909

A Swedish textile designer, Astrid Sampe was head of the textile design department in Stockholm's Nordiska Kompaniet from 1937 to 1972. Her work is characterized by its simple decoration and typically Swedish lightness and humanism.

Richard Sapper

b. 1932

After studying mechanical engineering, Richard Sapper worked for Mercedes-Benz in Stuttgart. In 1958 he left Germany to live in Milan, where he joined the office of **Gio Ponti** and worked in collaboration with **Marco Zanuso**. Sapper and Zanuso have between them been responsible for some of the most prized cult objects of the later twentieth century: the **BrionVega** 'Doney 14' television (1962, p. 247), the folding BrionVega radio (1965, p. 60), the Italtel 'Grillo' telephone (1965) and the BrionVega 'Black 12' television of 1969. On his own account Sapper has designed **Artemide**'s most successful product, the 'Tizio' low-voltage desk light (1972) and an espresso coffee percolator (pp. 161 and 219).

Sapper has brought German engineering thoroughness to the Milan manufacturers, who, in turn, have given him the opportunity to produce refined and sophisticated products. However, his 'Bollitore' kettle for Alessi, which came on to the market in 1983 – a working kettle, but nevertheless a luxury product – is evidence that a wilful type of formalism has overtaken international designers in the eighties. Although handsome and precious, Sapper's kettle has a handle that is too hot to hold before the water has even boiled. Since 1980 Sapper has been principal product design consultant to **IBM**. (See also p. 56.)

'Tizio' Light by Richard Sapper, 1978

Sapper's light was manufactured in huge numbers by Artemide. Low-voltage electrical power is fed through the metal construction, obviating cables. The slender shape is highly articulate and can be turned, at will, from a desk into a standard light.

'Bollitore' Kettle for Alessi, 1983; Model, 1982 (left)
Sapper's kettle relies for its effect on dramatically simple shapes and the richly expressive use of different metal finishes; it is a blend of High-Tech and Post-Modernism and an international cult object. Sapper says the sound of the whistle was inspired by an Amtrak train.

Timo Sarpaneva

b. 1926

Timo Sarpaneva studied as a draughtsman at Helsinki's Taideteollisuuskeskuskoulu (school of applied arts). Since 1950 he has been a consultant designer to the Iittala glassworks and, with **Tapio Wirkkala**, has come to be acknowledged as one of Finland's leading glass designers, since his work first gained international attention at the Milan **Triennales** in the early fifties. It is highly sculptural and expressive. He established his own office in 1962. (See also **Finnish design**.)

'Suomi' Coffee Service, 1976
Sarpaneva designed this porcelain coffee service for Rosenthal's Studio-Linie.

Sixten Sason

1912–69

Sixten Sason was born in the provincial Swedish town of Skovde. He was trained as a silversmith, a discipline which was at the time conventional grounding for a would-be designer. He became a technical illustrator and joined **SAAB** at the moment when its engineers were beginning to develop the company's first light car. He was responsible for the appearance of the SAAB 96, and the fame of this sophisticated car brought him more commissions from expanding Swedish industry. As a result he designed appliances for Electrolux and determined the appearance of the first Hasselblad cameras. Thus he was Europe's first design consultant to work in the American fashion on a diverse variety of products. Although his designs have all the characteristic Swedish qualities of care and responsibility, there is a strong element of Detroit flair in them too.

Sason's health had been poor since a flying accident in the thirties, but as a result he had the leisure to study engineering. He died just as his second great car design, the SAAB 99, was coming on to the market.

SAAB 92, 1947
The SAAB 92 was Sason's streamlined vision of a popular car. His adventurous styling was complemented by Gunnar Ljungstrom's sophisticated engineering and by the aircraft construction techniques employed by the manufacturer.

Electrolux Vacuum Cleaner, Drawing, 1945
Besides SAAB, Sixten Sason worked for many of the other leading Swedish corporations, including Electrolux, for whom he designed streamlined vacuum cleaners.

Hasselblad Camera, 1949
Sason's subliminal influence as a designer has been huge: for Victor Hasselblad he created the shape of the single lens reflex camera. Modelled first in wood and plaster, it became the stereotype of the professional camera.

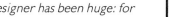

Ferdinand de Saussure

1857–1913

Ferdinand de Saussure was the founder of modern linguistics. His scientific analysis of language, with its inherent suggestion of the importance of structures and signs in our ways of thinking, laid the basis for **semiotics**, which in the hands of followers such as **Roland Barthes** has had a substantial effect on writing about design, and has helped bring the modern material world into the orbit of academic culture.
Bibliography R. & F. De George *The Structuralists* Doubleday, Garden City, New York, 1972

A B C D E F G H I J K L M N O P Q R S T U V W X Y Z

Afra and Tobia Scarpa

Tobia Scarpa was born in 1935, the son of **Carlo Scarpa**. From 1957 to 1961 he worked for **Venini** at their Murano glassworks. In 1960 he opened an independent office with his wife, Afra (b. 1937). Together they have designed furniture for **Cassina** and **Gavina** as well as lighting for **Flos**.

Chair, B&B Italia, 1967
Afra and Tobia Scarpa's furniture has a monumental presence. They frequently use natural materials, such as wood or leather, and the edges are given gentle, massive curves.

Carlo Scarpa

1906–78

Carlo Scarpa was born in Venice and in 1926 began an academic career at the University's Institute of Architecture. He designed glass for **Venini** between 1933 and 1947, but his speciality has been in interior and exhibition design, his major works including the Paul Klee exhibition in Venice (1948), the Venice Biennale of 1952, the **Frank Lloyd Wright** exhibition in Milan (1960) and the 'Frescoes from Florence' exhibition in London in 1969. Scarpa's numerous sophisticated interiors include the **Olivetti** showrooms in Venice, which display his interest in minimal, sculptural form, in a combination of glass, metal and marble.

Xanti Schawinsky

b. 1904

Alexander (Xanti) Schawinsky was born in Basle and studied at the **Bauhaus** from 1924 to 1929. From 1929 to 1933 he worked in Magdeburg, but then went to Italy where he began to work for **Olivetti**. Schawinsky was one of an entourage of artists and creative people employed by Adriano Olivetti, and in three short years he repaid Olivetti's faith in him by designing a remarkable poster for the 'MPI' typewriter and collaborating with Figini and Pollini on the design of the 'Studio 42' typewriter. In 1936 Schawinsky went to live in the United States, taught briefly at Black Mountain College, and retired to spend the rest of his life painting. (See also p. 199.)

Circus, Poster 1924 (top);
'Fliessende Architektur' Poster, 1927
These two posters show how influenced Schawinsky was by the geometrical rationale of Constructivism during the twenties. In the thirties his style matured and gained a richer visual vocabulary, typically combining photographic imagery in montage techniques for Olivetti and other clients.

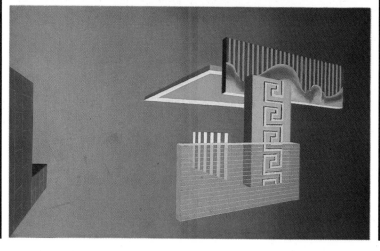

Elsa Schiaparelli

1890–1973

Elsa Schiaparelli produced a paradigm of her own career as a fashion designer when she invented the colour 'shocking pink'. Translated from wealth in Rome to poverty in Paris after an unsatisfactory marriage, Schiaparelli was forced to live off her creativity. Her first fashion design was for a sweater got up in *trompe-l'œil* so as to appear that the wearer was sporting a tie. Such designs quickly caught on and in 1935 she opened a shop which became a clearing house for ideas and for the people who crossed the barriers between fine art and fashion: Salvador Dali and Jean Cocteau were friends of hers and in turn they

Evening Dress and Wrap, 1937
Schiaparelli often designed her collections to a theme – here she uses the butterfly. She was known for the witty invention of her fabrics, as well as for her zany, yet highly sophisticated, designs.

collaborated on designs for embroideries and for fabrics. As well as **Surrealism**, Schiaparelli also introduced various exotic influences into the repertoire of Paris couture, including Peruvian Indian colours and North African patterns. She was consistently inventive and quick to experiment with new materials, using rayon and cellophane, and was also the first couturier to use the zip fastener (which she characteristically turned into a provocative motif).

Schiaparelli was patronized by Hollywood, including Marlene Dietrich, Lauren Bacall, Gloria Swanson and Mae West (whose plaster cast provided the inspiration for the bottle containing Schiaparelli's famous scent, 'Shocking'), but her great contribution to the language of clothes was to open up fashion to a wide variety of influences, from art, folklore and science.

The Schools of Design

Britain's first art schools, called the Schools of Design, were founded as a consequence of the Parliamentary Select Committee's *Report on Arts and Manufactures* of 1836. The idea was to establish in all Britain's manufacturing cities institutions half way between museums and schools to teach industrial artisans by example, in order to raise taste. Many manufacturers, however, expressed disappointment at the ability of the graduates, who seemed to have been more highly skilled in painting and sculpture than in industrial techniques.

Under **Henry Cole**'s direction ninety art schools with 16,000 students had been established by 1864. This was the basis for Britain's entire system of art education, still the most extensive in the world. **Bibliography** Quentin Bell *The Schools of Design* Routledge & Kegan Paul, London, 1963

Douglas Scott

b. 1913

Douglas Scott trained as a jeweller and silversmith at London's **Central School**. From 1936 to 1939 he worked in **Raymond Loewy**'s London office, opening his own studio at the end of the Second World War, at the same time as he created the Central's **industrial design** course. Scott has become a genuine *éminence grise*, for, while he is almost unknown as a personality, products which carry his distinctive 'handwriting' are familiar all over Britain. In 1953 he designed the 'Routemaster' bus for London Transport and in the early sixties the British Post Office's STD call box fittings. His other clients include Ideal Standard, Marconi and ITT. His work is characterized by its severe restraint, and although his forms are often very satisfying, they are rarely expressive. In writing that 'I have always designed for the market . . . [but] private and personal aesthetic are out of place in industrial design', Scott supplies the conceptual and practical link between his own training (at the hands of a stylish American) and his own background (which was essentially British).

'Routemaster' Bus, 1953
Scott's characteristic gentle curves help the huge vehicle look less aggressive.

Semiotics

Semiotics, sometimes (but particularly in France) known as semiology, is the science which studies the systems of 'signs' in language, literature and the material world. It is the linguistic part of a philosophy known as structuralism. Structuralism and semiotics evolved from the studies in linguistics by **Ferdinand de Saussure** and in social and cultural anthropology by Claude Lévi-Strauss, mixed together with the psychoanalysis derived from Freud. Its most highly regarded exponent was the French savant **Roland Barthes**, although Northrop Frye and **Marshall McLuhan** have also published texts which form a part of the international corpus of semiotics. Because semiotics has obvious ramifications in the media, ideas developed by Barthes and taught by his followers have had a formative influence on our awareness of structures and symbols in the modern, commercial world.

The anthropologist Edmund Leach has described the workings of semiology: 'any human creative act starts out as a mental operation which is then projected on to the external world . . . plays, ceremonials, religious rituals . . . carvings and paintings . . . All such creations are "designed" . . . The mental operations of any human designer are circumscribed, not only by the qualities of his materials and by his objectives, but by the design of the human brain itself.' It is the business of the structuralist to understand this and the business of the semiotician to analyse the details of the process. **Bibliography** Pierre Guiraud *La Sémiologie* Presses Universitaires de France, Paris, 1973

Peter Shire

b. 1947

The American designer Peter Shire was born in Los Angeles and studied at the Chovinard Institute of Art. In 1981 he contributed some furniture to **Memphis** and in 1983 made some designs in silver for Cleto Munari.

Joseph Sinel

1889–1975

Joseph Sinel was a New Zealand-born commercial artist who arrived in America in 1918. By 1921 he was taking on 'product improvement' jobs for the companies who were the clients of the advertising agency which was his employer. Having set up his studio almost eight years before **Raymond Loewy**, **Norman Bel Geddes**, **Walter Dorwin Teague** and **Henry Dreyfuss**, he claimed in later life that this gave him reason to call himself America's first industrial designer. In 1923 he published *A Book of American Trademarks and Devices*.

SIAD

The Society of Industrial Artists and Designers was founded by **Milner Gray** and others in 1930. Its first members came from the worlds of graphic and exhibition design and it was the first professional society of its kind in the world, and is still the largest. It was granted a Royal Charter in 1976. It publishes a monthly journal, *The Designer*.

Silver Studio

Wallpaper Frieze, 1903
Rex Silver specialized in a late form of Art Nouveau, shown in this wallpaper frieze. Later his studio became entirely eclectic, embracing every idiom except Modernism.

Arthur and Rex Silver (1853–96, 1879–1965), father and son, were designers of wallpapers and fabrics, the most famous of which is probably the 'Peacock Feather' pattern done for **Liberty**'s in the 1880s. The pair also produced designs for the so-called 'sanitary wallpapers' which became available during the following decade. These were printed on a fine surface which could be easily varnished and was thus washable. This was a great asset in the days when natural coal produced so much internal pollution that wallpapers had either to be 'sanitary' or to be replaced very often.

The Silver Studio produced a huge variety of designs in many different styles from its premises at Brook Green, Hammersmith, but many went out anonymously under the Liberty name. The studio was finally wound up in 1963.
Bibliography John Brandon-Jones *The Silver Studio Collection. A London Design Studio 1880–1963* Lund Humphries, London, 1980; 'The Decoration of the Suburban Villa' Broomfield Museum, London, 1983–4

Erich Slany

b. 1926

Erich Slany is an almost unknown German engineer with a small range of products, which nevertheless have helped popularize the hard-edged German technical style. His principal client has been Robert Bosch, for whom he has designed a whole series of more or less aggressive drills, with pistol-grips and general proportions resembling those of small arms (see p. 134). Slany's 'style' is very refined, seeming on the face of it to be pure engineering, but it is nonetheless an aesthetically determined manner.

Sony

In the fifties Sony became the first Japanese consumer manufacturer to be widely known in the West, and since then has consistently maintained a high profile for innovation and design.

The origins of the company lay in Tokyo Tsushin Kogyo Kabushikakaika (TTK, or Tokyo Telecommunications Engineering), a company founded, like **Honda**, just after the War. Its founders were Masaru Ibuka and Akio Morita, with a paid-up capital of $500. TTK started on its course of product innovation in 1950, when it designed, manufactured and marketed the first Japanese tape-recorder, the 'G' Type. This laid the foundation of the company's fortunes with guaranteed distribution through schools and courtrooms throughout the country. Characteristically, TTK found a novel way to market the machine, taking it on national tours in specially converted vans.

In 1954 TTK used Western Electric patents to manufacture the first successful transistor in Japan, and in 1955 the first transistor radio, the 'TR-55', appeared, shaped as a simple box. This machine bore the brand name 'Sony', which Morita had invented after a trip to America, when he had learnt that Ford was easier to say than Plymouth, and that 'Sony' both evoked the Latin word for 'sound' and the affectionate diminutive for 'son'. In 1958 TTK adopted Sony as its corporate name.

In 1959 Sony introduced the first transistorized television, the 'TV8-301', and another wave of product innovations followed: in 1961 the first transistorized video-recorder, in 1962 a 5-inch micro TV, the 'TV5-303', in 1964 the first domestic video-recorder, in 1966 the first integrated circuit radio, in 1968 the new technology 'Trinitron' colour television tube, in 1969 the U-matic colour video-cassette, in 1975 the domestic 'Betamax' video cassette recorder, in 1979 the 'Walkman' personal stereo, and in 1980 the digital audio disc.

Although it is only the forty-fifth largest corporation in Japan, Sony is the best-known one in the West, an achievement reflecting Akio Morita's dedication to Western ideas of marketing and public relations as well as his engineers' consistent ability to integrate different technologies. It was this ability that produced Sony's first clock radio in 1957 – a clockwork machine yoked to a small transistor radio – and its greatest money-spinner, the 'Betamax' video machine, which combined studio-standard engineering together with the convenience of the low-cost audio-cassette. Daring innovation from the design section was behind one of their great successes, the 'Walkman'.

More than any other company, Sony exemplifies the principles of **Japanese design**. (See also pp. 58 and 61–2).
Bibliography Wolfgang Schmittel *Design – Concept – Realization* ABC, Zürich, 1975; 'Sony Design' exhibition catalogue, The Boilerhouse Project, Victoria & Albert Museum, London, 1982

Masaru Ibuka
The co-founder of Sony with one of his first products, the world's first commercially successful tape-recorder. With an astuteness that would later be seen as characteristic, Ibuka and his partner Akio Morita realized a world market for tape-recorders which the German and American inventors had ignored. With equal foresight the company's name was changed to the European-sounding and euphonious 'Sony'. A succession of product innovations followed, each one more ingenious (and often more miniature) than its predecessor.

'Tummy' Trinitron, late 1960s
Throughout the sixties Sony used New York agency Doyle Dane Barnbach to create campaigns for its unique products.

Tape-Recorder, 1950; 'TV8–301' Television, 1959
Tokyo Tsushin Kogyo Kabushikakaika's first product was a tape-recorder, using American technology. By the mid-fifties Sony had abandoned the successful but clumsy machine in favour of a policy of miniaturization which continues today. First came a transistor radio in 1955, and this was followed four years later by the world's first transistorized television. These made Sony Japan's first international company.

At last. Tummy Trinitron.

Our 12" Trinitron has been doing very well since we introduced it last September.

But over the years, a lot of our customers have gotten used to little Sony's. The kind they could put on their breakfast tables, or on their tummies.

And we thought it was about time we had a Trinitron for them.

So we're making the KV-9000U. It's got a 9" diagonal screen. It weighs 19 pounds. And it sells for $309.95.

It's an easy television to carry around the house. Or even out of the house.

It's got automatic color control. And all-solid-state circuitry. And most important, it's got the same brighter, sharper Trinitron color that our 12" set has.

So why not keep a few on hand?

Because pretty soon, the people who bought our black-and-white tummy TV's will be wanting to put color on their stomachs.

And you might as well be ready for them.

9" Trinitron. Sony Color TV

A
B
C
D
E
F
G
H
I
J
K
L
M
N
O
P
Q
R
S
T
U
V
W
X
Y
Z

Ettore Sottsass

b. 1917

Ettore Sottsass, Junior, the son of an architect, was born in Innsbruck, Austria. The unusual name is a peasant corruption of 'sotto sasso' (under the stone). Sottsass became perhaps the most outstanding Italian designer of his generation, a pioneer of the post-War *ricostruzione* whose career continues to develop and take unexpected turns.

Sottsass studied architecture at Turin Polytechnic and set up his own office in the city in 1946. His first works were housing projects for the state run INA-Casa scheme, which were built in 1952–4, and he spent the following years working on interiors and small decorative objects. Since 1957 he has been continuously associated with **Olivetti** (although he does still maintain an independent identity as an architect and designer with his own practice). His principal works for Olivetti have been the 'Elea 9003' computer (1959), the 'Tekne 3' and 'Praxis 48' electric typewriters and the 'Dora' portable (1964), the 'Te 300' teleprinter (1967), the 'Lettera 36' electric portable, the 'Valentine' typewriter (1970, p. 169) and 'Synthesis 45' office furniture (1973).

Sottsass enjoys the role of both guru and intellectual delinquent. In the sixties he became very interested in **Pop**,

grew his hair and went to India. This phase of his life resulted in intense and profound studio ceramics and glassware designed for **Vistosi**. In 1979, while still working for Olivetti and still carrying out independent commissions for Poltronova and Alessi, Sottsass became involved with the avant-garde Milanese group **Studio Alchymia**. He contributed some bizarre furniture designs to their collection which was ironically called 'Bauhaus', but in 1981 broke away to form a radical group of his own which, in mock reference both to Egyptology and to rock'n'roll, he called **Memphis**.

Sottsass' work and thought is most of all characterized by formal and intellectual

irreverence. He has enjoyed designing a typewriter which can be used in a discotheque, just as a secretary's chair for Olivetti had feet intended to suggest Mickey Mouse (p. 54). These characteristics remain the same whether he is working on his own furniture, on modular systems for data processing, or on street furniture for Turin.

In 1980 Sottsass Associati was established with architects **Aldo Cibic**, **Matteo Thun** and **Marco Zanini**.

Bibliography Federica di Castro *Sottsass Scrapbook* Documenti di Casabella, Milan, 1976; Penny Sparke *Ettore Sottsass* Design Council, London, 1982; Andrea Branzi *The Hot House: Italian New-Wave Design* MIT, Cambridge, Mass., 1984

'Dora' Portable Typewriter for Olivetti, 1964

In his work for Olivetti Sottsass combines imagination and novelty with the constraints of designing for a largely conservative public. His 'Dora' portable typewriter is characteristic in its elegance of this aspect of his output.

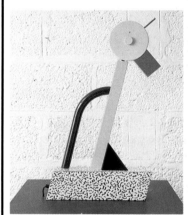

'Carlton' Dresser and 'Tahiti' Lamp, 1981

Memphis furniture is a realization of ideas Sottsass has been exploring since the end of the last war, unhindered by the more sober concerns of large corporations such as Olivetti. The 'Tahiti' lamp and 'Carlton' dresser are both characteristically colourful, eye-catching and outrageous.

Yves St Laurent

b. 1936

The fashion designer Yves St Laurent took over the house of his mentor, **Christian Dior**, when he was only twenty-one, and offered his first solo collection, the 'Trapeze Line', a year later in 1958. Drafted into the French army he had a nervous breakdown, and then suffered the indignity of seeing his second collection flop. Marc Bohan was made head designer of Dior in his place, and St Laurent sued the house. On the proceeds of the legal action, St Laurent set up his own house in 1962.

St Laurent's clothes are pretty, sexy and glamorous. In the sixties he was influenced by gypsy and North African motifs and these developed into the 'rich hippy' style that made him a celebrity during the seventies. He was one of the first genuine couturiers to take his inspiration from the streets. With American backing, he has also enjoyed astonishing success in merchandising his own ready-to-wear through his international chain of Rive Gauche shops, and in licensing his name to manufacturers of toiletries and perfumes.

'Broadway' Suit, 1978
A typical St Laurent design with its glamorous line, good cut and retrospective element.

Mart Stam

b. 1899

A Dutch architect, Mart Stam was born in Purmerend. In 1924 he was, probably, the first designer to conceive a tubular steel chair employing the **cantilever** principle. His initiative was taken up with more success after 1926 by the better equipped designers of the **Bauhaus**, **Marcel Breuer** and **Mies van der Rohe**. With Emil Roth and Hans Schmidt he ran the journal *ABC* from Zürich, promoting the solution of social problems by the use of technology and modern architecture. Stam's social commitments took him from the 'New Frankfurt' he was building with Ernst May to the Soviet Union from 1930 to 1934. From 1939 to 1945 he was director of the Institute voor Kunstnijverheidsondernijs in Amsterdam. He retired from active life in 1966.
Bibliography Mart Stam – *Documentizing his Work 1920–1965* RIBA Publications, London, 1970; Otakar Macel and Jan van Geest *Stühle aus Stahl* Walther König, Cologne, 1980

Stockholm Exhibition

The Stockholm Exhibition of 1930 was perhaps the most important activity organized by the **Svenska Sljödföreningen**, under its director **Gregor Paulsson**. Paulsson employed **Gunnar Asplund** to design the exhibition. Asplund turned what had been conceived as a metropolitan exhibition into an international advertisement for the **Modern Movement**, presenting architecture and design as essays in standardization, rationalization and availability. To English travellers like **Gordon Russell** and Morton Shand it was a revelation, and a whole generation of architectural students left the London and provincial schools to see what

Asplund had done. Before Stockholm, international exhibitions had attracted attention by their vulgar excess or ostentatious luxury. But such was the impact of Stockholm that the Swedish glass industry abandoned engraved glass in favour of simpler forms, while the ceramics manufacturers began to think more clearly about producing tableware that was easy to stack and easy to wash. Stockholm 1930 showed the rest of the world Sweden's humane and individual interpretation of Modernism.

Exhibition Buildings, 1930
The exhibition buildings were designed by Gunnar Asplund and introduced the International Style to Sweden. They were the first expression in buildings of the ideals of the Svenska Sljödföreningen.

Giotto Stoppino

b. 1926

Giotto Stoppino was born in Milan and studied architecture there. From 1953 he was involved (with **Vittorio Gregotti**) in Architetti Associati, until he opened his own office in 1968. Stoppino has produced furniture designs for Bernini and **Kartell**, but since the mid-seventies has worked almost exclusively with Acerbis International.
Bibliography Daniele Baroni *Giotto Stoppino dall'architettura al design* Electa Editrice, Milan, 1983

Streamlining

Streamlining is to **aerodynamics** what **styling** is to **industrial design**, that is, the glib and facile use of the language of aerodynamics purely for the sake of appearance. The streamlined style developed into a popular automobile aesthetic, but it also penetrated the world of domestic appliances, affecting the shapes of irons, toasters and refrigerators. It became the most familiar product style of the mid-century, its dissemination aided by the popularity of **plastics**, which could easily be shaped into the characteristic curved and furrowed forms.
Bibliography 'Streamline Style: how the future was' exhibition catalogue, Queens Museum, New York, 1984

Burney Prototype Car, 1928
The Burney was a bold, but unsuccessful, British experiment in air management. A commercial failure, it was a flawed monument to the marriage of art and science.

Studio Alchymia see p. 72

Styling

The term 'styling' is used dismissively (and with contempt) for an American approach to design in which a product's appearance was moulded for the purpose of increasing sales. It flourished in the thirties and forties. **Raymond Loewy** and **Harley Earl** were its masters.

Chevrolet 'Biscayne' by Harley Earl, 1958
Styling was the first 'tool' used by American industrial designers to increase the sales of their clients' products. In stagnant markets, the application of a dashing visual effect to a mundane product helped stimulate demand. Before the discovery of ergonomics, ecology and consumer protection, styling was the best evidence of the American designer at work. Earl's Chevrolet is characteristic of this approach to design. The appearance has nothing to do with the function; it is an exercise in pure form and in visual semantics – in fact, an exercise in style. (See also p. 133.)

Superstudio

Like **Archizoom**, Superstudio was one of the Italian avant-garde groups of architect-designers which was founded in the sixties and which matured into something less than radical, in this case obscurity, after a brief flourish of popularity. In 1970 Superstudio collaborated with Gruppo 9999 on the foundation of the Sine Space School for the study of conceptual architecture. All three are now defunct.

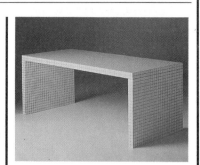

'Quaderno' Table, 1970
The 'Quaderno' table's design was a part of Superstudio's radical programme to find a 'neutral surface' for furniture. Their solution was to create an uncompromising design of orthogonal lines, screen-printed on to a laminate in 3cm squares. The idea was that so unconventional and unusual a surface treatment would allow the table to fit into any setting.

Surrealism

The fine-art movement Surrealism had a tangential effect on some designers and couturiers, notably **Piero Fornasetti** and **Elsa Schiaparelli**. The word was coined by a French poet, Guillaume Apollinaire, in 1917, and the 'movement' was founded by another poet, André Breton (1860–1966), in 1924. Like Freud, the Surrealists were interested in locating the bridges between the psyche and the 'real' world, but while Freud used psychoanalysis, the Surrealists used imagery and poetry. Surrealism promoted irrationality to the status of art, correspondingly demoting logic. So cerebral and so poetic a world-view as Surrealism proposed is at odds with the practicalities of design, but as the most highly organized, popular and successful of the movements in modern art, Surrealism has had a profound influence on public taste. By making the public aware that 'reality' was not necessarily what we perceive, and vice versa, Surrealism matched in art the strange discoveries being made in theoretical physics by Einstein and Heisenberg. In that sense, its dream world aesthetics are perhaps the ones most appropriate to the twentieth century. Surrealism has helped extend the repertoire of many graphic designers, from **Abram Games** and **Tom Eckersley** to **Milton Glaser**, as well as inspiring many exhibition displays.
Bibliography W.S. Rubin *Dada, Surrealism and their Heritage* Abrams, New York, 1968

Svenska Sljödföreningen

The Svenska Sljödföreningen is an art association founded in 1845. Its most important director was **Gregor Paulsson**, who ran it from 1920 to 1934. He once wrote that its purpose was to achieve 'a definitive change from the isolated production of individuals to the conscious work of a whole generation for a culture of form on a broad social basis'. It has now changed itself to **Foreningen SvenskForm**, or just SvenskForm for simplicity. The Sljödföreningen's greatest achievement was to organize the **Stockholm Exhibition** of 1930. It has acted as a design pressure group, being especially concerned since the war with ideal sizes for furniture and with methods of rationalizing activities in smaller homes.

Svenskt Tenn

Svenskt Tenn (which means 'Swedish Pewter') is the name of a shop founded by Estrid Ericson on Stockholm's Strandvagen. Its merchandise helped popularize the idea of 'Swedish grace' throughout the world, particularly in the United States, where to many of the **House & Garden** readership Svenskt Tenn became known as 'the most beautiful shop in the world'. Svenskt Tenn became the showroom for **Josef Frank**, the Austrian architect who did much to create the Swedish style, after his arrival in Stockholm in the mid-thirties.

One-piece Telephone on Cover of 'Ericsson Review', *1956*
Ericsson introduced this one-piece telephone, designed by Gosta Thames, in 1956. It was a remarkably inventive re-interpretation of the company's established table telephone.

Swedish design

Since the emergence of modern Sweden, native design has been associated with a respect for tradition, a sense of humanism and a concern for democratic values. This last commitment in particular lay behind the dominant 'beauty for all' principle, first announced by the writer Ellen Kay and picked up by **Gregor Paulsson** in 1915, who turned it into the motif of the **Svenska Sljödföreningen**. These ideas provided the ideological background against which companies such as **Gustavsberg**, **Rörstrand** and **Orrefors** initiated their policies of having practising artists work in their factories.

The **Modern Movement** in Sweden took a softer and more natural form than it did in other countries, and the style that became known as 'Swedish Modern', with its predominant use of beech, simply patterned textiles and small wooden objects, was described by a journalist visiting the 1939 New York World's Fair as 'a movement towards sanity in design'. The appeal of 'Swedish Modern' was widespread in the fifties and sixties, but since then the Swedes have found no formula of similar international appeal (although the nation's industries still dominate world markets in their production of factory-made crafts goods).

Aga Cooker by Gustav Dalen, 1922
This highly efficient Swedish design in cast iron has been in continuous production in England since 1932.

'Tech' Trolley by Innovator, 1982
This trolley is a mass-market version of the vogue for High-Tech.

A B C D E F G H I J K L M N O P Q R S T U V W X Y Z

T

Roger **Tallon**
Ilmari **Tapiovaara**
Taste
Taylorism
Walter
Dorwin **Teague**
Technès
Guiseppe **Terragni**
Benjamin **Thompson**
Michael **Thonet**
Matteo **Thun**
Total Design
Touring
Triennale
Jan **Tschichold**

Roger Tallon

b. 1929

The professional institution of design does not exist in the same way in France as it does in other countries, and Roger Tallon is one of the few identifiable, independent living French designers.

After meeting **Jacques Viennot** in 1953 he became director of research for **Technès** in Paris in 1960, but with the exception of the watches designed for Lipp in the late sixties and early seventies, most of his well-known work has been outside France, principally for **General Motors** and **Erco**. In France he is known to the public for his work on SNCF's 'Corail' railway locomotives, Essilor sports goggles, Gambin machine tools, and the OPL electronic microscope.

According to Tallon, who is a devotee of technical culture, the **Ford** Model T was a major turning-point in the history of the modern world: 'It meant that people stopped copying and started inventing. Industry designed its own objects.'

Development Drawings for Lipp Watches by Roger Tallon

Watches for Lipp, early 1970s
Tallon's watches designed for the doomed Lipp cooperative anticipated both Post-Modernist mannerism and Giorgio Giugiaro's highly articulate technical 'language'.

Ilmari Tapiovaara

b. 1914

The architect-designer Ilmari Tapiovaara was born in Tampere, Finland. As a student at Helsinki's Taideteollisuuskeskuskoulu (school of applied arts), Tapiovaara became familiar with modern methods of furniture production, working in Otto Korhonen's factory (where **Alvar Aalto**'s furniture was manufactured). On graduating in 1937 he got a job with the Asko-Avonius furniture factory, where his responsibility was to take creative charge of the product line. By the 1939 Finnish Housing Exhibition Asko was showing mass-produced, unpainted light wood furniture, suitable for both the urban middle-class home and the house of a small farmer. After wartime service Tapiovaara designed furniture for a student dormitory called Domus Academica (1946) and the 'Domus' chair (1947) effectively became his trademark. Because of its success, contract furniture for schools, universities and other public buildings became the mainstay of his design work throughout the fifties. Tapiovaara's furniture has all the 'traditional' virtues of **Finnish design** – elegant, simple and natural, but with subtle refinements. He has also designed various exhibitions, the **Olivetti** showroom in Helsinki (1954) and aircraft interiors for Finnair's Convairs and Caravelles (1957). He took part in a development project for Paraguay (1959) and designed some children's furniture for **Heal**'s (1960).
Bibliography 'Ilmari Tapiovaara' exhibition catalogue, Taideteollisuusmuseo, Helsinki, 1984

Taste

'Good taste' and 'bad taste' are relatively modern terms. They have emerged because a plurality of values has made it necessary to distinguish what constitutes 'good' in design.

The English word 'taste' derives from an old French term meaning 'to touch' or 'to feel', a sense that is preserved in the modern Italian word *tastiera*, which means 'keyboard'.

The modern concept of taste seems to have originated in France, and was first taken up in England by eighteenth-century men of letters, who no longer used it only to mean sensation in the mouth but as a metaphor for judgment. In the later eighteenth century, at the time when **Josiah Wedgwood** was separating his wares into 'useful' pieces, and 'ornamental' ones designed in the fashionable neo-classical manner, philosophical discussion of the nature of judgment became involved with the practical business of manufacture.

In the nineteenth century many efforts were made, some perverse, some wildly optimistic, to understand and control popular taste. **Henry Cole** was the first man brave enough to teach about 'bad' design. Later **Elsie de Wolfe** introduced the term 'good taste', but her definition had more to do with status than with academic standards, for her 'good taste' denoted the choice of a style of interior design that she felt had social *cachet*. At the same time the thinkers of the **Modern Movement** attempted to restore the academic standards that were lost in the commercial and spiritual confusion of the Victorian age, and tried to establish precepts for design in answer to the morally loaded question, 'What is good design?' Since the Second World War, with the explosion of mass communications, taste has become a fundamental, if unspoken, issue in all design. However, the standards of taste are even more uncertain than before the Modern Movement. 'Good taste' itself is held in suspicion in some quarters, where an excess of it is regarded as being as unwelcome as careless vulgarity, and many radical designers set out deliberately to offend against traditional standards. (See also **Kitsch**.)

Taylorism

Frederick Winslow Taylor was the author of *Principles of Scientific Management* (1911), a pioneering book which was an influence on **Henry Ford** and **Le Corbusier**.

Taylorism was a set of commonsense organizational principles, intended to replace authoritarianism and anarchy on the shopfloor. Taylor felt it would mean 'the elimination of almost all causes for dispute and disagreement' between employers and workmen. Some of Taylor's organizational theories were picked up by the Nazis.

Bibliography Judith A. Merkle *Management and Ideology* University of California Press, Berkeley and London, 1980

Walter Dorwin Teague

1883–1960

Walter Dorwin Teague was, with **Raymond Loewy**, **Henry Dreyfuss** and **Norman Bel Geddes**, one of the pioneers of the consultant design profession which established itself in New York during the later twenties.

Teague was born in Decatur, Indiana, the son of an itinerant Methodist minister. He studied ▶

Boeing 707 Sales Literature, late 1950s
The first Boeing jet interior was the product of a design consultancy's imagination: Teague built a 707 mock-up in a New York loft in order to demonstrate the possibilities of jet travel to potential customers. (See also p. 49.)

A B C D E F G H I J K L M N O P Q R S T U V W X Y Z

at the Art Students' League, becoming an advertising draughtsman before setting up his own consultancy in 1926. This early date, despite the contrary claims of Bel Geddes, gives Teague some claim to being the very first individual to open an **industrial design** office.

Teague's first job was a re-design of a Kodak camera, for which he produced a set piece of **styling**. Teague's other clients included **Ford**, US Steel, NCR, Du Pont, Westinghouse, Proctor & Gamble and Texaco, and he designed six different pavilions at the 1939 New York World's Fair. His work was characterized by a restrained businesslike quality. Like his contemporaries, all eager to establish themselves as legitimate members of the community, Teague wrote a book to celebrate the accomplishments of the industrial designer. *Design This Day*, published in 1940, was the most refined and sophisticated of the first generation of industrial design books to come out of America; it had a patrician, almost sacerdotal quality. But Teague had other literary interests too: commuting to his New York offices he would read Shakespeare on the train, and in mid-life he was the author of a book on agriculture as well as a modestly successful detective story.

After the Second World War Teague's office was effectively

run by his lieutenant, Frank del Giudice, whose own work concentrated on the interior design of all Boeing commercial transports; from his Stratocruiser through his 707, 727, 737, 747 and 757 to his 767, the inheritors of a twenties version of commercial style have moulded the world's perceptions of how aeroplane interiors should appear. The influence of the Teague office even extended to the actual appearance of the aeroplane itself – on the 707 del Giudice advised on the contours of the nose, fins and engine nacelles.

Such was Walter Dorwin Teague's reputation and his firm's successes that he had attained an almost scriptural presence in American industry. (See also pp. 44 and 48.)
Bibliography Walter Dorwin Teague *Design This Day – the technique of order in the Machine Age* Harcourt Brace, New York, 1940; Arthur J. Pulos *American Design Ethic* MIT, Cambridge, Mass., 1983

Texaco Service Station, 1935
During the mid-thirties Teague's studio took charge of the corporate identity of Texaco stations. To Teague, who had a visionary belief about the place of design in the modern world, the garage was to the twentieth century what the temple had been to Greece and Rome. His design remained essentially unchanged until 1983.

Technès

Technès is a design consultancy founded by **Jacques Viennot** in 1953 in Paris with offices on the Boulevard Raspail. Technès worked in both product and graphic design. In 1975 it combined with Atelier Maurandy to form a multidisciplinary office working in retail design.

Giuseppe Terragni

b. 1904

Guiseppe Terragni was born in Meda, in northern Italy. He was one of the founders of the 'Movimento Italiano per L'Architettura Razionale' and of the avant-garde Gruppo 7. His most celebrated building, the first pure exercise in Italy of the **International Style**, was the Casa del Fascio in Como (1932–6). A chair he designed in 1935 in lacquered wood and steel is now reproduced by **Zanotta**.

Benjamin Thompson

b. 1918

Benjamin Thompson is an American architect whose ideas about urban environment, and in particular about urban renewal, have had a profound effect on the world of design. Thompson was chairman of Harvard's department of architecture and a partner in The Architects' Collaborative (TAC), the firm founded in America by **Walter Gropius**.

Thompson has also conceived and designed for his own stores.

Fulton Hall, New York, 1984
Thompson Associates' reclamation of the derelict area of New York's South Street Seaport, like its reclamation of Boston's Faneuil Hall, exemplified the architectural and environmental concerns of the early eighties. The old buildings were preserved but given new life with an eclectic range of stalls, cafés and shops.

Called D/R (for Design Research) they were intended 'to communicate to the viewer a sense of the world, of joy-of-living, etc.' Growing out of the day-to-day architects' business of selecting furniture and fabrics, they evolved into an expression in the mercantile world of New York retailing of some of the educational ideas which Thompson developed in his courses at Harvard: 'D/R has to do with daily life, morning, noon and night, fresh daisies on the table, a good loaf of bread – the living environment.' It was Thompson who discovered **Marimekko** at European trade fairs in the late fifties, and invited **Armi Ratia** to organize an exhibition at his 'Design Research' store in Cambridge, Mass.

The most complete expression of Thompson's ideas about life and environment has been his rehabilitation of Boston's Faneuil Hall and Quincy Street Market into a brisk and popular urban meeting place which has restored life and business to a moribund part of the city. It was an influence on the redevelopment of London's similarly placed Covent Garden. Thompson's most recent scheme has been the redevelopment of New York's South Street Seaport, an ancient wharf area on the edge of the city's financial district.

Michael Thonet

1796–1871

Michael Thonet's bentwood 'Vienna' chair was one of the first examples of successful mass-production to reach the market, and has constantly been a symbol of excellence in design. Brahms used a Thonet chair at his piano, while composing. Lenin used them. **Le Corbusier** populated his interiors with them, because he felt they possessed 'nobility'. And they are used today in smart New York restaurants.

Michael Thonet was born at Boppard, near Koblenz, and trained as a cabinet-maker. In the 1830s he began to experiment with the technique of **lamination**, which was a cheaper and more effective way of making curved structures than hand-cutting. When his laminated chairs were exhibited at Koblenz in 1841 they were seen by Prince Metternich, who suggested he would be better off in Vienna. In July of the next year he was given an imperial monopoly on making these light, elastic laminated chairs, and duly set out for the Austrian capital. In 1849 Thonet chairs were used in the popular Viennese café, the Daum, and in 1851 Thonet exhibited in London at the **Great Exhibition**. In 1852 the firm Gebrüder Thonet was incorporated.

However, rising wages in Vienna started to make the labour-intensive lamination technique expensive, so Thonet continued to experiment. His next development was to bend solid wood with steam, which allowed the parts of the chair to be turned *before* they were steam-bent, and it was this technique that led to the real innovation in mass-production furniture. A new factory was built at Koritschan in Moravia in 1856 to make the *Vierzehner* (number 14) chair, which was the model that became the classic. Thonet applied sophisticated production techniques in the Koritschan factory and took the division of labour almost as far as **Henry Ford** was to. Thonet also provided schools and health insurance schemes for the workers in his factories (although when Le Corbusier visited the factory in 1932 he noted in the visitors' book that working conditions were like an 'inferno').

The *Vierzehner* was made out of six separate parts of beech. The section of each component continuously varies, according to the local demands

of the structure. The chair was awarded a bronze medal at the London exhibition of 1862, where the jury declared: 'An excellent application of a happy thought . . . they are not works of show, but practical furniture for daily use – they are simple, graceful, light and strong.' At the same exhibition **William Morris** was exhibiting pseudo-medieval designs.

By the mid-twenties it was estimated that more than one hundred million examples of the *Vierzehner* had been produced, but it was nonetheless clear to Thonet-Mundus (as the firm had become in 1906) that a new age called for the use of new materials, and the first tubular steel chairs by **Mart Stam**, **Marcel Breuer** and **Mies van der Rohe** were produced by Thonet in their Frankenberg factory, where the firm remains today. The original bentwood chairs are still manufactured in the old factory at Korycany in Czechoslovakia (Korycany is the Slavonic of Koritschan). **Bibliography** Ole Bang *Thonet – Geschichte eines Stuhles* Weitbrecht, 1981

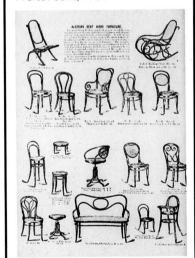

Thonet Chairs from Catalogue of 1885
Michael Thonet's bentwood chairs not only deliberately manifested the technique used in their manufacture, but were also products of the taste for the Rococo which influenced 1840s Viennese craftsmen.

Matteo Thun

b. 1952

Matteo Thun is a partner in **Sottsass** Associati and contributed to the first **Memphis** collection in 1981. He was born in Bolzano, studied at the Oskar Kokoschka Academy in Salzburg and at Florence University. Since 1982 he has taught product design at the Vienna Academy of Arts.

Total Design

Total Design is an Amsterdam design consultancy founded by **Friso Kramer** in 1962. His partners were Bennon Wissing and Wim Crouwel.

Its work is typical of the 'new' Dutch graphics. Although Wim Crouwel's work for Amsterdam's Stedelijk Museum shows a traditional, modern restraint, there are new elements coming into the studio's 'language'. Like other Dutch graphic designers, they tend to prefer 'grotesque' newspaper typefaces (and even newspaper layout) to the more refined 'Helvetica' of the Swiss School. Similarly, they use idioms and motifs which are deliberately anti-rational or at least unfunctional in the old-fashioned sense.

Post Office Signage, 1978–9
The biggest job undertaken by Total Design was a complete corporate identity scheme for the Dutch PTT (Post Office). Total chose a clean sans serif typeface instead of the more expressive letter forms favoured by some of their contemporaries.

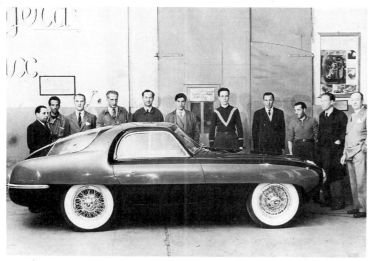

Touring

Carrozzeria Touring was founded in Milan in 1926 as a partnership between Felice Bianchi Anderloni and Gaetano Ponzoni. Since its inception Touring has been particularly concerned with lightness of construction, and the shop became associated with the term it coined for its own special method of construction: *Superleggera*. This is a system where hand-beaten metal panels are mounted on to a very light space-frame. The choice of the English word *touring* in the name instead of the Italian, *turismo*, betrays the taste of the founders, and the firm's best-known body design was for the English Aston Martin DB-4 (See also p. 160.)

Special Model, early 1950s
Lancias and Maseratis being Assembled, early 1960s
The Milan carrozzeria Touring has a distinguished record as a producer of elegant coach-work for exclusive cars. In its sixty-year history it has numbered many of the world's top sports and GT car manufacturers amongst its clients.

Aston Martin Spyder DB3, 1958
Even though Aston Martin is held to be the essence of Britishness, its famous sixties look was created in Milan by Touring.

Triennale

The Milan Triennale grew out of a tradition of bi-annual exhibitions which began in Monza in 1923 with the 'Prima Mostra Internazionale delle Arti Decorative' (First International Exhibition of Decorative Arts). The last Biennale was held in 1930 and the first Triennale in 1933, at Milan's Palazzo d'Arte.

At the first Triennale there was a celebration of **Futurism** side by side with examples of the work of **Le Corbusier**, **Walter Gropius** and some other leaders of the **Modern Movement**. The second Triennale, in 1936, was a Fascist event, redeemed by **Nizzoli**'s participation in the design of the 'Salone della Vittoria'.

The Triennale continued after the war and by the fifties had become the acknowledged showplace for modern design. It has contributed greatly to Milan's reputation as the leading international centre for design.
Bibliography Anty Pansera *Storia cronache della Triennale* Fabbri, Milan, 1978

Poster for IXth Triennale, 1951
From their inception in 1933 the Milan Triennales became the most important international showcases for Italian design. They resumed after the War, but there was a four-year gap between 1947 and the ninth one in 1951.

Jan Tschichold

1902–74

With **Stanley Morison** and **Herbert Bayer** Jan Tschichold was the most influential typographer of the twentieth century. He was born in Leipzig, the son of a signwriter, and as a young man was inspired by the first **Bauhaus** exhibition of 1923. As a result of this he published a manifesto, *Elementare Typographie*, in the same year. This polemic in the cause of new, uncluttered book design and layout was followed by a book, *Die neue Typographie*, in 1926. Like the Bauhaus masters, Tschichold had to leave Germany with the rise of Hitler, who thought that the new typography was an expression of *Kulturbolschewismus*. In 1935 he lectured in Denmark and then moved to London, where the publishers Lund Humphries arranged an exhibition of his work. In England he joined **Penguin Books** and established the distinguished standards of typography and layout which changed the face of British publishing and did as much to educate British taste as many well-funded public and educational institutions. In 1949 he retired to Switzerland.
Bibliography 'Penguin Books – the pictorial books 1960–1980' exhibition catalogue, Manchester Polytechnic, 1981

Unimark

Unimark was founded in Milan in 1965 by **Bob Noorda**, **Jay Doblin**, **Massimo Vignelli** and others; its New York office opened in 1966. It had a distinguished client list which included Gillette, **Olivetti** and McCormick.

Utility

'Utility' furniture was produced from 1943, under the auspices of the Board of Trade which had **Gordon Russell** as chairman of its Design Panel. The 'Utility' concept arose out of wartime conditions but its origins go back to 1938, when Russell had begun a private initiative to start an association to produce dignified furniture at low cost.

Just as many people later recalled that they had never eaten better than under rationing, so wartime privations stimulated an improvement in quality in British furniture design.

Russell employed designers such as **Enid Marx** to make 'Utility' fabrics, while he took

Dressing Table, 1947
The Board of Trade's draconian standards forced moderation in design, but the discipline could lead just as easily to mediocrity as to innovation.

charge of the furniture. Under Russell, the Board of Trade introduced high standards of integrity in design to a population that had been denied them by peacetime traditions in retailing. Although in style 'Utility' furniture and fabrics were somewhat bland and unexciting, sometimes betraying the drabness imposed by austerity, in general Russell offered goods of high quality at low prices, applying principles loosely derived from the **Arts and Crafts** and transferred to mass-production.

The furniture produced under Russell was, however, considered too daring by the furniture trade and too dated by the leaders in taste, like the **Architectural Review**'s writers. Russell expressed the ethos behind it when he said, 'I am never for forcing the pace, a limited advance and then consolidation is a sound principle, both in war and peace.'

**Unimark
Utility**

V

Pierre **Vago**
Gino **Valle**
Henry **van de Velde**
Harold **van Doren**
Andries **van Onck**
Victor **Vasarely**
Thorstein **Veblen**
Venini
Robert **Venturi**
Vespa
Victoria and Albert Museum
Jacques **Viennot**
Vittorio **Vigano**
Vignale
Massimo **Vignelli**
Vistosi
Vogue
Volkswagen
Volvo
Hans **von Klier**
C.F.A. **Voysey**
Vuokko

Pierre Vago

b. 1910

A French architect and town-planner, Pierre Vago was born in Budapest and was educated at the Ecole Spéciale d'Architecture in Paris. He became editor of the influential Parisian magazine *Architecture d'aujourd'hui* in 1932, just as it was discovering the **Modern Movement**. At the time, Vago's magazine was the only influential French periodical to feature articles on industrial design. Vago, who left *Architecture d'aujourd'hui* in 1948, has been a prominent member of juries judging architectural competitions, and was president of **ICSID** from 1963 to 1965. He has practised as an architect and town-planner in Belgium, Austria, France, Germany, Luxembourg, Israel and Italy.

Gino Valle

b. 1923

An Italian architect, Gino Valle gained his diploma of architecture in Venice in 1948 and then went to Harvard until 1952. With his wife Nani, and John Myer, he set up a workshop and experimented with prefabricated structures, but he is best known for the digital clocks and timetabling equipment he has designed for Solari. His 'Cifra' and 'Dator' timepieces and giant timetabling boards have become familiar features at railway and aircraft termini around the world. Valle's work for Solari won a **Compasso d'Oro** award in 1957.

Henry van de Velde

1863–1957

Henri van de Velde changed the spelling of his first name to its English form as a response to the Anglophilia which swept Europe in the late nineteenth century with the popularity of the **Arts and Crafts** movement among designers and architects.

He was influenced by **William Morris** as a young man, and, persuaded that art should become more directly connected with life, or perhaps the other way around, helped found a review called *Van Nu en Straks* (From Now and the Future) in 1893 to promote Arts and Crafts ideals. After his marriage in 1894 van de Velde designed his own house (and all its furniture) at Uccle. The house became a sensation and he was brought to the attention of influential taste-makers, men such as the entrepreneur Samuel Bing and the art critic Julius Meier-Graefe.

By the end of the nineteenth century van de Velde was successfully designing and manufacturing furniture in Brussels and exhibited regularly at a gallery called La Libre Esthétique. He moved to Berlin in 1900 from his native Antwerp, when he designed advertising graphics which were heavily influenced by the then current fashions in high art, in particular the symbolist style of painting practised with sinuous lyricism by Toorop and Beardsley. In 1901 he was taken on as a consultant by the Grand Duke of Saxe-Weimar, who asked him to run the Weimar Academy of Applied Arts. In this capacity van de Velde became one of the founders of the **Deutsche Werkbund**, but he refused to compromise what he felt to be the essential *artistic* element in design, and this led to a clash with **Hermann Muthesius**, who, along with most of the other members of the Werkbund, argued for *Typisierung*, or standardization and machine-manufacture of products. There was a fierce public debate at the time of the Werkbund exhibition at Cologne in 1914 and van de Velde resigned. Athough the mechanical-romantic zeal of the Werkbund vanquished his essentially nineteenth-century ideals, it was van de Velde who suggested that **Walter Gropius** replace him as director of the Weimar school, and so can be seen as a prime mover in the foundation of the **Bauhaus**. ***Bibliography*** Alfred Roth *Begegnung mit Pionieren* Birkhäuser, Zürich, 1974; 'Van de Velde – projets et réalisations' exhibition catalogue, Brussels, 1969; Robert Schmutzler *Art Nouveau* Thames & Hudson, London, 1960

Armchair, 1906
Arts and Crafts influenced this armchair from a suite produced by van de Velde, in the year before the foundation of the Deutsche Werkbund.

Harold van Doren

1895–1957

Like **Eliot Noyes**, who went straight from working in a museum to working in American industry, Harold van Doren brought culture to bear on the raffish body of the American **industrial design** profession.

Van Doren was born in Chicago of Dutch antecedents, the name having originally been van Doorn. After studying languages he worked in the Louvre in Paris, and his French was good enough to allow him to become the translator of Ambrose Vollard's *Paul Cézanne* (1923) and *Jean Renoir* (1934). He also wrote an unpublished novel, *The Love Pendulum*, and played a romantic role in Jean Renoir's film *La Fille de l'eau.* On his return to America he became assistant to the director of the Minneapolis Institute of Arts, but resigned when he had a chance to become an industrial designer so that he could, in his view, make a real contribution to the modern world. His first major job was in 1934 for the Toledo Scale Company of Toledo, Ohio, which he was given by the company's president, Hugh Bennett, an Englishman whom van Doren had known since his college days. Bennett had originally approached **Norman Bel Geddes** to style his product and, while Bel Geddes came up with many dramatic renderings (which he published in his futuristic book, *Horizons*, of 1934) and an astonishing plan for a factory of the future, the management soon became disenchanted with Bel Geddes' lack of practicality. Van Doren's design solution was, perhaps, less visually exciting, but it was more advanced in a truer sense, as he used a new plastic called Plaskon. This product earned for Toledo Scale the distinction of being the first major user of lightweight, large-scale plastic mouldings, and was for van Doren the first of many designs in new materials. As described by Seldon & Martha Cheney in 1937 'radios and kitchen equipment, laundry and heating machines, exquisite little perfume bottles, automobile tires, a gasoline pump, a long line of streamlined juvenile vehicles are but items in the steady flow of products from his studio'. His clients were Philco, MayTag and Goodyear (for whom he styled a tyre) – blue chips, indeed, but van Doren was aware of the limitations of his new craft.

In 1940 he published *Industrial Design: a practical guide* in which he described the practical side of working with new materials and their production techniques. His health failing, he retired to Philadelphia to devote himself to music and painting and it was there that he died. (See also p. 43.)

Bibliography Harold van Doren *Industrial Design: a practical guide* McGraw-Hill, New York, 1940; Jeffrey L. Meikle *Twentieth Century Limited* Temple University Press, Philadelphia, 1979; Arthur J. Pulos *American Design Ethic* MIT, Cambridge, Mass., 1983

Maytag Washing Machine and Egry Cash Dispensers Before and After Styling, late 1930s
The shamanistic 'before-and-after' sequence was a set-piece of designers' presentations to clients during the thirties. Harold van Doren was a master of the technique and his studio prepared elaborate airbrushed images of his design projects for the manufacturers who came to them.

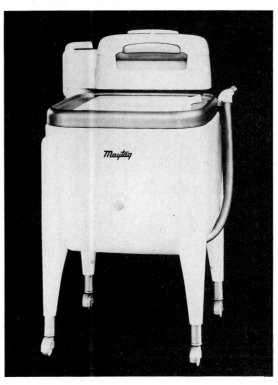

A B C D E F G H I J K L M N O P Q R S T U V W X Y Z

Andries van Onck

b. 1928

Andries van Onck was born in Amsterdam and studied at the Hague under **Gerrit Rietveld** and at Ulm under **Max Bill**. Roberto Olivetti noticed him as a promising student and invited him to Italy, where he worked with **Ettore Sottsass**. He opened his own studio in Milan (with his Japanese wife, Hiroko Takeda) and became fascinated by the problem of creating interesting design at accessible prices. He has described white goods as 'a Niagara of white cubes falling over Europe', adding 'We don't want those things to be ugly cubes, do we?' His clients include the chain store Upim and the manufacturer Zanussi, to whose refrigerators, freezers, cookers and washing-machines van Onck has applied a stylized version of German minimalism. With **Massimo Vignelli** in charge of graphics and **Gino Valle** in charge of its **corporate identity**, the Zanussi enterprise has one of the most thoroughgoing product design programmes in Europe; van Onck is responsible for designing three different ranges for them aimed at the different markets across Western Europe, each being replaced on a five-year cycle.

'Cusinaire' Oven for Zanussi, 1984
Van Onck brings a version of the Hochschule für Gestaltung's rational design to domestic interiors.

Victor Vasarely

b. 1908

The French painter, sculptor and graphic designer Victor Vasarely was born at Pecs in Hungary. His geometric paintings were an influence on Op-Art, one of the fashionable styles of painting in the sixties (which had a brief effect on advertising graphics). Vasarely designed an illusionistic, Op-Art badge for the state car company Renault in 1974, and in 1983 he designed some special bottles and labels for the private Taittinger champagne company.

Thorstein Veblen

1857–1929

Thorstein Veblen, an American sociologist and social critic, was educated at Carleton College, Minnesota, and Johns Hopkins and Yale universities. In 1899 he published what was to be his most celebrated work, *The Theory of the Leisure Class*. In it Veblen gave the expression 'conspicuous consumption' to the language and lent dialectical form to the notions of middle-class revolt which had already been sensed in England by **C.R. Ashbee** and others. Veblen's book was the first scientific study of popular taste, written just as the professional practice of design was beginning to emerge from the late Industrial Revolution.

His later books, *The Theory of Business Enterprise* (1904) and *The Instinct of Workmanship* (1914), have been entirely overshadowed by the success of *Leisure Class*, which has been continuously in print, both in Britain and the United States, since it was first published. Yet despite its popularity Veblen's spiky personality meant that he never enjoyed academic celebrity. **Bibliography** Joseph Dorfmann *Thorstein Veblen and his America*, Viking, New York, 1934

Venini

Since 1959 the Venini glassworks has been run by Ludovico de Santillana (b. 1931), the son-in-law of Paolo Venini (1895–1959), its founder. Venini has had a reputation for being 'progressive' ever since it abandoned traditional Venetian forms in favour of splashed and mottled surfaces. It has produced 'art glass' designed by **Tobia Scarpa**, **Pierre Cardin** and **Tapio Wirkkala**.

Robert Venturi

b. 1925

Robert Venturi is a Philadelphia architect-academic whose books, *Complexity and Contradiction in Modern Architecture* (1966) – delivered originally as papers at New York's **Museum of Modern Art** – and *Learning from Las Vegas* (1972), persuasively argued against what he maintained was the rigid formalism of the **Modern Movement** in architecture and design and, instead, sought to introduce eclecticism and variety. The doctrinaire versions of Modernism had already suffered intellectual depredations from **Pop**, in whose imagery and immediacy Venturi and his partners (his wife, Denise Scott-Brown, and Steven Izenour) looked for their new aesthetic.

They argued, amongst other things, for a return to native American tradition, and encouraged American architects and designers to see in the vernacular American townscape not confusion and visual chaos, but inspiration and excitement. The architectural and design culture they proposed was a reversal of and a complete reaction to the European influence of **Mies van der Rohe** and **Walter Gropius**.

In this sense Venturi can claim to be the originator of what was to be known as **Post-Modernism**, having written, for example, 'I like elements that are hybrid rather than pure, compromising rather than clean, distorted rather than straightforward . . .'

Coffee Service for Alessi, 1983
Robert Venturi's coffee service applies the mannered style of Post-Modernist architecture on a domestic scale.

Recently he has turned his attention to furniture, and in 1984 **Knoll** introduced a collection of chairs and tables designed by him. The range comprises a sofa, nine chairs and two table bases. Each type, like his architecture, used historical reference; the chairs, made of laminated wood, were cut with a jig-saw so that Queen Anne, Gothic Revival, or **Biedermeier** features could be presented on them as flat patterns. For Knoll it was an extraordinary departure from a formalist tradition which had its roots in the **Bauhaus**, but Venturi had sufficient ego to see the firm through: 'Mies did one chair – I did nine,' he remarked to a journalist from New York's *Metropolis* magazine.
Bibliography Robert Venturi *Complexity and Contradiction in Modern Architecture* Museum of Modern Art, New York, 1966

Chair for Knoll, 1984
Venturi put his Post-Modern theories into practice in his furniture for Knoll. Expensively made out of high quality laminates, his designs aped styles of the past.

Vespa

The Vespa motor scooter became a cult object. Its name is derived from the Latin for 'wasp' on account of the sleek housing for its rear-mounted engine and transmission. It was the first motor scooter to break away from the basic low running-board pattern, and its wasp-like shell made for a radically new appearance.

Created as a cheap means of mass transport for housewives in the Italian cities during the post-War years of *ricostruzione*, the Vespa was manufactured by the boat and aircraft concern of Rinaldo **Piaggio**, to designs by **Corradino d'Ascanio**. **Ettore Sottsass** has spoken evocatively about how to his generation (which was used to the new visual language being developed for other machines by **Pininfarina** and **Marcello Nizzoli**) the Vespa seemed a specially strong symbol of a new civilization. It also became the symbol of a new outlook in England and Terence Conran claims to have delivered his first furniture on one.

Victoria and Albert Museum

The Victoria and Albert Museum, in London's South Kensington, is the world's foremost museum of the applied arts. Although the present building is almost entirely Edwardian in fabric, the origins of the Museum go back to the early nineteenth century, and Aston Webb's bombastic architecture really only unites a number of separate building campaigns. Both in substance and in purpose, the V&A has grown by accretion.

The history of the Museum is inseparable from those other developments in British public life which led to the **Great Exhibition of the Industry of All Nations** and to the foundation of what became the **Royal College of Art**. Its spiritual origins lie with the *Report on Arts and Manufactures* by a Parliamentary Select Committee of 1836, which called for the setting up of exemplary collections of manufactured goods so that students and artisans might be better prepared to work to counter foreign imports. The Great Exhibition brought together all interested parties around Prince Albert including **Henry Cole**, who, as head of the Government's Department of Science and Art, was appointed director of the South Kensington Museum when it was established after the 1851 exhibition. The South Kensington Museum became the 'V&A' in 1899. (See also pp. 22–4.)

As Europe's first museum of the applied arts, the South Kensington Museum added to the international influence of Britain's **Arts and Crafts** movement and it was soon imitated abroad: museums in Hamburg, Oslo, Vienna and later in Zürich, all owe their origins to London's example. During the twentieth century the character of the V&A changed, and instead of being the reforming museum of the industrial arts which Cole and his contemporaries had intended, it became a vast custodian of the applied arts. This effect was mitigated in 1981 when the Boilerhouse Project was established in the Museum's old boilerhouse yard with the intention of reviving Cole's educational and missionary purpose by showing modern design.
Bibliography Nikolaus Pevsner *Academies of Art, Past and Present* Cambridge University Press, Cambridge, 1940; Quentin Bell *The Schools of Design* Black, London, 1947; Fiona MacCarthy *A History of British Design 1830–1970* Allen & Unwin, London, 1979; John Physick *The Victoria & Albert Museum* 1982

Jacques Viennot

1893–1959

Jacques Viennot was a French theorist and polemicist of design. He founded the Cabinet d'Esthétique Industrielle de **Technès** in 1953, and was a director of *La Revue de l'esthétique industrielle*. In 1951 he established the Institut de l'Esthétique Industrielle, dedicated to informing the French people of the significance of **industrial design** in the wealth-producing cycle. It was unsuccessful.

Vittorio Vigano

b. 1919

A furniture designer, Vittorio Vigano was born in Milan into a family with an artistic tradition. He studied architecture at Milan Polytechnic, and after 1944 worked first with **Gio Ponti** and then with BBPR. In 1947 he set up his own practice and designed quiet, restrained wood furniture for the straitened mass market. In 1949 he produced a bent **plywood** chair for Compensati Curvate and, in the same year, a dish-like chair in enamelled metal with a rush seat which, like **Harry Bertoia**'s similar design, was ideally suited to being pictured in the modernistic living rooms which appeared in the design magazines of the period. Vigano has also worked for **Arteluce** and contributed to the VIIth, IXth, XIIth and XIIIth Milan **Triennales**.
Bibliography Centrokappa (ed.) *Il Design Italiano degli anni '50* Domus, Milan, 1980; Paolo Fossati *Il Design in Italia 1945–1970* Einaudi, Turin, 1972; 'The New Domestic Landscape' exhibition catalogue, Museum of Modern Art, New York, 1972

Vignale

Alfredo Vignale emerged as an independent coach-builder after an apprenticeship with **Pininfarina**, whose shop he had joined when he was seventeen. He founded his own firm in 1946 and produced designs for Ferrari, **FIAT**, Maserati, Aston-Martin and Rolls-Royce.

Vignale specialized in producing both small runs of utilitarian vehicles which the mass manufacturers found uneconomic to produce, and unique designs for private clients or prototypes for industry. Among his first designs was a coupé version of the FIAT 100 of 1949. The firm produced coachwork for Ferrari racing cars throughout the early fifties, and elements from racing cars were incorporated into the series production Maserati 3500 of 1959, which is, perhaps, Vignale's best-known design. Through one of its young designers, **Giovanni Michelotti**, the studio also produced sketches for a sports car for Standard-Triumph which ultimately became the Triumph TR-4 of 1963. The sketches of the Maserati 3500 and the Triumph TR-4 of the same year are almost identical, and a comparison of the proportion, detail and character of the sketches and the production cars makes an instructive lesson in the differences between the Italian and British car industries.

Vignale's style tended towards a high-waisted solidity, lacking the flamboyance of some of his contemporaries. After Alfredo Vignale's death in a car crash near his Turin factory in 1969 Carrozzeria Vignale was taken over by **Ghia**, which was, itself, bought in 1974 by the **Ford** Motor Company.
Bibliography Angelo Tito Anselmi (ed) *La Carrozzeria Italiana – cultura e progetto* Alfieri, Turin, 1978

Triumph TR-3, 1958
The Triumph TR series of sports cars was the paradigm of the strong-armed British tradition in design. The eyebrows over the headlights, vestigial tail fins and mouth-organ grille of Vignale's design were idiosyncratic motifs. Slightly modified, this design went into production as the TR-4.

Massimo Vignelli

b. 1931

Massimo Vignelli has become a social phenomenon in American design, discussed and celebrated by people and concerns not hitherto excited by professional graphic designers.

Vignelli studied architecture in Venice, and then worked for **Venini** from 1954 to 1957, before opening an office with his wife, Lella, in Milan in 1960. He went to Chicago in 1964, worked for the Container Corporation of America (for which he designed a logo), and was one of the founders of **Unimark**, a company specializing in **corporate identity**. In 1971–2 he was retained by **Knoll**. Vignelli specializes in a certain sort of supergraphics which achieves its effects with colour planes and dramatic variations of scale and size. He designed the graphics for the Washington subway system.

Graphics for Knoll
The clean cut European look of Vignellis' graphics added huge dignity to the American furniture manufacturer.

Vistosi

Luciano Vistosi is an Italian glassware manufacturer based in Murano, the Venetian home of decorative Italian glass. Vistosi produced **Ettore Sottsass'** 'Aulica', 'Diodata', 'Dogaressa' and 'Faliera' decorative glassware, using strong shapes and strong colours to achieve dolmen-like effects of intensity and presence.

Vogue

Vogue magazine was founded as a weekly paper in 1892, like its contemporary *Harper's Bazaar*. **Condé Nast** acquired it in 1909 and turned it into the leading international magazine of fashion and, to a lesser extent, design and style. Its character has been moulded by strong and determined editors, but especially by Edna Woolman Chase, who was acquired along with the weekly paper and remained with the Condé Nast group until 1952. Under her editorship *Vogue* expanded internationally: a British subsidiary was set up in 1916, a French one in 1920 and Australian, Italian and Spanish editions have all appeared subsequently.

The magazine's reputation depends very much upon the adventurous qualities of the cover design and the high quality of photography inside. *Vogue's* continuing achievement has been to introduce ideas about high fashion and interior design to a financially independent audience. The *doyenne* of American fashion, Diana Vreeland, was editor from 1963 to 1972.
Bibliography Caroline Seebohm *The Man who was Vogue – the life and times of Condé Nast* Weidenfeld & Nicolson, London 1982; Viking, New York, 1982

Volkswagen

The first Volkswagen car is one of the greatest collaborative design exercises ever. The origins of the vehicle that became known over the world as the 'Beetle' or the 'Bug' lay in development contracts for a small car which Zundapp and NSU, both firms which were essentially motorcycle manufacturers, had placed with Ferdinand **Porsche**'s design bureau in Stuttgart in the early thirties. In 1933 Porsche sent a memorandum to the Minister of Transport outlining his ideas for a *Volkswagen*, literally a 'people's car', which was to be basically a four-wheeled motorbike produced cheaply through the application of sophisticated design. The idea of a people's car appealed to the German dictator, Adolf Hitler, who thought that a Volkswagen could be an industrial counterpart to the *Volkswohnung* ('people's housing') which his ministers were promoting. Porsche's private initiative was brought under state control with the establishment of the Volkswagen Development Corporation. Test cars, employing many ideas which were first seen in sketches made for Zundapp and NSU, were running in 1936; the first experimental line was operating at the Daimler-Benz factory in 1937; and the foundation stone of the Wolfsburg factory was laid in 1938. At the ceremony, without Porsche's foreknowledge, Hitler declared that the Volkswagen would be named after the Nazi recreational organization *Kampf durch Freude* (Strength Through Joy) and be known as the KdFwagen.

The Volkswagen was built down to a cost of 990 Marks, and there was to be no profit margin. This meant that hydraulic brakes could not be used because a licence fee would have had to be paid.

Porsche settled on a flat four air-cooled engine, developed originally by Josef Kales for NSU, but adapted for the Volkswagen by another member of Porsche's team called F.X. Reimspiess (who also designed the Volkswagen logo). The body of the Volkswagen was designed by **Erwin Komenda**.

The Second World War began exactly four weeks before Volkswagen production had been scheduled to start, and, although 100,000 military versions were built during the War, production of the People's Car did not begin until 1945, and then under the management of a British army major. Renamed the Volkswagen, with continuous development it was to replace the Ford Model T as the most popular car ever made.

However, its very success almost brought economic ruin to the German manufacturer because by the early seventies Volkswagen's managing director, Toni Schmucker, was faced with the problem of revitalizing a manufacturing plant too dependent on one product with vast, but diminishing, sales. He called in **Giorgio Giugiaro** and ItalDesign to develop the Golf, a new technology front-wheel-drive, water-cooled car that replaced the Beetle in all Western markets. The influence of Porsche, an Austrian, and Giugiaro, an Italian, has provoked more than one commentator to make the wry observation that Volkswagen's most successful products have never been designed by Germans.

Bibliography K.B. Hopfinger *Beyond Expectation – the Volkswagen Story* Foulis, London, 1954

VW 'Beetle', Prototype, 1936

VW Karmann-Ghia, 1961
Before Volkswagen discovered style in the early seventies, customers who wanted the traditional reliability and economy together with a degree of chic had only low-volume specials to choose from, styled by Ghia and built by the Karmann bodyshop.

Volvo

The Swedish car and truck manufacturer was founded by Assar Gabrielsson and Gustav Larson, two employees of the SFK bearings company. Their company became 'Volvo' in 1924 (the name is Latin for 'I roll').

Volvo picked up its design principles from American cars and has concentrated on solidity and reliability, often maintaining a single model on a very long production run rather than taking risks with adventurous engineering or interesting styling. Compared with its compatriot SAAB, for a long time Volvo's interest in design was only remote. However, the conservatism of Volvo design and the reliability of the firm's products have happily combined with a dedicated safety effort since the forties which has accelerated since the sixties. As a result, as well as the cars being safe no-one knows more than Volvo about how to make a car *look* safe. Volvo's head of design, Jan Wilsgaard, architect of the 'Amazon' of 1956, eschews any pursuit of 'fashion', although the Volvo Concept Car (VCC) which was developed in the late seventies by Volvo's head of research, Dan Werbin, has been criticized for its gimmickry. Similarly, the 760 series introduced in 1982 was a blatant appeal to the tastes of the large American market.

Model of the Volvo 760, 1982
The Volvo 760 was designed by Jan Wilsgaard.

Hans von Klier

b. 1934

Hans von Klier collaborated with **Ettore Sottsass** on numerous projects for **Olivetti** while working in his Milan offices from 1960 to 1968. He was born in Tetschen, Czechoslovakia and went to Ulm to study at the **Hochschule für Gestaltung**, graduating in 1959. In 1969 he became head of **corporate identity** for Olivetti.

C.F.A. Voysey

1857–1941

An English architect, Charles Frederick Annesley Voysey was born in Hessle, near Hull, the son of a clergyman. Voysey's whole career was to be associated with the **Arts and Crafts** movement. He set up his own office in 1884 and quietly developed a version of the Arts and Crafts philosophy, while remaining independent of the various guilds and societies which flourished at the end of the century.

Voysey's place in history was established when he was claimed as a pioneer of the **Modern Movement** by **Nikolaus Pevsner** in 1936. However, the architect always denied any avant-garde element in his work, and maintained to his death that he was solely preoccupied with vernacular British traditions in architecture and design. Indeed, his trademark was a combination of strong, original forms with an inspired interpretation of traditional, vernacular details.

Voysey began to design wallpaper, textiles and silver in 1888, and each displays his characteristic concern with natural pattern. Designs like 'Bird and Tulip' or 'Nympheas' use his favourite heart-shaped motif with a general decorative treatment like **William Morris**', but more stylized. Also like Morris, Voysey expounded ideals of truth to nature and truth to materials. In his most famous building, a house called The Orchard at Chorleywood, north-west of London, Voysey attempted to create a total

'Let Us Prey', Wallpaper Design

design where the architecture, decoration, fittings and furniture all combined to create a unified effect. Voysey is significant in the history of design not because of his legacy of novel formal ideas nor for his polemics, for each of these was largely derivative, but for his sustaining influence on the tradition of the Arts and Crafts which has had such a strong influence on the development of **industrial design** in Britain. Despite the fine theory – as in his adjuration of 1892: 'Begin by casting out all the useless ornaments . . . Eschew all imitations. Strive to produce an effect of repose and simplicity' – Voysey can be held responsible for having invented the suburban style.
Bibliography Duncan Simpson *C.F.A. Voysey* Lund Humphries, London 1979

Vuokko see **Vuokko Eskolin-Nurmesniemi**

242

Wilhelm Wagenfeld

b. 1900

Wilhelm Wagenfeld studied at the **Bauhaus**, where he was a pupil of **Laszlo Moholy-Nagy**, but Wagenfeld rejected his Bauhaus training and, like **Hermann Gretsch**, remained in Germany throughout the Nazi years. He taught at the Staatliche Kunsthochschule (state college of art) in Berlin from 1931 to 1935 and from 1935 to 1947 worked at the Lausitze Glassworks. He designs utilitarian objects such as glass and cutlery, his most popular and least recognized work being his 'Pelikan' ink bottle of 1938. He created the 'Atlanta' flatware for WMF in 1954–5, a series of architectural light-fittings for Lindner throughout the later fifties, and a melamine dinner tray and service for Lufthansa in 1955. Wagenfeld became a professor at Berlin's Hochschule für Bildende Künste, but since 1954 has run his own studio from Stuttgart. Wagenfeld has an uncompromising and unwavering commitment to both the aesthetic and to the social ideals of the **Modern Movement**. In 1955 he resigned from the **Deutsche Werkbund** as a protest against what he saw as its loss of idealism and its lack of character. His achievement has been to bring genuine Bauhaus standards to the design of readily available, mass-market glass and ceramics, although his style is severe and dry, even by the standards of contemporary **German design**.
Bibliography Wilhelm Wagenfeld *Wesen und Gestalt der Dinge um Uns* Eduard Stichnote, Potsdam, 1948; 'Industrieware von W. Wagenfeld. Kunstlerische Mitarbeit in der Industrie 1930–1960' exhibition catalogue, Kunstgewerbemuseum, Zürich, 1960

Glass Teapot and Cup, 1930
Wagenfeld specializes in glassware, produced mostly for the Jenaer Glaswerke and the Vereinigte Lausitze Glaswerk. Wagenfeld's unflinching dedication to the Modern Movement ideals of Functionalism produced designs that are awesomely pure.

Otto Wagner

1841–1918

Otto Wagner was one of the key figures in Viennese culture at the turn of the century. An architect and town-planner, he influenced an entire generation through his teaching at the School of Art between 1894 and 1912. His most important building was the Vienna Postsparkassenamt (Post Office Savings Bank) which he designed in an early version of **Functionalist** style. Wagner designed fittings and furniture for the Post Office, as well as a series of armchairs for **Thonet**.

Ole Wanscher

b. 1903

Ole Wanscher was one of the founders of the Copenhagen Cabinetmakers' Guild, an influential society which offered the first public showing of designs by **Børge Mogensen** and **Hans Wegner**.

Neville Ward

b. 1922

Neville Ward was educated at Liverpool School of Architecture and became a member of the Board of Trade Furniture Panel (under **Gordon Russell**) in 1946. His special concern has been with interior design, particularly of ships and exhibitions. He worked on the **Victoria and Albert Museum**'s 'Britain Can Make It' show of 1946 and on the Festival of Britain, and was responsible for the interior design of British Rail's 'Sealink' ferries. In 1972 he created Ward Associates.

Wilhelm **Wagenfeld**
Otto **Wagner**
Ole **Wanscher**
Neville **Ward**
Josiah **Wedgwood**
Hans **Wegner**
Weissenhof Siedlung
Gunnar **Wennerberg**
Werkbund
Wiener Werkstätte
Yrjo **Wiherheimo**
Tapio **Wirkkala**
Tom **Wolfe**
Wolff Olins
Frank Lloyd **Wright**
Russel **Wright**

Josiah Wedgwood

1730–95

A master-potter, inventor, industrialist and retailer Josiah Wedgwood has had his name turned into a trademark, the highest honour which industrialized culture can offer. He was a product of what the Marxist historian of the Industrial Revolution Francis Klingender called 'the Provincial Englightenment', conquering England and France from Burslem, Staffordshire, in the West Midlands: for a while in the eighteenth century the backwaters of England led the metropolitan centres of the world. Wedgwood, together with several of his near neighbours, saw his opportunity and took it. He summed up his achievement with characteristic poetry and asperity: 'I saw the field was spacious and the soil so good as to promise ample recompense to anyone who should labour diligently in its cultivation.'

The establishment of Wedgwood's 'manufactory' at Stoke-on-Trent was the beginning of an industrial, humanitarian and artistic career which was one of Britain's most original contributions to the Age of Reason. In its various aspects, Josiah Wedgwood's life was like an overture to the nineteenth century. In all things he was an essentially practical man: he used artists like Flaxman and Stubbs, not as a precious affectation, but as a shrewdly understood means of expanding his markets and his business; and his model village at Etruria was not solely a philanthropic gesture, for, like Lord Leverhulme, he realized that happy workers are good workers (see also pp. 13–14).

Among Wedgwood's practical innovations in the production of ceramics was his division of labour and of production into 'useful' wares, from his Burslem factory, and 'ornamental' wares, from his Etruria factory. His use of

artists anticipated **Gustavsberg** by a century and **IBM** by two. Innovation was almost an obsession with him, leading him to develop a stoneware pyrometer that could withstand furnace temperatures and to produce his own original designs, of which the Queen's Ware and Black Basalt ranges are still in production today.

But Wedgwood's devotion to art and science did not dull his commercial instincts. Like an impresario he displayed his monumental Portland vase (p. 14) at his showrooms in Greek Street, offering tickets for entry to see this ceramic wonder. The large production runs which his logically organized factories made possible were such that he invented sales catalogues for the public.

Queen's Ware Plate with 'Blue Weed' Pattern, c. 1775
Some of Wedgwood's ceramic designs have achieved a timeless quality: the Queen's Ware service came out of the Etruria factories in Staffordshire under Josiah Wedgwood's own supervision and is still in production today.

Hans Wegner

b. 1914

Now a furniture designer, Hans Wegner started his career as a cabinet-maker. Until 1943 he was an employee of **Arne Jacobsen**, and since then has designed furniture principally for Johannes Hansen. Wegner's chair '501' of 1949, known simply as 'The Chair', turned Danish furniture into an international phenomenon. Made entirely of natural materials, it is marked by a remarkable synthesis of simplicity, elegance and care in execution. Writing in *Mobilia* in 1960, **Poul Henningsen** pinpointed its qualities: 'This chair is the perfect solution of a task: the light, lowbacked armchair, sufficiently comfortable. It weighs nine pounds, just like a new-born child. An architect can gain a nice reputation for himself by making this chair five times as heavy, half as comfortable and one quarter as good looking. Look at it once more. It is completely faultless. Its form is spare and harmonious. It does not have any false or mendacious pretences. It fulfills its task in society with the modest conscientiousness expected of the good citizen.'
Bibliography Henrik Sten Moller *Tema med Variationer* Sonderjyllands Kunstmuseum, Tønder, 1979

'Ypsilon' Chair, 1951
The 'Ypsilon' was the successor to the famous 'The Chair'.

Weissenhof Siedlung

The **Deutsche Werkbund**'s exhibition of 1927 was an entire housing estate, in a village called Weissenhof just outside Stuttgart. Houses by **Mies van der Rohe**, **Mart Stam** and **Le Corbusier** were erected together for the first time, and in them were the first examples of tubular steel furniture to be seen by the public.

Gunnar Wennerberg

1863–1914

A Swedish painter, Gunnar Wennerberg studied painting in Paris and ceramics in Sèvres before becoming artistic director of the **Gustavsberg** factory in 1895. Wennerberg was one of the first artists actually to work in modern industry, and his freshly observed wild flower patterns replaced the oppressive funk of the National Romantic school which had dominated Gustavsberg's production before his appointment. Wennerberg remained artistic director of Gustavsberg until 1908, and was also designing for **Kosta** from 1898 to 1909.
Bibliography 'Art and Industry: a century of design in the products you use' exhibition catalogue, The Boilerhouse Project, Victoria & Albert Museum, London, 1982; 'Wennerberg' exhibition catalogue, Prins Eugens Waldemarsudde, Stockholm, 1981

Werkbund see Deutsche Werkbund

Wiener Werkstätte

The Wiener Werkstätte was an offshoot from the Vienna Secession. The Secession's exhibition in 1900 focused attention on the work of **C.R. Mackintosh** and **C.R. Ashbee**, and one of the Secession group, Koloman Moser, suggested setting up a workshop in Austria along the same lines as Ashbee's in London. Together with **Josef Hoffmann** he founded in 1903 the Wiener Werkstätte Produktiv-Gemeinschaft von Kunsthandwerken in Wien (The Viennese Workshops and Production Cooperative of Art Workers in Vienna). By 1905 it had over a hundred craftsmen. Its forte was hand-made metalware whose reductive style belied its dependence on hand production. However, a change in style around 1915 from Hoffmann's rectilinear one to a more florid, organic approach presaged its decline; it dissolved in 1933. (See p. 16.) *Bibliography* 'Die Wiener Werkstätte' exhibition catalogue, Museum für Angewandte Kunste, Vienna, 1967

Yrjo Wiherheimo

b. 1941

A furniture designer, Yrjo Wiherheimo has designed furniture for Haimi, Asko and Vivero, and **plastics** for Nokia. Wiherheimo is among the most respected of the younger generation of Finnish designers. In particular, his furniture for Vivero is admired for its combination of refined aesthetics with **ergonomic** precision.

Tapio Wirkkala

b. 1915

A widely various Finnish designer, Tapio Wirkkala worked for Iittala after 1947 and joined **Raymond Loewy** in 1955. His work became internationally known after it appeared at Milan **Triennales** during the early fifties. He has worked for **Venini** and **Rosenthal**.

'Variation' Coffee Service for Rosenthal

Tom Wolfe

b. 1931

The American journalist Tom Wolfe has been a substantial influence in raising the level of writing about popular culture. An inventor, with Hunter S. Thompson, of what both his critics and fans call 'the new journalism', Wolfe added a satirical Southern Gentleman's point of view to the gallimaufry of opinions that abounded during the sixties. He invented the name of the next ten years when he described it as the 'Me Decade'.

Wolfe thinks of himself somewhat as a modern Thackeray. His books, *The Kandy-Kolored Tangerine-Flake Streamline Baby*, *The Electric Kool-Aid Acid Test* (1968) and *The Right Stuff* (1979) were immensely popular, but his satire on fashions in twentieth-century architecture and design, called *From Bauhaus to Our House* (1981) raised the ire of an American establishment which was not accustomed to being mocked.

Wolff Olins

Wolff Olins was a London-based design consultancy, founded in 1965.

The founders are two very different personalities – Michael Wolff (b. 1933), a romantic who describes his recreation in *Who's Who* as 'seeing', and Wally Olins (b. 1930), who says he is the 'first design consultant who couldn't draw'. Wolff and Olins had had patchy careers before forming the consultancy, Wolff as a designer for the BBC and Olins as an executive for the advertising agency Geers Gross.

Wolff Olins specialized in **corporate identity** and was an English equivalent of American firms like **Lippincott & Margulies** and Anspach, Grossman and Portugal. The Wolff Olins style veered between a specialized whimsy, characterized by Michael Wolff's suggestion that the Bovis group of companies choose a humming bird as their corporate symbol, and a hard-edged slickness which the firm produced for BOC, Aral and VAG. Michael Wolff left the firm in 1983. (See also p. 110.) *Bibliography* Wally Olins *The Corporate Personality* Design Council, London, 1978

Frank Lloyd Wright

1869–1959

Frank Lloyd Wright was an immensely successful architect who has influenced the whole world of design through the novelty and power of his vision. Because he stood outside, way outside, the Euro-centric vision of the **Modern Movement**, Wright has been adopted as a hero by many diverse vested interests: **Tom Wolfe**, who perhaps sees him as an authentic American hero, and the historians of **Post-Modernism**, who see him as some kind of anticipator of the garish **Kitsch** that clogs the colour supplements.

Frank Lloyd Wright was born in rural Wisconsin, where his Welsh grandparents had emigrated a hundred years earlier. He studied engineering in Madison, the state capital, and then went to Chicago in 1887 to work as a draughtsman. He soon entered the architectural offices of Dankmar Adler and Louis Sullivan, and his career had begun. Sullivan's theories about organic building were a fundamental influence on Wright, and when he left the Adler & Sullivan office to set up his own in 1893 he took with him what he had learned from his first years as an architectural apprentice. He combined this with an appreciation of the traditional building of Japan and his own vision of the universe into an authentic, original philosophy of design. His ▶

A B C D E F G H I J K L M N O P Q R S T U V W X Y Z

house designs worked from the functional requirements of living accommodation towards the outside, and Wright never imposed a style robbed from reference books on to a predetermined structure. He thought about what he wanted his building to be and then worked it out from first principles. He was also always anxious to integrate any building into its natural environment, so it is no coincidence that the long, low Wright buildings, covering huge areas of ground, grew out of his experience of the vast plains of the Mid-West, later fortified by experience of the vast emptiness of the Arizona desert. He once said that no building should ever be made on a hill, it should be *of* the hill.

Wright also made many technical innovations in his buildings: his Larkin office building in Buffalo, New York (1905), was among the first anywhere to use plate-glass doors framed in metal, air-conditioning and bizarre metal furniture – which was made to Wright's own designs. In 1909 Wright travelled to Europe and his contact with German and Dutch architects gave a new dimension to the inchoate fermentation that we now see as the beginning of the **Modern Movement**. Drawings and photographs of his buildings were extensively published in Holland and Germany.

Wright took from his Welsh ancestors a prophetic, bardic, and chthonic interest in nature and folklore, naming his own houses after the druid Taliesin, and praising vernacular architecture at the expense of the formal. He wrote that 'humble buildings are to architecture what folklore is to literature'. It was this element of his thought, together with his insistence that architecture should be based on contemporary possibilities, that interested the Europeans. J.J.P. Oud, the Dutch architect, praised Wright for proposing

buildings that were economically possible and socially responsible (while criticizing him for never having produced any, save for some exquisite examples for rich men). Wright's vision of the future was that there should be houses spread across the United States, each integrated into its natural environment and each in an acre of ground, with 'the future city . . . everywhere and nowhere'.

C.R. Ashbee, who met him, did much to publicize his work in Britain.
Bibliography F. Gutheim (ed.) *Frank Lloyd Wright on Architecture* Duell Sloan & Pearce, New York, 1941; Charles Jencks *Kings of Infinite Space* Academy Editions, London, 1983

Oak Chair, 1908
This chair was designed by Wright for his assistant, Isabel Robert, who worked in his Oak Park, Chicago, office. It was one of a series of slat-back chairs that Wright made at the beginning of the century.

Russel Wright

b. 1904

Russel Wright was an American institution, of sorts. His work was seen first in Macy's store in New York and then in the **Museum of Modern Art**'s 'Machine Art' exhibition. In the words of Russell Lynes, author of the influential book *The Tastemakers*, 'Russel Wright was the answer for those of us who were brought up to accept the **Bauhaus** doctrine . . . but who could not afford to buy the expensive imports of **Le Corbusier** and **Mies van der Rohe** and **Marcel Breuer**.' Wright managed to balance in an odd, but effective, way, **Functionalism**, **Art Deco** and the vernacular Mission Style which so many American first-time buyers had picked up from junk and antique shops in the years between the Wars.

He was born in Lebanon, Ohio into a family of Quakers, and his values have always been located both in puritanism and the Mid-West (although each was somewhat adapted to meet the demands of consumption). He studied sculpture at the Art Students' League in New York and law at Princeton, but did not last the course in law, being drawn to the theatre. **Norman Bel Geddes** offered him a theatrical job which Wright turned down on the basis that the wages were too low (they were nil). Under the influence of his wife, Wright began to move away from the theatre towards a novel form of sculptural caricatures which, celebrated in **Vogue**, sold well. His first essay in **industrial design** was a set of spun **aluminium** bar tools, which also sold well, and which launched him on his new career. Wright enjoyed metals because of 'their easy workability' and 'permanent integral coloring', and began to design entire table settings in spun aluminium and spun steel. His wife would present these at department stores and trade shows

throughout the thirties. In 1932 Wright did a classic transformation job on a Wurlitzer radio, turning a solemn piece of funereal table architecture into a **Raymond Loewy** casket, and in 1934 introduced a sixty-piece range of furniture (manufactured by Heywood-Wakefield) at Bloomingdale's. In 1935 his hugely successful 'Modern Living' furniture line, with its characteristic blond maple, was introduced at Macy's. His wife's sense for public relations and his own theatrical background helped 'Modern Living' ease into a rut in the American imagination, together with the designer's name. He was the first designer to persuade Macy's to use his name in their advertisements, for which he became so celebrated that in 1951 *Advertising Age* ran an article headed 'Russel Wright Does Not Advertise, But Many Ads Give Him Top Billing'. In 1937 Wright began to concentrate on ceramics, his greatest success being the 'American Modern' line for Steubenville Pottery, which ran for twenty years after its launch in 1939.
Bibliography 'Russel Wright – American designer' exhibition catalogue, Gallery Association of New York State, 1983

'American Modern' Service for Steubenville Pottery, 1939
Wright's curvaceous and witty service remained in production for twenty years, and became a classic of popular design.

Sori Yanagi

b. 1915

Yanagi was born in Tokyo, but came into early contact with European modern design while he was an assistant in **Charlotte Perriand**'s office in Japan. In 1952 he founded the Yanagi Industrial Design Institute, and since 1977 he has been director of the Japan Folk Crafts Museum in Tokyo, two moves which suggest his dual commitment to the cultures of East and West. His approach to **industrial design** has an oriental, somewhat mystic quality: 'basic concepts and beautiful forms do not come from the drawing board alone'. His most famous design is a **plywood** and steel 'Butterfly' stool of 1956, a delightful mediation between modern techniques and ancient ideals.

Zagato

Ugo Zagato (1890–1968) was originally a mechanical engineering apprentice in Cologne, and set up his own bodyshop, Carrozzeria Zagato, in Milan. After his death it passed into the hands of his sons, Elio (b. 1921) and Gianni (b. 1929). Zagato has often produced exaggerated, even ugly, body designs which derive much of their character from the symbols and necessities of the racetrack. In particular, the firm has worked for **Alfa Romeo** and Lancia; for them it has produced the Lancia Flavia Sport (1963) and the Alfa Romeo Guilia TZ2 (1964).

Marco Zanini

b. 1954

Marco Zanini, a partner in **Sottsass** Associati, studied architecture at the University of Florence, travelled in the United States, and joined Sottsass as an assistant in 1977. He contributed to the first two **Memphis** collections. (See p. 54).

Zanotta

Zanotta is one of the leading firms of Milanese furniture manufacturers, producing side chairs, easy chairs and tables. Based at Nova Milanese, Zanotta abandoned the traditions of Italian furniture manufacture and turned to design patronage in the early fifties, devoting itself to the search for aesthetic and functional solutions to the problems of the modern interior. Zanotta is a commercially astute company and has an important presence at the annual furniture fairs in Milan, Paris, Cologne and Kortrijk. It produces **Giuseppe Terragni**'s 'Follia' chair of 1935 and **Achille Castiglioni**'s 'Mezzadro' stool of 1957 (p. 102). (See also p. 133.)

'Sella' Stool by Achille Castiglioni, 1957
Castiglioni's design, derived from a bicycle seat, uses Surreal incongruity to startling effect.

Marco Zanuso

b. 1916

Marco Zanuso was born in Milan and graduated in architecture from Milan Polytechnic in 1939, then joining its staff. He was editor of *Casabella* and designed all the Milan **Triennales** from VIIIth to XIIIth. His product designs have a remarkable sense of form which, while minimal, always achieve strong presence: for both his 1956 Borletti sewing-machine and his 1962 **BrionVega** television (p. 60) he won a **Compasso D'Oro** award, and he continued this sculptural tendency with his 'Black' television for BrionVega and his 'Hastil' and 'Thesi' pens for the Aurora company. He has designed factories and offices for **Olivetti** at Segrate, São Paulo, Buenos Aires and Caserta, and children's **plastic** furniture for **Kartell**.

'Doney 14' Television, 1964, and 'Black 13' Television, 1969
Working with Richard Sapper, Zanuso has designed a remarkably distinguished range of appliances in the Italian High Style, including the 'Doney' and 'Black' televisions. Zanuso has also designed kitchen scales for the French firm, Teraillon (p. 56). His designs are most effective in high-quality, injection-moulded plastics.

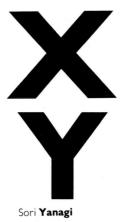

Sori **Yanagi**

Zagato
Marco **Zanini**
Zanotta
Marco **Zanuso**

General Bibliography

Design is not one subject but a great many different ones, including engineering and materials science at one end, styling and marketing at the other. For this reason there have been few synoptic treatments of international design because writing them requires the command of a variety of subjects. Throughout the *Conran Directory of Design* specific bibliographical references have been attached to entries where it was relevant to do so, and, for those with a specialist interest, these can be supplemented by popular treatments of individual disciplines within the totality of design: furniture, graphics, ceramics, and so on. More specialist material is available from trade journals and business magazines, which are frequently more authoritative than magazines ostensibly devoted to design.

What follows is a list of the general surveys of design.

Banham Reyner, *Theory and Design in the First Machine Age* Architectural Press, London and New York, 1960 (and many subsequent editions)
Banham Reyner (ed. Penny Sparke) *Design By Choice* Rizzoli, New York, 1981; Academy Editions, London, 1982
Bayley Stephen, *In Good Shape: Style in Industrial Products 1900–1960* Design Council, London, 1979
Benton Tim and Charlotte, with Dennis Sharp *Form and Function: A Source Book for the History of Architecture and Design 1890–1939* Open University Press, Milton Keynes, 1975
De Noblet Jocelyn, *Design: introduction à l'histoire de l'évolution des formes industrielles de 1820 à aujourd'hui* Stock-Chène, Paris, 1974
Doblin Jay, *One Hundred Great Product Designs* Van Nostrand Reinhold, New York, 1970
Dorfles Gillo, *Il Disegno industriale e la sua estetica* Capelli Editore, Bologna, 1963
Drexler Arthur, and Daniel, Greta, *Introduction to Twentieth Century Design from the Collection of the Museum of Modern Art* Museum of Modern Art, New York, 1959
Ferebee Ann, *A History of Design from the Victorian Era to the Present Day* Van Nostrand Reinhold, New York, 1970
Garner Philipe (ed.) *The Encyclopaedia of the Decorative Arts 1890–1940* Van Nostrand Reinhold, New York, 1979
Garner Philipe, *Contemporary Decorative Arts from 1940 to the Present* Van Nostrand Reinhold, New York, 1980
Giedion Sigfried, *Mechanisation Takes Command: A Contribution to Anonymous History* Oxford University Press, New York, 1948 (and many subsequent editions)
Heskett John, *Industrial Design* Thames & Hudson, London, 1980; Oxford University Press, New York, 1980
ICOGRADA/ICSID *World Design Sources Directory/Repertoire des sources d'information en design* Pergamon Press, Oxford, various editions
Jervis Simon, *Dictionary of Design and Designers* Penguin Books, Harmondsworth, 1984
Pevsner Nikolaus, *Pioneers of Modern Design* Penguin Books, Harmondsworth, 1960 (and many subsequent editions)
Philadelphia Museum of Art (ed. Kathryn B. Heisinger) *Design Since 1945* exhibition catalogue, Philadelphia Museum of Art, Philadelphia, 1983; Thames & Hudson, London, 1983
Selle Gert, *Ideologie und Utopie des Design. Zur Gesellschaften Theorie der Industriellen Formgebung* DuMont Schauberg Cologne, 1968
Sparke Penny, *Consultant Design* Pembridge Press, London, 1983

Museums and Institutions

The universal nature of industrial production has made design into an international subject. There are a number of museums, societies and other institutions in all parts of the world which either have permanent collections or can make available specialist material for students of design.

AUSTRALIA

Industrial Design Council of Australia
114 William Street
Melbourne
Victoria 3000
exhibitions and design awards

AUSTRIA

Museum für Angewandte Kunst
Stubenring 5
1010 Wien
permanent collections

Österreichisches Institut für Formgebung
Salesianergasse 1
1030 Wien
exhibitions and design awards

BELGIUM

Design Center
51 Galerie Ravenstein
1000 Bruxelles
exhibitions, competitions, design index

Ecole Nationale Supérieure d'Art et des Arts Visuels
21 Abbaye de la Cambre
1050 Bruxelles
documentation of product design

ICSID
45 avenue Legrand
1150 Bruxelles
international collective of industrial design societies

CANADA

Centre de Recherche Industrielle du Quebec
333 rue Franquet
Case Postale 9038, Ste Foy
Quebec
G1V 4C7
computerized database on product design

CZECHOSLOVAKIA

Institut Prumysolveho Designu
Na porici 24
Praha 1
exhibitions and documentation

Umeleckoprumyslove Muzeum
Ulice 17
Listopadu 2
Praha 1
permanent collection

DENMARK

Dansk Designrad
Industrihus
H.C. Andersens Boulevard
DK 1053 Kobenhavn V
exhibitions, awards

Det Kongelige Danske Kunstakademi
Kongens Nytorv 1
DK 1050 Kobenhavn V
documentation on furniture and product design; permanent collection of furniture

FINLAND

Taideteollisuusmuseo
Korkeavuorenkatu 23A
00130 Helsinki 13
exhibitions, permanent collection

Teollisuustiteen Liitoo Ornamo
Pohj. Esplanadi 25A
00100 Helsinki 10
exhibitions, documentation, awards

FRANCE

Centre de Création Industrielle
Centre Nationale d'Art et Culture Georges Pompidou
75191 Paris
exhibitions

Bibliothèque Forney
Hotel des Archevêques de Sens
1 rue du Figuier
75004 Paris
documentation of textiles and wallpapers

Musée de l'Affiche
18 rue de Paradis
75010 Paris
posters

Musée des Arts Décoratifs
107 rue de Rivoli
75001 Paris
the applied arts department of the Louvre; exhibitions

GERMANY (Democratic Republic)

Amt für industrielle Formgestaltung
Breitstrasse 11
102 Berlin
exhibitions, competitions, awards

GERMANY (Federal Republic)

Bauhaus-Archiv
Klingelhoferstrasse 13–14
1000 Berlin 30
documentation and exhibitions

Design Center Stuttgart
Kanzleistrasse 14
7000 Stuttgart 1
exhibitions

Deutsche Werkbund
Alexandraweg 26
6100 Darmstadt

Deutsche Werkbund Archiv
Schlosstrasse 1
1000 Berlin 19
documentation of Werkbund and popular culture

Deutsches Architekturmuseum
Schaumankai 43
6000 Frankfurt
exhibitions

Deutsches Museum von Meisterwerken der Naturwissenschaft und Technik
Museumsinsel 1
8000 München 22
permanent collection

Haus Industrieform Essen
Steelerstrasse 29
4300 Essen 1
permanent collection

Rat für Formgebung
Eugen-Brandtweg 6
61 Darmstadt
exhibitions, competitions, awards

HUNGARY

Iparmuveszeti Muzeum
IX Ulloi ut 33/37
H-1091 Budapest
museum of applied arts with an interest in industrial design

IRELAND

Kilkenny Design Workshops Ltd
Kilkenny
exhibitions and documentation, largely about craft-based design

ISRAEL

The Israel Museum
POB 1299
Jerusalem 91012
exhibitions

ITALY

Associazione per il Disegno Industriale
via Montenapoleone 18
20121 Milano
documentation, competitions

Triennale di Milano
Palazzo dell'Arte
viale Alemagna 6
20121 Milano
exhibitions

JAPAN

Japan Industrial Design Promotion Organization
World Trade Center
Annexe 4th floor
PO Box 101
2–4–1 Hamamatsu-cho
Minato-ku
Tokyo 105
permanent collection, awards

Osaka Design Center
Senba Center Building
2–2 Senbachuo
Higashi-ku
Osaka
exhibitions and awards

NETHERLANDS

Stedelijk Museum
Paulus Potterstraat 13
Amsterdam
permanent collections, exhibitions

NORWAY

Konstindustrimuseet
Saint Olavsgate 1
0165 Oslo 1
permanent collections, exhibitions

Nordenfjelske Konstindustrimuseet
Munkegarte 5
7000 Trondheim
permanent collections, exhibitions

SWEDEN

Rohsska Konstslojdmuseet
37–39 Vasagatan
41137 Goteborg
permanent collections, exhibitions

Design Center Malmo
Gustav Adolfs Torg 51
21139 Malmo
exhibitions, awards

Foreningen Svenskform
PO Box 7404
10391 Stockholm
exhibitions, documentation

Nationalmuseum
Sodra Basieholmshamnen
11148 Stockholm
permanent collection

SWITZERLAND

Alliance Graphique Internationale
c/o Graphis
Dufourstrasse 107
8088 Zürich
international society of graphic designers, elected on merit

Kunstgewerbemuseum
Austellungstrasse 60
8031 Zürich
exhibitions

UNITED KINGDOM

Art Gallery & Museum
Northgate House
Church Street
Brighton BN1 1VE
permanent collections

Design Council
28 Haymarket
London SW1Y 4SU
exhibitions

Victoria and Albert Museum
Exhibition Road
London SW7 2RL
permanent collection, exhibitions

UNITED STATES OF AMERICA

Cooper-Hewitt Museum
2 East 91st Street
New York
NY 10028
permanent collection, exhibitions, important documentation

Museum of Modern Art
11 West 53rd Street
New York
NY 10019
permanent collection, exhibitions

USSR

Vsesojnzy Naucho Isledovatelski Institut Techniceskoj
VNIITE
Moscow 129223
exhibitions, awards

Acknowledgments

The publisher would like to thank the following photographers and organizations for providing the photographs in this book (a. – above, b. – below, bt. – bottom, c. – centre, l. – left, r. – right, t. – top):

10–11 City of Derby Museum & Art Gallery; **12** Boilerhouse; **13** a. and b. r. Josiah Wedgwood & Sons Ltd; **13** b. l. National Portrait Gallery, London; **14** a. Michael Holford; **14** b. Josiah Wedgwood & Sons Ltd; **15** Ann Ronan Picture Library; **16** Angelo Hornak; **17** AEG Telefunken (UK) Ltd; **18** R.A. Gardner; **20** Trustees of the Victoria and Albert Museum/E.T. Archive; **21** a. r. National Portrait Gallery, London; **21** b. The Photographers' Library; **22** a. Mansell Collection; **22** c. l. Trustees of the Victoria and Albert Museum; **23** a. The Victorian Society; **23** c. r. Peter Roberts; **24** BBC Hulton Picture Library; **25** Hoover PLC; **26** Arthur Sanderson & Sons Ltd; **28** c., and c. l. Trustees of the Victoria and Albert Museum; **28** c. r. William Morris Gallery; **29** a. Royal Commission on Historical Monuments (England); **29** c. l. Angelo Hornak/Philippa Lewis and Juliet Scott; **29** c. r. Trustees of the Victoria and Albert Museum; **30** c. l. Trustees of the Victoria and Albert Museum; **30** c. r. Boilerhouse; **30** b. courtesy Messrs Hazlitt Gooden & Fox Ltd; **31** Angelo Hornak; **32** courtesy of the Fogg Art Museum/Purchase – Louise E. Bettens Fund; **34** Michael J. H. Taylor; **35** a. l. Boilerhouse; **35** c. Bauhaus-Archiv; **35** c. r. Tim Benton; **36** Bauhaus-Archiv; **37** Robert Vickery/Architectural Association; **38** a. Boilerhouse; **38** c. l. Trustees of the Victoria and Albert Museum; **38** c. r. London Lighting Company; **39** Library of Congress; **40–41** © The Art Institute of Chicago; **42** Boilerhouse; **43** l. American Telephone & Telegraph; **43** a. r. Boilerhouse; **44** a. l. Walter Dorwin Teague Association Inc; **44** c. r. Boilerhouse; **44** b. The Queens Museum/Phyllis Bilick; **45** Boilerhouse; **46** Boilerhouse; **47** Boilerhouse; **48** b. c. Knoll Overseas; **49** Boilerhouse; **50** Bob Noorda; **53** Le Grandi Automobilie; **54** c. Olivetti; **54** c. r. The Design Council; **55** Piero Fornasetti/Casa Vogue; **56** a. ItalDesign; **56** c. l. RCL Ltd; **56** c. r. Olivetti; **57** a. r. ItalDesign; **58** Boilerhouse; **60** b. l. Boilerhouse; **61** a. Boilerhouse; **61** c. l. Boilerhouse; **62** Braun AG; **63** b. Technics; **64** a. Boilerhouse; **64** b. l. Ford (UK) Ltd; **64** b. r. Boilerhouse; **65** Bartle Bogle Hegarty; **68** Artek Oy; **69** a. r. Boilerhouse; **69** l. Eero Aarnio; **69** c. AEG Telefunken (UK) Ltd; **70** a. ERCO Lighting Ltd; **70** b. l. Daimler-Benz AG; **70** b. r. Otl Aicher; **71** l. AID Ltd; **71** c. Marco Albini Franca Helg Antonio Piva Architetti Associati; **71** r. Knoll International; **72** r. Industrie Pininfarina; **73** c. Emilio Ambasz Design Group Ltd; **73** b. Boilerhouse; **74** a. The Coca-Cola Company; **74** c. The Museum of Modern Art, New York; **74** b. Boilerhouse; **75** r. The Design Council/Henry Dreyfuss Associates; **75** c. l. Landor Associates; **75** b. l. Anspach Grossman Portugal; **75** bt. l. Eliot Noyes Industrial Design Inc; **76** b. l. Oy Wärtailä Ab Arabia; **76** c. Royal College of Art; **76** r. Architectural Association/Peter Cook; **77** a. r. Abet Laminati; **78** a. Rosenthal; **78** b. Royal Commission on Historical Monuments (England); **79** a. r. Angelo Hornak; **79** b. r. Trustees of the Victoria and Albert Museum; **79** b. l. Trustees of the Victoria and Albert Museum/Angelo Hornak; **80** a. r. Artemide GB Ltd; **80** c. Flos & Arteluce/Environment; **80** c. r. Artemide

Index of Products and Designs

The letters a, b, c and d that follow the page references indicate the four columns on each page, reading from left to right. Page references in italic type indicate illustrations.

A

advertisements
Audi, 65
Gae Aulenti furniture, 171
'Black America' programme, 118
BMW, 94
in Das Andere, 179
Knoll fabrics 171
Knoll furniture, 171
Memphis, 185
Olivetti Lexicon, 80, 196
Sony 'Walkman', 59, 61
see also posters
aircraft
'Air Pullman', 34
Boeing, 48, 231, 232b
Douglas, 46, 118c–d
Finnair, 230d
helicopters, 113b,c
interiors, 48, 116d, 201a, 201, 230d, 231, 232b
Lockheed, 116d, 165a–b, 165, 197b
SAAB, 218b, 218
U2, 165a, 165
'Vega', 197b
Vickers Viking, 201a, 201
Zeppelin, 164a
by Clarence L. Johnson, 165a–b, 165
by John K. Northrop, 197a–b
by Piaggio, 113b, 205c
by William Stout, 34
airlines, colour schemes and logos for, 87b
architectural decoration, ornament, 166a–b, 179a–b
architectural ironmongery, 143b, 143, 155b
architecture and architectural drawings (see also exhibition design; interior design)
AEG Turbine Hall, 91
Art Nouveau, 79, 146d, 146, 158c
Arts and Crafts, 81
AT&T building, 165c–d, 165
Avenue Rapp, Paris, 31, 79
Bauhaus building, 88b,c, 88
Buckler's Hard, 81
Casa del Fascio, 232c
Castel Béranger flats, 146d, 146
De Stijl, 37, 114c
Deutsche Werkbund exhibition building, 144a
'Dymaxion' house, 131a–b
E-1027, 141b, 141
English, Muthesius on, 193c–d
Fagus factory, 144a
Fulton Hall, New York, 232
Geodesic dome, 131b
Giedion and, 136a
Glasgow Art School, 180b–c
Great Exhibition 1851, 142a
Holtshanger, 153d
Hoover Factory, 25
'House of an Art Lover', 85a, 85, 180
International Style, 158b, 158
La Rinascente store, 71b–c, 160
Larkin office building, 246a
Métro entrances, 146d

Modern Movement, 188d, 189
Moller House, 179
Museum of Modern Art, 193a–b, 193
Palais Stoclet, 155a
Pirelli Tower, 208a
Plug-in-City, 76d, 76
post-modern, 140d, 165d, 165, 209b–c, 238d
Public Services Building, Portland, Oregon, 140d
Schroeder House, 37, 214c
Seagram Building, 186d, 189
Stockholm Exhibition, 227b–c, 227
Torre Velasca, 90d
'University Node', 76
Villa Savoie, 158
by Franco Albini, 71b–c
by Archigram, 76d, 76
by Art Workers' Guild, 80a
by Gunnar Asplund, 83a, 227b–c, 227
by M. H. Baillie-Scott, 85a–b, 85
by BBPR, 90d
by Peter Behrens, 90d–91a, 91
by Pierre Chareau, 103c
by Wells Coates, 106c–d
by Maxwell Fry, 130c–d, 130
by Buckminster Fuller, 131a–b
by Gaudí, 133a–b
by Ernest Gimson, 137a
by Alexander Girard, 137b
by Philip L. Goodwin, 193a
by Michael Graves, 140d
by Walter Gropius, 144a–145a, 158b
by Gruppo Strum, 145c
by Hector Guimard, 146d, 146
by Oliver Hill, 153d
by Josef Hoffmann, 154d–155a
by Hans Hollein, 155b
by Arne Jacobsen, 162b–c
by Philip Johnson, 165c–d, 165, 193b
by Le Corbusier, 145a, 158b, 158, 176b–177a
by Adolf Loos, 179b, 179
by Charles Rennie Mackintosh, 180b–c
by Robert Mallet-Stevens, 182b
by MARS, 183b
by Roberto Menghi, 185d
by Mies van der Rohe, 145a, 186b–d
by Keith Murray, 193a,b
by George Nelson, 194c–d
by Cesar Pelli, 193b
by Gio Ponti, 208a
by Jean Prouvé, 210a, 210
by Pugin, 20–1, 210c
by Gerrit Rietveld, 37, 214c
by Eero Saarinen, 219a–b
by Eliel Saarinen, 111c
by Ettore Sottsass, 226a
by Edward Durrell Stone, 193a
by Superstudio, 228c
by Giuseppe Terragni, 232c
by Benjamin Thompson, 232d–233a, 232
by Pierre Vago, 236b
by Gino Valle, 236b
by Robert Venturi, 238c–d
by C. F. A. Voysey, 242b–d
by Otto Wagner, 243d
by Frank Lloyd Wright, 245d–246b

B

beds
'Bislet', 157
'Cabriolet, 108
hospital, 76
by Rutger Anderson, 157
by Joe Colombo, 108
bed/sofa, by Børge Mogensen, 189c
bicycles
by Piero Fornasetti, 55
by Alex Moulton, 99
book design
Bauhaus booklet, 88
Das Englische Haus, 193
The House Book, 106
Penguin Books, 203c–d, 203, 235a
Wren's City Churches, 181a
Yellow Book, 79
by A. H. Mackmurdo, 181a
by Laszlo Moholy-Nagy, 190a, 190
bookcases
'tensistructure', 71b
by Gaetano Pesce, 204c
bottles
Fanta, 74
'Pelikan' ink bottle, 243a
Taittinger, 238b
by Victor Vasarely, 238b
bowls
by Ashbee's Guild of Handicrafts, 82
by Sergio Asti, 83
by Enzo Mari, 182
buses
Greyhound, 74
'Routemaster', 223b, 223
by Norman Bel Geddes, 91

C

cabinets
by Gropius, 30
by Ponti and Fornasetti, 160
calculators, 65
Braun ET44, 62–3, 63
Casio 'SL-800', 63
Olivetti 'Divisumma', 56, 92a, 196b
Olivetti 'Logos', 92a
cameras
Hasselblad, 221b, 221
Kodak, 140c, 232a
Leica, 86c, 86
Minox 35EL, 126c
Nikon, 57, 138b, 138
Olympus, 122a, 163
by Oscar Barnack, 86c
by Kenji Ekuan, 122a
by Giorgio Giugiaro, 138b, 138
cars
aerodynamics and, 63–4, 70b, 70, 164a, 167c–168a
Alfa Romeo, 72c–d
Alfa Romeo 1750 6c Gran Sport, 160
Alfa Romeo 2500S cabriolet, 72
Alfa Romeo 2500 coupé, 206
Alfa Romeo Alfasud, 72d, 138a
Alfa Romeo Giulia GT, 138a
Alfa Romeo Giulia TZ2, 247a
Alfa Romeo Giulietta Sprint, 93d, 93
Alpine Renault, 186a
American, in the fifties, 73, 74b
'Ape', 113b
Aston-Martin DB-4, 234c
Austin 1100, 206b
Austin A30, 84a

Austin A40, 206b
Austin Atlantic, 84a
Auto-Union, 172b
Benz, 23
BMW, 94c
British Leyland, 84b, 93d
Buick 'Y' Job, 121c
Burney prototype, 228
Cadillac, 46, 73, 121, 133d
'Capsula', 138b
Chevrolet, 194b, 228
Chrysler, 70b, 97a, 97, 104b
Citröen, 70b
Citröen 2CV, 94a, 96a, 104d, 105
Citröen BX, 93d, 105c
Citröen CX, 126a
Citröen DS, 94a, 105a–b, 105
Citröen Traction Avant, 94a, 96a, 104d, 105a, 143a
Citröen Type A, 104d, 105
Citröen Type C, 104d
CNR, 126a
Daf, 186a
Datsun Prince Skyline, 186a
de Tomaso Mangusta, 135a
'Dymaxion', 131b, 131
ergonomic properties, 123
Ferrari 308 GTB, 206b
Ferrari 330GT, 206b
Ferrari Daytona, 126a, 206b
Ferrari 246 GTS, 206
Ferrari 308, 93d
Ferrari Mondial, 126a
Ferrari racing cars, 240a, 240
FIAT 100 coupé, 240a
FIAT 124, 128 and 130, 135d
FIAT 127, 124b
FIAT 131 Super Mirafiori, 95a
FIAT 500 series, 52, 124, 135d
FIAT 1100, 124
FIAT 2100S Coupé, 135
FIAT Ballila, 124
FIAT Panda, 138a, b–c
FIAT Uno, 124b
FIAT 'Zero A', 135
Ford, 135a
Ford Capri, 128a
Ford Consul, 128a
Ford Cortina, 63, 64, 128a
Ford Edsel, 127d, 128a
Ford Fairline, 127d
Ford Model 40, 143a
Ford Model T, 127c, 127, 128a, 230c
Ford Model T Roadster, 127
Ford Sierra, 63, 64, 70b, 84b, 84c, 128b, 128
Ford Thunderbird, 143a, 143
Ford V8, 127d
Ford Zephyr, 128a
Ford Zodiac, 128a
General Motors, 133c–d, 165a, 188b
Ghia, 135a
Hino Contessa, 186a
Honda, 155c
La Salle, 121c
Lamborghini, 93d, 174d, 234
Lancia, 206b, 206, 234, 247a
Land-Rover, 84a, 84
Lotus, 103b–c, 103
Maserati, 135a, 240a–b
'Medusa', 138b
Mercedes-Benz, 70, 134, 219c, 219
Morris, 159a, 159
Motoramas, 192a
Opel, 175a

Peugeot, 126a, 206b
Porsche, 70b
Porsche 91, 172b
Porsche 356, 172b, *172*, 209a
Porsche 911, *209*
Porsche 928, 175a
Range Rover, 84b
Renault, 95b–c, *95*, 159a, 238b
Rover, 84a,b
SAAB, 122c, *122*, 218b–c, *218*, *219*, 221b, *221*
Studebaker, 178a
Toyota Corolla A1, *163*
Triumph, 186a, *186*, 240a–b, *240*
Vespa 400, 113c
Volkswagen, 172b–c, 209a
Volkswagen 'Beetle', *241*
Volkswagen Golf, 138a, *138*, 159a, 241b
Volkswagen Karmann-Ghia, 135a, *241*
Volvo, 242a, *242*
by Giulio Alfieri, 174d
by David Bache, 84a–b, *84*
by Uwe Bahnsen, 84c
by Nuccio Bertone, 93d, *93*, 174d
by Flaminio Bertoni, 94a, 105b
by Rodolfo Bonetto, 95a
by Michel Boué, 95b–c, *95*
by Pierre Boulanger, 104d, *104*
by Carl Breer, 97a, *97*
by Colin Chapman, 103b–c
by Luigi Colani, 107a
by Corradino d'Ascanio, 113b–c
by Harley Earl, 74b, 121b–c, *121*, 133d, 165a, 192a–b, *228*
by Bjorn Envall, 122c, *122*, *219*
by Leonardo Fioravanti, 126a
by Buckminster Fuller, 131b, *131*
by Giacinto Ghia, 135a, *135*
by Dante Giacosa, 135c–d, *135*
by Giorgio Giugiaro, 103c, 124b, 138a–c, *138*
by Eugene Gregorie, 143a
by Alec Issigonis, 159a, *159*
by Wunibald Kamm, 167c–168a
by Erwin Komenda, 172b–c, *172*
by Anatole Lapine, 175a
by Giovanni Michelotti, 186a, *186*
by Bill Mitchell, 188b
by Pininfarina, *72*, 124b, 133d, 206a–b, *206*
by Bruno Sacco, 219c, *219*
by Sixten Sason, 218b–c, 221b, *221*
by Carrozzeria Touring, 234c, *234*
by Vignale, 240a–b, *240*
by Zagato, 247a
cartoons, by Disney, 117c–d, *117*
ceramics
  'American Modern', 246d, *246*
  Art Deco, 106a, *106*
  'Bizarre', *106*
  'Drop' service, 107a, *107*
  Finnish, 125a, *125*
  'Ivory', *215*
  'Kilta', 129b
  'LB', 177c
  'Praktika', 147a–b, *147*, 167b
  'Pyro', *147*, 167b
  'Ruska', 129b, 210a
  'Servus', 177c
  'Teema', *129*
  'Tema e Variazione', *128*, 129a
  by Arabia, 76b, *76*, 125a, *125*, 129b, *129*, 210a

by Alison Britton, *111*
by Clarice Cliff, 78c, 106a, *106*
by Luigi Colani, 107a, *107*
by Henry Cole, 107a
by Piero Fornasetti, 128d, *128*, 129a
by Kaj Franck, 129b, *129*
by Berndt Friberg, 130a
by Walter Gropius, *144*, 215d
by Gustavsberg, 147a–b, *147*, 167a, 177c, 244d
by Habitat, 148b
by Edward Hald, 149a
by Wilhelm Kåge, 147a–b, *147*, 167a–c
by Stig Lindberg, 147b, 177c, *177*
by Keith Murray, 193a, *193*
by Thure Oberg, *125*
by Ulla Procopé, *125*, 210a
by David Queensberry, 211c
by Rörstrand, 215b, *215*
by Rosenthal, *78*, 107a, *107*, *144*, 215c–d, *221*, 245
by Steubenville Pottery, 246d, *246*
by Wedgwood, 13–14, *14*, 193a, *193*, 244a–b, *244*
by Gunnar Wennerberg, 244d
by Russel Wright, 246d, *246*
chairs
  '005', *197*
  '24', 244c
  '40-in-4', 216a, *216*
  'Aluminum', 120c
  'Ant', *162*
  'Antelope', 109c, 212b, *212*
  'Ball', 69b
  'Barcelona', *187*
  'basculant', 176d
  'Blow', 114c
  'Brno', *48*
  'Bruno Mathsson', 183c
  'Cab', *54*
  campaign, 112c
  'Camponino', 104a
  'Cesca', 97c, *171*
  'Chief', 166d
  deck (by Klint), 112c, *112*, 170d
  'Djinn', 192a–b
  'Domus', 230d
  'Egg', 162c, *162*
  'Elda', 108c
  'Eva', *183*
  'Follia', 247b
  'Gazelle', 212b
  'Grand Confort', *176*
  'Grasshopper', 219a
  'Gyro', 69b
  'Hammond', *170*
  high (children's), *118*
  'Jigsaw', *108*
  'Joe', *114c*
  'Karuselli 412', 173b, *173*
  'Kimara', *69*
  'Landi', 72d, 109d, *109*
  'Mies' (by Archizoom), 77c
  'MK16', 172a
  'Model B33', *38*
  'Modello 115', *181*
  'MR', 93b, *186*
  office, 54, *117*, *173*
  'Omkstack', 169c
  'Pan', *181*
  paper, 208c, *208*
  'Penilla', *183*
  'Plaano 435 U', *125*
  'Plia', 206c, *206*

'Polypropylene', 113d, *113*, 207b
'Primate', 247d
'Red-Blue', 37, 214b, *214*
'Sacco', 133a, *133*, 208d
safari, 170d, *170*
'Selene', *80*, 181c
'Senna', *83*
'Sindbad', *101*, 181c
'Slim', *157*
'Sof-Tech', 216a
'Springbok', 109c
stacking (by Albinson), 71d, *71*
stacking (by Eames), *121*
stacking (by Jacobsen), 162c
stacking (by Kinsman), 109d, *201*
stacking (by Panton), 202c
stacking (by Rowland), 216a, *216*
steel wire, *93*
'Superleggera', 104b, 208a–b, *208*
'Supporto', *154*
'Swan', 162c
'TI', 169c
'Torso', 115a
'Transat', 141b
'Tulip', 219a, *219*
'Vertebra', 73a, *73*, 206c
'Vienna', 233a
Vierzehner, 233b
'Wassily', 68d, *97*, 171
Windsor, 123a, *123*
'Wink', *101*
'Zig-Zag', 214b
by Alvar Aalto, 68d, *68*
by Eero Aarnio, 69b, *69*
by Emilio Ambasz, 73a, *73*
by Archizoom, 77c
by Gunnar Asplund, *83*
by Harry Bertoia, 93b, *93*
by Marcel Breuer, *38*, 97b, *97*
by Joe Colombo, 108c, *108*
by Hans Coray, 72d, 109d, *109*
by Robin Day, 113d, *113*
by De Pas, D'Urbino, Lomazzi, 114c
by Deganello, 115a, *115*
by Niels Diffrient, 117a, *117*
by Nana Ditzel, *118*
by Charles Eames, 71d, 86d, 120c, *120*, *121*, 187c–d
by Ercol, 123a, *123*
by Josef Frank, 130a
by Michael Graves, 140d
by Eileen Gray, 141b
by René Herbst, 152c
by Arne Jacobsen, 162b,c, *162*
by Finn Juhl, 166c–d, *166*
by Rodney Kinsman, 109d, 169c, *201*
by Toshiyika Kita, *101*
by Kaare Klint, 112c, *112*, 170d, *170*
by Mogens Koch, 112c
by Yrjo Kukkapuro, *125*, 173b, *173*
by Vico Magistretti, *80*, *101*, 181c
by Mies van der Rohe, *48*, 93b, 186
by Børge Mogensen, *113*, 189
by William Morris, *98*
by Olivier Mourgue, 192a–b
by Peter Murdoch, 208c, *208*
by Antii Nurmesniemi, 123d, *123*, 197d, *197*
by Verner Panton, 202c, *202*
by Parker-Knoll, 171a
by Gaetano Pesce, 204c
by Gio Ponti, 104a–b, 208a–b
by Ernest Race, 109c
by Richard Riemerschmid, *214*
by Gerrit Rietveld, 72d, 214b,c, *214*

by David Rowland, 216a, *216*
by Eero Saarinen, 76d, 219a, *219*
by Fred Scott, *154*
by Giuseppi Terragni, 232c
by Thonet, *38*, 233a–c, *233*, 243d
by Henry van de Velde, *236*
by Robert Venturi, 239a, *239*
by Vittorio Vigano, 239d
by Otto Wagner, 243d
by Hans Wegner, 244c, *244*
by Frank Lloyd Wright, *246*
chaises-longues
  'Djinn', 192a–b, *192*
  by Marcel Breuer, *171*
  by Poul Kjaerholm, 170a, *170*
  by Le Corbusier, 176c–d
clocks
  'Cifra', 236b
  'Dator', 236b
  'Secticon', 182c, *182*
  'Sfericlock', 95a
  by Max Bill, 94b
  by Rodolfo Bonetto, 95a
  by Gino Valle, 236b
clothes, *see* fashion; knitwear
cocktail cabinet, by Hille, *154*
cocktail shaker, *169*
coffee pot, by Richard Sapper, *161*, 219, 220b
coffee services
  by Michael Graves, *57*, 140d
  by Alessandro Mendini, *185*
  by Rörstrand, *215*
  by Rosenthal, 245
  by Timo Sarpaneva, *221*
  by Robert Venturi, 238
  by Wiener Werkstätte, *16*
coffee tables
  by Poul Kjaerholm, 170a
  by Isamu Noguchi, *196*
computer, by Olivetti, 226a
cooking ware, 177c, 197d, 220a
corporate identity, 17, 69c, 74b, 90d, 152b, 177d
  AEG, 17, 69c, 110a
  Alitalia, *110*
  American Motors, *177*
  Braniff, 137b–c
  British Rail, 119d, *119*
  Chase Manhattan Bank, 103d
  Dutch Post Office, *233*
  Emery Air Freight, *75*
  Grand Union Supermarket, *110*
  IBM, 74b, 110a, 1976–c, 213a
  ICI, *110*
  London Transport, 205d, *205*
  Minolta, 87b, *110*
  Mowlem, 106b
  Olivetti, 242b
  P&O Ferries, *110*
  Peter Dominic, 106b
  Peter Robinson, 106b
  Quaker Oats, 87b
  Royal Bank of Scotland, 99
  SAS, *110*
  Texaco, *110*, 232
  United Airlines, 87
  Westinghouse, 213a
  Zanussi, 238a
couture, *see* fashion
cutlery
  'Chinese Ivory', *184*
  'DRY', *161*
  'Embassy', 184b
  'Pride', 184b

Index of Products and Designs

'Thrift', 184b
by Achille Castiglioni, *161*
by David Mellor, 184b–c, *184*
by Wilhelm Wagenfeld, 243a
see also flatware

D

desk sets
'Carvacraft', *85*
by Bruno Munari, *192*
dictating machine, by IBM, 197c
diesel engine, by Eliot Noyes, *75*, *197*
disabled, equipment for, 69b, 123b, *123*, 147b
dispensers
cash, *237*
Coca-Cola, 178a, *178*
divan, inflatable, *114*
domestic appliances and accessories, 96a, 96b–c, 108a, *108*, *123*, 155b, 185d, *206*, *229*, *238*; *see also* electrical goods; kitchen equipment
dressers
'Carlton', *228*
by Peter Behrens, *81*
by Memphis, *226*
Ettore Sottsass, *226*
dressing tables
'Plaza', 140d
Utility, *235*
by Eileen Gray, *141*
duplicators, Gestetner, *45*, 178a

E

electrical goods
food mixer, 140c, *140*, 212d
heater, *17*
razors, 62, *62*, 126c, *134*
toothbrush, *96*
see also radios; record players; television; vacuum cleaners; video equipment; white goods
exhibition design
Olivetti, 83c, *83*
Stockholm Exhibition (1930), 83a, 227b–c
by Franco Albini, 71b, *71*
by Gae Aulenti, 93c, *83*
by Misha Black, 94b
by Gropius, 116b
by Innovator, 157d
by Hermann Muller-Brockmann, 192c
by Carlo Scarpa, 222a

F

fabrics, textiles
'Aurinko', *125*
'Bird and Tulip', 242c
'Contemporary', 109b–c
'Côte d'Azur', *107*
Finnish, 125a, *125*
'Flotilla', *98*
for London Transport, 183b
'Freesia', *175*
'Havana', *107*
'Huuto', *123*
'Ianthe', *177*
'Iso Sana', *125*
'Iso Tasaraita', *123*
'Jäävvoret', *183*

'Maisema', *125*
'Moon & Stars', *104*
'Nympheas', 242c
'Peacock Feather', 224b
'Primavera', *129*
'Sana', *125*
Utility, 183b, *183*, 235b–c
'Vusi Raita', *125*
by Barron and Larcher, 87a
by Fede Cheti, 104a, *104*
by Stafford Cliff, 106b
by Collier Campbell, 107c, *107*
by Lucienne Day, 98, 113d
by Nana Ditzel, 118a
by Elio Fiorucci, *126*
by Kaj Franck, 129b, *129*
by Josef Frank, 130a
by Alexander Girard, 137b, *137*
by Group of Ten, 145b, *145*
by Habitat, 148b
by Fujiwa Ishimoto, *183*
by Dora Jung, 166d
by Knoll, *171*
by Jack Lenor Larsen, 175b–c, *175*
by Liberty's, 177b, *177*
by Stig Lindberg, 177c
by Marimekko, 125a, *125*, 183a, *183*
by Enid Marx, 183b, *183*
by Astrid Sampe, 220a
by Silver Studio, 224b
by Vuokko, 123d, *123*, 125a, *125*
by C. F. A. Voysey, 242c, *242*
fashion
mini-skirt, 211a
'New Look', 100c, 117b, *117*
'sack' dress, 86a
by Giorgio Armani, 78a
by Cristobal Balenciaga, 86a, *86*
by Benetton, 92d
by Brooks Brothers, 175d
by Pierre Cardin, 100c, *100*
by Chanel, 102d–103a, *103*, 174b
by Chloé, 174b, *174*
by Dior, 117b, *117*
by Fiorucci, 126b
by Mariano Fortuny, 129a
by Katharine Hamnett, 149b, *149*
by Deryck Healey, 150b
by Kenzo Takada, 168d–169a, *169*
by Calvin Klein, 170a–b, *170*
by Karl Lagerfeld, 174b, *174*
by Ralph Lauren, 175d
by Missoni, 188a, *188*
by Issey Miyake, 188b–c, *188*
by Hanae Mori, 190d
by Paul Poiret, 208a–c, *208*
by Emilio Pucci, 210b
by Mary Quant, 221a–b, *211*
by Yves St Laurent, 117c, 227a, *227*
by Schiaparelli, 222c–223a, *222*
films
credits and titles by Saul Bass, 87b, *87*
by Charles Eames, 120d
flatware
'Atlanta', 243a
by David Mellor, 184b, *184*
by Roberto Sambonet, 220a
by Wilhelm Wagenfeld, 243a
see also cutlery; tableware
furniture
American, in the fifties, 74a
anthropometrics in, 75b
Bauhaus, 88c
Biedermeier, 94a

'Contemporary', 109b–c
Danish, 112c–d, *112*, 118a, 170c–d
Finnish, 125a, *173*
from Chiavari, 104a–b
G-Plan, 140a, *140*
laminated, 92c, 175a, 207d, 233b
'Maestri' series, 101c
'Modern Living', 246d
'moderne', 189
office, *96*, 114b, 116d, *117*, 169b, *173*, 226a
Pop, 208c–d
post-modern, 209c, *209*
tubular steel, 38, *38*, 78a, 97b, *97*, 100b, 152c, 158d, 203b, 227b, 233c, 244d
Utility, 235b–c, *235*
wire, 207d
by Alvar Aalto, 68d, *68*, 207d
by Franco Albini, 71b,c
by Studio Alchymia, 72a, *72*, 209b, 226b
by Emilio Ambasz, 73a, *73*
by Bruce Archer, *76*
by Archizoom, 77c, *77*
by Artek, 80a
by Artemide, 80c, *80*, 137d
by Gunnar Asplund, 83a, *83*
by Gae Aulenti, 83c, *171*
by Barnsley Brothers, 86d
by J. H. Belter, 92c
by Harry Bertoia, 93b, *93*, 158d
by Cini Boeri, 95a, *95*
by Andrea Branzi, 96b
by Marcel Breuer, 97b–c, 133c, *144*, 158d, *171*
by Cassina, 101c, 115a, *161*, 181c, *181*, 204c
by Achille Castiglioni, 102a–b, *102*, 247b
by Pierre Chareau, 103c
by Aldo Cibic, 104c
by Wells Coates, 158d
by Gino Colombini, 168b
by Joe Colombo, 108c, *108*, 168b
by Robin Day, 154b
by Michele de Lucchi, 114b, *114*
by Paolo Deganello, 115a, *115*
by Donald Deskey, 116a
by Nana Ditzel, 118a, *118*
by Jan Dranger, 118d
by Henry Dreyfuss, 75b
by Driade, *115*
by Charles Eames, 71d, *74*, 120b–c, *120*, *121*, 158d, 187c–d, 207d
by Ercol, 123a, *123*
by Ergonomi Design Gruppen, 75b
by Piero Fornasetti, 128d–129a, *160*
by Kaj Franck, 129b
by Josef Frank, 129c, 130a
by Dino Gavina, 133c
by Ernest Gimson, 137a
by W. H. Gispen, 137d
by Giorgio Giugiaro, 138b
by Eileen Gray, 141a, *141*
by Habitat, 148b–d, *148*
by Heal's, 149c–150b, *150*
by Robert Heritage, 152c
by Hille, 113d, *113*, 154a–b, *154*
by Johan Huldt, 155d, *157*
by IKEA, 157a, *157*
by Innovator, 155d, 157d, *157*, *229*
by Isokon, 158d
by Betty Joel, 164d
by Finn Juhl, 112c

by Kartell, 108a, 168b, *168*
by Rodney Kinsman, 109d, 169c, 201a
by Poul Kjaerholm, 170a, *170*
by Kaare Klint, 75b, 112c, *112*, 170c–d
by Knoll, 48, 74a, 83c, *93*, 133c, 171a–b, *171*, 207d, *209*, 219a, *219*, 239a, *239*
by Friso Kramer, 173a, *173*
by Shiro Kuramata, 173c, *173*
by Le Corbusier, 176c–d, *176*
by Charles Rennie Mackintosh, 180b, c–d
by A. H. Mackmurdo, 181a
by Vico Magistretti, 181c, *181*
by Louis Majorelle, 182a, *182*
by Carl Malmsten, 182c
by Bruno Mathsson, 183c, *183*
by Memphis, *54*, 96b, 104c, 114b, *114*, 137d, *168*, 183b, 184d, 209b, *226*, 226b, *228*
by Mies van der Rohe, 48, 93b, 158d, 186d, *186*, *187*
by Herman Miller, 74a, 187c–d, *187*
by Børge Mogensen, 112c, 189c, *189*
by Olivier Mourgue, 192a–b, *192*
by Isamu Noguchi, 196c, *196*
by OMK, 201a, *201*
by Verner Panton, 202c, *202*
by Parker-Knoll, 171a, 202d
by PEL, 203b
by Charlotte Perriand, 204a–b, *204*, *210*
by Gaetano Pesce, 204c, *204*
by Giancarlo Piretti, 206c, *206*
by Warren Plattner, 207d
by Gio Ponti, *160*, 208a–b, *208*
by Jack Pritchard, 209d
by Jean Prouvé, 210a
by Ernest Race, 158d, 212b, *212*
by Rasch Brothers, 213b
by Richard Riemerschmid, 214b, *214*
by Gerrit Rietveld, 214b–c, *214*
by Terence Harold Robsjohn-Gibbings, 215a
by Gordon Russell, 217b–c
by Ero Saarinen, *74*, 219a, *219*
by Afra and Tobia Scarpa, 222a, *222*
by Ettore Sottsass, 226b, *226*
by Giotto Stoppino, 228a
by Superstudio, *228*
by Svenska Sljödföreningen, 229b
by Ilmari Tapiovaara, 230d
by Thonet, 207d, 233a–c, *233*, 243d
by Henry van de Velde, 236c, *236*
by Robert Venturi, 209b, *209*, 239a, *239*
by Vittorio Vigano, 239d
by Otto Wagner, 243d
by Hans Wegner, 112c, 244c, *244*
by Yrjo Wiherheimo, 245b
by Frank Lloyd Wright, 246a
by Russel Wright, 246d
by Zanotta, 133a, *133*, 247b
by Marco Zanuso, 168b, 247c
see also chairs; tables; *and other types of furniture*

G

garages, filling stations, *47, 232*
glassware
  Art Nouveau, 79b, *79*, 132b, 174c
  'Aulica', 240d
  'Diodata', 240d
  'Dogaressa', 240d
  'Faliera', 240d
  Favrile, *79*
  Finnish, 125a
  by Emile Gallé, 79b, 132b, *132*
  by Edward Hald, 149a, 201c, *201*
  by Jenaer Glasverein, 164a
  by Henning Koppel, 172d
  by René Lalique, 174c
  by Adolf Loos, 179b
  by Keith Murray, 193a
  by Orrefors, 201c, *201*
  by Timo Sarpaneva, 125a, *125*, 221a
  by Carlo Scarpa, 222a
  by Tobia Scarpa, 222a
  by Louis Comfort Tiffany, 79b, *79*
  by Venini, 222a, 238c
  by Vistosi, 240d
  by Wilhelm Wagenfeld, 243a,b, *243*
  by Tapio Wirkkala, 125a
graphic design
  Festival of Britain, *109*, 132d
  London Transport, *121*, 166a, *166*,
    168c, 205d, *205*
  Mobil, 103d
  Olympic Games, 70c, *70*, 130d, *139*,
    168f
  Pop, *208*
  by Otl Aicher, 70c, *70*
  by Aubrey Beardsley, *79*
  by Chermayeff & Geismar, 103d
  by Stafford Cliff, 106b, *106*
  by Lou Dorfsman, 118c, *118*
  by Alan Fletcher, 126c
  by Shigeo Fukuda, 130d
  by Abram Games, 132c–d, *132*
  by Milton Glaser, *110*, 139a–b, *139*
  by Milner Gray, 141d
  by Henrion, 152a–b
  by Edward Johnston, 166a, *166*
  by Herb Lubalin, 179d, *179*
  by Laszlo Moholy-Nagy, 77
  by Bruno Munari, 192d
  by Bob Noorda, 196d
  by Michael Peters, 204d, *204*
  by Paul Rand, 213a
  by Total Design, 233d, *233*
  by Unimark, 235b
  by Massimo Vignelli, 240c, *240*
  see also logograms; posters;
    typography
helicopters, by d'Ascanio, 113b,c
hi-fi system, by Braun, 63
household appliances, *see* domestic
  appliances
houses, *see* architecture

I

industrial design, 43, 73c–74b
  Central School of Arts and Crafts
    and, 102a
  Victor Papanek and, 202d
  by Emilio Ambasz, 73a
  by Peter Behrens, 17, *17*, 90d–91b,
    91
  by Norman Bel Geddes, 91c–d, 157b
  by Misha Black, 94b

by Achille Castiglioni, 102a–b, *102*
by Henry Dreyfuss, 119c, 157c–d
by Kenji Ekuan, 122a
by Kenneth Grange, 140c, *140*
by Hans Gugelot, 146a–b, *146*
by Erik Herlow, 152d
by Raymond Loewy, 178a–b, *178*
by Peter Muller-Munk, 192c
by Marcello Nizzoli, 196a–b
by Eliot Noyes, 197a–b, *197*
by Richard Sapper, 220b, *220*
by Douglas Scott, 223b
by Joseph Sinel, 157b, 223d
by Roger Tallon, 230b, *230*
by Walter Dorwin Teague, 157c–d,
  232a–b, *232*
by Harold van Doren, 157c–d,
  237a–c, *237*
by Jacques Viennot, 239d
by Russel Wright, 246c–d
by Sori Yanagi, 247a
by Marco Zanuso, 247c, *247*
interior decoration
  by Colefax & Fowler, 107b
  by Omega Workshop, 220c–d
interior design
  Art Deco, 78, 116a, *116*, 127a
  Art Nouveau, 78
  Biedermeier, 94a
  Broadcasting House, 106d
  Charleston, Sussex, 220c–d
  'Contemporary', 109b
  Fonda del Sol restaurant, 137b, *137*
  Gropius' room at Bauhaus, *144*
  High-Tech, 153b, *153*
  Milan underground, 71c
  Radio City Music Hall, 116a, *116*
  Strand Palace Hotel, 78
  by Franco Albini, 71b,c
  by Gunnar Asplund, 83a
  by Ward Bennett, 93a
  by Aldo Cibic, 104c
  by Wells Coates, 106b
  by Joe Colombo, 108c
  by Elsie de Wolfe, 115b
  by Donald Deskey, 78c, 116a, *116*
  by Nana and Jorgen Ditzel, *112*
  by Paul Follot, 127a
  by Piero Fornasetti, 129a
  by Josef Frank, 129c–130a
  by Maxwell Fry, 130d
  by Alexander Girard, 137b
  by Milton Glaser, 139b
  by Habitat, 148b, *148*
  by Heal's, *150*
  by David Hicks, 153a
  by Shiro Kuramata, 173c
  by Charles Rennie Mackintosh,
    180b–c, *180*
  by Syrie Maugham, 184a
  by William Morris, *191*
  by George Nelson, 195c–d
  by Antii Nurmesniemi, 197d
  by Warren Plattner, 207d
  by Gio Ponti, 129a
  by Terence Harold Robsjohn-
    Gibbings, 215a
  by Carlo Scarpa, 222a
  by Henry van der Velde, 78
  by Neville Ward, 243d

J

jewellery, by René Lalique, 174c

K

kettles
  'Bollitore', 220b, *220*
  Russell Hobbs, 99
  by Peter Behrens, *17*
kitchen equipment, 56, 140c, *140*,
  146c, 184c, *229*, 237c, *238*; *see also*
  cooking ware; domestic
  appliances; electrical goods;
  white goods
knitwear
  by Benetton, 92d
  by Kenzo Takada, *169*
  by Missoni, 188a, *188*

L

lacquerwork, by Eileen Gray, 141a,b
leatherware, by Gucci, 145d, *145*
lighting
  'Arco', 102a,b
  'Bestlite' lamp, *38*
  'Jill', 80
  'Kandem' night light, 96
  'Osiris', 73a, 206c
  paper lampshades, 196c
  'Papillona', *126*
  'PH', 151b, *151*
  'Tahiti' lamp, 228
  theatrical, 129a
  'Tizio' desk light, 220b, *220*
  'Toio', 102b
  by Arteluce, 80b, *80*
  by Artemide, 80, 220b, *220*
  by Sergio Asti, 83b
  by Cini Boeri, 95a
  by Achille Castiglioni, 102a,b, 126d
  by Joe Colombo, 108c
  by Concord, 152c, *152*
  by Erco, 73a, 122d
  by Flos, 102a,b, *102*, 126d, *126*, 169b
  by Carlo Forcolini, 80
  by Kaj Franck, 129b
  by Josef Frank, 130a
  by Poul Henningsen, 151b, *151*
  by Robert Heritage, 152c, *152*
  by Memphis, *226*
  by Isamu Noguchi, 196c
  by Richard Sapper, 220b, *220*
  by Afra and Tobia Scarpa, *126*, 222a
  by Ettore Sottsass, *226*
  by Wilhelm Wagenfeld, 243a
liners, interiors for, 201a
logograms, logotypes
  AEG, 69
  Aluminum Corporation of America,
    87b
  American Motors, *177*
  AT&T, 87b
  Chevrolet, *133*
  Citibank, 75
  Electrolux, 44, *122*
  Erco, *70*, 122d
  Festival of Britain, 132d
  Girl Scouts, 87b, *87*
  IBM, 213a
  London Transport, *205*
  Mother and Child Store, *179*
  Olivetti, *200*
  Warner Communications, 87b, *87*
  Westinghouse, 213a
  by Otl Aicher, *70*, 122d
  by Saul Bass, 87b, *87*
  by Peter Behrens, 69

K

by Abram Games, 132d
by Lippincott & Margulies, 177d,
  177
by Herb Lubalin, *179*
by Paul Rand, 213a
by Sixten Sason, *122*
lorries, *see* trucks

M

machinery, machine art, 33–9
  Constructivism, 109a
  Futurism, 131, *192*
  Horatio Greenough, 142c–d
  MoMA's 'Machine Art' exhibition,
    38, 46–8, 86d
  Amedée Ozenfant, 201d
  Herbert Read, 213d
magazines
  Architectural Review, 77
  designed by Milton Glaser, 139a
  Kritisk Revy, 151b–c, *151*
  New York, 139a
  Oz, *208*
  Paris Match, 139a
  Vogue, *194*
maquettes, by Henry Dreyfuss, 75b,
  75
medical equipment, by Niels
  Diffrient, 116d
microcomputer, by Olivetti, 92a
models, by Giovanni Sacchi, 92b, *92*,
  195, 219a, *219*
motorcycles
  BMW K100RS, *94*, *134*
  Honda, 155c, *155*
  Yamaha RD350, *163*
motor scooters
  Lambretta, 174d
  Vespa, 113b,c, 205c, *205*, 239b

N

newspapers
  design for, by Itten and Dicker, *161*
  typeface for *The Times*, 191a, *191*

O

office equipment, furniture
  by IBM, 156b, *156*
  by Knoll, 116d
  by Olivetti, 114b, 169b, 200a–b,
    226a
  chairs, *54, 117, 173*
  desk fan, 96
  stapler, 44
  see also typewriters *and other
    types of office equipment*
ottoman, by Charles Eames, 120c, *120*

P

packaging
  Bowyers, *110*
  IBM, 213a, *213*
  Lucky Strike cigarettes, *73*, 178a
  Typhoo tea, *71*
  by AID, 71a, *71*
  by Egmont Arens, 77d
parking meter, 140c
pasta, by Giorgio Giugiaro, *138*
pens
  Parker '25', 140c
  by Marco Zanuso, 247c

Index of Products and Designs

photography, by Herbert Matter, 184a
pictograms, for Olympic Games, 70
posters
 Amber Musical Festival, 139
 Bauhaus, 36, 89, 90a
 BP, 132c
 Chemin de Fer du Nord, 101
 Citröen, 105
 Compagnie des Wagons-Lits, 101a
 Deutsche Werkbund, 116
 FIAT, 124
 Heal's, 149
 'Home Exhibition', 167
 London Transport, 121, 168c
 Memphis, 185
 Milan Triennale, 234
 Ministry of Information, 132c–d, 152a, 152
 'MPI' typewriter, 199, 222b
 Olympic Games, 139
 Pirelli, 51, 196d
 'Pride and Prejudice', 103
 Shell, 99, 132c, 168
 Stedelijk Museum, Amsterdam, 173
 Swiss Transport Office, 184a
 War Office, 132c, 132
 by Herbert Bayer, 88
 by Cassandre, 101a–b, 101
 by Chermayeff & Geismar, 103
 by Marcello Dudovich, 124
 by Tom Eckersley, 121d, 121
 by Abram Games, 132c–d, 132
 by Milton Glaser, 139
 by Henrion, 152a, 152
 by Edward McKnight Kauffer, 168c
 by Herbert Matter, 184a
 by Laszlo Moholy-Nagy, 36
 by Alfonso Mucha, 192c
 by Bob Noorda, 51, 196d
 by Xanti Schawinsky, 199, 222b, 222
 by Joost Schmidt, 89
 by Graham Sutherland, 99
 see also advertisements
pottery
 by Arabia, 76b
 by Bernard Leach, 176a, 176

R

radios
 'Concept 51K', 130
 Ecko, 106d, 106
 hinged, 98a
 'Mobile', 71b
 Murphy, 217d
 Phonola, 102a
 RCA, 91c
 Sony TR-55, 224d
 'TS 502', 60, 247
 by Norman Bel Geddes, 91c
 by Castiglioni brothers, 102a
 by Wells Coates, 85d, 98c, 106
 by Frogdesign, 130
 by Richard Sapper, 220b
record players
 'Beogram 4000', 164b, 164
 BrionVega '126', 98
 'Phonsuper', 146a–b
 SK4, 212
 by Castiglioni, 98a, 98
refrigerators
 Coldspot, 178a
 Electrolux, 122b, 122
 Philco, 43
revolver, by Colt, 21, 22, 24

S

screens
 by Archizoom, 77
 by Vanessa Bell, 200
 by Eileen Gray, 141a,b
 by William Morris, 191
seats, seating
 'Aluminum', 187d
 'Luterma', 68d
 'Soft Pad', 187d
 'Strips', 95a
 tandem, 120c
 see also chairs and other types of seating
sewing-machines
 'Borletti', 247c
 'Logica', 56
 'Mirella', 195a, 195, 196b
 by Diffrient and Zanuso, 116d
 by Giorgio Giugiaro, 56, 138b
 by Necchi, 56, 195a, 195, 196b
 by Marcello Nizzoli, 196b, 197
ships, see liners
sideboard, by Alessandro Mendini, 72
silverware
 by Ashbee's Guild of Handicrafts, 82
 by Christopher Dresser, 119
 by Georg Jensen, 164b, 164
 by Henning Koppel, 164, 172d
 by Enzo Mari, 182
 by Jean Puiforcat, 210c
slide projector, by Kodak, 146b, 146
sofas
 'Dublin', 54
 'Fiandra', 175
 'Grandma', 209
 'Lido', 114
sofa/bed, by Børge Mogensen, 189c
stage design, see theatre design
staircase, in Strand Palace Hotel, 78
stereo equipment
 Sony 'Walkman', 59, 61, 225a
 Technics '315', 63
stools
 bar, 168
 'Butterfly', 247a
 kneeling, 102a
 'Mezzadro', 102, 247b
 stacking, 68d–69a, 125
 by Achille Castiglioni, 102a, 102
storage trolley, 108
storage wall, 187c, 195
stoves, Aga, 229

T

tables
 hospital side table, 77
 'Il Colonnato', 161
 lacquerwork, 141a
 'Malibu', 95
 Nenuphars', 182
 'Pan', 181
 'Quaderno', 228
 'Super-Ellipse', 151a, 151
 by Mario Bellini, 161
 by Michael Graves, 140d
 by Eileen Gray, 141a
 by Piet Hein, 151a, 151
 by Poul Kjaerholm, 170a
 by Bruno Mathsson, 151a, 151
 by Isamu Noguchi, 196
tablescapes, 153a

tableware
 Model 1382, 143d
 by Sergio Asti, 83b
 by Hermann Gretsch, 143d
 by Georg Jensen, 164b, 164
 by David Mellor, 184b–c, 184
 by Jean Puiforcat, 210c
 by David Queensberry, 211c
 by Russel Wright, 246c
 see also cutlery; flatware
tape-recorders, by Sony, 61, 163, 224d, 225
tea-machine, by Wolfgang Tumpel, 89
teapots
 'TAC 1', 144
 by Marianne Brandt, 96a
 by Christopher Dresser, 119a–b, 119
 by Wilhelm Wagenfeld, 243
telephone call box, 223b
telephone exchange (c. 1900), 24
telephones
 Bell, 43–4, 43, 119c, 119
 Ericsson, 150c–d, 150, 229
 'F78', 113
 'Grillo', 220b
 by DCA, 99
 by Henry Dreyfuss, 43–4, 43, 119c, 119
 by Jean Heiberg, 85d, 150c, 150
 by Gosta Thames, 229
teleprinter, by Olivetti, 226a
televisions
 BrionVega 'Black 12', 98a, 220b, 247c, 247
 BrionVega 'Doney 14', 98a, 220b, 247
 Sony Trinitron, 163
 Sony TV5-303, 224d
 Sony TV8-301, 224d, 225
text editing system, 92a
textiles, see fabrics
theatre design, 91c, 119b–c, 122a, 169a
tiles
 by William de Morgan, 29
 by William Morris, 28
timepieces, see clocks
timetabling boards, 236b
tools, 100d, 100, 134, 224c
torch, by Nick Butler, 98
trains
 'Corail', 230b
 Inter-City 125, 140c
 'Twentieth Century Limited', 119c
trolleys
 'Hilton', 183b
 storage, 108
 'Tech', 229
 by Alvar Aalto, 68
 by Artek, 68
 by Joe Colombo, 108
 by Innovator, 229
 by Javier Mariscal, 183b
trucks, Leyland, 198d, 198
tureens, 125
typewriters
 IBM, 156, 197c
 Olivetti 'Dora' portable, 226a, 226
 Olivetti Editor 2, 195d
 Olivetti ET series, 92a–b, 92
 Olivetti Lettera 22, 196b
 Olivetti Lettera 36, 226a
 Olivetti Lexicon 80, 196b, 196, 199
 Olivetti Lexicon 83, 92a
 Olivetti M1, 199a

 Olivetti MP1, 199a–b, 199, 222b
 Olivetti Studio 42, 199b, 222b
 Olivetti Valentine, 139b, 169b, 169, 226a
 Remington (1870s), 24
 by Mario Bellini, 92a, 92
 by Eliot Noyes, 156
typography
 London Transport, 166a, 166
 The Times, 191a, 191
 by Herbert Bayer, 88, 90a
 by Adrian Frutiger, 130c
 by Eric Gill, 136c–d, 136, 191a
 by Edward Johnston, 166a, 166
 by Herb Lubalin, 179d
 by Stanley Morison, 191a
 by Total Design, 233d, 233
 by Jan Tschichold, 235a

V

vacuum cleaners
 Electrolux, 122b, 178, 221
 Hoover, 44
vases
 'Marco', 83b
 Savoy series, 69a
 by Josef Hoffmann, 154
 by Bernard Leach, 176
 by Stig Lindberg, 177
vehicles
 design by Ogle, 198d
 Jeep, 164a
 see also aircraft; cars; and other types of vehicle
video equipment, 224d, 225a

W

wallpaper
 'Bird and Tulip', 242c
 'Fruit', 27
 'Garden Tulip', 98
 'Let Us Prey', 242
 'Nympheas', 242c
 'Peacock Feather', 224b
 'sanitary', 224b
 by Josef Frank, 130a
 by A. H. Mackmurdo, 181
 by William Morris, 27, 98
 by Pugin, 210
 by Rasch Brothers, 213b
 by Silver Studio, 224b, 224
 by C. F. A. Voysey, 242c, 242
washing machines, 237
watches
 'Tank', 35
 by Louis Cartier, 35
 by Giorgio Giugiaro, 138b, 138
 by Roger Tallon, 230b, 230
white goods, 237, 238a, 238; see also refrigerators

THE CONRAN DIRECTORY OF DESIGN

Text set in Monophoto Gill Sans Light (362) Medium (262) Bold (275)
and Extra Bold (321) in 11/12 pt and 10/11 pt on a Monophoto Laser-
comp MK III by Servis Filmsetting Limited

Illustrations reproduced on a Crosfield 645 IE Scanner with page
make up on a Crosfield 820 page make up unit by Minervahscan of
London and Colourscreens of Hong Kong

Printed Web offset by Jarrold and Sons of Norwich on Nimrod
125gsm Matt coated art paper

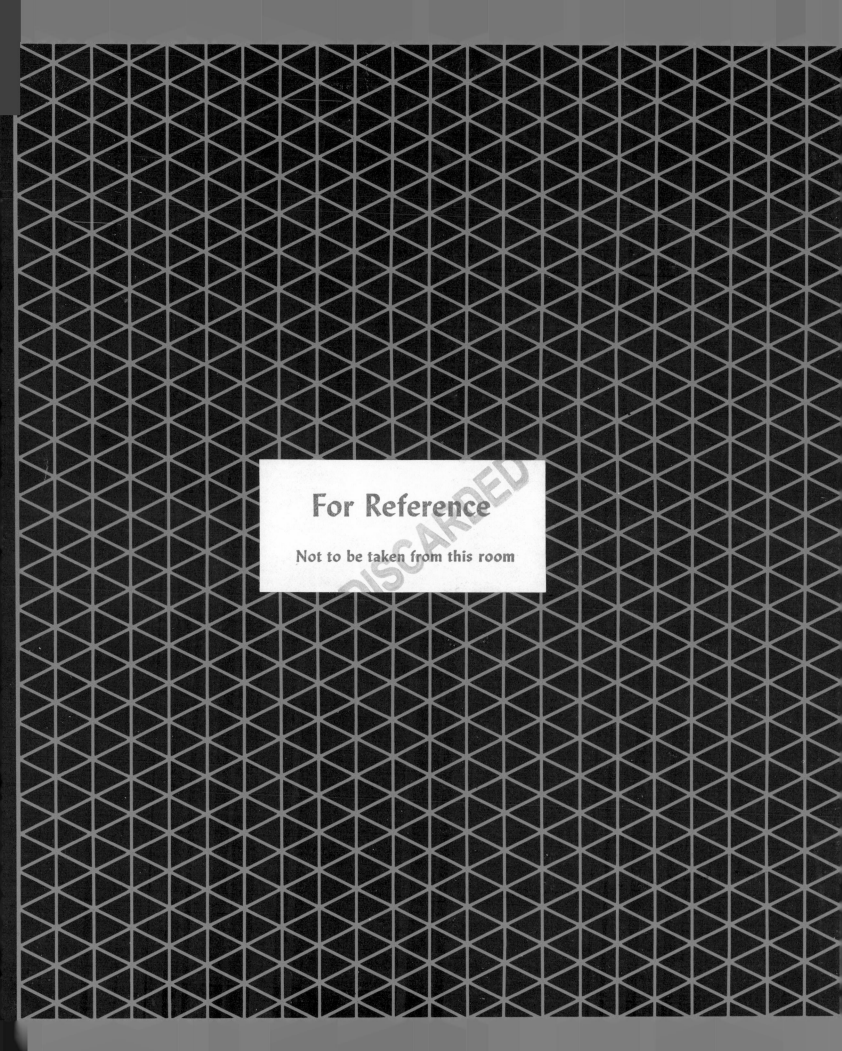